CHILD SLAVERY NOW

CHILD SLAVERY NOW

A contemporary reader

Edited by Gary Craig

LEARNING
RESOURCES
CENTRE

This edition published in Great Britain in 2010 by

The Policy Press
University of Bristol
Fourth Floor
Beacon House
Queen's Road
Bristol BS8 1QU
UK

Tel +44 (0)117 331 4054
Fax +44 (0)117 331 4093
e-mail tpp-info@bristol.ac.uk
www.policypress.org.uk

North American office:
The Policy Press
c/o International Specialized Books Services (ISBS)
920 NE 58th Avenue, Suite 300
Portland, OR 97213-3786, USA
Tel +1 503 287 3093
Fax +1 503 280 8832
e-mail info@isbs.com

British Library Cataloguing in Publication Data
A catalogue record for this book is available from the British Library.

Library of Congress Cataloging-in-Publication Data
A catalog record for this book has been requested.

ISBN 978 1 84742 609 3 paperback
ISBN 978 1 84742 610 9 hardcover

The right of Gary Craig to be identified as editor of this work has been asserted by him
in accordance with the 1988 Copyright, Designs and Patents Act.

Cover design by The Policy Press
Front cover: image kindly supplied by Magnum Photos
Printed and bound in Great Britain by Hobbs, Southampton
The Policy Press uses environmentally responsible print partners

Contents

Acknowledgments and dedication

Putting an international reader together can be a difficult task. This one has been made relatively straightforward by the willingness of the writers to meet deadlines, often in the midst of frantic timetables and, in many cases, faced with the competing (and far more important priorities) of responding to day-to-day events in the murky, horrific and dangerous territory of child slavery. As editor I am extremely grateful to the contributors, who in nearly every case gave me little cause to panic and who responded rapidly to queries and requests for revisions. I am also grateful to staff at The Policy Press who received the proposal enthusiastically, harried me gently during the course of its writing and saw it through to production with the minimum of hassles. Any responsibility for the content of the final product lies with me. I am also grateful to colleagues at, and visitors to, WISE (Wilberforce Institute for the study of Slavery and Emancipation), who provided a supportive and comradely environment in which debates about modern slavery were strongly profiled.

The book is dedicated to all those who work, often with little recognition, on the ground, sometimes facing injury and death, often with little to sustain them other than the knowledge that they are engaged in the most moral of all struggles, to give dignity and a secure, free future to millions of children worldwide working in conditions of slavery. It is dedicated particularly to the memory of Neil Kearney, a trades union official, who died late in 2009 at an undeservedly early age, from a heart attack. Neil worked tirelessly for many years to combat modern slavery in his field of expertise, leather and footwear. Characteristically, he died whilst on a field trip to sweatshops in South Asia. The abolition of contemporary slavery requires many things to be in place: laws, people (in the police and judiciary) to ensure they are implemented, committed politicians, advocates and campaigners in the field, and a wider recognition that this is a truly global evil. Neil was a highly committed campaigner who effectively gave his life over to combating slavery. I hope that this book can bring that goal a little closer.

Notes on contributors

Hakan Acar is a lecturer in the Department of Social Work at Hacettepe University, Ankara, Turkey. His work focuses on child welfare, youth policy and street children.

Yüksel Baykara Acar is an assistant professor in the Department of Social Work at Hacettepe University, Ankara, Turkey. She specialises in work on juvenile delinquency and justice, street children and family policy.

Jason Aliperti is an independent researcher and a New York-certified teacher with an MA in International Relations and an MA in TESOL (Teachers of English to Speakers of Other Languages). He has travelled extensively and has over five years of experience as an educator, including work with the Peace Corps-Ukraine and Amnesty International in India and Japan.

Patricia Aliperti is an independent researcher and a certified teacher and school counsellor in the US with an MEd in Counselling/Student Services and an MA in Public Administration. She has volunteered in Peru, taught in Japan and served as a Peace Corps-Ukraine teacher trainer. She is a Rotary World Peace Fellow-V.

Kevin Bales is an expert on modern slavery and President and Co-Founder of Free the Slaves, the US sister organisation of Anti-Slavery International (the world's oldest human rights organisation). He is Emeritus Professor of Sociology at Roehampton University in London, Visiting Professor at the Wilberforce Institute for the study of Slavery and Emancipation (WISE), University of Hull, as well as serving on the Board of Directors of the International Cocoa Initiative.

Jonathan Blagbrough has worked on child labour issues since 1989, managing Anti-Slavery International's child labour programme from 1995 to 2006. He is now an independent consultant, specialising on child domestic labour, undertaking research and developing policy, lobbying and advising governments, United Nations agencies and non-governmental organisations (NGOs). He is Senior Visiting Research Associate at the Wilberforce Institute for the study of Slavery and Emancipation (WISE), University of Hull.

Farhat Bokhari has extensive experience in human rights research and advocacy, having worked for ECPAT UK (End Child Prostitution, Child Pornography and the Trafficking of Children) and Human Rights Watch.

In 2009, a research fellowship with the Wilberforce Institute for the study of Slavery and Emancipation (WISE), University of Hull, led to a groundbreaking report on child trafficking.

Brenda Oude Breuil is a cultural anthropologist and criminologist, and lecturer at the Willem Pompe Institute for Criminal Law, Utrecht University, Netherlands. She is researching adult and child trafficking and transnational labour migration to West European cities, within the broader context of economic migration and global inequalities. She participated in a European study on child trafficking in Marseille. Her research interests include child begging, prostitution migration and exploitation of child migrants.

Bill Brookman is a street theatre performer and musician and director of Bill Brookman Productions, based in Leicestershire, where he also runs a children's performing arts group. As well as work for the United Nations, his work includes several seasons with the National Circus Project of America, and in Japan, Russia, India and Thailand.

Trevor Buck is Professor of Socio-Legal Studies at the Leicester De Montfort Law School, De Montfort University. He has three areas of research: international child law, administrative justice and the Social Fund (UK). He is currently completing the second edition of *International child law* (Routledge/Cavendish), due for publication in 2010.

Claire Cody is holder of the Oak Foundation Fellowship on the recovery and reintegration of children affected by sexual abuse, exploitation and trafficking, based at the University of the Highlands and Islands Centre for Rural Childhood in Inverness. She previously researched (at Plan International's headquarters) birth registration, trafficking and broader child rights issues.

Gary Craig is Associate Fellow and Emeritus Professor of Social Justice at the Wilberforce Institute for the study of Slavery and Emancipation (WISE), University of Hull, where he led the team working on issues of modern slavery; and Visiting Professor at the University of Durham. He was President of the International Association for Community Development for nine years, for which he is now International Ambassador.

Katherine Darton began adult life as a flautist and flute teacher. Experience as a music therapist led her to study medical sciences, after which she did a PhD and postdoctoral research. She now works in mental health and still plays the flute.

Serdar M. Degirmencioglu is Professor of Developmental Psychology at the Department of Psychology, Cumhuriyet University, Turkey. He has served as coordinator of the Children's Rights Coalition of Turkey and as President of the non-governmental organisation (NGO)/UNICEF Regional Network for Children in Central and Eastern Europe, Commonwealth of Independent States (CIS) and Baltic States. He is currently associate editor of *Education, Citizenship and Social Justice*.

Birendra Raj Giri was born in rural Nepal, but obtained an International Baccalaureate Diploma from the International School of Amsterdam, a BA (Honours) from Utrecht University College, Netherlands, an MA from the Universiteit van Amsterdam and MSc and PhD degrees from The Open University, UK. Research interests include (bonded) child labour, poverty and inequality, development aid, migration and refugees and non-governmental organisation (NGO) movements.

Hans van de Glind works with the International Labour Organization's International Programme on the Elimination of Child Labour (ILO-IPEC) in Geneva, coordinating work against child trafficking globally, and is (co) author of various related publications. He has been with the ILO since 1997, with prior postings in the Mekong Subregion and China, designing/ managing anti-trafficking projects. Prior to ILO he worked with the International Organization for Migration (IOM) on irregular migration and human trafficking, and with non-governmental organisations (NGOs) in South Asia.

Aarti Kapoor is a qualified international lawyer. She worked against human trafficking and child exploitation in Asia and the UK and is currently Chief Policy Adviser with the Child Exploitation and Online Protection Centre (CEOP). In Asia, Aarti developed extensive experience working with non-governmental organisations (NGOs), the Asian Development Bank and the United Nations (UN).

Emma Kelly is a social worker with 10 years experience of practice and training in safeguarding children. Since 2006 Emma has developed a strong interest in child trafficking leading to work with ECPAT UK (End Child Prostitution, Child Pornography and the Trafficking of Children), and publications in this area.

Joost Kooijmans works as a senior legal officer in the International Labour Organization's International Programme on the Elimination of Child Labour (ILO-IPEC) in Geneva and was posted for some years for the ILO in Southern Africa. He has worked for the United Nations Office of the

High Commissioner for Human Rights (UNOHCHR) and as an expert for the European Commission.

Esben Leifsen is a social anthropologist, and currently a senior lecturer at the Department of International Environment and Development Studies at the Norwegian University of Life Sciences in Norway. Research interests span the Andean indigenous economy and global integration, child abandonment and care, the governance of reproduction, child trafficking and children in transnational migration.

Aidan McQuade is Director of Anti-Slavery International, the oldest international human rights organisation in the world. Before joining Anti-Slavery International, he worked in humanitarian response and development in Ethiopia and Eritrea (on rural water supply and soil conservation), and Afghanistan, in war-displaced persons camps. In Angola, at the end of the civil war, he managed an emergency relief programme in interior cities and worked with the United Nations (UN) on civilian human rights protection.

Virginia Murillo Herrera is a sociologist with an MA in development. She is a researcher, evaluator and consultant on human rights, international cooperation, violence against children, local development and institutional building capacities. She is a United Nations High Commissioner on Human Rights (UNHCHR) expert and board member of the UN Voluntary Fund on Contemporary Forms of Slavery. She is Executive President of DCI (Defence for Children International) Costa Rica.

Andrea Nicholson is a senior lecturer at Nottingham Law School, leading modules on public law, public international law and international human rights. She is an editor for the *Nottingham Law Journal*. Her research interests concern the law relating to contemporary forms of slavery and slavery-like practices, and human rights.

Cecilia Flores Oebanda faced great difficulties as a child labourer, leading her to dedicate her life to catalysing innovative efforts to protect, uphold and promote the rights and dignity of Filipinos. Her efforts aim to help them find work without the risk of abuse and exploitation, and to have the freedom to explore opportunities without fear of being enslaved.

Evelyn Omoike is a doctoral researcher involved in researching different forms of child labour. She is currently exploring fostering in relation to child domestic work in West Africa and is interested in children's interpretation and experiences of the Convention on the Rights of the Child's (CRC) notion of best interest.

Enrique Restoy is Programmes and Advocacy Team Manager at Anti-Slavery International. He was previously Programmes Manager at the International Child Soldiers Coalition and a researcher for West Africa at Amnesty International.

Padam Simkhada is Lecturer and Programme Coordinator for the MSc in International Health and Management at Aberdeen University, and Visiting Professor for Manamohan Institute of Health Science, Purbanchal University, Nepal. He publishes extensively on health issues in Nepal and elsewhere and has a PhD from the University of Southampton.

Jonathan Todres is Associate Professor of Law at Georgia State University College of Law, Atlanta, US. His research focuses on children's rights issues, particularly trafficking and commercial sexual exploitation. He has authored numerous publications on children's rights, co-editing a book on the Convention on the Rights of the Child (CRC).

Catherine Turner is Child Labour Programme Coordinator at Anti-Slavery International, researching and advocating on child slavery issues there since 2002. She has been Deputy Representative to the United Nations (UN) in Geneva for Amnesty International, and worked for the Foreign and Commonwealth Office and the Quaker UN Office. She has a Master of Laws (LLM) in International Human Rights Law from the University of Essex and an MA in International Relations and European Studies from the Central European University, Budapest.

List of abbreviations

AAC	area advisory council
ACRWC	African Charter on the Rights and Welfare of the Child
ANPPCAN	African Network for the Prevention and Protection against Child Abuse and Neglect
ASE	Aide Sociale à l'Enfance (French Child Welfare Agency)
ASEAN	Association of South East Asian Nations
BBA	Bachpan Bachao Andolan (Save the Childhood Movement, India)
BMG	Bal Mitra Gram [child-friendly village]
CDD/CDI	*contrat durée déterminée/indéterminée* (temporary/ indeterminate job contract)
CDW	child domestic worker
CEDAW	Convention on the Elimination of all forms of Discrimination Against Women
CEOP	Child Exploitation and Online Protection Centre
COSECODENI	Coordinadora de ONGs para la Defensa de los Derechos de la Niñez y la Adolescencia (NGO group for the Defence of the Rights of Children and Adolescents)
CPN(M)	Communist Party of Nepal (Maoist)
CRC	Convention on the Rights of the Child
CSR	corporate social responsibility
DCLC	district child labour committees
DCI	Defence for Children International
ECHR	European Convention on Human Rights
ECPAT	End Child Prostitution, Child Pornography and the Trafficking of Children
EU	European Union
FGM	female genital mutilation
FMU	Forced Marriage Unit
GC	Global Compact
GDP	gross domestic product
ICCPR	International Covenant on Civil and Political Rights
ICESCR	International Covenant on Economic, Social and Cultural Rights
IDFM	internal displacement due to forced migration
IEC	information, education and communication
ILC	International Labour Conference

ILO	International Labour Organization
IOM	International Organization for Migration
IPEC	International Programme on the Elimination of Child Labour
ITC	International Training Centre (ILO)
LRA	Lord's Resistance Army (Uganda)
NAFTA	North American Free Trade Agreement
NAP	national action plan
NGO	non-governmental organisation
OATIA	Oficina de Atención y Erradicación del Trabajo Infantil y Protección al Trabajador Adolescente (Office for the Elimination of Child Labour and the Protection of Working Adolescents)
OPAC	Optional Protocol on the Involvement of Children in Armed Conflict
OPSC	Optional Protocol on the Sale of Children, Child Prostitution and Child Pornography
SCREAM	Supporting Children's Rights through Education, the Arts and the Media (programme)
SPARC	Society for the Protection of the Rights of the Child
UN	United Nations
UNDP	United Nations Development Programme
UNODC	United Nations Office on Drugs and Crime
UNOCHA	United Nations Office for the Coordination of Humanitarian Affairs
UNOHCHR	United Nations Office of the High Commissioner for Human Rights
UPDF	Ugandan People's Defence Force
WISE	Wilberforce Institute for the study of Slavery and Emancipation (University of Hull)

List of boxes, figures, tables and photos

Boxes

Figures

Tables

Photos

Introduction: Child slavery worldwide

Gary Craig

Origins

This book has its origins in two international conferences that I organised in 2006 and 2008[1] at the Wilberforce Institute for the study of Slavery and Emancipation (WISE) at the University of Hull, where I was then Associate Director and Professor of Social Justice, leading the team working on issues of contemporary slavery. The first conference was organised as a counterpoint to a series of events held in Hull and nationally to commemorate the 200th anniversary of the British Act of Parliament that had abolished the slave trade (although, sadly, not slavery itself), an Act that followed the parliamentary campaign led by William Wilberforce, sometime Member of Parliament (MP) for Yorkshire (including Hull), and whose name was adopted when WISE was founded (see www.hull.ac.uk/WISE). This bicentennial was dominated by discussion, particularly in the UK, other western European countries, North America and Africa, of the transatlantic slave trade and its historical legacies, and provided few opportunities to review the ongoing existence of slavery. Some of the papers given at the 2006 conference raised issues about child slavery and these, with other commissioned papers, found their way into a special issue of the journal *Childhood and Society*, published in mid-2008.[2] Following discussions with those active in this area of work, it appeared that there would be more than sufficient interest to organise a follow-up conference focused entirely on the issue of childhood slavery. This proved to be the case and the follow-up 2008 conference drew academics, activists, policy makers and politicians together from across the world, to examine the question of child slavery worldwide.

It is common for conferences to lead to edited collections of papers and this was the case here. Many of the following chapters, however, were not delivered at the conference but specially commissioned for this book. This book has, however, a more pressing agenda than a purely academic one. Child slavery, as we shall see, is not only developing new forms (for example, child soldiers or cannabis cultivation), but it is also increasingly shaped by the processes of globalisation in ways that were not possible even 20 years ago. Obvious influences are the greater possibilities for mobility (as a result of cheaper travel), the re-emergence of criminal gangs linking supply of human beings to demand, and the growth of trade serving northern consumers of cheaper products, such as clothing, footwear, stone, jewellery and minerals and foodstuffs, produced by children working in slavery conditions in the global South.

Despite a range of international and national legislation, child slavery does not appear to be on the wane. Indeed, it appears that there remains large-scale unawareness that it is a major global problem (despite evidence facing consumers daily purchasing foreign-made goods at ridiculously low prices) or, in many cases, that child slavery exists at all. Archbishop Emeritus Desmond Tutu, first patron of WISE, elegantly expressed this lack of public awareness in the foreword to a report scoping the extent of modern slavery in the UK (Craig et al, 2007, frontispiece):

> Slavery ... I didn't know about all these forms that existed. I think it's largely because we aren't expecting it. It is hidden. Generally people would not believe that it is possible under modern conditions. They would say 'No I think you are making it all up', because it's just too incredible.[3]

The pressing political agenda of this book then, is to help raise levels of public and political awareness of the issue of child slavery and to help in the process of its abolition.

Themes

Bales has argued elsewhere (Bales, 2007) that the resources required to abolish modern slavery as a whole are relatively modest, certainly in comparison with the gross domestic product (GDP) of a single major industrialised economy, and he repeats this argument in the Afterword to this volume. However, resources by themselves are clearly not enough to abolish slavery: there are many examples worldwide where attempts to free slaves have failed because their rehabilitation was not undertaken holistically. It is not just a question of releasing slaves from whatever form of bondage they are in or even giving them a financial package to restart their lives. Former slaves need psychological, material, physical, emotional and local community support if they are to rebuild their lives. Most of all, they need the structural context in which they became slaves to change, and this requires much more broad-based political, economic and cultural change, and a concerted attack on poverty, inequality, discrimination, political and economic corruption and crime.

What we probably need least of all are changes in the law. Virtually every country in the world – with the exception only of international pariahs such as Myanmar (Burma) – has either signed up to international legislation or protocols making child slavery illegal or has developed its own parallel legislative framework. To take the most obvious example, in India, federal legislation, much of it binding on local states, has been in place, making forced labour and trafficking illegal since 1976 and 1954 respectively. Child domestic labour for those under 14 years of age has been illegal under federal legislation since 2004. Nevertheless, millions of children – the largest single numbers of anywhere in the world – live in India under conditions of slavery, as chapters in this book demonstrate, a result of a combination of a lack of political will, the impact of the hugely discriminatory caste system, the powerful economic interests of India's growing middle classes and widespread legal and judicial corruption. Child slavery is effectively embedded in the country's culture and economy and it will require more or less revolutionary policies and practices to abolish it.

The same story can be repeated, with differing emphases, in most other countries in the world. In the UK, for example, awareness of child slavery is only just appearing on the radar of policy and politics. However, the issue of trafficking has become distorted by the fact that the discourse is often dominated by the overriding concern of government and other political parties to be seen to be tough on immigration. As a result, trafficking victims – often entering the country legally but then tricked by criminals or gangmasters – tend to be viewed more through the lens of policing initiatives to track criminals than seen as subject to the brutal manipulation of criminal gangs; and the question of forced labour in southern countries (and indeed in the UK itself; see Craig, 2010) is pushed to one side in the search for ever-cheaper goods and services, regardless of the conditions under which they are produced. Clearly, one necessary prerequisite is that there should be an absence of corruption in official circles. This, as several chapters point out, is a counsel of excellence: officials who may themselves be living in poverty can often see opportunities for enhancing their income by acting as brokers or conduits for information or for children themselves.

One frequently occurring theme in the chapters is that of definitions and boundaries. This is not just an academic nicety. On the one hand, ever more sophisticated and precise definitions have been developed in protocols and conventions; on the other, too rigid definitions lead to inflexible responses that sometimes cannot address new manifestations of child slavery. The difficulty is that without clear definitions of what is and what is not child slavery, the issue, as one writer puts it, is 'diluted', leading to a situation where policy responses are vague or undermined. Public credibility is lost and hostile media attacks can lead people to believe that the issue does not exist, a process exemplified in Archbishop Desmond Tutu's earlier quote. There can be no doubt that child slavery exists, but its parameters need to be kept clearly in mind to avoid both confusion in policy and service responses, or political antipathy. The search for quantitative certainty has little meaning; for an activity that is so covert, it is literally a waste of time to try and achieve anything other than rough orders of magnitude.

A systemic approach to child slavery is clearly needed, an argument supported by many chapters included here. This means a system where the various elements – police, judiciary, politicians, statutory professionals (and in many differing welfare sectors), non-governmental organisations (NGOs) and activists, and the media too – understand the nature of the problem, share intelligence and work collaboratively towards common goals and within a common value system. This is not always the case. For example, in multicultural countries, there is often confusion about the value base of certain practices ascribed to cultural groups. References back to the basics – for example the values underpinning the Convention on the Rights of the Child (CRC) and the framework of basic human rights in the 1948 United Nations (UN) Declaration – should resolve such confusions but often do not, especially where cultural relativism is at work. The impact of casteism in India and the familial exploitation of children in West Africa are examples of situations where 'traditional' practices frequently remain unchallenged because they are accepted as 'normal' practices.

It also requires an approach that spans national borders, since trafficking, by definition, involves movement across borders. There are a few examples of such international collaboration, between 'sending' and receiving countries, mentioned within this book, but much more information is needed both in policy, politics, action and research. This systemic approach needs to be supported by adequate resources: many writers detail how an analysis of the problem and recommendations for action fail because the issue is not taken seriously enough in terms of resources. If there were adequate resources, there could be a much wider range of interventions to add to those described here. Critical too is the international monitoring and supervision undertaken by organisations such as the International Labour Organization (ILO), so the worst performers can be brought up to the standards of the best. However, the most important contributors to a systemic approach are policy and political interventions to address the roots of slavery, outlined earlier.

Finally, but certainly not least, there is a role for the public in every country. Most child slavery is 'invisibilised', but for those who wish to find it, the evidence of child slavery is there to be seen, whether it be in the manifestly low prices of consumer goods marketed in rich countries (prices reflecting the low or no wages paid to child workers in poor countries), the appearance of unusual activity in a neighbourhood, which requires explanation (Pai, 2009) but is often disregarded by neighbours who prefer 'not to get involved', the disappearance of children, or examples of maltreatment needing properly to be investigated. In many cases, in fact, it is members of the public who first observe these unusual phenomena and they have a key role in making the 'invisible' visible. Their interest needs to be aroused by public education and community awareness campaigns,[4] some described in this volume. It is often awareness at a community level that first alerts officials or the police to a situation that may result in the release of those held in slavery.

At the centre of any attempt to abolish child slavery must be a focus on the children themselves. This means that the process of 'rescue' and rehabilitation must be holistic, paying attention to their social, economic, psychological and physical needs and to providing sustainable alternatives to the context of exploitation from which they have been freed. But it must also be remembered that children have agency: they can play a part both in their own rehabilitation and in that of others; this is especially important in situations where family have been colluding in slavery. Typically their struggle to free themselves is part of wider collective efforts and this should also be remembered by those active on the ground. It is also important to respond to how different forms of child slavery are heavily gendered when planning interventions – girls are more vulnerable, more open to cultural pressures to conform to certain roles and are often less well supported in their struggles to achieve independence.

Child slavery is without doubt one of the most heinous crimes of present times. It occurs in different forms across the world and in ways that link countries in often unseen ways. Most of the elements are in place to combat it effectively: laws, conventions, activists, intelligence, committed politicians and policy makers and models of good practice. These are, however, rarely brought together in one place and as we have noted, the resources to help them do their work effectively are often also not in place.

Faced with the evidence gathered in this volume, and the numbers of those estimated to be in childhood slavery, it is tempting to assume that the problem is intractable. People often ask 'but what can I do?'. In fact history shows that many important and indeed revolutionary changes have occurred as a result of the actions of relatively few people. There is a role for everyone, from Presidents to ordinary members of the public, in challenging childhood slavery and, viewed through a positive lens, the chapters in this volume show many ways in which this can be done. At the local level, Fairtrade campaigns and anti-slavery education – in schools and with the general public – is significant. At the other end of the scale, global collaboration can set targets and frameworks that drive programmes in all countries focused on the abolition of slavery. The Worst Forms of Child Labour Convention No 182 sponsored by the ILO and the Dutch government in May 2010, discussed in Chapter Two, which brought together 400 actors from every country and every sector, is one leading example of such international collaborative action. Regional organisations such as the African Union, the North American Free Trade Agreement (NAFTA), the European Union (EU) and the Association of South East Asian Nations (ASEAN) can also take a much more prominent role in leading debate and change within their regions. Within virtually every country of the world, there are NGOs and campaigns accessible to all who wish to engage in the struggle to abolish childhood slavery. The issues are becoming much clearer as a result of the research of dedicated scholars and activists, many of them represented in this volume. We hope this book, based on some of the cutting-edge work in this field, will go at least a little way towards helping support the global campaign against child slavery worldwide.

Outline

The book is divided into two main sections, an introductory section of eight chapters, which reviews issues relating to child slavery in a strategic way, and a second section of 11 chapters, each of which deals with one aspect of childhood slavery in some detail and from differing perspectives or in different locations. The chapters as a whole draw on material from across the world, underlining the point that childhood slavery is indeed a global problem, both in terms of being present in every country of the world but also by virtue of the links, in the trades of goods, services and human beings, occurring between different countries. A Resources section is provided at the end of the book covering details of other organisations, websites, events and other useful literature to supplement references given at the end of each chapter. The present part of this introductory chapter reviews the contents of the individual chapters, while the earlier part has drawn out key issues from the book as a whole. These issues are also reviewed in an Afterword, kindly contributed by Professor Kevin Bales, one of the world's leading authorities on modern slavery and sometime colleague at WISE.

The ILO is the pre-eminent international body tasked with addressing issues of exploitation in the labour market, and one section, IPEC (International Programme on the Elimination of Child Labour), is responsible for monitoring the global situation vis-à-vis the exploitation of children. In Chapter One, IPEC analysts Joost Kooijmans and Hans van de Glind review the extent and nature of child slavery, tracing the history of the concept of slavery and the first attempts at abolition through to the range of conventions and protocols that emerged during the 20th century. These provide a range of definitions of child slavery that are increasingly wide-ranging and sophisticated at the same time, moving from those shaped very much by the notion of chattel slavery ('the status or condition of a person over whom any or all of the powers attaching to the right of ownership are exercised', p ??) to understanding slavery in a more modern context, playing catch-up with its new manifestations of slavery and child slavery alike. Today, as they say, 'the prohibition of slavery and various slavery-like practices is well enshrined in international and regional human rights treaties', the term 'slavery-like practices' being introduced specifically to refer to contemporary forms of slavery. Increasingly, international conventions (such as the 2000 Palermo Protocol and ILO Worst Forms of Child Labour Convention No 182) have developed definitions specifically addressing child slavery, identifying in particular forms of forced labour and trafficking pertinent to childhood. Increasingly, too, it has been necessary to distinguish between child slavery and forms of child exploitation that, while 'illegal and reprehensible', are not strictly slavery.

Chapter One also reviews what we know about the quantitative dimensions of child slavery. Because it is illegal, accurate data will always be difficult to obtain: the authors' best estimate is of approximately six million children in slavery worldwide, although larger estimates are available reflecting more wide-ranging definitions of childhood slavery. The authors review the scope of childhood slavery as encompassing forced labour, trafficking (for forced labour or sexual exploitation), debt bondage, serfdom, child soldiers and children forced into a range of illicit activities. These are all examined in detail in subsequent chapters in the book. Finally, they examine the current state of political and policy response, pointing to the need for clear enforceable legal frameworks, effective use of supervisory mechanisms by agencies such as the ILO, better and more targeted research, and wider mobilisation, including of the public at large, businesses and trade unions. Key goals for victims are for their empowerment, and effective multidimensional rehabilitation and reintegration. This programme needs to be supported by a global action plan, driven forward by the ILO-IPEC staff, working within a clear timetable.

In Chapter Two, Trevor Buck and Andrea Nicholson, both UK legal academics, examine in depth the international legal framework. Questions of definition remain problematic conceptually and legally, and this in turn leads to difficulties both in quantifying the extent of the problem of child slavery and in policing it. Narrow definitions such as in the 1926 Slavery Convention suggest that child slavery is a limited phenomenon; on the other hand, thinking of the wider term 'exploitation' leads us to a position where the notion of slavery becomes heavily diluted, thus losing 'any analytical integrity or functionality'. In the modern context, there is no sense in distinguishing between slavery and servitude, for example, and the same challenge may need to be made regarding the distinction between slavery and forced (child) labour. One helpful development over the past century has been the emergence of child-specific rights, challenging the notion of the child as entirely at the whim of adults, focused most of all on the 1989 UN CRC, endorsed by all countries in the world except, infamously, the US and Somalia, 'providing a near-global normative legal standard, customised specifically to children'.

The legal frameworks relating to child labour and child trafficking are examined in detail, the authors commenting on the current failings of international supervision to enforce the protocols and conventions that have allegedly been endorsed by individual signatory states. Even where states are politically willing to act effectively, the covert nature of child slavery can undermine these attempts; for those less politically compliant, the hidden nature of slavery provides an easy means for avoiding their responsibilities. The authors conclude guardedly that 'the movement from generic rights to the creation of treaties concerned with more distinct practices, and a focus on child-specific rights, has led to the positive construction of measures that go beyond criminalisation and are aimed at providing more comprehensive assistance to the victim and the recognition of children as active rights holders'; they also argue that much more needs to be done.

The two main forms of child slavery numerically are now forced (child) labour and child trafficking, usually for sexual exploitation, although also for forced labour. The following two chapters provide overviews of child labour. In Chapter Three, Catherine Turner, Aidan McQuade and Enrique Restoy, from Anti-Slavery International, the longest-standing UK anti-slavery organisation within the UK, evaluate the effectiveness of one of the conventions identified in Chapter One, the ILO Worst Forms of Child Labour Convention No 182. They do this by examining outcomes of a 'snapshot' fieldwork study undertaken in Costa Rica, Kenya, Pakistan and Togo, in collaboration with local activist partner organisations, a study that included reviewing literature and policy documents and interviews with individuals and group discussions. This kind of study helps to establish just how effective international protocols and conventions are in changing the situation on the ground. It confirms, as we noted earlier, that the problem on the ground is often not a question of a lack of law or policy but lies in the inability or unwillingness of the police, the judiciary and policy makers to address the activities of criminal gangs, and to confront the phenomenon in the private sector where much of the abuse remains hidden but is often more extreme. Overall, despite a few successes and some positive case studies, often following concerted campaigns, including publicity and the removal of barriers to children having real alternatives open to them – particularly education – the impact of the Convention at local level in these areas was disappointing. Gathering data was often problematic, potential key actors such as trade unions were not as effectively involved in campaigning as might be hoped and international conventions were sometimes not fully incorporated into national laws. At a structural level, the impact of poverty, natural disasters and large-scale migration were critical in generating conditions under which child labour became a significant local phenomenon.

Jonathan Blagbrough, in Chapter Four, then focuses on child domestic labour, examining detailed evidence, again based on fieldwork, from a wide range of countries, including Peru, Togo, the Philippines and Tanzania. Child domestic work is one of the most widespread, dangerous and exploitative forms of child work in the world today, and one of the most difficult to tackle. Children are hard to reach not only because they work behind the closed doors of their employers' homes, but also because societies often see the practice as normal and – in relation to girls – important training for later life. One major shift required then is in cultural attitudes within many societies. The issue is not simply the fact that many children have to start work at a young age, thus foregoing education and the normal transitions from childhood to adulthood, but the conditions – often of physical, emotional and not infrequently sexual exploitation – under which they work. Not all employers of child domestic workers are cruel or highly exploitative but many are, and unlike many child labourers, child domestic workers start work at a very young age. The hidden nature of the work makes interventions difficult and Blagbrough argues that many of these interventions should be targeted at employers, requiring them to improve the conditions under which children work; in particular, allowing them access to education, recreation and contact with their peers, normal requirements for children in any civilised society. Once again, the impact of family poverty is significant in driving children into this kind of work, often serving wider family needs, and thus occupying roles that are doubly inappropriate. The growth of the middle classes in hitherto very poor countries has led to increased demand for cheap servants. This demand is often highly gendered, with an emphasis on girls who are seen culturally as more expendable and fulfilling roles culturally sanctioned as 'women's work'.

Some national legislation, action by NGOs and increasing consideration at international levels may help to change this situation. Access to education is key, and Blagbrough sees a role for children themselves as agents for change. There is indeed much evidence worldwide of the ability of children, using community development techniques, to change the context in which they live (Craig, 2002).

The following four chapters then provide different strategic takes on the issue of child trafficking. In Chapter Five, Hans van de Glind provides a detailed overview of the issue of child trafficking, to complement the more wide-ranging review of child slavery in Chapter Two. Children, he argues, and especially those on the margins of societies, are very vulnerable to trafficking, as their isolation and separation from their families and communities leaves them in places where they may not speak the language or have any legal status. The key centres for child trafficking are Asia, Latin America and the Caribbean, but it is a worldwide phenomenon. Although the recruitment and movement involved in trafficking may appear voluntary at first, they eventually take on aspects of coercion by third parties; girls, as with child domestic labour, are affected disproportionately, both for commercial sexual exploitation and domestic labour, whereas boys are more likely to be trafficked for forced labour. Critically, sexual exploitation, although dominant, is by no means the only form of child trafficking. A significant number of boys are also trafficked – both internally and externally from any one country – for sexual and other forms of exploitation. In the UK for example, Vietnamese young boys have been trafficked to farm cannabis in domestic settings throughout the country. The balance between differing types of child trafficking varies from one context to another.

Van de Glind provides a numerical analysis of child trafficking, suggesting that many more than one million children are trafficked at any one time, and reviews key treaties, protocols and conventions from 1949. The ILO considers that what makes child trafficking distinct from other forms of child slavery is the element of movement; as a result of easier migration both within and beyond national borders, and the activities of international criminals, child trafficking has become a very significant phenomenon. The question of consent is irrelevant for children and this, theoretically at least, makes it easier for law enforcement agencies to ensure that child traffickers are punished. However, child trafficking can take many forms, taking place in a home community, at a transit point or at a final destination. Third parties – acting criminally – are always involved, but they may take different forms, and family members may collude in the trafficking process.

National endorsement of international trafficking legislation is rather more patchy than with other conventions on child slavery and this yet again makes the relationship between trafficking and poverty, structural unemployment and the impact of natural and man–made disasters (such as war) significant: van de Glind notes, for example, that seasonal floods in Bihar, India, were followed by a surge in child trafficking.

Combating trafficking requires subtle responses, informed by good intelligence. Criminal gangs continually shift the way in which they work, responding to new forms of demand but also to attempts by policing agencies to control them, by developing new methods and new routes. All depend, however, on manipulation and deceit and on the vulnerability of those being trafficked. Governments need to understand the meaning of vulnerability and identify the range of risk factors making trafficking of children more likely. Stronger law enforcement tools, stricter, less ambiguous laws, labour inspection, corporate social responsibility (CSR) mechanisms, specialised knowledge and outreach to workers' and employers' organisations, can all contribute to the protection of families whose children are at risk of (re)trafficking. Education and the agency of children themselves can be important obstacles to the crime of trafficking.

In Chapters Six and Eight, the authors examine aspects of trafficking in a strategic way through the experience of the UK, a not untypical 'developed' and industrialised country that is both the destination and transit country for children being trafficked. Aarti Kapoor, in Chapter Six, examines, from her experience of the UK government-sponsored innovative Child Exploitation and Online Protection Centre (CEOP), ways in which child exploitation is being monitored and policed, and provides a detailed conceptual and policy analysis of the UK experience. Although the wider concept of exploitation is analysed here, it is accepted that this largely focuses on the fact of child trafficking, with numerous forms of child exploitation as the end purpose of trafficking, including sexual exploitation, domestic servitude, benefit fraud, cannabis cultivation, labour exploitation/forced labour, drug trafficking/ smuggling/dealing, illegal adoption, servile/forced marriage, street crime and begging. These, as van de Glind notes in Chapter Five, all involve the process of movement of the child, but Kapoor reminds us that other forms of child exploitation may exist, not involving movement. There remain arguments about definition and boundaries, and the growth of sectional and sectoral interests does not help the process of developing coherent and clear responses. For example, where trafficking becomes interwoven with political concerns about immigration, the clear focus on the needs and rights of victims may become obscured. Kapoor attempts to unravel and clarify these contested conceptual (and political) debates by locating the UK experience in the context of international conventions, notably the Palermo Protocol referred to earlier. While trafficking is associated with movement and thus often with crossing national borders, this does not make the task of identifying trafficked children much easier, particularly where enforcement officials have poor or no training. While definitions are important for the police and judiciary, it is important not to lock ourselves into a tight legal definition, not least because this impedes developing and flexible responses.

Jonathan Todres examines the issue of trafficking through the lens of a human rights approach in Chapter Seven. If we can analyse the rights of the child, for example through the CRC, the failure of national governments (backed or pushed by international legislation) to pay attention to the cumulative effect of protecting the key individual rights of the child, for example freedom from discrimination, birth registration rights (see Chapter Ten), rights to education, healthcare and t protection in the labour market, illuminates the cumulative effect of this lack of rights leading to vulnerability to trafficking and indeed to other forms of exploitation. This is the root cause of trafficking, supporting the argument advanced in other chapters that a multi-organisational or multisectoral approach to child trafficking is required, one that does not depend on narrow policing, immigration or social welfare interventions. Such an holistic approach will reduce vulnerability to trafficking and offer wider benefits such as increasing development and strengthening communities.

Finally, in this group of more strategic overviews, in Chapter Eight, Farhat Bokhari and Emma Kelly, both former members of the UK branch of ECPAT (End Child Prostitution, Child Pornography and the Trafficking of Children), an international network of prominent anti-child trafficking NGOs, analyse the grounded experience of children trafficked into the UK, including those – such as an identifiable group of girls and young women –

who are then trafficked on into other European countries. Even in a country such as the UK, with a well-developed policing and monitoring system, largely free from corruption, providing accurate data remains problematic, a lacuna exploited recently in hostile media coverage challenging the notion that trafficking is a serious problem at all. The consensus, however, is that hundreds, and more likely thousands, of children are trafficked into the UK annually, and that this is not solely for sexual exploitation but for a much wider range of purposes. Known numbers are also probably deflated by the fact that cultural confusion among policing agencies – seemingly a result of increasing ethnic diversity within the UK – leads some social services and related professionals to perceive certain forms of trafficking as acceptable cultural practices. This view was challenged – but certainly not totally demolished – by the death of Victoria Climbié, a young West African child trafficked into the UK (under the guise of being fostered by an 'auntie'), and later beaten to death by her putative foster parents.

The drivers for trafficking in sending countries are the familiar litany of absolute and relative poverty, and the exploitation and manipulation of criminals who present a life of 'better opportunities' for children, facilitated by the increasingly easier opportunities for children to be migrated from one country to another. The notion of informal fosterage (see Chapter Twelve) – often used to conceal exploitation and child domestic labour within African countries – has been an important tool for traffickers to convey a sense of respectability and legality in their intentions towards children. Other key areas needing further scrutiny and policing include the practice of diplomatic families, typically from the Gulf States and the Horn of Africa, trafficking girls into their embassies under the guise of family membership to act as servants and/or to be sexually exploited (which has begun to attract media attention), and that of forced marriages, under the pretence of family reunion, the focus of a separate study by Bokhari.

Trafficked children themselves, as a result of deception but also in common with victims of domestic abuse, may not see their experience as exploitative, and this makes the problem, of monitoring and policing child trafficking, more complicated. Children may not be aware of their rights and where they are, are unwilling to pursue them or distrustful of authority; a patient process of building trust is often necessary but often precluded by lack of resources or political imperatives. There are a number of ways in which policy, practice and political perspectives need to be changed, both to verify the extent of child trafficking and to underpin effective responses to it.

Part II contains a wide range of more detailed and focused chapters, exploring different aspects of or themes related to child slavery from across the world, and drawing on the perspectives of activists, policy makers, academics and support groups. These are summarised below.

In Chapter Nine Jason and Patricia Aliperti discuss how education for all children is one of the most important tools in abolishing child trafficking. There are also international conventions covering the issue of education, notably in the UN CRC, but while most countries such as India, the case study discussed here, have signed up to these conventions, in practice the desire of parents to send their children to school, thus opening up opportunities to better themselves, is overwhelmed by major structural factors such as family poverty, illiteracy and the cultural and historical ties of debt bondage. The authors' approach to education is based on the Freirian notion of education as empowerment and the development of critical consciousness (Freire, 2002), illustrated through case studies collected in a fieldwork study. In these case studies, they explore how critical consciousness can be developed to confront factors making villages more prone to child trafficking. How, too, can children and their wider communities be empowered to act as agents for social change rather than necessarily relying on the interventions of external agents?

In Chapter Ten, drawing on the experience of Plan International, Claire Cody describes the utilisation of what is, on the face of it, a remarkably simple tool to prevent child trafficking, that of birth registration. For countries with sophisticated systems of record keeping, this may seem an unremarkable claim. Yet in many countries, because of a failure of government resources, inadequate administrative procedures, family poverty, a lack of awareness, limited political will and corruption, failure to register births often happens on a large scale. Parents are also often discouraged by the prospect of taxation or even by the fear that registered children become, in due course, 'visible' for conscription into armies or slave armies. Yet this registration is the key to claiming a host of rights: in a sense it defines the child as existing at all, hence its enshrinement in the CRC (Articles 7 and 8). It opens the way to healthcare, education, nationality and to the formal labour market. As we know, child trafficking relies on obscured and hidden activities; it is hardly surprising that the failure to register a child's birth contributes to the conditions sought by traffickers.

Using the example of irregular North African child migrants in the port city of Marseille, France, Brenda Oude Breuil explores, in Chapter Eleven, some boundaries of the meaning of trafficking. Many of these young people may not start their journey as trafficking victims, believing stories passed back to them that migration may offer the route to a better life than is available in the Maghreb. Whether or not they actually cross other borders, they enter what the author characterises as liminal 'borderlands'. Interestingly, given Cody's discussion of birth registration, these migrants are not *sans papiers* in the sense of being refused leave to remain in the French system but are *harragas* ('those who burn their papers'): they destroy their identity in the search for the excitement and danger that a liminal existence offers. Some may operate almost autonomously, albeit staying ahead of the immigration authorities; others are 'managed' by agents who control their supply of goods to sell (in this case, cheap cigarettes). They live in the borderland of two statuses, 'child victim of trafficking' and 'illegal migrant', and we see here some of the difficulties that local policing and welfare agencies face as a result.

Evelyn Omoike, in Chapter Thirteen, has another perspective on the boundaries of trafficking, and looks in detail at one of the aspects of child trafficking touched on earlier by Kelly and Bokhari, that of fostering. She examines the practice of fostering in the West African context, and the extent to which it overlaps with the phenomenon of child domestic work, very extensive in many West African cities. She argues that current child labour policies and interventions that focus primarily on the nature of work those children undertake, described earlier in detail by Blagbrough, for example, fail to properly take into account the nature of domestic work; this work, often undertaken under the guise of 'fosterage', frequently but not necessarily through kinship networks, is a common cultural phenomenon. Failure to understand how this operates and overlaps with child domestic work more generally reinforces the exclusion and exploitation African child domestic labourers face. Traffickers can take advantage of this system to place children in exploitative situations, for example. Because children then lack supportive networks, they can be open to horrific abuse: Omoike agrees that the exploitation of children arises from the situation in which they live and work, and not just the work they do. Unlike most other forms of child slavery, there is yet no convention explicitly targeted on child domestic labour.

In Chapter Thirteen, Serdar M. Degirmencioglu, Hakan Acar and Yüksel Baykara Acar analyse the nuances within another national context, Turkey, where children are moved from their homes, often with the collusion of family members, to other – rural or urban – labour markets where they work under conditions of forced labour. Two little known forms of child labour in Turkey are described and examined. The process through which these children are made to work is revealed as closely related to slavery practices. One, involving forced labour, is a long-standing practice from northwestern Turkey of parents hiring children to better-off farmers. The other, a more recent phenomenon, involves children being trafficked to big cities and forced to join criminal rings. Both forms are consequences of poverty but the possibilities for exploitation are enhanced by the instability and lack of monitoring associated with the internal displacement of families. Here, the authors note that agencies are becoming aware of the problem but their response is compromised by having little understanding that forced migration underpins many of the difficulties children face.

Birendra Raj Giri provides a parallel example in Chapter Fourteen, from Nepal, showing how a bonded labour system has existed for hundreds of years where children are used by parents to pay off debts incurred to landlords by offering their own children's labour to the landlords. This labour might be repaid by a mixture of cash or kind, including foodstuffs and clothing, to help families eking out a meagre existence on poor land. While away from their home, children – particularly girls – are open to a variety of forms of physical, sexual and psychological abuse and struggle to maintain their work responsibilities alongside their desire to stay in education and improve their lot. Again, laws exist in Nepal to ban this system of *kamaiya*, yet the forms of childhood abuse are so extensive that they fall within the ILO definition of the worst forms of child labour (see Chapters One and Four). What had been an adult form of debt bondage has shifted, as a result of pressures of poverty, into a system based now as much on children as adults, with the political system turning a blind eye to the practice. Not all of the landlord class are deeply exploitative, but those attending to the children's needs seem relatively rare.

Chapter Fifteen, by Padam Simkhada, provides a companion piece looking at child (girl) trafficking from Nepal to other countries, mainly India. He points to the difficulties of obtaining accurate figures, although it is known that the scale of the problem is considerable. Programmes have been developed to address child trafficking but there has been recent criticism of national and local political apathy on the issue, and the continued chronic lack of law enforcement to address this problem. Girls who are trafficked are typically unmarried, non-literate, coming from rural backgrounds and very young, factors making them very vulnerable. Often trafficking occurs with the collusion of parents or carers. Promises are made about the possibilities of work and the push of poverty drives many young girls to put themselves in the hands of experienced, manipulative traffickers. Simkhada suggests that there is still a lack of precise knowledge about the 'who', 'how' and 'why' of trafficking. He argues for an increase in community-level initiatives and for more holistic rehabilitation schemes that again involve the community in helping those who have been trafficked to reintegrate into normal life.

Bill Brookman and Katherine Darton, in Chapter Sixteen, discuss an innovative programme of work in relation to a peculiarly modern form of child slavery, that of child soldiers. Wars in Central and West Africa in recent years have been characterised by the use of captured children, both as direct protagonists but also as sexual slaves for adult combatants. The SCREAM programme, sponsored by the ILO, uses the arts to educate children about their rights with respect to all forms of work. The exercises include role-plays, creative writing, drawing and painting, theatre projects, debates and so on. Many can be extended to involve the whole community, depending on the context, and Brookman and Darton describe piloting the programme's use in Nepal and Uganda, both sites of vicious civil wars involving thousands of enslaved children.

This is an experimental approach to the rehabilitation of children traumatised by violence and abuse and, as with all such programmes, needs generalising and building on, involving a programme to train trainers, including teachers, advocates and peer educators, who can take the ideas and the material into communities to raise the level of awareness of the issues involved. The authors point out that it would be more helpful still, although more difficult, to use the programme in areas where there is an identified risk of future conflicts occurring.

Esben Leifsen, in Chapter Seventeen, examines another aspect of the difficulties associated with definitions, with boundaries and with judicial and official manipulation in the context of international adoption, in Ecuador. International adoption involves a number of policy, service and legal actors operating within a policy and legal framework. Where officials are corrupt (even if, in their defence, they are driven to be so by their own poverty) or do not fully understand the niceties of that framework, agencies and individuals can manipulate the system to their own advantage. What can be presented by clever operators as an adoption process is, in reality, child trafficking, involving children who have been stolen or removed from parents by a combination of threats and promises. Where cases are exposed by activists, mis-representation of the case can lead the public to perceive the issue as of one or more miscreants rather than being based on a systemic failure. The issue is, in reality, not about a series of 'irregular acts' by criminals acting alone; as Leifsen puts it, 'the most useful cases are those where it is possible to externalise the problem of the irregular, and localise the problem in a restricted set of actors, institutions and types of actions', but the focus on the particular obscures the systemic dimension. Legislation misses the point and is in any case undermined by paltry levels of resources given over to scrutinising the issue.

This section concludes with two shorter chapters from activists in key NGOs. Chapter Eighteen takes us to the Philippines, with a general discussion of child slavery in South and South East Asia. Cecilia Flores Oebanda, of the Visayan Forum Foundation, reviews a familiar listing of structural factors driving the existence of child slavery, and notes again the fact that it is facilitated not by a lack of legislation – laws banning child labour do exist in the Philippines for example – but by weak political will and in many instances, poor governance or ineffectual implementation by those charged with acting on anti-slavery laws and policies. Oebanda notes that internal migration and migration to other countries – the Philippines being a prominent exporter of labour – are of such a scale that child labour is seen as an almost 'normal' process; with agents willing to manipulate, deceive and coerce young people, tens of thousands find themselves in situations of debt bondage or being sexually exploited (or both). An interorganisational approach is needed, reflecting the interconnectedness of the issues; a mix of cultural, economic, social and political factors all reinforce the problem of trafficking. This requires responses from many partners and at many levels in the judicial and welfare systems.

In the final chapter, Chapter Nineteen, Virginia Murillo Herrera describes the process of trafficking into, within and through Central America. Relative poverty is the key driver, with the US to the north a beacon for those seeking economic betterment. The violence of recent civil wars, and of criminal gangs and growing social inequality, create a context for huge levels of out-migration. Within these processes of migration there are, often hidden, substantial numbers of children either seeking an improvement in their own lives or, at least, to rejoin adult family members who migrated earlier also in search of work and a better life. The particular geography of the region makes it a bridge for trafficking and it has come to be seen as a good destination for the commercial sexual exploitation of minors, with accelerating numbers of ever-younger children and adolescents being drawn into the trafficking nexus. Recent laws are driving the problem underground as traffickers find ever more devious ways – using corrupt or ignorant officials, lawyers and professionals – of operating within the broader current of population flow. Countries in the region are attempting to harmonise legislation and at the grassroots level NGOs are also engaging in concerted actions. However, the structures in place in most states are too weak to engage in effective enforcement. There remains a lack of belief in and, consequently, of resources to address the scale of the problem.

The book concludes with a Resources section, which we hope will provide pointers to readers wanting to know more or to become engaged in campaigns and lobbying around the issue; and with an Afterword, contributed by Professor Kevin Bales, who reminds us that the resources devoted to fighting child slavery are far too small, that there exists a range of actions that can be taken and that, with coordinated political, policy and community/NGO action, at local, national and international levels, childhood slavery can be abolished and the gift of childhood given back to the millions of children who are currently enslaved.

Notes

[1] I was assisted enormously in their organisation by Jane Ellison and Charlotte Hursey respectively, who, despite many difficulties being placed in their path that were beyond their control, ensured that both events were highly successful.

[2] Several of the papers for the special issue were rewritten for the present publication and we are grateful to Wiley and Sons for permission to reproduce them, where relevant.

[3] The portrayal of child slavery by the film 'Slumdog Millionaire' was widely greeted with disbelief, and in India, also with denial.

[4] See, for example, the UK Blue Blindfold campaign at www.blueblindfold.co.uk

References

Bales, K. (2007) *Abolishing slavery*, Berkeley, CA: University of California Press.

Craig, G. (2002) 'Children's participation through community development: lessons from international experience', in C. Hallet and A. Prout (eds) *Hearing the voices of children*, London: Routledge, pp 38-56.

Craig, G. (2010) '"Flexibility", xenophobia and exploitation: modern slavery in the UK', *Social Policy Review 22*, Bristol: The Policy Press.

Craig, G., Wilkinson, M., Gaus, A., Skrivankova, K. and McQuade, A. (2007) *Contemporary slavery in the UK: Themes and issues*, York: Joseph Rowntree Foundation.

Freire, P. (2002) *Pedagogy of the oppressed*, New York, NY: Continuum.

Pai, H.H. (2009) *Chinese whispers*, Harmondsworth: Penguin.

Part I
Strategic overviews

one

Child slavery today

Joost Kooijmans and Hans van de Glind[1]

Concept of child slavery

Historical background

Slavery – of adults and children – is probably one of the most horrific human rights violations. History shows that slavery was a feature of virtually all major civilisations. Slaves were captured in wars and slave raids across Europe, the Middle East, Africa and Asia, in practically every era, and the use of slaves in private households was considered normal practice, often a sign of status and affluence. Slave labour was frequently also an important factor in the economies of these civilisations. While not all societies treated their slaves equally badly, slavery always meant that the victim lacked rights and freedoms in all respects: freedom of choice, freedom of self-determination, freedom to own property, freedom to enjoy the fruits of one's labour and many other rights and freedoms now considered inalienable to any human being, as for example in the US Constitution.

Perhaps because slavery has been such a well-known and widespread phenomenon and a particularly serious violation of human rights, it also became one of the first causes of international action to abolish it. The year 2007 saw the 200th anniversary of the abolition of the slave trade by the UK. Even though the trade continued for many decennia after 1807, this Act by the UK government (following Denmark) proved to be the beginning of the end of the western slave trade. By 1815, a first international document – the 1815 Declaration Relative to the Universal Abolition of the Slave Trade – was adopted by the six countries of the Vienna Congress. Many international agreements to abolish the slave trade followed in the ensuing century, although none of them were fully effective (Weisbrodt and Anti-Slavery International, 2002). In 1926, member states of the League of Nations adopted the Slavery Convention, which for the first time defined slavery internationally, and set globally binding rules to abolish it. The Convention defined the phenomenon thus:

> **Box 1: Slavery**
>
> (1) Slavery is the status or condition of a person over whom any or all of the powers attaching to the right of ownership are exercised.
>
> (2) The slave trade includes all acts involved in the capture, acquisition or disposal of a person with intent to reduce him to slavery; all acts involved in the acquisition of a slave with a view to selling or exchanging him; all acts of disposal by sale or exchange of a slave acquired with a view to being sold or exchanged, and, in general, every act of trade or transport in slaves.
>
> *Source*: 1926 Slavery Convention, Article 1

From 'slavery' to 'slavery and practices similar to slavery'

The Slavery Convention also introduced another form of labour considered analogous to slavery: forced labour (1926 Slavery Convention, Article 1). At roughly the same time, member states of the International Labour Organization (ILO) adopted the 1930 Forced Labour Convention No 29. This Convention defines forced labour as 'all work or service that is exacted from any person under the menace of any penalty and for which the said person has not offered himself voluntarily' (Article 2(1)). The Convention permits few exceptions from the general prohibition against forced labour, such as compulsory military service, normal civic obligation, and work done in prisons following conviction in a court of law (see Article 2(2)). Today, Convention No 29 has been ratified by 174 ILO member states. It remains the most specialised international instrument on forced labour, even though most of its provisions were transitory in nature – aiming gradually to abolish forced labour, then common in many colonial systems. These transitory provisions can no longer be invoked by governments to justify forced labour: nowadays forced labour *must* be prohibited under national law (see ILO, 2007, para 10).

In further recognition of the fact that slavery has many faces, the 1956 Supplementary Convention on the Abolition of Slavery, the Slave Trade, and Institutions and Practices Similar to Slavery introduced a number of further practices considered analogous to slavery, namely debt bondage, serfdom, forced marriage and the sale of wives or children (see www2.ohchr.org/english/law/slavetrade.htm). Thus, discussion on slavery was gradually no longer considered as merely concerning the phenomenon as defined in the 1926 Slavery Convention, but came to encompass other slavery-like forms.

Today, the prohibition of slavery and various slavery-like practices is well enshrined in international and regional human rights treaties. The legally non-binding but politically and historically important 1948 Universal Declaration of Human Rights (UN General Assembly Resolution 217 A [III] of 10 December 1948) establishes the principle of the prohibition of slavery in all its forms, while Article 8 of the 1966 International Covenant on Civil and Political Rights (ICCPR) (UN General Assembly Resolution 2200 A [XXI] of 16 December 1966) – a legally binding treaty – prohibits slavery in all its forms, including servitude and forced labour. European, inter-American and African regional human rights treaties contain similar provisions. Thus, today, the concept of slavery encompasses a range of practices seen as contemporary forms of slavery, which will be referred to below as 'slavery-like practices'.

What is 'child slavery'?

In respect of children, the concepts that together define slavery and practices similar to slavery have been further specified in a number of international instruments: the UN Convention on the Rights of the Child (CRC), the ILO child labour Conventions Nos 138 and 182 and the Palermo Protocol on trafficking in persons. These instruments are described below. Box 1 (above) and Box 2 (below) provide further definitions of the various concepts and relevant sources.

Convention on the Rights of the Child and its Optional Protocols

The special plight and vulnerability of children in the case of slavery and similar practices was recognised explicitly in the 1956 Supplementary Convention on the Abolition of Slavery, the Slave Trade and Institutions and Practices Similar to Slavery, outlawing the sale of children. To increase international protection of children's human rights, member countries of the United Nations (UN) adopted the 1989 CRC. Today the CRC has been ratified by all UN member states save two, Somalia and the US (as at 1 January 2010). This Convention is the main human rights instrument for children; it contains provisions covering all their human rights in a child-specific context, and is the point of reference for all questions relating to children"s rights. It contains several provisions relating to slavery and similar practices in respect of children, most notably Article 32, which recognises the right of the child to be protected from economic exploitation. Slavery and slavery-like practices to an important extent are also expressly covered, where the Convention provides for the right of children to be protected from illicit production and trafficking of drugs (Article 33), sexual exploitation (Article 34), trafficking (Article 35) and use in armed conflict (Article 38).

The 'sale of children and sexual exploitation' and 'children involved in armed conflict' are further elaborated in two Optional Protocols to the

CRC (Article 3(a) of Convention No 182). The Optional Protocol on the Sale of Children, Child Prostitution and Child Pornography requires the criminalisation of these practices and emphasises the importance of fostering increased public awareness and international cooperation in efforts to combat them. It defines the sale of children as 'any act or transaction whereby a child is transferred by any person or group of persons to another for remuneration or any other consideration'. The Optional Protocol on Involvement of Children in Armed Conflict prohibits the participation of children under the age of 18 in armed conflict, and governs both voluntary and forced recruitment of minors. With respect to the use of children in armed conflict it is noteworthy that the 1998 Rome Statute of the International Criminal Court qualifies the recruitment of children below 15 years for use in armed conflict as a war crime (Statute of the International Criminal Court, Article 8(2)(e)(vii)).[2]

ILO child labour Conventions

The ILO child labour Conventions complement the CRC and its Protocols[3] and provide the most specific legal framework in respect of the exploitation of children through slavery and slavery-like practices. While, generally, child labour is defined within the parameters of the ILO 1973 Minimum Age Convention No 138,[4] the 1999 Worst Forms of Child Labour Convention No 182 provides a definition of what constitutes slavery and slavery-like practices. It defines them in Article 3 as:

> (a)   all forms of slavery or practices similar to slavery, such as the sale and trafficking of children, debt bondage and serfdom and forced or compulsory labour, including forced or compulsory recruitment of children for use in armed conflict.

Other worst forms of child labour are further defined as:

> (b)   the use, procuring or offering of a child for prostitution, for the production of pornography or pornographic performances;
> (c)   the use, procuring or offering of a child for illicit activities, in particular for the production and trafficking of drugs as defined in the relevant international treaties;
> (d)   work which, by its nature or the circumstances in which it is carried out, is likely to harm the health, safety or morals of children. (Convention No 182, Article 3)

Thus child slavery and practices similar to child slavery can be defined as 'classical' child slavery, forced labour of children, the sale and trafficking of children, debt bondage and serfdom, and compulsory recruitment of children for use in armed conflict ('child soldiers'). Categories (a)-(c) are absolute worst forms of child labour because improving working conditions cannot make these forms more acceptable.[5] Thus slavery and similar practices can in no way be justified and should categorically be prohibited and eliminated.

ILO Convention No 182 covers all children under the age of 18 (Article 2) in line with the CRC definition of the child.[6] ILO Convention No 182, accompanied by Recommendation No 190, reflects a global consensus that there should be an immediate end to the worst forms of child labour. It calls for urgent 'immediate and effective measures to secure the prohibition and elimination of the worst forms of child labour.' (CRC, Article 1). Today, with 154 ratifications,[7] Convention No 138 remains the basic framework for both legislative and policy measures to combat child labour. Convention No 182, entered into force on 19 November 2000, has enjoyed an unprecedented rate of endorsement, having been ratified by 172 member states,[8] more than 90% of the ILO membership.

Not all forms of child exploitation are forms of slavery or similar practices. For example, child labour as defined under Convention No 138 is not always slavery or forced labour, even though it is an illegal and reprehensible phenomenon. Children may have to resort to child labour because of compelling conditions, such as poverty or social exclusion. Only where child labour is performed under the conditions defined in Article 3(a) of Convention No 182 can it be regarded as slavery or slavery-like. Likewise, the sexual exploitation of children is categorised in Article 3(b) as a separate worst form of child labour. That means that such exploitation of children is to be prohibited and eliminated even where the child victim in question was not forced into prostitution or pornographic acts. In other words, the Convention recognises that not all commercial sexual exploitation of children can be described as forced labour or slavery, but requires its prohibition and elimination anyway, thereby enhancing the range of protective measures applicable to children in sexual exploitation. The same applies to children in illicit activities: only if these activities are performed under the conditions defined in Article 3(a) of Convention No 182 do they qualify as 'slavery'. It is important to make this distinction. If all exploitation of children were to be simply categorised as slavery or slavery-like practices, the concept would be diluted, insufficient attention being paid to those in dire need.

Child slavery versus forced labour by children

It may seem a contradiction that slavery was traditionally dealt with in the ILO system under the scope of the Forced Labour Convention No 29, while in the general international system, forced labour is considered a 'slavery-like' practice. The reason why, in the ILO, slavery was treated like a 'forced labour-like' practice is because the ILO system of international labour standards never incorporated a slavery convention. In 1930, the adoption of such an instrument in the ILO was considered unnecessary, given the 1926 Slavery Convention. Later on, the supervisory ILO system (see later) successfully addressed slavery under Convention No 29 and the need for separate instruments was obviated.

In respect of children, the terminology of Convention No 182 – defining forced labour by children as a 'slavery-like practice' – fell back into line with the general international approach. Following the Convention's adoption in 1999, the supervisory ILO Committee of Experts on the Application of Conventions and Recommendations addressed the question of child slavery and forced labour exclusively under Convention No 182, 'since the protection of children is enhanced by the fact that the later Convention requires ratifying States to take immediate and effective measures to secure the prohibition and elimination of the worst forms of child labour as a matter of urgency.' (ILO, 2007, para 47). However, as some member states have not yet ratified Convention No 182, for these countries forced labour imposed on children continues to be examined within the framework of supervision associated with Convention No 29 (ILO, 2007, para 113).

'Palermo Protocol' on trafficking in persons

Child trafficking is an internationally recognised form of slavery (addressed in more detail in later chapters). The UN Convention against Transnational Organised Crime and its additional Protocol to Prevent, Suppress and Punish trafficking in persons, especially women and children (the 2000 Palermo Protocol [UN General Assembly Resolution 55/25 of 15 November 2000]), defines trafficking as:

> ... the recruitment, transportation, transfer, harbouring or receipt of persons, by means of the threat or use of force or other forms of coercion, of abduction, of fraud, of deception, of the abuse of power or of position of vulnerability or of the giving or receiving of payments or benefits to achieve the consent of a person having control over another person, for the purpose of exploitation.

In the case of children (that is, under 18 years of age), the Protocol further specifies, 'the recruitment, transportation, transfer, harbouring or receipt of a child for the purpose of exploitation shall be considered "trafficking in persons" even if this does not involve any of the means set forth in the definition'. This means that to qualify a case as one involving child trafficking, it is not necessary that 'threat or use of force or other forms of coercion, of abduction, of fraud, of deception' were used in the trafficking process. In other words, children are considered to be victims of trafficking even where this took place without them being deceived or coerced. Not only does this take into account their special vulnerability, but it also makes it easier for law enforcement agencies and prosecutors to provide evidence to ensure that child traffickers are duly punished.

Ensuring that international agreements are put into action?

How are the application of the CRC and the ILO Conventions monitored?[9] Both the UN and ILO have supervisory mechanisms, based on governments' regular reports submitted to each respective body. CRC reports are due every five years, while reports for both Convention No 138 and No 182 should be submitted biennially. Countries that have not ratified the two ILO Conventions are required to report annually to the ILO on how they realise the Conventions' principles and what obstacles remain hindering ratification.[10] These reports, together with other information, such as the country's legislation, employers' and workers' comment, and information by non-governmental organisations (NGOs), are examined by independent expert bodies, that is, the UN Committee on the Rights of the Child (www2. ohchr.org/english/bodies/crc/) in the case of the CRC, and the Committee of Experts on the Application of Conventions and Recommendations[11] for the ILO. These Committees' reports are submitted to the main political organs of these organisations, that is, the UN General Assembly and the ILO's International Labour Conference (ILC). In practice, particularly relating to the ILO system, the Committee's findings prompt discussions on individual country cases at the ILC, regularly highlighting certain situations in countries with respect to slavery and slavery-like practices. For example, the forced labour of children in informal gold mining in Niger was first raised by the Committee of Experts, later debated in the ILC, resulting in an intensified dialogue with the government and other stakeholders, and quickly led to the implementation of technical cooperation programmes by the ILO to end child labour in gold mining. Likewise, trafficking practices have been the focus of debate in the Conference, helping the initiation of projects against child trafficking in various regions and countries.

Box 2: Practices similar to slavery (slavery-like situations)

Sale of children

Any institution or practice whereby a child or young person under the age of 18 years, is delivered by either or both of his natural parents or by his guardian to another person, whether for reward or not, with a view to the exploitation of the child or young person or of his labour. (1956 Supplementary Convention on the Abolition of Slavery, the Slave Trade, and Institutions and Practices Similar to Slavery)

Sale of children means any act or transaction whereby a child is transferred by any person or group of persons to another for remuneration or any other consideration. (2000 Optional Protocol on the Sale of Children, Child Prostitution and Child Pornography)

Trafficking

(a) 'Trafficking in persons' shall mean the recruitment, transportation, transfer, harbouring or receipt of persons, by means of the threat or use of force or other forms of coercion, of abduction, of fraud, of deception, of the abuse of power or of a position of vulnerability or of the giving or receiving of payments or benefits to achieve the consent of a person having control over another person, for the purpose of exploitation. Exploitation shall include, at a minimum, the exploitation of the prostitution of others or other forms of sexual exploitation, forced labour or services, slavery or practices similar to slavery, servitude or the removal of organs;

(b) The consent of a victim of trafficking in persons to the intended exploitation set forth in subparagraph (a) of this article shall be irrelevant where any of the means set forth in subparagraph (a) have been used;

(c) The recruitment, transportation, transfer, harbouring or receipt of a child for the purpose of exploitation shall be considered 'trafficking in persons' even if this does not involve any of the means set forth in subparagraph (a) of this article;

(d) 'Child' shall mean any person under eighteen years of age.

(2000 Protocol to Prevent, Suppress and Punish trafficking in persons, especially women and children, supplementing the UN Convention against Transnational Organised Crime)

Debt bondage

The status or condition arising from a pledge by a debtor of his personal services or of those of a person under his control as security for a debt, if the value of those services as reasonably assessed is not applied towards the liquidation of the debt or the length and nature of those services are not respectively limited and defined. (1956 Supplementary Convention on the Abolition of Slavery, the Slave Trade and Institutions and Practices Similar to Slavery)

Serfdom
The condition or status of a tenant who is by law, custom or agreement bound to live and labour on land belonging to another person and to render some determinate service to such other person, whether for reward or not, and is not free to change his status. (1956 Supplementary Convention on the Abolition of Slavery, the Slave Trade and Institutions and Practices Similar to Slavery)

Forced or compulsory labour
... all work or service which is exacted from any person under the menace of any penalty and for which the said person has not offered himself voluntarily. (1930 Forced Labour Convention, No 29)

Magnitude and appearances: a global overview

As child slavery is often hidden, reliable statistics are scarce. An ILO report notes that 'more than any other worst form of child labour, this is an area beset with severe problems of quantifications' (ILO, 2002a). Some figures on worst forms of child labour exist nonetheless. The ILO's recent global report on child labour estimates that over six million children worldwide are in slavery (ILO, 2002b). This includes an estimated 5.7 million children in forced and bonded labour and 300,000 children forced into 'child soldiering'. Some argue that children in prostitution and pornography should also be considered slave-like practices, hence adding an estimated 1.8 million children in sexual exploitation to this figure of six million. Furthermore, an unknown percentage of the 600,000 children in illicit activities – drug trafficking, other criminal activities and forced begging – work in slave-like situations. An estimated 1.2 million children, trafficked across various ages and both genders, some of them into forced and bonded labour or armed conflict, are excluded to avoid double counting.

Global forced labour statistics shed further light. The ILO (2005a, p 36) estimates a total 12.3 million people in forced labour, including an estimated 2.45 million trafficked into forced labour, and that children comprise an estimated 40%–50% of all forced labourers worldwide, or between 4.92 and 6.15 million children, consistent with the 5.7 million children in forced/ bonded labour estimated in the 2002 ILO global report (ILO, 2002b). To put the scale of forced labour in a different perspective, the ILO's 2009 global report on forced labour estimated that the total cost of forced labour, including slavery, to workers worldwide was US$21 billion (ILO, 2009, p 32).[12]

Numbers given are minimum estimates, as the studies from which they were derived were cautious in validating sources. Bales, an expert on modern-day slavery, has estimated this figure at a much larger 27.9 million people (Bales, 2007). Excluding Asia and the Pacific, both data sets are largely congruent by region. In Asia, however, Bales found a total of 26.4 million labourers, a number 16.9 million higher than the ILO's estimate of 9.5 million Asian forced labourers. These higher numbers probably result from use of a definition of slavery broader than that of ILO Convention No 29[13] and use of different methodology.[14] Regardless of these discrepancies, the ILO 2002 global estimates on child labour (ILO, 2002b) indicate that the region with the largest incidence by far of children in forced labour is Asia and the Pacific, where the estimated number of children in forced and bonded labour was 5.5 million and in armed conflict 120,000 – which, if combined, is about 15 times greater than the corresponding number in the rest of the world combined (ILO, 2002a, Table 10). In Latin America and the Caribbean, 30,000 children were forced into armed conflict and a staggering 750,000 children work in prostitution – most of them indeed in slave-like situations. Africa had 210,000 children working in forced or bonded labour and 120,000 children were forced into armed conflict. With regards to developed industrialised economies, an estimated 420,000 children work in prostitution and pornography. From this point, information regarding specific regions becomes more difficult to find. Around 200,000 children were known to be trafficked in Eastern Europe and former Soviet republics. Numerous cases of child trafficking for camel jockeying and domestic labour are reported in the Middle East.

Overview by type of child slavery

Forced or compulsory labour

Children are often coerced into labour by employers or even parents; the absence of chains does not preclude the child from being considered enslaved. Typically, employers may harass children by means of threats, usually in the form of physical violence to the victim or his/her family. Trafficked children are especially vulnerable, as employers will often threaten to expose them to local or immigration authorities or confiscate their identity papers. Threats of non-payment of wages are also used. Sweatshop workers are often threatened with the prospect of losing all their wages if they do not work long hours. Victims typically enter this type of labour through trafficking or deception; many victims assume they will be working for a legal and well-paid job only later to discover the true nature of the work. One example is Jenny, a 14-year-old Nigerian girl, who left her native country for the US to work in the home of a couple, also originally from an African country. She thought she would be paid to look after their children, but the reality was very different. For five years her employer raped her and her employer's wife physically assaulted her, sometimes with a cane, on one occasion with a high-heeled shoe (USDS, 2007).

Children often enter forced labour due to difficult family situations such as debt or illness. Parents often give up children in order to lessen their own financial burden and repay debts. The example of Margaret, a 15-year-old agricultural labourer forced to work in Ghana, illustrates this:

> "My dad is a gardener and my mum makes olive oil to sell at the market," she explained. "They don't make a lot of money and we are a family of six children. My brother fell gravely ill and had to be hospitalised. Since my parents didn't have enough money to pay the hospital, they had to borrow. But my mother could not refund the loan in time. Then a man began to harass and insult us, and threaten my mum. To stop the threats from coming, my parents decided that he could take me and all my siblings, except for the youngest child. I had to stop going to school. I didn't have any idea that I would be forced to work for him." (Quoted in ILO-IPEC, 2006a)

Child trafficking

Child trafficking violates fundamental human rights and exploits innocent people. It involves the sale of human beings as commodities. Men, women and children can be sold multiple times and in multiple ways for profit. Child trafficking occurs to and from all regions of the world. The routes are complex, ranging from domestic to cross-border trafficking, involving even global trade.

While both sexes are trafficked, boys are typically trafficked for labour relating to commercial farming, the drug trade and other illicit activities, while trafficking of girls often relates to domestic service or sexual exploitation. Trafficking represents 20% of all forced labour, and over 43% of victims are trafficked for sexual exploitation. Of all trafficking victims worldwide, between 40% and 50% are children.[15] Their vulnerability, as well as the economic hardships that may make family members complicit or even hopeful of better prospects in cities, results in a greater risk of being trafficked.

Debt bondage and serfdom

Debt bondage and serfdom arises when a worker is coerced by their debt to their employer. It typically occurs when a person needing a loan, having no assets, offers their labour for an unspecified or specified amount of time, without wages or for less than the minimum wage, as security for a loan. In some cases, interest on the loan may be impossibly high, or it may be determined that the bonded person's work repays the interest on the loan but not the principal. The loan becomes inherited and perpetuated, and can become intergenerational (USDL, 2005, p xli). Almost two thirds of forced labour in Asia and the Pacific is related to debt bondage, while around 20% is imposed by states (e.g. men forced to work on the railways by states or governments, such as in Myanmar [Burma]) (ILO, 2005b, pp 12, 25). Privatised economic exploitation constitutes 75% of all forced labour in Latin America and the Caribbean, largely in the form of debt bondage.

'Bonded labour' is a particularly controversial practice in South Asia. Pre-existing debt is often inherited from parents or grandparents, resulting in child slavery. The rooted traditions of a stratified society do little to improve the situation. Bonded labour is seen as a cyclical phase, families entering and leaving it at different points of their lives. The lender often offers an advance for the rights to the parent's child, the advance is accepted, and the cycle begins anew (HRW, 2002). In Nepal an estimated 33,000 children work under debt bondage (Sharma, 1999), 95% in the agricultural sector (ILO, 2005c). Trafficking often augments this problem, as traffickers demand a transportation 'fee' from the childrens' salaries; the children are thus forced to work for one to two years without pay. In Pakistan, measures have been taken to ban bonded labour, but the practice continues due to insufficient monitoring and lacklustre action in the legal system. The ILO has made some advances in the country, notably the elimination of bonded labour in the manufacture of footballs, but many domestic industries still suffer from this problem and are difficult places to facilitate change.

Children forced into armed conflict

Reliable statistics are not available, but boys constitute the majority of soldiers, with an average age of 15–17 years. Girls taken in conflicts must often fight in combat and serve as sex slaves to soldiers (USDS, 2007). Children are often recruited through bogus measures such as a 'penalty' for not having identification. In Myanmar, Ko Aung reported that he was recruited by force against his will:

> "One evening while we were watching a video show in my village, three army sergeants came. They checked whether we had

identification cards and asked if we wanted to join the army. We explained that we were underage and hadn't got identification cards. I said no and came back home that evening but an army recruitment unit arrived next morning at my village and demanded two new recruits. Those who could not pay 3,000 kyats (US$9) had to join the army, they said. My parents could not pay, and altogether 19 of us were recruited and sent to Mingladon [an army training centre]." (Quoted in USDS, 2007)

Once recruited into armed conflict, it is difficult to escape due to psychological pressure, threats of physical violence and other reprisals. Addiction to drugs such as amphetamines, marihuana and 'brown brown', a mixture of cocaine and gunpowder, creates further dependency.

Children forced into sexual slavery

The abundance of anecdotal evidence from many different sources makes it safe to assume that commercial sexual exploitation of children below 18 years is a serious and widespread problem. Many children are forced into this practice.

In Sri Lanka, for example, children often become the prey of sexual exploiters through friends and relatives. The prevalence of boys in prostitution here is strongly related to foreign tourism (ILO, 2002c, p 79ff). An estimated 12,000 Nepalese children, mainly girls, are trafficked for commercial sexual exploitation each year within Nepal or to brothels in India and other countries (ILO, 2001a, p 17ff). Some 84% of girls in prostitution interviewed in Tanzania reported having been battered, raped or tortured by police officers and *sungu sungu* (local community guards). At least 60% had no permanent place to live. Some girls started out as child domestic workers (ILO, 2001b, p 29). In El Salvador, one third of the sexually exploited children between 14 and 17 years of age were boys. The median age for entering into prostitution among all children interviewed was 13 years. They worked on average five days per week, although nearly 10% reported that they worked seven days a week (ILO, 2002d, p 42). In Madagascar, 80% of children interviewed no longer attended school, and some 65% were engaged exclusively in commercial sexual exploitation (ILO, 2002e, p xiii). In Vietnam, family poverty, limited family education and family dysfunction were found to be primary causes for commercial sexual exploitation. Sixteen per cent of the children interviewed were illiterate, 38% had only primary-level schooling and 66% said that tuition and school fees were beyond the means of their families (ILO, 2002f, p 26ff).

Children forced into illicit activities

Many of the children working in illicit activities, such as forced begging, drug trafficking or organised crime, effectively work as forced labourers. Psychological pressure, threats of physical violence and reprisals on family members in case of escape effectively force children to continue this work. In Brazil 'it is not uncommon for children to experience threats (both verbal and with fire arms), physical abuse, intimidation, pressure and rape' (de Sousa e Silva and Urani, 2003, p 27). Addiction to glue or drugs creates further dependency. Anecdotal evidence from a range of countries suggests that many children trafficked into illicit activity did not initially choose to begin drug use, but rather were the victims of drugging that created an addiction. Due to drug dependence, the children continue illicit activities in order to make enough money to continue usage (ILO–IPEC, 2010: forthcoming).

Responses

In a world where most people have adequate incomes, the majority are educated and have a range of communication devices at their disposal, where technology reaches virtually all its corners, how is it possible that millions of its children still toil in slavery? Where are we failing and what can be done to stop this severe violation of children's rights?

Clear and unambiguous legal frameworks at a national level

Clear, specific and unambiguous national laws against child slavery are crucial if it is to be addressed effectively and should include specific prohibitions against children in slavery, forced labour, bondage and trafficking. However, international instruments, and their translation into national laws, are not without ambiguity, and often, national laws do not cover the full scope of slavery-like practices. For instance, child trafficking is often not fully defined, hampering effective law enforcement. Another problem in laws relating to trafficking in many regions is that they cover trafficking for sexual exploitation only, and not trafficking for other forms of labour exploitation, limiting their applicability.

Law enforcement

Laws against child slavery mean little if they are not enforced vigorously. Effective law enforcement implies clarity in roles and responsibilities of responsible agencies, exchange of information and collaboration among them, well-equipped law enforcement officials trained in relevant laws and policies relating to child slavery, and sufficient staff to monitor and intervene where necessary.

Interventions should aim at protecting victims of child slavery and prosecution of the culprits, followed, where convicted, by credible punishment. Too often, however, perpetrators are not punished or punishment is too light, sending the wrong signal to society. Interventions should also go beyond punishment and, through law enforcement, eliminate the source of exploitation by confiscating the assets of the culprits and dismantling the mechanisms they use to exploit children. In weak states with large illegal sectors this is a significant challenge.

Capitalising on international supervisory mechanisms

Supervisory bodies of international instruments such as the CRC and the ILO Conventions (discussed earlier) can play a valuable role in more effective law enforcement, pointing at weaknesses in legislation, application and enforcement. They give guidance to governments, but also provide a list of 'what is to be done' for international agencies and NGOs. For anyone concerned with child slavery issues, the comments of the UN and ILO Supervisory Committees are important information resources. Moreover, there are several ways in which concerned individuals and organisations can contribute to the Committees' work, by bringing to their attention information on issues and practices relating to child slavery.[16]

Better research methodology and more targeted research

Reliable statistics on child slavery are scarce. It is a notoriously difficult subject to research given its clandestine nature, and yet extremely important to ensure effective responses. Although research aimed at determining national estimates is important as a basis to advocate for policy attention, the value of localised but in-depth research that provides information on children's profiles and root causes should not be underestimated. Such specific information can be immensely valuable in identifying effective local responses. A combination of research methods, both quantitative and qualitative, should allow for obtaining useful data. Mapping of workplaces where children work in slavery-like situations based on analysing proxy data, focus group discussions with key informants and direct observations and primary data gathering that does not put the children at risk may result in geographically targeted information and minimum basic estimates.

Public intolerance and social mobilisation

Research findings should be utilised to raise public awareness and fight public tolerance of child slavery. The media, workers' and employers' organisations and civil society play important roles in challenging public indifference to child slavery, thus creating incentives for responsive governments to take remedial action. An effective mobilisation tool could be the promotion of 'child slavery-free' villages, districts, cities and eventually provinces and countries. This could contribute to a global movement against child slavery.

Engaging workers' organisations

Child slavery undercuts profit margins by 'clean'[17] companies and puts pressure on wages of regular workers, so it is in the interest of workers' organisations to fight such exploitation. More broadly, well-functioning dialogue between workers' and employers' organisations serves as a crucial impediment to child slavery.

Engaging business

In a globalising world, international companies make use of increasingly complex sub-contracting arrangements and are hence at risk of 'benefiting' from and thus contributing to child slavery at the other end of supply chains. Stringent monitoring by independent, well-resourced agencies is crucial, along with adherence to a code of ethics by all those involved in supply chains, without subjecting children to slavery or slavery-like practices. For instance, companies operating in Brazil, in areas that typically benefit from slave labour such as the beef, iron, sugar, coal and soy industries, have signed agreements to ban any form of involvement with business people listed in the *lista suja* (the bad list) (ILO, 2010: forthcoming). Another example is the Global Compact (GC) (www.unglobalcompact.org/AboutTheGC/TheTenPrinciples/index.html) to support environmental and social principles – a UN initiative – which includes multinational and other companies pledged to advance the principles of the GC, including the elimination of all forms of forced and compulsory labour, and the effective abolition of child labour. This initiative offers opportunities to enlarge and deepen mobilisations against child slavery.

Fight marginalisation and exclusion

Children in slavery tend to be from disadvantaged populations, such as poor/indebted families, minority ethnic groups and other socially excluded groups. The situation of such children is compounded by cultural values and practices that rank children low in status, encouraging others to disregard their rights. Their marginalisation often excludes them from accessing services such as basic education and healthcare. Such exclusion and discrimination plays into the hands of those wanting to exploit children. It is therefore important that in addition to law enforcement that targets perpetrators, basic services – including free, compulsory, quality education – are offered to all children, irrespective of origin, ethnicity or level of affluence. Registration at birth is crucial to make children visible and accounted for, creating the basis for access to social services (see Chapter Ten, this volume).[18]

Empowerment

Children at risk of ending up in slavery, and their families and communities, should furthermore be targeted for assistance to recognise child slavery and be made aware of their rights and how to exercise them, while acknowledging the different needs of boys and girls. In particular, in situations where law enforcement is malfunctioning, it is crucial that children, families and communities can protect themselves from slavery before it happens and are able to mobilise relevant authorities to undertake remedial action.

Rehabilitation and reintegration of victims of child slavery

In addition to measures that prevent child slavery, rehabilitation and reintegration assistance to rescued child victims is needed. Such assistance should be child-centred, and include individual needs assessment followed by tailor-made remedial action. Care providers should be experienced professionals able to rebuild trust and overcome children's trauma, before offering socioeconomic reintegration including life skills training sustained until no longer needed (that is, until an alternative life has been built up and the risk of re-entering child slavery has abated) (ILO-IPEC, 2006b).

Global Action Plan: time-bound targets

Finally, in working with national authorities, reference can be made to the Global Action Plan against Worst Forms of Child Labour.[19] This plan commits all ILO member states (currently 183) to eliminate the worst forms of child labour, including child slavery, by 2016.

Conclusion: looking ahead

The list of responses above suggests that the route to eliminating child slavery exists but that not enough action is being undertaken. The goal of 2016 should serve as a benchmark and constant reminder that actions against this worst form of child labour need to be intensified and better coordinated among the various actors and stakeholders. This is not any easy task, given the diversity of required interventions and actors.

The 2010 Global Conference on Child Labour in the Netherlands – 10 years after Convention No 182 came into force and six years before the global target of 2016 – served as an important opportunity to redouble our commitment to actions to eliminate child slavery in all its forms. The Conference – attended by more than 90 countries – adopted the Roadmap for achieving the elimination of the worst forms of child labour by 2016. The Roadmap spells out a series of priority actions that have been proven to make a difference in fighting the worst forms of child labour, including child slavery, along with initiatives to monitor progress and hold governments accountable.

With this comprehensive global policy tool, it is now up to all actors to carry forward the messages of the Roadmap and live up to the commitment to action to eliminate the scourge of child slavery.[20]

Notes

[1] The views expressed in this article are those of the authors.

[2] The Optional Protocol on the Involvement of Children in Armed Conflict (came into force on 13 February 2002) and the Optional Protocol on the Sale of Children, Child Prostitution and Child Pornography (came into force on 18 January 2002).

[3] Both Protocols to the UN CRC refer in their preambles to the ILO Worst Forms of Child Labour Convention No 182.

[4] The framework as per the ILO Minimum Age Convention No 138, is as follows:

	General	For developing countries ('where economy and education facilities are insufficiently developed') This flexibility for developing countries is optional and needs to be used at the time of ratification
General minimum age (Article 2)	Not less than the end of compulsory schooling, 15 years or more	14 years
Light work (Article 7)	13 years	12 years
Dangerous work (Article 3)	18 years (16 years under certain conditions)	18 years (16 years under certain conditions)

[5] The term 'worst forms of child labour' encompasses both hazardous work and 'absolute' worst forms of child labour. The difference is that while hazardous work, through changes in the work environment and the work itself, can sometimes be modified to remove the hazardous aspects, the absolute forms can, under no circumstances, be considered acceptable.

[6] A slight difference between ILO Convention No 182 and the definition of a child in Article 1 of the CRC is that whereas the latter defines a child as 'every human being below the age of eighteen years *unless under the law applicable to the child, majority is attained earlier*', the ILO Convention requires that every person below the age of 18 is protected from each and every worst form of child labour (as defined in Article 3), irrespective of whether, according to law, they attain majority at an earlier age.

[7] As at 1 January 2010. For up-to-date information regarding the ratification of ILO Conventions, see the ILOLEX database at www.ilo.org

[8] As at 1 January 2010.

[9] For more information on the manner in which the implementation of the Palermo Protocol is monitored, see www.unodc.org

[10] For more information, see www.ilo.org/declaration/thedeclaration/lang--en/index.htm

[11] The comments on the application of a particular Convention by a particular country made by the Committee of Experts can be found www.ilo.org through 'International Labour Standards' by using either the APPLIS or ILOLEX databases.

[12] This estimate comprises unpaid wages, recruitment fees, etc.

[13] Bales (2007) measured the incidence of slavery as defined by 'a social and economic relationship marked by the loss of free will where a person is forced through violence or the threat of violence to give up the ability to sell freely his/her own labour power'.

[14] Bales' methods involve the aggregation of country-estimations from secondary sources, later validated by country experts. His country-estimates include a figure of 22 million people in slavery in India (or 83% of the total estimate for Asia) (Bales, 2007).

[15] ILO (2005a) estimates that 2.45 million people are trafficking victims.

[16] For more information on the procedures to be followed, the websites of the relevant organisations should be consulted. For ILO, see www. ilo.org/global/What_we_do/InternationalLabourStandards/ ApplyingandpromotingInternationalLabourStandards/lang--en/index.htm. For CRC, see www2.ohchr.org/english/bodies/crc/index.htm

[17] Page 36.

[18] The Minimum Age Recommendation No 146, which accompanies Convention No 138, provides in paragraph 16(a) that 'public authorities should maintain an effective system of birth registration, which should include the issue of birth certificates'.

[19] Formally endorsed by the ILO Governing Body in November 2006.

[20] See www.ilo.org/ipecinfo/product/viewProduct.do?productId=13453

References

de Souza e Silva, J. and Urani, A. (2003) *Situation of children in drug trafficking: A rapid assessment. Brazil*, Geneva: International Labour Organization.

HRW (Human Rights Watch) (2002) *Small hands of slavery: Bonded child labor in India*, Delhi: HRW/India.

ILO (International Labour Organization) (2001a) *Nepal: Trafficking in girls with special reference to prostitution: A rapid assessment*, Rapid Assessment No 2, Geneva: ILO.

ILO (2001b) *Tanzania: Children in prostitution: A rapid assessment*, Rapid Assessment No 12, Geneva: ILO.

ILO (2002a) *Every child counts*, Geneva: ILO.

ILO (2002b) *A future without child labour: Global report under the follow up to the ILO Declaration on Fundamental Principles and Rights at Work*, Geneva: ILO.

ILO (2002c) *Sri Lanka: The commercial sexual exploitation of children: A rapid assessment*, Rapid Assessment No 18, Geneva: ILO.

ILO (2002d) *El Salvador: La explotación sexual comercial infantil y adolescente: Una evaluacion rapida*, Rapid Assessment No 30, Geneva: ILO.

ILO (2002e) *Madagascar: Les enfants victimes de l'exploitation sexuelle à Antsirana, Toliary et Antananarivo: Une évaluation rapid*, Rapid Assessment No 25, Geneva: ILO.

ILO (2002f) *Viet Nam: Children in prostitution in Hanoi, Hai Phong, Ho Chi Minh City and Can Tho: A rapid assessment*, Rapid Assessment No 16, Geneva: ILO.

ILO (2005a) *Minimum estimate of forced labour in the world*, Geneva: ILO.

ILO (2005b) *A global alliance against forced labour: Global report under the follow-up to the ILO Declaration on Fundamental Principles and Rights at Work*, Geneva: ILO.

ILO (2005c) *Combating child labor in Asia and the Pacific*, Geneva: ILO.

ILO (2007) *General Survey concerning the Forced Labour Convention, 1930 (No 29) and the Abolition of Forced Labour Convention, 1957 (No 105)*, 96th Session, Report III (Part 1B), Geneva: ILO.

ILO (2009) *The cost of coercion: Global report under the follow-up to the ILO Declaration on Fundamental Principles and Rights at Work*, Geneva: ILO.

ILO (2010: forthcoming) *Combating child trafficking for labour exploitation: A resource kit for policy makers and practitioners*, Geneva: ILO.

ILO-IPEC (International Programme on the Elimination of Child Labour) (2006a) 'Le travail des enfants en servitude. Mecanismes, contraintes et caracteristiques', Unpublished paper, Geneva: ILO.

ILO-IPEC (2006b) *Child-friendly standards and guidelines for the recovery and integration of trafficked children* (TICSA), Geneva: ILO.

ILO-IPEC (2010: forthcoming) *Children in illicit activities*, Geneva: ILO.

Sharma, S. (1999) *Rapid assessment investigation of Nepal*, Katmandhu: National Labor Academy, Nepal.

USDL (United States Department of Labour) (2005) *2005 findings on the worst forms of child labour*, Washington, DC: USDL.

USDS (United States Department of State) (2007) *Trafficking in persons report*, Washington, DC: USDS.

Weisbrodt, D. and Anti-Slavery International (2002) *Abolishing slavery and its contemporary forms*, New York, NY: United Nations.

two

Constructing the international legal framework

Trevor Buck and Andrea Nicholson

Introduction

As noted earlier, and in other writing (for example, Walvin, 2007; Quirk, 2009), slavery has been a feature of virtually all major civilisations in history and children have been caught up in traditional forms of slavery across different cultures. Indeed, children have often been 'born into' slavery, that is, regarded as the possession of a slave owner from birth. Equally, practices of selling children into slavery for economic reasons have been ubiquitous over time and across different countries and cultures. The phenomenon of 'child slavery' has been persistent, even after the formal international legal abolition of slavery in the 19th century in most parts of the world. 'Modern' forms of child slavery may include, for example, severe forms of child labour, child trafficking and child sexual 'exploitation' (see Chapter Five, this volume), or a combination of these.

A rational approach to the construction of international legal regimes will need to take stock of the nature and extent of such practices in the real world. However, despite the best efforts of international organisations such as UNICEF and the International Labour Organization (ILO), the covert character of such practices does not make for easy or reliable empirical evidence to be gathered to measure the extent of child slavery. The nature of the problem is also difficult to define conceptually. The existence of modern forms of child slavery depends in part on one's view of the parameters of meaning attached to our concept of child slavery. Taking a narrow view, perhaps based on the legal definition found in the 1926 Slavery Convention, the 'problem' of child slavery becomes associated with a concern about a smaller subset of occurrences of the phenomenon, so defined, around the world. On the other hand, an over-liberal definition, perhaps based more on the notion of 'exploitation' – the dominant language used in the Convention on the Rights of the Child (CRC) – might include such a broad range of such practices that it loses any analytical integrity or functionality.

To some extent, the international legal framework relating to child slavery has struggled to provide a sensible balance between these two positions, but, as will be seen, globalisation has not produced a coherent, uniform system of international legal protection. Our changing social recognition of the phenomena of *slavery, servitude, enslavement, forced labour* or *practices similar* to these has given rise to a parallel (but not always coterminous) development of such key concepts in international legal instruments, which are fundamental to the construction of the international legal framework. It should be noted, for the purposes here, that the 'construction' of this framework carries a dual meaning: it includes both the historic manner in which this framework has been built up and the normative sense of how this framework *ought* to be built.

Prohibition of slavery

The prohibition of slavery was finally established in the 1926 Slavery Convention, and subsequently reinforced under Article 4 of the 1948 United Nations (UN) Declaration of Human Rights. While Article 1 of the Convention still provides the accepted definition of slavery (see Chapter One, this volume), the realisation that many practices were not subsumed within its definition led to the implementation of the 1956 Supplementary Convention on the Abolition of Slavery, the Slave Trade and Institutions and Practices Similar to Slavery, which provided for the abolition of a variety of practices similar to slavery under Article 1 of the Slavery Convention. These include debt bondage, serfdom, the inheritance of a woman and extreme forms of child labour. These two Conventions were not specifically directed at the rights of the child, but recognised and prohibited a number of practices that applied to both adults and children. Numerous subsequent related treaties have served to crystallise the prohibition of slavery, enhancing the view that it has achieved *jus cogens*[1] status, the International Court of Justice defining the prohibition of slavery as an obligation '*erga omnes* arising out of human rights law' (see *Barcelona Traction, Light and Power Co Ltd [Belgium v Spain]*, 5 February 1970, ICJ Reports 1970, p 32), an obligation owed by a state to the international community as a whole.

The progressive growth of treaties relating to slavery and servitude reflects the international community's awareness of 'contemporary forms of slavery' and has also moved over time to address the protection of women and children in particular, as those most vulnerable and likely to be subjected to such practices. Thus, states are subject to an extensive range of obligations with regard to the prohibition of child slavery and similar practices. The provisions of the CRC and its Optional Protocols, the ILO Worst Forms of Child Labour Convention No 182, and the Protocol to the Convention against Transnational Organised Crime to Prevent, Suppress and Punish trafficking in persons, especially women and children (hereafter the Palermo Protocol; see other chapters, especially Chapters One, Five and Six), together with international and domestic judicial discourse, demonstrate a concerted attempt to prohibit, in particular, all possible forms of child exploitation. The forms most commonly linked to slavery include debt bondage, child trafficking, forced marriage, sexual exploitation and the more extreme forms of child labour.

However, as the extent of child exploitation has become more apparent, the term 'slavery' has understandably been appropriated by the anti-slavery non-governmental organisation (NGO) community, which has sought to draw attention to the problem by subsuming the breadth of identified practices within the meaning of slavery, thereby benefiting from the stigmatisation attached thereto, even though the practice may not genuinely amount to slavery in strict legal terms.

Slavery and servitude

The accepted definition of slavery, drawn from Article 1 of the 1926 Slavery Convention,[2] provides that slavery is 'the status or condition of a person over whom any or all of the powers attaching to the right of ownership are exercised'.[3] An examination of the *travaux préparatoires* to the Slavery Convention indicates that it was not intended as a means to combat all forms of exploitation (Allain, 2008), and a narrow interpretation synonymous with chattel slavery has previously been adopted by the European Court of Human Rights (*Siliadin v France* [2006] 43 EHRR 16). However, more recent case law (see *R v Tang* [2008] HCA 39) and current academic discourse demonstrates this as an unnecessarily restrictive interpretation (Cullen, 2006; Allain, 2009; Nicholson, 2010: forthcoming); an absolute definition may impact on immigration law and result in lengthy attempts to bring the particular facts within the confines of definition (Cullen, 2006, pp 591-2). A concept of slavery as chattel slavery, that is, *legal* ownership (the law does not know of any right of ownership over a person), also does not take into account the full wording of the definition. Taken as a whole to include the preceding words 'any or all powers attaching to [the rights of ownership]', the definition can instead be interpreted to encompass *de facto* slavery (Allain, 2009, p 274). This interpretation is borne up by the court in *R v Tang* [2008] (see *R v Tang* [2008] HCA 39) and by an analysis of the *travaux préparatoires* to the 1926 Convention, and is seen in the Rome Statute of the International Criminal Court, which adopts the definition of slavery from the 1926 Convention to define the act of enslavement, but adds '… and includes *the exercise of such power* in the course of trafficking in persons, in particular women and children',[4] an approach that is further supported by the International Criminal Court on interpretation of Article 1 of the 1926 Convention in *Kunarac* (2001) (see *Kunarac et al [IT-96-23-T & IT-96-23/1-T] Judgment*, 22 February 2001, at 117–18).

Instead, a more general concept of child slavery would have the result that forced domestic service, and many other practices similar to slavery, would fall under current legal provisions on slavery without further analysis. The social context of child slavery has shifted and traditional notions of absolute ownership may no longer be relevant. In practice, child slavery has become a generic term for a range of offences – child trafficking, forced marriage, sexual exploitation and extreme forms of child labour. Some of these practices may in reality be subsidiary to the 'true' concept of slavery as envisaged by the drafters of the 1926 Convention, but many will fall within the meaning of servitude. Little justification can be made out for a distinction between slavery and servitude. Indeed, many international and regional treaties place these two terms consecutively within the same provision, unlike slavery and child labour, which are often treated separately (Nicholson, 2010: forthcoming). Thus, slavery may instead have to be determined via one or more of the following notions: the capability to sell or dispose of a person; the disempowerment of the individual; the denial of bodily integrity; or the devaluation of the person (noting that children have traditionally not been granted full rights as persons).

Slavery, servitude and forced labour

There nevertheless remains a significant overlap in identified practices falling within the meaning of servitude and forced labour. Most practices outlined in ILO Convention No 182 could amount to child slavery or servitude, but it is also clear that Article 3(d), which provides for work likely to harm the health, safety or morals of children, may not reach the standard for slavery or servitude. The sale and trafficking of children, debt bondage, serfdom and forced and compulsory labour are stated as forms of slavery or practices similar to slavery under Article 3(a) of ILO Convention No 182, yet the 2005 Action Punishing Trafficking in Human Beings Convention provides that, *inter alia*, trafficking *may* include slavery or servitude. Thus there is recognition that these practices *may* amount to slavery or servitude, but they are not in themselves routinely regarded as such, perhaps instead being linked to forced labour or other related practices. This begs the question whether any distinction is necessary. However, child labour is not considered as yet to have achieved *jus cogens* status: the existence of qualifications to forced and compulsory labour under ILO Conventions Nos 29 and 105 may enable a state to classify that its practices fall within an exception,[5] thereby avoiding responsibility and leaving the victim with little avenue for redress. The Slavery Convention itself does not prohibit forced labour for public services, but under Article 5, the parties are to 'recognise that recourse to compulsory or forced labour may have grave consequences and undertake … to take all necessary measures to prevent compulsory or forced labour from developing into conditions analogous to slavery'. Conversely, there can be no such qualification to the prohibition of slavery and servitude.

Accurate and consistent interpretation as to which offence has been carried out will influence the measures implemented to assist the child's psychological and physical recovery, additionally impacting on sentencing. Recognition that the *mens rea* for slavery or servitude may be distinct from that of similar practices, more certainly of the 'lesser' forms of forced labour, will mean that the penalty will need to reflect the offender's state of mind and parallel the seriousness of the harm. If a legal distinction does exist between slavery and servitude on the one hand, and forced or compulsory labour on the other, a variance in protection may therefore arise, further compounded by issues of cultural relativity, varying notions of childhood and disparate domestic laws on the rights of the child (see Chapters Two and Five).

Ultimately the problem with determining slavery as an identifiable practice or collection of practices distinguishable from 'lesser' harm may soon be rendered irrelevant in the light of the proliferation of legal instruments on recognised practices relating to child exploitation. International law has become saturated with treaties attempting to tackle these exploitative practices. There is a significant move towards protecting women and children given their weakened status in society and the resultant vulnerability of their position. It is perhaps time to view the Slavery Conventions as essentially inert: these are Conventions that provide essential definitions and an understanding of the development of human rights law on slavery, but beyond that, a precise meaning of slavery may well vanish in favour of a prohibition of more distinct practices, with specific and appropriate measures for protection and reparation, such as those within the Palermo Protocol.

Inception of child-specific rights

While the 19th-century abolitionist movements did not usually make distinctions between adults and children, the 20th century has seen not only a general sophistication of international texts on human rights protection, but also a focus on the welfare and rights of *children* specifically. Two years prior to the first Slavery Convention, a (non-binding) Declaration of the Rights of the Child was adopted by the League of Nations in 1924, prompted by armed conflict in the Balkans. This brief five-point document had first been promulgated by the non-governmental Save the Children International Union led by the British campaigner, Eglantyne Jebb (1876-1928). It was in fact the first declaration of human rights adopted by an intergovernmental organisation and preceded the (strictly speaking, non-binding) UN Universal Declaration of Human Rights 1948[6] by a generation. The 'Jebb' Declaration was a product of international concern, in the wake of the First World

War, of children's particular vulnerability in times of armed conflicts and famines. As one commentator put it, 'the devastation of the war gave new credence to the child in distress as the symbol of the problems of social life' (Marshall, 1999, p 145). Then came the expansion of this text into a 10-point Declaration of the Rights of the Child, 1959, promulgated by the UN's General Assembly. 'The essential theme underlying all of these non-binding declarations was that children need special protection and priority care' (Cantwell, 1992, p 19). Although it was not technically binding in international law, 'its unanimous adoption by the General Assembly gave it a significant moral authority' (Buck, 2008, p 48), becoming the text on which the first drafts of the (binding) 1989 CRC was based 30 years later.

The origins and development of the CRC form a significant and revealing story in its own right (see Hammarberg, 1990; Cantwell, 1992; van Bueren, 1995). Five of its general features can be noted. It contained, for the first time in international law, an attempt to produce a comprehensive and coherent account of children's rights, both 'first generation' civil and political and 'second generation' social, economic and cultural rights. Although the language deployed has changed – the words 'slavery' and 'servitude' do not appear at all in the text of the CRC – it includes provisions aimed at addressing exploitative behaviours and practices in respect of children analogous to older legal concepts found in the 1926 and 1956 Slavery Conventions.[7] Second, the CRC reflects a construction of the child as a more active and distinct rights holder, in contrast to the image of children as passive objects of concern in need of special protection and care contained in older declarations. Third, spurred on by the UN's International Year of the Child in 1979, the working group developing the text of the CRC met over a lengthy period and was remarkable for the high level of NGO participation (Cohen, 1990; Cantwell, 1992; Detrick 1992) in its work. Participation of NGOs has been reflected in the reporting process of the Convention machinery – NGOs may be consulted and contribute to the examination of a member state's official periodic reports (CRC, Article 45(a)). Fourth, this reporting process to a Committee on the Rights of the Child established under the CRC remains the only process whereby member states can be sanctioned for practices departing from CRC standards; there is otherwise no court forum.

Finally, the CRC is famously the international instrument with the largest number of ratifications among the whole body of international treaties. The only states not to have ratified are Somalia and the US. Somalia's non-ratification is largely due to its failure to maintain regular government infrastructures familiar in the international community. There has been an expanding literature to explain the failure of the US to ratify despite its active interest and participation in the early drafting of the Convention (Cohen and Davidson, 1990; Kilbourne, 1998; Todres et al, 2006). In the past there has been a strong suspicion in the US that 'children's rights' were in competition with 'parents' rights', and that the Convention in certain respects threatened the privatised realm of parent–child relationships. This concern is reflected structurally to the extent that family and child law is generally left as a matter for state legislatures rather than federal institutions. Consequently there are concerns that ratification would inappropriately federalise an area of activity traditionally associated with state competences. The absolute prohibition on capital punishment or life imprisonment without possibility of release (Article 37 of the CRC) sat uneasily with a country where several states had permitted capital punishment of under-18-year-olds in certain circumstances. However, a decision of the US Supreme Court in 2005 held, by a 5–4 majority, that it was unconstitutional to impose capital punishment for crimes committed while under the age of 18 (*Roper v Simmons*, 543 US 551 [2005]). That decision overruled a previous ruling (*Stanford v Kentucky*, 492 US 361 [1989]) upholding capital punishment for persons at or over the age of 16. In any event, such objections, based on the US Constitution, are not insuperable. Where there are potential conflicts, the US could always ratify with appropriate 'reservations, understandings and declarations' (see Article 51 of the CRC). It is also the case that no treaty can override the US Constitution (*Reid v Covert*, 354 US 1 [1957]). In any event, it is arguable that the CRC is not a 'self-executing' treaty, that is, it would need *state* legislation to progress its implementation. The CRC contains little by way of direction as to how to *implement* the various rights, so the perceived threat to US state sovereignty is without rational foundation. At the time of writing, it would appear that, prompted by a vigorous campaign to do so, the Obama administration might yet achieve US ratification of the CRC.[8]

The central importance of the CRC in providing a near-global normative legal standard, customised specifically to children, has been further strengthened by the addition of two Optional Protocols to the CRC machinery in 2000: the Optional Protocol on the Sale of Children, Child Prostitution and Child Pornography (OPSC) (entered into force in international law on 18 January 2002) and the Optional Protocol on the Involvement of Children in Armed Conflict (OPAC) (entered into force in international law on 12 February 2002, known as 'Red Hand Day'). Interestingly, the US *has* ratified both of these Optional Protocols. OPSC has two overall aims: to strengthen international criminalisation and to provide welfare protection for child victims. It is arguably the case that while the Protocol may have assisted in the process of international criminalisation, its implementation appears to have had a weaker impact on the protection of child victims (Buck, 2008, p 176). Article 38 of the CRC had reiterated states' international duties to respect humanitarian law in armed conflicts relevant to children and to take 'all feasible measures' to ensure that persons under the age of 15 do not participate directly in hostilities and to refrain from recruiting under 15-year-olds into their armed forces. The CRC also contains a duty on states to take 'all appropriate measures' for the recovery and social reintegration of children who have been victims of a range of exploitative behaviour including armed conflicts.[9] OPAC builds on these provisions, highly controversial during the drafting of the CRC, and further details the standards against the use of children in armed conflict, in addition raising the minimum age of participation to 18 years.

Indeed, the gathering authority of the CRC on matters of international child law has prompted commentators to argue that it can be regarded as having entered into the body of international customary law, and that the parts of the CRC that, in effect, prohibit child slavery or practices analogous to slavery, can be regarded as *jus cogens*[10] and cannot be derogated from, even by countries that have not ratified it (van Bueren, 1995, pp 53-7).

Child labour

Certain ILO Conventions[11] complement the CRC and its Optional Protocols with a developed international regulation of exploitative child labour. Smolin (2000) indicated that there have been four distinct stages of development associated with the history of international legal protection against exploitative child labour. First, five specific areas of work were identified for minimum age in employment regulation between 1919 and 1932.[12] Second, progress was made to raise the minimum age from 14 to 15 years via a number of Conventions.[13] Third, there followed a consolidation of these efforts in the form of the 1973 Minimum Age Convention No 138. Fourth, and most recently, the overall tendency has been for the international community to make efforts to *mainstream* child labour issues within the ILO, a process that eventually led to the current 'market leader' international instrument in this field, the 1999 Worst Forms of Child Labour Convention No 182 (see especially Chapter Three, this volume). In particular, the concept of the 'worst forms of child labour' comprises four categories including one that, in effect, assumes that the form of work is intolerable because of the work *relationships* involved:

> ... all forms of slavery or practices similar to slavery, such as the sale and trafficking of children, debt bondage and serfdom and forced or compulsory labour, including forced or compulsory recruitment of children for use in armed conflict. (Article 3(a))

A second and third category assumes the *nature* of the work itself is intolerable, for example, child prostitution and child pornography and using, procuring or offering a child for illicit activities, in particular the production and trafficking of drugs (Articles 3(b) and (c)). A fourth, residual category refers to 'work that, by its nature or the circumstances in which it is carried out, is likely to harm the health, safety or morals of children' (Article 3(d)). No doubt reflecting the difficulties of achieving international consensus in this area, the definition of what type of work might belong to this residual category is left to national governments to consider after consulting with the guidance on 'hazardous work' contained in the (non-binding) 1999 Worst Forms of Child Labour Recommendation No 190.

The 1999 Convention has provided a model of child protection that arguably reveals a more widespread impetus within the international community to frame international instruments that strike a sensible balance between universalism and cultural relativity. While the CRC can be described as a paradigm of global standard setting, a focus on child labour inevitably draws in very difficult issues of cultural relativity. The diversity of children's lives across different cultures and located within differing economic and social conditions does not necessarily lead to single, universal answers to the difficult questions, such as how we identify when children's work becomes 'exploitative'. This is of course especially evident in some developing countries where children's work to support the family household unit and its economic survival generates rather different normative values than found elsewhere in the world. The 1999 Convention in essence represents an agreement about *priorities* rather than following the absolutist solution of a policy of outright banning of the employment of children represented by the various minimum age Conventions. There is a significant scholarly literature around the conflict between universalism and cultural relativity (for example, Donnelly, 1984; Renteln, 1990), and many commentators have concluded both that 'human rights practice essentially has to learn to operate in the middle ground' (White, 1999, p 136) and that one must find 'approaches which involve neither the embrace of an artificial and sterile universalism nor the acceptance of an ultimately self-defeating cultural relativism' (Alston, 1994b, p 2).

Child trafficking

The international community has also seen considerable movement in attempts to tackle trafficking in human beings; globalisation and increasing demand for cheap labour and for prostitution means child trafficking is a highly profitable economic crime often concomitant with gender discrimination (see Chapter Five, this volume). Here it is the human rights of the child at issue; however, the trafficking of children will also impact on economic, social and cultural rights.

Child trafficking is not limited to sexual exploitation, but it is concerned with such practices. The sexual exploitation of children is already addressed in

Article 34 of the CRC and in Articles 2 and 3 of its OPSC. These have since been enhanced by the 2005 Action Punishing Trafficking in Human Beings Convention and the Palermo Protocol. The latter Convention and Palermo Protocol were extraordinary in that they were implemented as a means of tackling transnational organised crime, and not principally as human rights instruments. However, as a proportion of transnational organised crime is premised on trafficking and sexual exploitation, the human rights provisions are a fortunate and necessary byproduct.

The Palermo Protocol has become particularly important in this regard, clarifying and extending the meaning of trafficking and in particular dealing with the important issue of consent (as irrelevant) (see Article 3(b)), providing for distinct measures to be implemented to assist the victim (Article 6). The accepted meaning of trafficking is now significantly wider and is contained within Article 3 of the Palermo Protocol (see Chapters One and Five, this volume). Human trafficking is expressed as comprising three elements: the operation (recruitment, transportation, transfer, harbouring or receipt of persons), means (abduction, fraud, deception, etc) and purpose (exploitation). In order for an adult to be recognised as a victim of trafficking therefore, one or more of the criteria for each of these elements must be fulfilled. However, a distinction arises where children are concerned. Subparagraph (c) provides: 'The recruitment, transportation, transfer, harbouring or receipt of a child for the purpose of exploitation shall be considered "trafficking in persons" even if this does not involve any of the means set forth in subparagraph (a) of this article'. This recognition of the particular vulnerability of a child and their incapacity to give informed consent means that a child will be considered a victim of trafficking so long as the act (for example, transportation) and the consequence (exploitation) can be shown. There is no need to prove *how* the child was placed in an exploitative position; the fact that he or she has been recruited *for the purpose* of exploitation is sufficient (from which it can be inferred that exploitation does not have to occur for the trafficker to have committed the crime, although there are likely to be evidential issues for the proof of victim status). The definition is therefore so wide that it is most likely already supported by existing domestic law on prostitution and child labour.

A common error is to perceive of trafficking as a practice that requires border crossing or as a practice that relates solely to sexual exploitation. Neither is correct. It is clear that the definition makes no such requirement. Trafficking can therefore occur within a state if the above criteria are fulfilled. A distinction can be made between the treaties concerning migration and those that concern trafficking. Migration involves the voluntary movement of people across borders, and not coercion or deception of an individual for the purpose of exploitation.

The explicit mention of prostitution was purposefully included to recognise the additional harm that occurs here. Not only is the child subjected to trafficking by the trafficker, but they also suffer the additional and particularly grave harm of forced sexual abuse by the user (Huda, 2006). An examination of the discussions on the draft Protocol indicates that the word 'prostitution' was carefully selected (rather than 'sex work') so as to avoid interpretative debate and to emphasise the particular vulnerability of children, and girls in particular. The terms 'exploitation of others' and 'other forms of sexual exploitation' were also carefully chosen so as to enable states to determine the legality of prostitution within their domestic laws. However, state policy on prostitution is irrelevant where children are concerned. Any sexual practice to which a child is subjected will not be viewed as legal, although sexual exploitation is not the only criterion.

There is an absence of global consensus on the meaning of exploitation, but children subjected to the practices outlined in the Protocol (for example, prostitution and forced labour) would automatically fall within protective legal provisions by virtue of their status as children; there can be no argument of true autonomy, understanding or consent. However, the focus of the Protocol and its related Convention is on the buyers causing demand and the traffickers themselves, which, it has been argued, diverts attention from the wider economic, social and political context of the sex industry, that is, the role of residency, employment and migration policy (Anderson and Andrijasevic, 2008, p 140).

Nevertheless, the trafficking provisions exemplify the law's development in the field of children's rights. The recent and more overt recognition of the vulnerability of the child, in particular in relation to gender, is reflected in a new emphasis on special measures for the protection and support of victims. Article 6 of the Palermo Protocol provides quite prescriptive measures in an effort to secure the physical, psychological and social recovery of victims of trafficking. This includes the provision of appropriate housing, counselling, psychological and material assistance, employment, education, training opportunities and compensation. Under Article 7, states should also consider adopting measures to enable the reintegration and resettlement (repatriation) of victims. This potentially indicates a new era of human rights obligations, moving from the formalisation of overarching values and generic rights to the establishment of more precise obligations. This has important implications for the state that is likely to be concerned to protect its sovereignty. It may also prove harder to see such specific measures consistently observed in domestic laws in the light of cultural and legal divergences.

Implementation and enforcement

As we have seen, the construction of an international legal framework to address modern forms of child slavery has been challenging both in terms of the conceptual and legal definitional difficulties. These difficulties are further compounded by the complexities of implementation and enforcement of such international instruments at global, regional and national levels of operation. Both the CRC and the ILO Conventions, for example, lack the clarity of a discrete court enforcement mechanism where distinct legal remedies may be available to a state and/or individual litigant. The sanctions for breach of the Conventions discussed here are rather to be found in their reporting mechanisms (see Chapter One, this volume). The way in which the performance of individual states is exposed to political and diplomatic scrutiny and negotiation within nation states and on the international stage, in UN institutions and elsewhere, should be appreciated, but equally not overestimated. The 'naming and shaming' function of international law remains an important prompt to states to comply with international law. Unfortunately, although some of the international instruments discussed here have obtained a very good record of ratifications by countries,[14] this in itself is unlikely to guarantee compliance. Hathaway's 'integrated theory' of international law predicts, perhaps counter-intuitively, that countries with very poor human rights records can be as likely or even more likely to ratify treaties as countries with better records, but that, unlike those with better records, they are unlikely to comply with those commitments – which are, in fact, the patterns found (Hathaway, 2005).

However, any assessment of the effectiveness of these instruments should be prefaced by a proper consideration of the criteria by which such evaluation is made. This is not only problematic because, as we have seen, the covert nature of modern forms of slavery make it difficult to establish a reliable empirical research base for appropriate action, but it is contestable as to what time periods to use for any such evaluation. The CRC, for example, has some very long-term programmatic goals to raise general standards of children's rights, but wide areas of discretion are necessarily left to states to deliver such improvements. The expectation of short- or even medium-term gains, may inevitably lead to a negative verdict about their effectiveness.

The treaties discussed earlier do not all provide for an absolute prohibition; ILO Convention No 29 requires states merely to 'suppress the use of forced or compulsory labour within the shortest possible time' (Article 1(1)). The Palermo Protocol merely requests that states ensure *to the extent possible* implementing the measures provided under Article 6 to assist the victim, and *consider* introducing those in Article 7.

Ultimately the method of complying with obligations will continue to be subject to interpretation based on the existing social, economic and cultural concerns of the state. Perceptions that the law in place to protect children is ineffective emerge due to the impossibility of accurate monitoring of these practices, legal ambiguity, a lack of enforcement mechanisms and lack of global consensus as to the notion of childhood and related ethics of child labour. However, the value of the law is as a means of setting global standards and driving reform by the formal identification of universal human rights; states are encouraged to acknowledge normative values and human rights principles and so reflect them in domestic law. There has been widespread ratification of treaties protecting the child, the verbatim adoption of definitions and the implementation of suggested support measures in domestic legislation.

The new approach to obligations evident in more recent treaties reveals that international law has much to contribute to the debate about the protection of children subject to exploitation. International law continues to develop beyond the basic recognition of rights, and to streamline common understandings of the human rights of the child, endeavouring to construct a collective and transparent schema for children's protection and rehabilitation.

Conclusion

The widespread ratification of treaties discussed here indicates that there is now an extensive legal structure in place to address the problem of child slavery and child exploitation, evidenced by the increased promulgation of related domestic legislation. Given the varying jurisdictions, signature, ratification and adoption (and interpretation) of international and regional legal instruments, consistency of definition may become more important in the future; any ambiguity is likely to extend to states' internal organs, with the result that domestic law may become less effectual.[15] In particular it is clear that there is considerable variance on the meaning of child exploitation, complicated by issues of cultural relativity.

Nevertheless, the movement from generic rights to the creation of treaties concerned with more distinct practices, and a focus on child-specific rights, has led to the positive construction of measures that go beyond criminalisation and are aimed at providing more comprehensive assistance to the victim and the recognition of children as active rights holders. Such measures, although only proposals and therefore reliant on state policy, do much to address criticisms that human rights treaties provide little by way of reparation other than through the medium of compensation.

While questions as to the effectiveness of international treaties will no doubt continue given the lack of enforcement mechanisms, this is somewhat contra-indicated by the growth of treaties on children's rights, the extensive ratification status of existing treaties and the increased promulgation of related domestic legislation. This trend is likely to continue.

Notes

[1] A norm accepted by the international community as being so fundamental that there can be no derogation from it. Accepted examples include genocide and piracy.

[2] Amended in 1953 by the Protocol amending the Slavery Convention signed at Geneva on 25 September 1926 (approved by General Assembly Resolution 794 [VIII]).

[3] Article 1(1) of the 1926 Slavery Convention. Article 1(2) provides: 'The slave trade includes all acts involved in the capture, acquisition or disposal of a person with intent to reduce him to slavery; all acts involved in the acquisition of a slave with a view to selling or exchanging him; all acts of disposal by sale or exchange of a slave acquired with a view to being sold or exchanged, and, in general, every act of trade or transport in slaves'.

[4] Rome Statute of the International Criminal Court, 17 July 1998, Article 7(1):'For the purpose of this Statute, "crime against humanity" means any of the following acts when committed as part of a widespread or systematic attack directed against any civilian population, with knowledge of the attack: ... (c) enslavement'. The definition of the 1926 Slavery Convention is adopted under Article 7(2) but adds 'and includes the exercise of such power in the course of trafficking in persons, in particular women and children'.

[5] See, for example, the representations of Myanmar (Burma) to the UN that children and adults are required to work on road construction, despite clear witness reports from Amnesty International indicating that its actions are a clear breach of the ILO Conventions.

[6] The 1948 UN Declaration of Human Rights, Article 4, states that:'No one shall be held in slavery or servitude; slavery and the slave trade shall be prohibited in all their forms'. A near identical prohibition of slavery and the slave trade was contained in the (binding) 1966 International Covenant on Civil and Political Rights, Article 8(1).

[7] For example, protection from economic exploitation (Article 32), illicit production and trafficking of drugs (Article 33), sexual exploitation (Article 34), trafficking (Article 35), 'all other forms of exploitation prejudicial to any aspects of the child's welfare' (Article 36) and children's involvement in armed conflict (Article 38).

[8] See the Campaign for US Ratification of the Convention on the Rights of the Child at http://childrightscampaign.org/crcindex.php

[9] 'States Parties shall take all appropriate measures to promote physical and psychological recovery and social reintegration of a child victim of: any form of neglect, exploitation, or abuse; torture or any other form of cruel, inhuman or degrading treatment or punishment; or armed conflicts. Such recovery and reintegration shall take place in an environment which fosters the health, self-respect and dignity of the child' (CRC, Article 39).

[10] See note 1 above. Article 53 of the Convention on the Law of Treaties provides that a treaty will be void 'if, at the time of its conclusion, it conflicts with a peremptory norm of general international law'. This rule, known as *jus cogens*, 'will also apply in the context of customary rules so that no derogation would be permitted to such norms by way of local or special custom'. Such peremptory norms probably include the unlawful use of force, genocide, slave trading and piracy (Shaw, 2003, p 117). 'If the prohibition on slavery amounts to *jus cogens*, the argument that the institutions and practices similar to slavery also amount to *jus cogens*, becomes very compelling' (van Bueren, 1995, p 56).

[11] 1930 Forced Labour Convention No 29; 1973 Minimum Age Convention No 138; 1999 Worst Forms of Child Labour Convention No 182.

[12] 1919 Minimum Age (Industry) Convention No 5; 1920 Minimum Age (Sea) Convention No 7; 1921 Minimum Age (Agriculture) Convention No 10; 1921 Minimum Age (Trimmers and Stokers) Convention No 15; 1932 Minimum Age (Non-Industrial Employment) Convention No 33.

[13] 1936 Minimum Age (Sea) Convention (Revised) No 58; 1937 Minimum Age (Industry) Convention (Revised) No 59; 1937 Minimum Age (Non-Industrial Employment) Convention (Revised) No 60; 1959 Minimum Age (Fishermen) Convention No 112; 1965 Minimum Age (Underground Work) Convention, No 123.

[14] State ratifications as at September 2009: CRC, 193 parties; ILO Worst Forms of Child Labour Convention, 171 parties; International Covenant on Civil and Political Rights, 164 parties; ILO Minimum Age Convention, 154 parties; OPSC, 132 parties; OPAC, 130 parties; Protocol to Prevent, Suppress and Punish trafficking in persons, especially women and children, supplementing the UN Convention against Transnational Organised Crime, 133 parties.

[15] Confusion as to the correct interpretation can already be seen in the judgment of the Court in *Hadijatou Mani Koraou v The Republic of Niger* (2008) Judgment No ECW/CCJ/JUD/06/08, 27 October 2008.

References

Allain, J. (2008) *The Slavery Conventions: The travaux préparatoires of the 1926 League of Nations Convention and the 1956 United Nations Convention*, Leiden and Boston: Martinus Nijhoff.

Allain, J. (2009) 'The definition of slavery in international law', *Howard Law Journal*, vol 52, pp 239-75.

Alston, P. (ed) (1994a) *The best interests of the child: Reconciling culture and human rights*, Oxford: Clarendon Press/UNICEF.

Alston, P. (1994b) 'The best interests principle: towards a reconciliation of culture and human rights', in P. Alston (ed) *The best interests of the child: Reconciling culture and human rights*, Oxford: Clarendon Press/UNICEF.

Anderson, B. and Andrijasevic, R. (2008) 'Sex, slaves and citizens: the politics of anti-trafficking', *Soundings*, vol 40, pp 135-46.

Buck, T. (2008) 'International criminalisation and child welfare protection: the Optional Protocol to the Convention on the Rights of the Child', *Children and Society*, vol 22, no 3, pp 167-78.

Cantwell, N. (1992) 'The origins, development and significance of the United Nations Convention on the Rights of the Child', in S. Detrick (ed) *The United Nations Convention on the Rights of the Child: A guide to the 'travaux préparatoires'*, Dordrecht, Boston, MA and London: Martinus Nijhoff, pp 19-30.

Cohen, C.P. (1990) 'The role of nongovernmental organizations in the drafting of the Convention on the Rights of the Child', *Human Rights Quarterly*, vol 12, no 1, pp 137-47.

Cohen, C.P. and Davidson, H.A. (eds) (1990) *Children's rights in America: UN Convention on the Rights of the Child compared with United States law*, Chicago, IL: American Bar Association, Center on Children and the Law.

Cullen, H. (2006) '*Siliadin v France*: positive obligations under Article 4 of the European Convention of Human Rights', *Human Rights Law Review*, vol 6, no 3, pp 585-92.

Detrick, S. (ed) (1992) *The United Nations Convention on the Rights of the Child: A guide to the 'travaux préparatoires'*, Dordrecht, Boston, MA and London: Martinus Nijhoff.

Donnelly, J. (1984) 'Cultural relativism and universal human rights', *Human Rights Quarterly*, vol 6, no 4, pp 400-19.

Hammarberg, T. (1990) 'The UN Convention on the Rights of the Child – and how to make it work', *Human Rights Quarterly*, vol 12, no 1, pp 97-105.

Hathaway, O.A. (2005) 'Between power and principle: an integrated theory of international law', *University of Chicago Law Review*, vol 72, no 2, pp 469-536.

Huda, S. (2006) *Report of the Special Rapporteur on the human rights aspects of victims of trafficking in persons, especially women and children*, United Nations Commission on Human Rights, 20 February, E/CN4/2006/62.

Kilbourne, S. (1998) 'The wayward Americans – why the USA has not ratified the UN Convention on the Rights of the Child', *Child and Family Law Quarterly*, vol 10, no 3, pp 243-56.

Marshall, D. (1999) 'The construction of children as an object of international relations: the Declaration of Children's Rights and the Child Welfare Committee of League of Nations, 1900–1924', *The International Journal of Children's Rights*, vol 7, no 2, pp 103-47.

Nicholson, A. (2010: forthcoming) 'Silidain v France: slavery and definition', *International Journal of Human Rights*.

Quirk, J. (2009) *Unfinished business*, Paris: UNESCO.

Renteln, A.D. (1990) *International human rights: Universalism versus relativism*, London: Sage Publications.

Shaw, M. (2003) *International law* (5th edn), Cambridge: Cambridge University Press.

Smolin, D. (2000) 'Strategic choices in the international campaign against child labour', *Human Rights Quarterly*, vol 22, no 4, pp 942-87.

Todres, J., Wocjik, M.E. and Revaz, C.R. (eds) (2006) *The UN Convention on the Rights of the Child: An analysis of treaty provisions and implications of US ratification*, Ardsley, NY: Transnational Publishers Inc.

van Bueren, G. (1995) *International law on the rights of the child*, Dordrecht, Boston, MA and London: Martinus Nijhoff.

Walvin, J. (2007) *A short history of slavery*, Harmondsworth: Penguin.

White, B. (1999) 'Defining the intolerable', *Childhood*, vol 6, no 1, pp 133-44.

three

Just out of reach: the challenges of ending the worst forms of child labour

Catherine Turner, Aidan McQuade and Enrique Restoy

Introduction

Anniversaries often provoke reflection. So in 2008, in the approach to the 10th anniversary of the adoption of the International Labour Organization's (ILO) Worst Forms of Child Labour Convention No 182 by the 1999 International Labour Conference (ILC), Anti-Slavery International, with local non-governmental organisation (NGO) colleagues in Costa Rica, Kenya, Pakistan and Togo, undertook a snapshot review of progress in implementing this Convention in these countries.[1] This study allows us to explore the extent to which international conventions are embedded in local practice.

The study examined progress made towards ending child slavery and slavery-like practices, which, while relatively small in number compared with other worst forms of child labour,[2] are commonly where the most egregious violations of human rights occur. Although a snapshot review could not be expected to cover all other areas included in ILO Convention No 182, it examined a further five areas critical for ending the worst forms of child labour in general and hence, by implication also, child slavery. These were: (1) harmonisation of national laws; (2) government consultations and coordination; (3) data gathering; (4) civil society and the media; and (5) child participation. These areas are not only identified in ILO Convention No 182 and/or its accompanying Recommendation No 190, but featured in an initial project undertaken by Anti-Slavery International and the same local NGO partners from 2002–04,[3] thereby affording the 2008 review a baseline in these areas against which to measure progress.

Following brief descriptions of ILO Convention No 182 under international law and the study methodology, governments' progress in implementing measures to eradicate child slavery and slavery-like practices under the Convention as well as the other areas cited above are examined in turn to identify where implementation has enabled effective combating of the worst forms of child labour, or how failures to implement have impeded and constrained national efforts to eradicate it. While particularly relevant to the four countries involved, these findings provide useful strategic insights and recommendations to help policy makers and practitioners advance the protection of the millions of children who are still being exploited around the world.

Worst forms of child labour under international law

As laid down in ILO Convention No 182, the worst forms of child labour refer to all forms of slavery and slavery-like practices, such as trafficking, debt bondage and forced or compulsory labour, including for use in armed conflict, prostitution or pornography, for use in illicit activities such as drug trafficking, or work likely to harm the health, safety or morals of children (Article 3(a)-(d)). The Convention also provides for governments to determine which types of work to classify as hazardous, and consequently work that children should be prohibited from doing, based on clear and widely agreed guidelines contained in the Convention's accompanying Recommendation No 190. Governments are supposed to make this determination on the basis of consultations with employers' and workers' groups, and should take into account relevant international standards (Article 4(1)-(3)). This Convention applies to all children under 18 years of age (Article 2).

The United Nations (UN) Convention on the Rights of the Child (CRC) sets norms on all aspects of childhood, and obliges states that have ratified it to protect children and promote their well-being in the wide range of areas that it covers. It also applies to all children under 18 years of age. To date it has been ratified by almost all states in the world. Rights in this treaty that are particularly relevant to the worst forms of child labour include: the right to be free from economic exploitation or performing any work that is hazardous, affects a child's education or harms their development (Article 32); and the right to protection from all other forms of exploitation (Article 36).

A brief note on methodology

In each of the countries involved, the 2008 snapshot study combined literature reviews by partner organisations into national laws and policies along with individual interviews and group discussions with a wide range of key stakeholders, including central and local government officials, trade union and employer representatives, NGOs and community groups and, in some cases, informal actors such as tribal chiefs and religious leaders as well as children and young people themselves.[4]

Extent of ILO Convention No 182 implementation

Teresa's story

Teresa[5] is 15 years old and works as a domestic worker in Cartago, Costa Rica. She describes her day: "I work by the hour. I have to arrive at six thirty in the morning and I have to be punctual. I sweep the floor, I dust the house, clean the toilet, do the washing up and iron everyone's clothes, I cook lunch, I have to watch the children when they come back from school, I feed them, do the washing up and I leave dinner ready. The lady comes at around five. Then I can go home. I have to take two buses." (quoted in Blagbrough, 2008, p 13)

Child slavery and slavery-like practices

As noted, slavery and slavery-like practices are explicitly prohibited in the text of ILO Convention No 182, governments being required to tackle them as a matter of urgency. Perhaps the most striking point emerging from the research, however, is that governments concerned do not appear to be prioritising or even paying much attention to measures to combat child slavery and slavery-like practices, with the notable exceptions of efforts to tackle trafficking for sexual exploitation and in some cases the exploitation of child domestic workers.

Many participants thought that child slavery issues were often overlooked, both in terms of gauging the true extent of the problems and taking action against them. This is either because they commonly have criminal links (such as forced begging and prostitution) or take place in the private or informal sphere (such as children in domestic work and agriculture) where scrutiny is much harder to guarantee. For example, several participants in Pakistan and Costa Rica commented that legislation and labour inspections target only a few work environments, notably factories and shops. However, many sectors known to be vulnerable to incidences of the worst forms of child labour, such as agriculture, fisheries, the carpet industry, stone cutting and child domestic workers, are ignored.[6] It was also felt that there was very little that employers' organisations or trade unions could do in these cases, since they only operate in the formal economy.[7] As one participant from the group discussion in Lahore, Pakistan, put it, "in informal industries, things become invisible".

The data even stress confusion and disagreement among policy makers and other research participants about what constitutes the worst forms of child labour. For some Kenyan actors, for instance, child begging (even forced) is hardly considered a crime, and early marriage is widely accepted.

In Costa Rica, some respondents also found it difficult to identify sexual exploitation as a child labour issue.

The study also highlighted emerging issues, meriting further research. Data from Pakistan indicate cases of children being recruited by Islamic militant groups as suicide bombers, either by force or through extremist teachings on the internet and in *madrassas* (Qur'anic/Islamic religious schools). For example, the Society for the Protection of the Rights of the Child (SPARC), coordinating the research in Pakistan, interviewed two juvenile prisoners aged 11 and 13 in South Waziristan, having been apprehended with explosive material strapped to them. The boys claimed that they had been abducted by armed men from their village and transported to an unknown place, where the explosives were attached to them, and they were then taken to a nearby city (Bannu City) where police intercepted them (SPARC, literature review and interview with NGO). Other children are becoming directly involved in tribal wars, for example in Sindh (interview with NGO, Pakistan).

While the overall picture in terms of tackling child slavery and slavery-like practices under ILO Convention No 182 was disappointing, some notable successes came to light. For example, while it appeared that little has been done about many aspects in Costa Rica, there have been targeted efforts to tackle the sexual exploitation of minors, including sex tourism, since ratification of the Convention. This has resulted in an overall increase in the number of criminal sentences passed in sexual exploitation cases. There have also been examples of successful intergovernmental cooperation: in 2004, for the first time, the US government extradited to Costa Rica one of its citizens accused of sex-related crimes against minors (DCI literature review).

In Togo, a reduction in the number of under-15-year-olds entering domestic work since ratification of the Convention was reported following a comprehensive range of NGO-led measures, including awareness raising in homes, reduced school fees and the professionalisation of the sector. There were also good examples of the government and NGOs working together, notably labour inspectors accompanying NGOs to inspect the conditions of domestic workers in private homes (WAO Afrique literature review and group discussion, Togo).

These success stories, albeit sporadic, suggest that although work in these areas is beset with difficulties, it should be possible to act to combat child slavery and slavery-like practices given a detailed understanding of the particular issues and a genuine determination to tackle them by governments, and with the support of other relevant actors.

Harmonisation of national laws and their enforcement

Like any other international treaty, for ILO Convention No 182 to be applied nationally it must first be incorporated into national legislation with appropriate penalties introduced for perpetrators contravening those laws. Indeed, the text emphasises that each member state will take all necessary measures to ensure the effective implementation of the Convention itself, including the provision and application of penal sanctions (Article 7[1]).

In 2004, project partners reported that ILO Convention No 182 had not been fully incorporated into national law. Pakistan stood out as one of the countries where domestication of the Convention was most needed. By 2008 the situation had barely changed. General prohibitions punishable with fines and imprisonment against slavery, forced labour and trafficking in human beings exist, such as in the Pakistani Constitution (Articles 9, 11(1)-(2) and 15) and Penal Code (Sections 370 and 374), but serious gaps remain. For example, Pakistan has long failed to address fundamentally the issue of debt bondage for adults and children (Upadhyaya, 2008). Further, child pornography falls under general bans on obscene materials as there is no specific legislation to combat electronic or digital child pornographic images, nor to punish those possessing such material or using children in this way (SPARC literature review).

More positively, Kenya had embarked on a thorough domestic legislative programme from the outset, although some areas still need to be addressed. For example, although Section 1 of the 2007 Employment Act defines a child as a person under 18 years old, Section 2 identifies a 16- to 18-year-old as a 'young person', thereby potentially excluding 16- and 17-year-olds from protection against working conditions prohibited for 'children' (ANPPCAN literature review). In Costa Rica, there have been no new laws since 2001, but there are two Bills awaiting passage through the legislative assembly,[8] which, although greatly delayed since 2005, would, if passed, increase significantly legal protection provided to children in the worst forms of child labour.

There was insufficient information available to partners to draw firm conclusions about current levels of enforcement in each of the countries, although from the data that could be accessed, prosecution and conviction rates appeared to be low compared with the likely scale of the problem. For example, a large number of NGO discussion participants in Lahore, Pakistan, believed that there have been too few convictions: "Why have there been almost no convictions? Awareness and publications cannot work alone."[9] In Costa Rica, partners found evidence of just two verdicts since ratification against employers relating to hazardous working conditions (one case involving injury to a child handling dangerous machinery and another relating to a child working in a circus; DCI literature review), although there has been an increasing annual conviction rate for sexual exploitation-related crimes (DCI literature review).

Penalties available do not always seem to match the severity of the crimes perpetrated. Under the 1991 Pakistani Employment of Children Act, any person, police officer or labour inspector can file a complaint in any court with relevant jurisdiction. However, even government representatives acknowledge the problems: "Slow court procedures hinder the elimination of worst forms of child labour and courts do not take the issue seriously – which also discourages labour inspectors – cases mostly end up with a Rs 50–100 [approximately 40–80 pence] fine, which is not a solution" (government representative, Peshawar, Pakistan).

The Kenyan 2001 Children's Act prohibits the economic exploitation of children in its many forms, including child trafficking, sexual exploitation and using children for illicit activities. However, it provides for penalties 'not exceeding' 12 months' imprisonment or a fine 'not exceeding' 50,000 shillings (£423). The failure of Kenya to enforce laws against child labour also appears to be a serious problem. For instance, the government's law enforcement agencies reported no investigations, prosecutions or convictions of child trafficking-related crimes in the whole of 2006 (ANPPCAN literature review).

Government consultations and coordination

ILO Convention No 182 establishes that each member state shall as a priority design and implement programmes of action to eliminate the worst forms of child labour in consultation with relevant government institutions and employers' and workers' organisations, taking into consideration the views of 'other concerned groups' (Article 6). This opened the possibility for involving NGOs and community-based organisations working on these issues, as well as children and young people affected by the worst forms of child labour themselves and their families.

In 2008, study participants noted an increase in relevant government officials' awareness of the treaty and worst forms of child labour since ratification. However, coordination among relevant governmental structures and between government, employers' associations and trade unions appears still to be an important challenge and progress here has been patchy. WAO Afrique (Togo) reported a successful experience for the most part. They noted that the government had consulted the ILO, trade unions and NGOs as a matter of course, with examples also of joint initiatives particularly between the government, NGOs and religious groups. This was echoed in the group discussions. While employers are reportedly invited to official meetings on child labour, representatives do not attend regularly (WAO Afrique literature review).

The African Network for the Prevention and Protection against Child Abuse and Neglect (ANPPCAN) in Kenya witnessed the strongest progress in this regard at the time of the original project, helped by external factors, notably a change of government. One important step was the revitalisation of the National Steering Committee, bringing together government departments and civil society organisations dealing with child labour issues in a regular and systematic way. However, it appears that a promising start has not been maintained. The National Steering Committee apparently met twice in 2007 and failed to meet at all by mid-2008 when the research was undertaken, due primarily to budget constraints, according to the Department of Labour (ANPPCAN literature review). Group discussion participants from Embakasi, Kenya, also criticised poor coordination by the government at national level.

In Pakistan, the National Committee of Child Welfare and Development indicated that the last national-level tripartite meeting was held in August 2006, having been postponed since 2004 (SPARC literature review). One local government informant in Karachi, Pakistan, noted that "Conventions have been ratified but there is no coordination and no focal person. People get transferred which is also a hindrance. There is no continuity of the programmes and NGOs need to have collaboration with government."

Although the ILO Steering Committee is supposed to meet regularly each year in Costa Rica, there appear to be problems getting the tripartite group to sit down together in practice.[10] Nevertheless, despite many, mainly NGOs, expressing frustration about the levels of commitment and collaboration between the government and key stakeholders (according to four NGO representatives in COSECODENI, Costa Rica), other actors consulted in Costa Rica were more positive (representative from OATIA, a trade union group and NGO representative, COSECODENI, Costa Rica).

The organisations involved in this study have been promoting awareness of the importance of ILO Convention No 182 at the grassroots since 2002, to help ensure that it amounts to more than unimplemented policy and reaches beyond capital cities. This was of course particularly critical for countries the size of Pakistan and Kenya. So SPARC in Pakistan and ANPPCAN in Kenya sought at that time to help promote the devolution of responsibilities to local government level and to increase coordination among implementing actors as part of project activities. Notably, nationwide networks of area advisory councils (AACs) on child protection, combined with district child labour committees (DCLCs) in Kenya, proved particularly effective at bringing district government officials together with other local key stakeholders regularly to review the situation of children in their area and to formulate programmes aimed at combating child labour in a way that was appropriate to the district and community-level context.

Since then, despite one or two positive examples, participants in group discussions in Pakistan, which were held in each of the provinces, Karachi, Lahore, Peshawar and Quetta, expressed disappointment at the rate of progress locally and many felt isolated from central activities. In contrast, in Kiambu, Kenya, where ANPPCAN also held group discussions outside the capital, Nairobi, participants indicated that the formalised AAC/DCLC approach appears to still be working very well.

Civil society and the media

While governments must take the lead in implementing ILO Convention No 182, such a large and complex problem as the worst forms of child labour can be tackled only with the widest possible alliance of relevant actors working together. Since ratification, civil society organisations have been instrumental, for example, in informing, sensitising and mobilising the general public; conducting training for their own representatives as well as for other professionals, such as relevant government personnel, especially inspectors and law enforcement officials, and raising the issue in the media. An NGO informant in Togo described some of their work: "Convention 182 is now our bible. We ... go door to door to sensitise the general public.... We also actively try to identify child domestic workers who are suffering and take them to the [NGO shelter] with a view to reintegrating them back into families, school or apprenticeships."

NGOs appear to have remained active in all of the countries examined, for example by rehabilitating survivors of the worst forms of child labour; promoting education or running scholarship or income-generating schemes, and conducting training among labour inspectors, magistrates, lawyers, judges, police and other NGOs. This could be a reflection of the fact that the researchers for this study were NGOs and so more familiar with those activities, although this impression was supported by remarks from various group discussion participants. NGOs themselves also identified areas in need of improvement; for example in Costa Rica NGOs thought they could do more to reach agreements among themselves and coordinate better to present a more unified front to government (NGO representative, COSECODENI, Costa Rica). Civil society groups in Costa Rica also noted that "we need to do more awareness raising through the media to generate public opinion [and] we still need to work with business owners, at least as a sector" (group discussion with representatives from four NGO members of COSECODENI).

Trade unions seem to have a difficult role when it comes to the worst forms of child labour as children do not form part of their constituency. Some workers' organisations nevertheless appear to be active. Costa Rican trade unions seemed to be particularly well informed about the issue and committed to tackling it, including in 'non-traditional' trade union areas, such as the Confederation of Workers Rerun Novarum (Confederación de Trabajadores Rerun Novarum), who work to promote awareness about child labour in the agricultural sector and the Movement of Costa Rican Workers (Central del Movimiento de Trabajadores [as] Costarricenses), who run day care centres for children of street sellers.[11] In Togo, the trade union representatives who took part in the research also appeared to be active and knowledgeable. However, they and worker representatives involved in group discussions in Pakistan acknowledged that as trade unions do not operate in the informal sector or have direct contact with children as part of their function, some members did not prioritise child labour and so lacked motivation (individual interview, trade unionist, Togo, and trade union representative, Karachi, Pakistan). Trade unions have undertaken several activities in Kenya, yet, although they were invited, no representatives attended the Kenyan group discussions. Other participants did not think that they took the matter seriously (Maragua and Kiambu group discussions, Kenya).

With some exceptions, the most reticent as a group overall in the 2002–04 project appeared to be employers, in part due to a relative lack of coherence as a body and therefore more difficult to coordinate when implementing activities. From the research in 2008, it appears that employers as a group have made efforts to promote action against the worst forms of child labour among their members, also in collaboration with others. For example, in Togo they appear to have been active in publicising new employment codes and organising seminars and training programmes to educate their members (WAO Afrique literature review), and in Costa Rica employers' groups have published articles and issued internal memos (DCI literature review). However, in general, fewer examples surfaced through the review process than for either NGOs or trade unions. This may be due to the fact that employers simply do not publicise their efforts as well as the other groups or because the constraints identified in the original project remain.

Of particular interest is the successful mobilisation of informal civil society groups in some countries, notably religious groups and traditional tribal chiefs in Togo, who have undertaken numerous activities locally, including campaigns, training and education about the worst forms of child labour, as well as incorporating information on the issue into church sermons. Before ratification of ILO Convention No 182, a tribal chief from Togo commented in an interview:

> For a long time we sent our children, especially girls … to town
> or abroad [to Gabon] to work as domestics. It even made us proud
> as parents to have our children working in town…. But thanks
> to many sensitisation campaigns and information from NGOs

and government we began, bit by bit, to realise the risks we were exposing our children to. Many cases revealed that children placed in town or sent abroad were often victims of exploitation and abuse of every sort. The Convention enabled us to inform ourselves better about the different types of work that are dangerous for children. So we began to join the struggle [against worst forms of child labour] by setting up a vigilance committee in our local area.

Getting non-traditional partners such as these on board is of course particularly important for reaching children and families at the grassroots level. At the start of the original project in 2002, there was a very low level of public awareness to which the chief's comment above testifies. So targeting the general public through the media, particularly radio in local languages, rallies, theatre groups and so forth, formed a major part of partners' project activities. The project partners then noted the need to expand grassroots awareness raising and training to reach vulnerable children and their families and communities. Today, the majority perception from survey participants in all countries involved in the review was that the general public were more aware than had been the case before ratification. One informant in Kenya, a volunteer children's officer from the Embakasi group discussion, pointed out that, "We have many support groups raising awareness on children's issues including child labour.... Now if a child is ... working in exploitative work ... people know it is bad. Initially people brought girls in from up-country to work as house helps. But now awareness on this has increased and many people have stopped the practice." But a great deal of frustration was expressed at how much more was still needed to tackle the worst forms of child labour at the grassroots.[12] Another Kenyan informant noted that cases of all forms of child labour were still high, as "parents see using children in work as a means of making additional money" (orphanage coordinator, Embakasi group, Kenya).

Sensitising and mobilising the media has been a key contribution to wider awareness raising of the issue and in general also appears to have achieved positive results. In Pakistan, for example, SPARC reported for this review that English and Urdu print and electronic media at both national and local levels have played an important role in maintaining the profile of the issue in people's minds since the last project, for example by highlighting the need for quality education and problems with law enforcement (SPARC literature review).

Child participation

In addition to ILO Convention No 182's request for governments to solicit children's views where appropriate (Article 6), it also recalls the UN CRC, which sets meaningful participation of children as one of its overriding principles, stating that 'State Parties shall assure to the child who is capable of forming his or her own views the right to express those views freely in all matters affecting the child' (CRC, Article 12(1)).

Four years on, in 2008, while there has clearly been some progress, the level of child participation was rated very differently in the countries concerned, and in all cases there is still a long way to go for participation to be fully integrated and meaningful in public life. It is also interesting to note that both WAO Afrique in Togo and DCI in Costa Rica were able to involve young people in group discussions to get their views for this review.

There were no significant examples of child participation to report in Pakistan beyond NGO initiatives, although a survey among relevant professionals conducted by SPARC indicated that children were raising more questions about child labour, suggesting that awareness raising directly among children had had some effect.[13] But this did not reflect everyone's experience, as an NGO participant in the group discussion in Lahore stated, "Children do not know about ILO Convention 182 and their rights, in which case how can they claim their rights?"

ANPPCAN noted that child participation was not prominent in government programmes, apart from some campaigns featuring children. But many NGOs involve children, including through child rights clubs to raise awareness and national celebrations, where they can participate in raising the profile of the issue (ANPPCAN literature review).

In Togo, children have been involved in seminars and sensitisation meetings, and through the organised youth group, Enfants Jeunesse Action, whose young members conduct awareness-raising activities (WAO Afrique literature review).

In Costa Rica, DCI did not find evidence of any formal child participation before the government ratified ILO Convention No 182. However, following ratification, the government undertook a nationwide consultation among children and adolescents in a total of 35 workshops involving both rural and urban districts. Their views were incorporated into the second National Plan of Action for the Prevention and Elimination of Child Work, 2005–10 (DCI literature review). Interestingly, however, the young people who took part in the research thought that while the main responsibility was with the government to tackle the problem, adolescents could play a greater part, helping to sensitise their peers through "campaigns, passing information to friends, giving advice to those who are working, but it has to be done well otherwise they will take it as a telling off". They added:

"Through children, society can be better informed. The children go home and tell their parents what they have learned in school."[14]

Data gathering

ILO Convention No 182 does not refer to the importance of detailed information and statistical data for successful implementation. ILO Recommendation No 190, however, stresses the need for disaggregated data to serve as a base for determining priorities for national action on the abolition of child labour and that relevant data concerning violations of national provisions against child labour should be compiled, kept up to date and referred to the ILO's Offices (ILO Recommendation No 190, Article 5(1)-(3)).

One of the main conclusions that the NGO partners reached in 2004 was the desperate need for governments to compile or at least have access to accurate and reliable data on the worst forms of child labour, which is essential for action to be properly targeted and the impact of those actions to be accurately evaluated. Four years on, our research indicates that there is still a serious lack of accurate information in all of the countries, either because current estimates do not reflect the whole picture or the data simply do not exist. This is particularly the case for child slavery and slavery-like practices, perhaps in part because of the greater difficulty involved in examining this area due to its largely hidden or criminal nature.

For instance, our partners in Pakistan noted that the last national survey on child labour was undertaken by the government in 1996, estimating that there were 3.3 million children in child labour in the country. A more recent survey into the labour force was conducted in 2007, but failed to analyse the situation of working children under 10 years of age (SPARC literature review). In Kenya, national surveys carried out in 1999 and 2005 indicated very encouragingly that child labour had fallen from 1.9 million to 1.01 million overall. However, in neither case were data disaggregated to reveal whether there was a concurrent reduction in any of the worst forms of child labour. In Costa Rica, partners noted that data are limited to children between 12 and 17 years of age and look at formal employment only, thus excluding all children in the informal sector. So while research shows a drop in formal employment of adolescents between 2003 and 2007, there is no way of knowing the full picture. Indeed, one research interviewee commented that some sample NGO investigations into the number of children in the worst forms of child labour in the informal sector, which were not included in official government statistics, could be an "alarming figure" (individual interview with an NGO, COSECODENI, representative, Costa Rica). At the time of the review, the Togolese government was only then planning to start a study on the issue to produce a national database, so no figures were available (WAO Afrique literature review).

Clearly this marked absence of targeted and accurate data on all aspects of the worst forms of child labour seriously restricts efforts by governments and other actors to respond meaningfully to the problem. It could also be an indicator that the governments concerned lack either the political will or capacity to prioritise the worst forms of child labour in practice.

Further obstacles to the effective implementation of ILO Convention No 182

In addition to the problems already discussed earlier in relation to data gathering, legal gaps and the lack of emphasis on the informal economy, survey participants raised several other obstacles. Unsurprisingly, their surveys highlighted chronic poverty, natural disasters and the migration flows associated with them as major causes of the worst forms of child labour, as well as factors holding back the implementation of ILO Convention No 182. One participant in Pakistan, an NGO informant from Lahore, noted "The reasons for the programmes [on worst forms of child labour] not being successful include poverty feudalism and forced labour. Political parties do not have [this] on their agendas." Another participant in Costa Rica, from COSECODENI, noted that "[The] main causes of poverty are not tackled effectively: most poor families receive support for [a] better quality of life in some areas, such as housing and health, but nothing effective is done to get them out of poverty."

Specific groups were identified as being particularly vulnerable to exploitation and therefore requiring particular attention, for example indigenous peoples in Costa Rica and street children and internally displaced people in Pakistan. Participants in Kenya and Togo emphasised that the increase in orphans as a result of the HIV/AIDS pandemic forced many children to drop out of school and enter the labour market prematurely in order to survive. In most cases, it appears to be the lack of viable alternatives for children and their families to survive that perpetuates the practice. These particular findings echo more general ones found by Anti-Slavery International in other research, which has identified that those who are subject to slavery and slavery-like practices are generally from groups who are also subject to wider societal prejudices (Kaye, 2008; Upadhyaya, 2008; Delap, 2009).

The need to combat poverty and adopt an holistic approach by improving the financial stability of parents – for example, by improving and regulating adult employment conditions and offering social, welfare and housing support for families, combined with education reform – was stressed by participants in one way or another in all countries. WAO Afrique and other research participants in Togo commented that they had noticed that there were problems in encouraging children to enrol and then to stay in school when there were poor prospects for employment on graduation (WAO Afrique literature review and group discussion). While some participants commented that the "whole education system" was in need of reform, more specific problems cited included: the lack of better targeted and widely available literacy and vocational training and the costs involved in attending school, such as transport and materials or in some cases fees (trade union group, Costa Rica; group, Lahore, Pakistan; and groups in Embakasi and Maragua, Kenya).

This study revealed a widespread perception in all four countries that implementation of ILO Convention No 182 has been set back by the fact that it is still not seen as a priority in government policies or, to a lesser extent, not fully understood by all government officials, putting the eradication of the worst forms of child labour to the bottom of the pile in terms of attention and necessary resources for implementation.[15] This was raised repeatedly as a factor in interviews and group discussions in Costa Rica. "Corruption at all levels" (NGO representative, group discussion, Togo) was also cited as a reason for side-tracking attention away in Pakistan and Togo, and diminishing the resources available to governments at central and local levels, for example to collect data, carry out inspections and to staff and equip rescue centres (Lahore group, Pakistan and group discussion, Togo).

Despite some positive examples, such as the success of the AAC/DCLC networks in Kenya and comments made by the tribal chief earlier, several participants still viewed cultural assumptions as an ongoing problem, blocking the elimination of the worst forms of child labour. One Pakistani NGO representative from Lahore asked: "Can you release child labourers in a feudal system? In other sectors, everyone wants a domestic servant and they prefer a child. For example, in carpet-weaving children work quickly and on low wages.... We need to change the mind sets." Another NGO informant from the Lahore group, Pakistan, pointed to a culture of corruption again: "People who are running brick kilns and tanneries also have relationships with those who implement programmes to tackle the worst forms of child labour." Participants in Kenya commented on the "get rich culture". Young people taking part in Costa Rica also highlighted the need to combat peer pressure among children to have nice things, and an "envy of others" that makes them vulnerable to exploitation (participants in working adolescents group, Costa Rica, and group, Kiambu, Kenya). This was echoed by comments from participants in Togo:

> "Trafficking victims [sometimes] return to villages with city clothes ... bank notes ... a bicycle, or are able to [fix] the roof to the family home ... [this exerts] powerful psychological pressure

which can push children, who are suffering, to leave the village or poor parents to allow them to do it, if [the parents] themselves do not make them to go. With time, they forget the cases of trafficked children who return sick or die [elsewhere] in anonymity" (taken from an interview with an employer, Togo).

Conclusion and recommendations

ILO Convention No 182 has enjoyed an impressive ratification rate. At the time of writing (25 August 2009), 171 states have ratified the treaty, suggesting a strong desire by these signatories to be seen at least to be prioritising the eradication of all worst forms of child labour.

The review underscores this by pointing towards a number of improvements in the countries involved in this research since they ratified the Convention. It is arguable that these advances would not have taken place and certainly without the same level of momentum if this standard did not exist. These include, but are not limited to: (1) important steps in law reform better to protect children; (2) the establishment of national action plans against the worst forms of child labour; (3) an increase in children's enrolment in schools thanks to wider access to primary education; (4) the work done by trade unions and, to a lesser extent, employers' associations towards combating worst forms of child labour; and (5) the active involvement of NGOs and other concerned groups, notably a range of non-traditional actors and in some cases at least, the participation of young people themselves.

The ILO (2006) recently identified significant drops in child labour and the worst forms of child labour since 2000. Yet stories like Teresa's remain tragically commonplace across the globe. There is a long way to go and a central obstacle remains the failure of governments to prioritise this issue and to lead on the actions required across society to address the causes and consequences of the problem. As was noted by a discussion participant in Costa Rica, a government ministry official, "[There is] no political will in practice to implement Convention 182".

This review has highlighted the following areas as requiring concerted and immediate action by policy makers and practitioners if ILO Convention No 182's aim of prohibiting and eliminating all worst forms of child labour as a matter of urgency are to be fully realised:

- Governments have made great strides in harmonising national legislation with ILO Convention No 182. However, after 10 years it is high time that any outstanding laws are passed without further delay. Furthermore, governments must ensure that in all cases the penalties provided for are commensurate with the severity of the crimes perpetrated and a greater effort is made across the board strictly to enforce those penalties.

- Governments and others must turn their attention to the informal and private spheres to be sure of tackling all worst forms of child labour and not just the small proportion in the formal sector easiest to find and regulate. Lessons could be learned from successes already achieved, for example, in combating sexual exploitation in Costa Rica and approaches to reducing incidences of young children in domestic work in Togo.

- Governments must also focus attention on communities and groups that are likely to be particularly vulnerable to exploitation. These include any poor communities against whom there is a wider societal prejudice, and may include, as identified in this study, children from families affected by HIV/AIDS, migrants and the internally displaced populations as well as communities in areas prone to drought or other factors leading to the consequent push for people to migrate. Other research by Anti-Slavery International identifies that ethnic and religious minorities and children from 'scheduled castes' in South Asia are particularly vulnerable to slavery and exploitation.

- Communities at the grassroots in particular remain relatively unaware of the worst forms of child labour. Awareness raising at all levels needs to be continuously sustained, particularly among the general public, including children, for example through local media, schools, religious groups and local events. Regular and organised consultation and coordination at the local level between government officials, trade unions, employers' organisations, as well as NGOs, informal actors, such as religious leaders, families and, more importantly children themselves, is crucial. Understanding the local specificity of child labour is essential when offering children and their families viable alternatives to entering the worst forms of child labour.

- Progress on education is welcome, and efforts must also ensure the quality of education and its usefulness for children in the labour market after graduation.

- All root causes of child labour must be addressed, notably poverty and discrimination. Income-generating schemes and securing and regulating conditions of employment for parents and young people leaving school can contribute to this and break the long-term cycle of poverty and prejudice that contributes to all worst forms of child labour.

- The lack of systematic, updated and disaggregated data undermines seriously the process of identification of children vulnerable to or engaged in the worst forms of child labour and prevents governments from adequately targeting and evaluating the effectiveness of their programmes. This is particularly serious in the case of slavery and slavery-like practices: while they are likely to be numerically relatively few, these children tend to be the most marginalised and hidden and where the most egregious human rights violations occur. All governments should review and invest resources in improving their targeted data-gathering efforts including among those who are typically the hardest to reach, calling on the assistance of the ILO, other agencies and other governments to achieve this where necessary.

The history of the last 10 years, since ILO Convention No 182 came into force, shows that the goal of ending child slavery and worst forms of child labour is achievable. But in order for this to happen, governments must prioritise the issue with the dedication and above all urgency called for by the Convention. It is high time that all governments finally make good the commitment they made to the international community and, above all, to their own citizens when they ratified ILO Convention No 182.

Notes

[1] This study was made possible due to the generous financial support of Ms Rikki Bewley, who, inspired by the life of William Wilberforce, was motivated to support work to end slavery in the modern world. To conduct this study Anti-Slavery International worked with the following partners: Defence for Children International (DCI), Costa Rica; the African Network for Prevention and Protection against Child Abuse and Neglect (ANPPCAN), Kenya; the Society for the Protection of the Rights of the Child (SPARC), Pakistan; and WAO Afrique, Togo. For information on these organisations see the Resources section at the end of this book.

[2] The ILO's 2006 global report on child labour estimates that there are 126 million children (under 18 years old) around the world in the worst forms of child labour. The ILO did not update figures for children in slavery, trafficking, debt bondage and other forms of forced labour in this report, but its 2002 global report put this number at an estimated 8.4 million (ILO, 2002).

[3] 'Advocacy for Effective Implementation of ILO Convention 182 on the Worst Forms of Child Labour', 1 September 2002 to 31 August 2004, funded by the UK's Department for International Development Civil Society Challenge Fund.

[4] In addition to literature and policy reviews, the snapshot review included 19 individual interviews and 15 group discussions across the four countries involving over 120 individuals from the various stakeholder groups described. Comments reported are from interviews or group discussions.

[5] The name has been changed to protect the child's identity.

[6] Based on group discussions in Lahore, Karachi and Quetta, Pakistan, and COSECODENI (Coordinadora de ONGs para la Defensa de los Derechos de la Niñez y la Adolescencia [NGO group for the Defence of the Rights of Children and Adolescents]), and group discussion and individual interview, Costa Rica.

[7] This issue was raised in Karachi, Pakistan, and in Kiambu, Maragua and Embakasi, Kenya.

[8] The Bill of Law on the Prohibition of Hazardous and Unhealthy Work for Adolescent People and the Bill of Law for the Reform of the Code of Childhood and Adolescence, and Protection of the Rights of Adolescent People in Domestic Service (May, 2005), unofficial translation.

[9] Also drawing on data from other participants, Lahore and Peshawar, Pakistan.

[10] OATIA (Oficina de Atención y Erradicación del Trabajo Infantil y Protección al Trabajador Adolescente [Office for the Elimination of Child Labour and the Protection of Working Adolescents]) and trade union group discussions, Costa Rica.

[11] Numerous examples were provided by participants in the trade union group from Costa Rica and also reflected in DCI's literature review.

[12] In the Karachi and Lahore groups, Pakistan; Maragua and Kiambu groups, Kenya, and an interview with an NGO representative, Kenya; COSECODENI and congressional committee discussions, Costa Rica.

[13] SPARC conducted the survey in 2008 during the most recent of their annual Child Labour Free Weeks, a series of mass mobilisation events involving children and including rallies and discussions that take place simultaneously throughout the country.

[14] Group discussion with six working adolescents aged 15–18 from the Entre Campos project took part. The group comprised females (working as domestics either at home or in other households) and males (who help their families, for example by street selling). All of the participants were enrolled in school.

[15] Interview with an employer, Kenya; congressional, COSECODENI and ministries groups, and interviews with a trade unionist and Ministry of Labour representative, Costa Rica; second group discussion, Togo. Lack of resources allocated to the problem was also specifically identified for example in the Lahore and Quetta groups, Pakistan; Kiambu group, Kenya; congressional group and COSECODENI member and Ministry of Labour interviews, Costa Rica; and both groups, Togo.

References

Blagbrough, J. (2008) *They respect their animals more: Voices of child domestic workers*, London: Anti-Slavery International/WISE.

Delap, E. (2009) *Begging for change: Research findings and recommendations on forced child begging in Albania/Greece, India and Senegal*, London: Anti-Slavery International.

ILO (International Labour Organization) (2002) *A future without child labour*, Geneva: ILO.

ILO (2006) *The end of child labour: Within reach?*, Geneva: ILO.

Kaye, M. (2008) *Arrested development: Discrimination and slavery in the 21st century*, London: Anti-Slavery International.

Upadhyaya, K.P. (2008) *Poverty, discrimination and slavery: The reality of bonded labour in India, Nepal and Pakistan*, London: Anti-Slavery International.

four

Child domestic labour: a global concern

Jonathan Blagbrough

Introduction

Child domestic labour is one of the most widespread, exploitative forms of child work in the world today, and one of the most difficult to tackle. Child domestic workers (CDWs) are hard to reach not only because they work behind the closed doors of their employers' homes, but also because society sees the practice as normal and – in relation to girls – important training for later life (Black, 2002).

The practice warrants particular attention because of the conditions under which CDWs – most living with their employers – are working. Time and again, CDWs report that their daily experience of discrimination and isolation in the household is the most difficult part of their burden. Their live-in situation also makes them highly dependent on their employers for their basic needs. This seclusion and dependency makes CDWs particularly vulnerable to exploitation and abuse, routinely resulting in physical, psychological and sexual violence (Blagbrough, 2008).

> "As a domestic worker, you have no control over your life. No one respects you. You have no rights. This is the lowest kind of work."
> (CDW, Indonesia, quoted in HRW 2006, p 1)

According to the International Labour Organization (ILO), there are more girls under the age of 16 in domestic service than in any other category of child labour (ILO-IPEC, 2004a). Pre-pubescent and older boys are also engaged as domestic workers in significant numbers (Blagbrough, 2008). Despite their large numbers, CDWs' cultural and physical 'invisibility' continues to result in a dearth of understanding and action about their situation.

The experiences and views of CDWs themselves remain particularly unheard, despite such voices offering critical insights into their individual circumstances, motives and means for their effective assistance. This chapter therefore draws heavily on the experiences and views of CDWs in various settings – in particular, findings from research undertaken by Anti-Slavery International and local non-governmental organisations (NGOs) with CDWs in several countries.[1]

Who are child domestic workers?

CDWs are those under 18 working in households other than their own, doing domestic chores, caring for children, tending the garden, taking care of animals, running errands and helping their employers run small businesses, among other tasks. This includes children who 'live in' and those who live separately from their employers, as well as those who are paid for their work, those who are not paid and those who receive 'in-kind' benefits, such as food and shelter.[2]

> "I wake up at 5am, prepare the children and escort them to school. Returning home I do the housework. Later, I pick the children up from school. Usually I sleep at 9pm." (CDW, Tanzania, quoted in Blagbrough, 2008, p 2)

A CDW is as likely to be working for a relative as for a stranger, blurring lines regarding their relationship with the employing family. In these situations the child is working, but is not considered a worker. They live as part of the family, but are not treated as a family member. The key issue for a child in domestic service is that, as a consequence of their ambiguous relationship to others in the household, the child is ultimately no one's responsibility. The familial and legal 'care vacuum' that results, coupled with the child's physical and emotional isolation in the household, creates particular vulnerability to exploitation and abuse.

> "I started to work at 12 years old. Since then, I never saw my family. Homesickness is my greatest enemy. My mother only saw me when my employer finally told her where I was working in Manila. They did not allow anybody to see me because they always beat me. I always wanted to tell my parents how difficult my life was, but there was no chance…." (CDW, Philippines, quoted in Blagbrough, 2008, p 2)

Unlike many other forms of child labour, children are often pressed into domestic service from a very young age. While many contextual factors will determine the age when a child begins work, recent studies in various locations have determined that most CDWs began their working lives well before puberty. The ILO estimates that more girls under 16 are in domestic service than in any other type of work, with recent statistics indicating that

CDWs are in the many millions worldwide (ILO-IPEC, 2004a). Despite the involvement of considerable numbers of boys, domestic service remains heavily gender-biased, with girls forming about 90% of all CDWs (ILO-IPEC, 2004a).

CDWs are isolated from their families and from opportunities to make friends, and are under the total control of employers whose primary concern is often not in the child's best interests. Despite some children entering domestic labour in the hope of continuing their schooling, most are deprived of opportunities for education and are working in conditions that can be considered among the worst forms of child labour. Worldwide, many have been trafficked, or are in situations of servitude.

Although being a CDW is a good experience for some, the typical view expressed by CDWs is that their jobs compare unfavourably with those of other child workers. This is usually due to their sense of inferiority, their isolation and their powerlessness against the behaviour of their employers.

> "It wears you out. It is tiring, all that sweeping, cleaning, shaking […] and then there is the walking to work; and on top of all that when you say to people 'I work at home' they look at you in a funny way; if you don't tell them they look at you quite normally, but the moment you say 'I am a home help', you are discriminated against. I never said I was a home help […] I just said, 'I work'."
> (CDW, Peru, quoted in Blagbrough, 2008, p 38)

How and why do children become domestic workers?

While there are often remarkable similarities in the circumstances and experiences of CDWs within and between countries, there are also many contextual factors at play that make each situation different, creating considerable complexity for those seeking to assist them.

> "My father died when I was three years old and a few months later my mother became mentally ill. As she lost her mind, she could no longer take care of me, so I was sent away as a domestic." (CDW, Benin, quoted in Blagbrough, 2008, p 10)

It almost goes without saying that poverty invariably underlies a child's vulnerability to this form of exploitation. However, other so-called 'push' factors such as gender and ethnic discrimination, social exclusion, lack of educational opportunities, domestic violence, rural-to-urban migration, displacement and the loss of close family members as a result of conflict and disease are also important triggers. There may also be several factors 'pulling' a child − especially a girl − into domestic work, including: a demand by employers for cheap, flexible labour; increasing social and economic disparities; the perception that the employer's household is a safe environment; and the illusion that becoming a CDW may provide more opportunities for advancement (Blagbrough, 2008).

> "Because all the members of my family except my old grandma passed away [due to conflict] and I had to earn bread for myself and grandma." (CDW, Nepal, quoted in Blagbrough, 2008, p 10)

In some locations, particularly South Asia, it is not uncommon to find children working as domestics to repay family loans (see Chapter Fourteen, this volume), while others cited alcoholic fathers as a catalyst for leaving home to find work. CDWs, particularly in some African countries, recounted that they were forced into domestic work on the death of family members from HIV/AIDS, as they had no reliable relatives to care for them.

> "Because we were [HIV/AIDS] orphans, our relatives took everything from us." (CDW, Tanzania, quoted in Blagbrough, 2008, p 10)

Poverty

The majority of CDWs come from poor families, and are sent to work to supplement their family's income or simply to lessen the financial strain at home. It remains a popular coping strategy for poor families; the job requires no education or training, and is considered useful preparation for a girl's later life (UNICEF-ICDC, 1999).

> "I came with my mum, she left me at my aunt's house, she told me I was going to stay there because it was better for me, because at home we didn't have so many things." (CDW, Peru, quoted in Blagbrough, 2008, p 11)

Poverty among populations displaced by conflict and natural disasters, devastated by HIV/AIDS or suffering the backlash of economic globalisation, is forcing more poverty-stricken young women and children into domestic work far from their homes. In many societies, uneven patterns of economic development create more demand for young domestic workers, which then generates more supply. Economic expansion in urban centres has meant increased employment in these areas, and a corresponding decrease in the local workforce available for domestic labour. This gap is often filled by younger women and children from families impoverished by the same modernisation process.

"My mother entrusted me to an employer. She had to work as a domestic abroad. Since then, I only saw her once when she came home for a vacation. She stayed for only one week, then left again." (CDW, Philippines, quoted in Blagbrough, 2008, p 11)

Culture and traditions

Children become domestic workers primarily as a result of their families being poor, but also because the practice is seen as normal and, indeed, beneficial for girls who will one day become wives and mothers. Powerful and enduring myths surround the practice, encouraging its continuance. Parents believe, for example, that a daughter working for a wealthier family might bring opportunities for her and her own family. Social restrictions on girls mean that domestic work is one of the few types of employment considered appropriate. It is also widely believed that domestic work is less arduous than other kinds of labour and that work in the home offers a protective environment for girls and for younger children. Employers of CDWs, far from seeing themselves as exploiters, consider that they are helping the child and her family by taking her in. In many cases employers believe that they are treating these children as 'part of the family' (Black, 1997).

"The lady once said to me that I could not be in the living room when they had visitors, that I was not part of the family. I started crying alone. It was her daughter's birthday. The lady only looked at me, nothing else." (CDW, Peru, quoted in Blagbrough, 2008, p 19)

At the same time, employers often seek out children and adolescents in particular because they are cheaper to hire than adults, are more malleable and cost less to support. CDWs interviewed in Nepal recounted that it was hard to continue working as a domestic worker above the legal minimum working age of 14 as employers had told them older children were more trouble and able to bargain for higher salaries and other rights.

For the children and adolescents themselves their age and dependence on their parents means that they are usually unable to resist plans to send them away. Such children also feel obligated to go from a sense of duty towards their parents, but they may also enter domestic service of their own volition, in order to escape from difficult home situations, or to continue their education.

"My aunt, you see. One day I couldn't register in school but she came and said 'you help me out with the house work and I will give you the money'. But she doesn't give me much. I add this and that and that's what I buy my books with." (CDW, Peru, quoted in Blagbrough, 2008, p 10)

In the Philippines, cases have emerged of children who were asked by their teachers if they wanted to work in exchange for their schooling. Some teachers were known to have made such an offer when they observed pupils struggling at school and lacking support from their families.

> "My teacher commissioned me as a dishwasher during her daughter's wedding reception. They asked me to stay a little bit more. I stayed in their provincial home for one month. Then her brother in law needed a domestic worker in Manila, so they took me there." (CDW, Philippines, quoted in Blagbrough, 2008, p 12)

Gender

Understanding child domestic labour in the context of child rights alone gives a partial perspective. CDWs are linked to wider patterns of exploitation and abuse, not only because they are children but also because they are girls. Evidence shows that the practice is hugely gender-biased, in large part due to entrenched societal notions of domestic work as fundamentally the domain of women and girls (Plan UK, 2009). Across the world, domestic work is an important source of employment for adults as well as children. In Asia, it has been estimated that employment in households accounts for approximately a third of female employment (Blagbrough, 2008). At the same time, domestic work, including childcare, is seen as economically unproductive and is consequently given little or no value. Typically, because domestic work is the assumed role of women, it is not recognised as 'work', and therefore outside the ambit of labour legislation in many countries (Ramirez-Machado, 2003). Despite the importance of domestic work to the functioning of economies and society, its sheer commonness and ordinariness conspire to maintain its continued invisibility.

> "My eldest sister was the first one to come. Once here I managed to talk to her so she could help me to find a house. She told me to come; she said I could stay with her while we find something. I spent three weeks with her and her children until I finally found a house where I work by the hour." (CDW, Costa Rica, quoted in Blagbrough, 2008, p 11)

CDWs often become adult domestic workers as it is seen as girls' training for later life. In many cases their lack of education and ability to develop other skills leaves young domestic workers with few options other than continuing in domestic service, but also, their experiences of child domestic labour absorbed during that time stay with them and may serve to strengthen their low self-esteem and inertia.

Generally speaking, the low status of domestic work and the circumstances under which it is carried out serve to make those who do it intrinsically vulnerable to exploitation and abuse. This vulnerability is likely to be even greater among those who have moved or who have been trafficked far from home. Recruitment of workers for domestic work has become an important business, both nationally and internationally, with recruitment and movement often unregulated and linked to organised smuggling and trafficking operations. Because of the acceptability of domestic work, in some places it is also commonly the lure for the recruitment of women and young girls into commercial sexual exploitation (Blagbrough, 2008).

Legal context

International legal standards such as the 1999 ILO Worst Forms of Child Labour Convention No 182 (see Chapters One and Three, this volume) draw attention to child domestic labour. ILO Convention No 182 has been instrumental in getting child domestic labour onto national agendas in many countries. Nevertheless, specific local regulation and enforcement remains almost non-existent because of a perceived conflict of interest with regard to privacy laws, inherent difficulties in regulating informal sector activities, backed up by continuing societal assumptions that children are well protected in private households. Despite these obstacles, legislative progress has been made in some countries. In India in 2006 employing children under 14 years (the legal minimum working age) as domestic workers became illegal when the practice was added to the list of proscribed activities under India's 1986 Child Labour (Prohibition and Regulation) Act and there is a national organisation campaigning for CDW rights.

While it is clear that neither national nor international laws will by themselves stop the exploitation and abuse of CDWs, their existence is important in setting a benchmark and is a useful way of highlighting the issue. As a sector, domestic work is often not covered by, or is specifically excluded from, national labour legislation; domestic workers are then devoid of the protection provided to other workers and are unable to access their rights. An ILO study of national laws in 65 countries revealed that only 19 of them have enacted specific laws or regulations dealing with domestic work. These laws often afford lower protection to domestic workers than to other categories of workers. In Peru, for example, a Domestic Workers Law was passed in 2003. While the law goes some way to protecting adult and adolescent domestic workers (in conjunction with existing legislation to protect children), it does not grant them the same rights as other workers.

Under this law, it is not mandatory to pay domestic workers the legal minimum wage; without the minimum wage, they cannot access the social security system. The ILO study also found that there have been very few convictions of abusive employers or intermediaries involved in trafficking domestic workers (Ramirez-Machado, 2003).

In some African countries, the inability of legal systems to adequately protect CDWs from abuse and exploitation has led to the development in a number of countries of 'codes of conduct' in order to regulate the age at which a child can work, as well as the conditions and treatment of CDWs. While not legally enforceable, codes of conduct often carry moral weight encouraging adherence to them – particularly because parents, employers and local communities are often involved in their development, and have a stake in their successful operation. In Tanzania, for example, a code of conduct for the treatment of CDWs – in line with Tanzanian legislation – was developed several years ago by a Mwanza-based NGO, and approved by the Ministry of Labour and Youth Development. In parts of Dar es Salaam, this code has been adopted by and is enforced through a local Association of Responsible Employers (Blagbrough, 2008).

In West Africa, where thousands of children are trafficked across borders, many of them for domestic service, bilateral agreements have been negotiated between countries (often with the assistance of multilateral agencies such as the ILO, IOM [International Organization for Migration] and UNICEF) to curtail the flow. In Togo in 2004, a local NGO developed a voluntary code of conduct concerning the employment of CDWs covering: minimum age for admission to employment; working conditions; recruitment methods; and education and vocational training of the child. In addition to Togo, six other neighbouring countries are also committed to using the code as a guiding principle for programme and policy actions (Blagbrough, 2008).

Codes of conduct have also been developed in some Asian countries (for example, in Sri Lanka), while focusing on advocacy to gain formal legal recognition for domestic work – either through changes in existing legislation, as in India, or by developing new laws specific to the particular needs of the sector, as in the Philippines. Here, legislative efforts at the national level have centred round the development and promotion of the *Batas Kasambahay*, or Magna Carta of Household Helpers. This draft national legislation sets out to protect domestic workers from exploitation and abuse, and to improve their working conditions by formalising the labour relationship between worker and employer. It has been developed to highlight the sector, as well as to plug gaps in existing labour code legislation on the issue (ILO-IPEC, 2005).

Alongside efforts to secure national legislation, local ordinances requiring the registration of all domestic workers have been enacted in several cities in the Philippines in an attempt to make adult and child domestic workers more visible and less isolated. Early indications suggest that the ordinances have been successful in identifying exploited workers, monitoring working conditions, increasing awareness among domestic workers of their rights and assisting in the formation of domestic workers' associations in many localities.

In Latin America and the Caribbean, many countries have recently developed legislation to protect domestic workers, including CDWs, but enforcement of these laws remains weak. A number of initiatives here focus on the need for written contracts, for granting full employment rights and for fulfilling obligations with regard to labour legislation.

In an important new initiative, the ILO's Governing Body recently agreed to consider the need for new international standards to strengthen legal protection for domestic workers (ILO Governing Body, GB301/2, 301st Session, March 2008). The process for developing the new standards began with the ILO's publication of a report in early 2009 analysing current law and practice among its member states. Accompanying this report was a questionnaire sent to governments, trade unions and employers' organisations (the ILO's tripartite constituents) requesting input on the elements of a new convention. Based on the replies, delegates to the ILO's annual International Labour Conference (ILC) in 2010 will develop a first draft of the convention, for further discussion. A final text will be debated in 2011, likely to result in the adoption of new standards, open for states to ratify and implement locally.

While the adoption of new standards on domestic work may not have an obvious immediate impact on the situation of the many children in domestic service, it has the potential to become a powerful tool to stimulate international and local debate about the challenges faced by domestic workers. It will also increase the pressure on governments to protect them. For the issue of child domestic work, the development of the new standards presents an opportunity to increase understanding of the issue as a labour, gender and child rights concern, and to argue the need for the special protection of CDWs from exploitation and abuse.

Child domestic labour: some key concerns

Discrimination and isolation

> "We don't get treated properly. We are discriminated against because of our race or our culture. That's how my employer's eldest daughter treats me, as inferior." (CDW, Peru, quoted in Blagbrough, 2008, p 19)

Significant power inequalities exist between CDWs and employers. For a start, the child is a child, probably a girl. She is far from home with little or no support network and likely to be from a family with fewer economic resources than the employing family. She may be of a different ethnic origin (typically perceived of lower status) and of a lower social class. She may have been trafficked and will be in unfamiliar surroundings (Blagbrough, 1995).

> "On the way back from the market with my employer, we decided to take a taxi. But the taxi was full and we had to sit together on the front seat. But my employer refused and said she cannot sit together with her domestic, in front of everyone else. So I had to take another taxi. I was very shocked." (CDW, Togo, quoted in Blagbrough, 2008, p 20)

As mentioned earlier, CDWs most often report that the daily experience of discrimination and their isolation in the employer's household are the most difficult part of their burden. Even if their relationship with members of the household is good, these relationships are not on equal terms (UNICEF-ICDC, 1999). A typical manifestation of this discrimination is that the employer's children go to school while the CDW cannot. CDWs often have to eat separately from the employing family, and may have to eat food of inferior quality. While CDWs may sleep in the same room as the employer's children, they may equally end up in the kitchen or on the veranda (UNICEF-ICDC, 1999).

> "Some days I stayed without food. I was not allowed to share the table with the family and to touch anything. I used to eat in the kitchen." (CDW, Tanzania, quoted in Blagbrough, 2008, p 19)

While most employers make some effort to assist CDWs in times of ill health, there are persistent reports of CDWs receiving little or inadequate treatment. Employers often prefer to treat CDWs themselves, rather than taking them to a doctor or hospital. In more extreme cases, employers may send CDWs home to avoid them being a burden.

CDWs have limited freedom of movement, living in their employers' houses and subject to their rules. Commonly, CDWs are told not to leave the house by employers, who frighten them with stories of what they will face on the outside. Even if they are paid, they may not handle their wages or have enough money to escape. While most employers do not take on CDWs with the express intention of perpetuating violence against them, research from many regions indicates that some employers prefer children to adults because they perceive them to be more 'submissive' and 'easier to control' (Blagbrough, 2003).

Violence and abuse

> "They hurt me, spank me, throw things at me, use hurting words – maybe just to shame me in front of other people." (CDW, Philippines, quoted in Blagbrough, 2008, p 21)

The child's isolated situation and their indistinct role in the employer's household makes them particularly vulnerable to physical, verbal and sexual abuse. If violence does occur, their dependency on their employer for basic needs and their acceptance of violence as an occupational hazard makes them far less likely to report it.

> "My punishment was not being able to see my family; they knew my family was my weak point." (CDW, Peru, quoted in Blagbrough, 2008, p 21)

There are broad similarities with regard to the incidence and range of violence against CDWs, although differences exist in local manifestations of violent behaviour towards them. For example, in some countries research has indicated that girls tend to suffer more from verbal bullying and boys more from physical violence. Commonly, CDWs experience various kinds of violence. Verbal violence takes the form of name calling, insults, threats, swearing, shouting and screaming. Numerous types of physical violence towards CDWs are regularly reported, including beating, kicking, whipping, pinching, scalding, overwork and denial of food. In a 2006 study of 500 CDWs in West Bengal, 68% had faced physical abuse, with almost half suffering severe abuse leading to injuries. Eighty-six per cent of CDWs had experienced emotional abuse. The study also found that nearly a third of families had no idea where their daughters were working, and 27% admitted they knew that they were being beaten and harassed (Save the Children UK, 2006).

> "One day, I went to fetch water. When I came back, my employer hit me on the back and pulled me on the ground because the bowl was not filled to the top. She continued slapping me even after I fell on the ground." (CDW, Togo, quoted in Blagbrough, 2008, p 21)

The labels used to describe CDWs are important components in reinforcing their low self-esteem. In Haiti the term to describe CDWs, *restavèks* ('stay-withs'), has come to mean someone motherless or unwanted, often used as an insult to describe someone without a personality or life. Some employers routinely change the given name of CDWs, as in Nepal (Camacho et al, 1997).

> "If something broke, like dishes or a glass, they would take the money out of my pay and they beat me. They used an electrical cord.... Both the husband and the wife were mean to me." (CDW, Morocco, quoted in HRW, 2006, p 13)

Sexual violence towards CDWs, due to the child's vulnerability and isolation, is relatively common. For example, in Haiti *restavèk* girls are sometimes called *la pou sa*, a Creole term meaning 'there for that'. They are accepted sexual outlets for the men or boys of the household (NCHR, 2002). In the West Bengal study, a third of CDWs reported having had their private parts touched by members of their employing family. Twenty per cent had been forced to have sexual intercourse (Save the Children UK, 2006). In El Salvador, an ILO-IPEC study showed that more than 15% of CDWs changing their employers had done so because of sexual harassment or abuse (Godoy, 2002).

> "Oh yes, the man wanted to take advantage. I lived in and had a room; he must have known that I was on my own. The lady had gone out, he arrived and he just came into my room. I was asleep, I had a gown on and the sheet but my chest was bare; I could feel somebody touching me. I got up and just then his mother-in-law came into the room and beat him with a broomstick.... I left after that, I was scared...." (CDW, Peru, quoted in Blagbrough, 2008, p 23)

It has been established that more than a quarter of girls being commercially sexually exploited in Dar es Salaam (Tanzania) are former CDWs, many of them sexually abused by members of the family they were working for (Mwakitwange, 2002; and author correspondence with local NGO). In cases where girls become pregnant, they are often thrown out of the house and forced to fend for themselves on the streets, as the shame of their situation makes it difficult for them to return home. Many families reject these 'spoiled girls' because their behaviour has brought dishonour to the family. In these instances, domestic work typically becomes a precursor to prostitution, as the girls and young women have few other available options (UNICEF-ICDC, 1999). In addition, traffickers of children into the sex trade routinely deceive children and their families about what will happen to them by promising them attractive jobs as CDWs. In the Philippines most of the children and young women trafficked to Manila from rural areas in search of work are assured jobs as domestic workers, but a significant number of cases end up in the sex trade (Flores-Oebanda et al, 2001; see also Chapter Nineteen, this volume).

The attitudes of CDWs themselves with regard to violence are also important to consider. The CDWs may themselves expect and/or accept violence for various reasons: they may have a background of abuse; they are likely to feel a strong sense of duty to their parents to make the situation work out; they may accept violence as an occupational hazard up to a certain point; they may not see any alternatives to their situation; or they may simply fear the consequences of speaking up (Blagbrough, 2003).

> "… it is very risky. Many of my friends, who work like me, tell me what happens to them […] that sometimes the man tries to go too far, and sometimes he does, and because they are afraid they don't want to say anything." (CDW, Peru, quoted in Blagbrough, 2008, p 22)

Loss of education

Numerous studies have shown how child domestic labour directly impedes the child's right to education. Most CDWs themselves attach great importance to getting an education and, in some cases, consider that being a domestic worker is a way of continuing their studies. In reality their situation is, more often than not, a serious obstacle to studying. Commonly, this is simply because employers do not allow them to go to school, or renege on an initial agreement to do so.

> "I work as a domestic but used to attend school. Before going to school every morning, I had to take a big pot full of cooked rice to the roadside. One day, the pot fell down and the rice was spoiled. My employer was angry and decided not to pay my school fees. So, I dropped out of school but continued working for her for a long time." (CDW, Togo, quoted in Blagbrough, 2008, p 17)

However, even when CDWs are given the opportunity, the long working hours and requirements of their job often make it impossible to take up education. In Lima, for example, some CDWs persevere with night schools, but report that they have little time for homework and are frequently tired at school, which makes it difficult to progress. Similar issues are commonly reported among CDWs elsewhere.

> "I was going to study this year but my employer said it wasn't possible; we couldn't leave the children alone. Both he and his wife go out to work." (CDW, Peru, quoted in Blagbrough, 2008, p 18)

The inflexibility of the formal education system is seen as another obstacle to continuing their education, as is poor teaching quality in some schools and the difficulty in affording school books, equipment, uniform and in paying school fees. Many CDWs also end up dropping out during the school year because of these problems, and are discouraged from returning to formal education because of the need to earn money for their families.

> "Even if my employer encouraged me to go to school, I decided not to enrol because I wanted to save money that I can send back to my family." (CDW, Philippines, quoted in Blagbrough, 2008, p 18)

In addition to being a tool for advancement, a recent study indicates that education is a key factor in protecting CDWs, 'because it denotes the support of their parents, community and teachers and allows them to participate, grow and have aspirations' (Meyers, 2008, p 74).

Impact of child domestic labour on children

Aside from violence, CDWs are exposed to a variety of other household dangers. Hazardous household chemicals (such as cleaning fluids), kitchen knives, irons, boiling water and the use of unfamiliar household appliances have caused many CDWs serious injuries and even death, especially among younger children and those already exhausted from a full day's work. There are also likely to be long-term health impacts of chronic sleep deprivation, and being 'on-call' 24 hours a day, as well as effects resulting from heavy tasks such as water collecting (UNICEF-ICDC, 1999). ILO found in Indonesia that CDWs perform the same amount of work as adult workers, which is inappropriate to their physical capacity and stamina. The long hours of work and little time for rest, recreation or socialising impacted on these children's mental, physical, social and intellectual development (ILO-IPEC, 2004b, pp 70-1).

In general, concern about the impact of work on children has tended to focus on aspects of the child's physical health from exposure to physical and environmental hazards, rather than their psychosocial well-being. However, when it comes to child domestic labour, where the circumstances in which the child is working are at least as much of concern as the work itself, understanding the psychosocial effects of the children's situation is vital to forming a comprehensive picture of their condition (Blagbrough, 2008).

In its reports on the situation of CDWs in El Salvador, Guatemala, Indonesia, Morocco and Togo, Human Rights Watch has found that, almost without exception, interviewees suffered some form of psychological abuse. It concludes that 'employer abuse, combined with isolation at the workplace, excessive work demands, and financial pressures may contribute to intense anxiety and depression' (HRW, 2006, pp 10-11).

> "I did not like my employer because she would shout at me, call me a 'Tai' [shit] and 'Anjing' [dog]. I did not feel comfortable. Why am I being treated this way? I could not stand my employer's treatment of me." (CDW, Indonesia, quoted in HRW, 2006, p 10)

In Kenya, one of the few studies that specifically looked at the psychological impact of child domestic labour found that CDWs experienced significantly more manifestations of psychological problems than other working and non-working children. Bedwetting, insomnia, nightmares, frequent headaches, withdrawal, regressive behaviour, premature ageing, depression and phobic reactions to their employers were common (Bwibo and Onyango, 1987). Depression among CDWs has also been reported in Bangladesh (Rahman, 1995) and in Latin American countries (Salazar, 1998) (see also Blagbrough, 2008).

More recently, an Ethiopian study in 2006 concluded that 'childhood mental and behavioural disorders were more common in domestic child labourers than in the non-labourers or other categories of labourers'. Researchers concluded that this was due to CDWs being under the control of employers; excessive hours of working; lack of personal freedom; and physical, verbal and emotional abuse (cited in Meyers, 2008).

Conclusion

CDWs today comprise a large group of uniquely vulnerable and violated workers whose situation is easy to ignore because the institution of child domestic work is so widely accepted, their exploitation takes place behind closed doors and the majority are girls. The low status of domestic work and the circumstances under which it is carried out render domestic workers intrinsically vulnerable to exploitation and abuse. This vulnerability is likely to be even greater among those who have moved or who have been trafficked far from home. Moreover, because of a lack of education and opportunities to develop other skills, and low self-esteem reinforced by their employers, young domestic workers often continue as domestics into adulthood.

In the absence of adequate legal protection for CDWs in many countries, international standards such as ILO Convention No 182 (see Chapter Three, this volume) have been instrumental in putting child domestic labour on various national agendas. National and local legal provision for CDWs remains a policy priority, both because it establishes minimum standards of protection and because it makes it easier to make the issue visible. The ILO's development of standards specific to domestic workers is likely to be a critical further step towards highlighting the inherent vulnerability of domestic workers, protecting them from exploitation and abuse.

CDWs have clearly articulated that their vulnerability to exploitation is directly due to the isolation and discrimination they face in their employers' households. Maintaining contact with their own families, and socialising with other children of their own age (other than their employer's children), is vital to countering such abuse, as might be the establishment of local support groups where domestic workers, young and old, can support each other and fight collectively for improvements in their working conditions and treatment. Again, evidence indicates that access to education (schooling or vocational training) is a priority for CDWs. Schools must adapt to the realities of older children who combine work with study by providing them with appropriate material and academic support. In addition, while it is easy to demonise employers, CDWs often indicate that the most effective form of protection is to enlist their employers' cooperation.

CDWs themselves must be involved directly as agents for change. It is beholden on practitioners and policy makers to learn from children who have found ways of mitigating the exploitation to which they are subject. Moreover, providing a context in which children can articulate their experiences is crucial to their personal development and ability to 'move on'. Enabling CDWs to meet and organise in self/mutual help groups, as well as being involved in the operation of services for their benefit, increases the likelihood that their needs will be met.

Finally, and most fundamentally, a seismic shift in societal attitudes (especially those of parents and employers) is needed if progress is to be made to protect children from exploitation of this kind. The seeds of change are being sown in many parts of the world to effect this crucial social transformation. These seeds, and the individuals and organisations who have planted them, must be nurtured to ensure an end to the exploitation and abuse of CDWs.

Notes

[1] During 2004 and 2005, Anti-Slavery International and local partners undertook consultations, including individual interviews and group discussions, with more than 400 current and former child domestic workers in over 20 locations in Africa, Asia and Latin America. The resulting full research report (Blagbrough, 2008) can be found at: www.antislavery.org/english/resources/reports/download_antislavery_publications/child_labour_reports.aspx

[2] It is also recognised that many children – particularly girls – carry significant domestic workloads in their own homes, and face similar issues to CDWs. However, their situation is different from CDWs in at least one major respect: these children

are under the control of adults for whom the child's best interest is, in the main, their primary concern. The situation of children, particularly of girls, expected to work long and hard and often denied an education also warrants attention, but is not the subject of this chapter.

References

Black, M. (1997) *Child domestic workers: A handbook for research and action*, London: Anti-Slavery International.

Black, M. (2002) *Child domestic workers – Finding a voice: A handbook on advocacy*, London: Anti-Slavery International.

Blagbrough, J. (1995) 'Child domestic work in Indonesia: a preliminary situation analysis', Unpublished mimeo, Geneva: ILO-IPEC.

Blagbrough, J. (2003) 'Violence against child domestic workers', Paper presented at 'Towards a Strategy to Address Corporal Punishment of Children in Southeast Asia Pacific' Workshop, 6-9 October, Bangkok: Save the Children Alliance.

Blagbrough, J. (2008) *They respect their animals more: Voices of child domestic workers*, London: Anti-Slavery International/WISE.

Bwibo, N.O. and Onyango, P. (1987) *Final report of the child labour and health research*, Nairobi: University of Nairobi.

Camacho, A.Z.V., Flores-Oebanda, C., Montano, V., Pacis, R.R. and Robidillo, R. (1997) 'The phenomenon of child domestic work: issues, responses and research findings', Paper presented at the Asian Regional Consultation on Child Domestic Workers, Manila, 19-23 November.

Flores-Oebanda, C., Pacis, R. and Montaño, V. (2001) *The Kasambahay – Child domestic work in the Philippines: A living experience*, Manila: ILO and Visayan Forum Foundation.

Godoy, O. (2002) *El Salvador. Trabajo infantil doméstico: Una evaluación rápida*, Geneva: ILO-IPEC.

HRW (Human Rights Watch) (2006) *Swept under the rug: Abuses against domestic workers around the world*, Human Rights Watch, 27 July.

ILO-IPEC (2004a) *Helping hands or shackled lives? Understanding child domestic labour and responses to it*, Geneva: ILO.

ILO-IPEC (2004b) *Flowers on the rock: Phenomenon of child domestic workers in Indonesia*, Jakarta: ILO.

ILO-IPEC (2005) *Child domestic labour in South East and East Asia: Emerging good practices to combat it*, Bangkok: ILO-SRO.

Meyers, A. (2008) 'Psychosocial impacts of domestic child labour in India: through the lens of a Save the Children development education resource', Unpublished MA dissertation, Institute of Education, University of London.

Mwakitwange, R. (2002) *Fighting commercial sexual exploitation of children: Study of good practices in interventions in Tanzania*, Vol III, Dar es Salaam: ILO-IPEC.

NCHR (National Coalition for Haitian Rights) (2002) *Restavèk no more: Eliminating child slavery in Haiti*, New York, NY: NCHR.

Plan UK (2009) *Because I am a girl (the state of the world's girls 2009): Girls in the global economy: Adding it all up*, London: Plan UK.

Rahman, H. (1995) *Child domestic workers: Is servitude the only option?*, Dhaka: Bangladesh.

Ramirez–Machado, J.M. (2003) *Domestic work, conditions of work and employment: A legal perspective*, Conditions of Work and Employment Series No 7, Geneva: ILO.

Salazar, M.C. (1998) 'Child work and education in Latin America', in M.C. Salazar and W.A. Glasinovich (eds) *Child work and education: Five case studies from Latin America*, Aldershot: Florence and Ashgate Publishing Ltd.

Save the Children UK (2006) *Abuse among child domestic workers: A research study in West Bengal*, West Bengal: Save the Children UK.

UNICEF-ICDC (1999) *Child domestic work*, Innocenti Digest No 5, Florence: UNICEF International Child Development Centre.

five

Child trafficking: a modern form of slavery[1]

Hans van de Glind[2]

Modern-day trafficking in persons has become a truly international phenomenon, widely considered to be one of the most significant manifestations of slavery today, and reducing victims to mere 'commodities' to be bought, sold, transported and resold. Children in particular are vulnerable to trafficking, as their isolation and separation from their families and communities leaves them in places where they may not speak the language or have any legal status. Although the recruitment and movement involved in trafficking may appear voluntary at first, they eventually take on aspects of coercion by third parties.[3] These third parties are more likely to target the most vulnerable children through violence, workplace confinement and even theft of wages. Girls are affected disproportionably, and are generally trafficked for commercial sexual exploitation and domestic labour. Boys are believed to be trafficked in particular for labour in agriculture, plantations, mines, drug trafficking and other illicit activities and armed conflict. Children excluded from society are particularly vulnerable to trafficking. These include minority ethnic groups, orphans (in particular those affected by HIV/AIDS), homeless children, children not registered at birth, migrant children without legal status and children with disabilities. Attempts to escape are often met with legal reprimands if they have no legal status, punishment (including corporal) and sometimes death.

The International Labour Organization (ILO) estimates that there are at least 1.2 million trafficked children at any given point in time (Belser et al, 2005), yet only recently has the international community begun to acknowledge that the practice is not only a human rights issue, but an economic and labour one (ILO, 2005). International treaties have covered the problem for years: the 1949 United Nations (UN) Convention (UN General Assembly, 1949) addressed sex trafficking within the context of slavery, the Palermo Protocol[4] lists exploitation as including 'slavery or practices similar to slavery' (see also Chapters One, Two and Six, this volume), and the ILO Worst Forms of Child Labour Convention No 182 (www.ilo.org/public/english/standards/relm/ilc/ilc87/com-chic.htm; see Chapter Three, this volume) lists slavery, including 'the sale and trafficking of children, debt bondage and serfdom and forced or compulsory labour, including forced or compulsory recruitment of children for use in armed conflict', as part of the worst forms of child labour (Article 3). However, the language used to discuss trafficking has changed much since then, and even today there are disagreements on what constitutes child trafficking. The first part of this chapter outlines the definition of child trafficking within both conceptual and legal frameworks. The next part then contextualises the problem, providing a global overview of child trafficking with regional insights as to which children are the most vulnerable to trafficking. Finally, the chapter addresses a range of interventions demonstrated to be effective in fighting child trafficking.

Understanding child trafficking

All children should enjoy the rights accorded to all human beings. Article 4 of the Universal Declaration of Human Rights (1948) reminds us that 'No one shall be held in slavery or servitude', Article 1 asserting that 'all human beings are born free and equal in dignity and rights' (UN General Assembly, 1948). The UN Convention on the Rights of the Child (CRC) (UN General Assembly, 1989) complements this by stating that every child 'without discrimination of any kind, irrespective of the child's or his or her parent's or legal guardian's race, colour, sex, language, religion, political or other opinion, national, ethnic or social origin, property, disability, birth or other status', is born with the same rights. By its very nature, child trafficking threatens these rights. Yet approaching the issues surrounding child trafficking is a complex process, requiring a broad understanding of the legal frameworks that have come to define this problem in an international context. There are many international instruments implemented in various countries to protect people from being trafficked. However, there have been disagreements as to what defines key aspects of trafficking or as to what the concept of trafficking implies. Consequentially, international conventions and legislations have at times provided varied or conflicting definitions.

Concepts and understanding of child trafficking as related to slavery have evolved over time. For many years, people thought of child trafficking in a very narrow sense, usually involving the kidnapping, abduction and selling of children. Yet the experience gained in numerous projects by non-governmental organisations (NGOs) and governments to combat child trafficking have shown that the problem is considerably more complex, involving multiple causes, risk factors and manifestations. Today, the Palermo Protocol (UN General Assembly, 2000) has given states the most authoritative definition of human trafficking (including child trafficking). The Protocol calls for the criminalisation of corruption on the part of public or other officials that allows trafficking to occur. This ranges from border guards ignoring irregular documentation to civil service agents providing illegal documents – for example a copy of someone else's birth certificate, so that the trafficked child's age can be hidden – and others who, in various ways, contribute to trafficking.

The concepts that together define child trafficking, slavery and practices similar to slavery have been further specified by the ILO child labour Conventions. Under Article 3(a) of ILO Convention No 182, child trafficking is listed as a form of slavery alongside the sale of children, debt bondage, serfdom, forced labour and the compulsory recruitment of children for use in armed conflict. Although these crimes are similar in nature, there are several important distinguishing factors. For example, child trafficking begins when a child is recruited (whether forcibly or not) to a different location.

The ILO considers that what makes child trafficking distinct from the other forms of child slavery and slave-like practices enumerated in Article 3(a) of ILO Convention No 182 is the element of movement; there must be a third party involved that relocates a child, as a rule to an unfamiliar location and away from protection, with the explicit intention of exploitation. Threat or use of force or other forms of coercion, abduction, fraud or deception, or the abuse of power or a position of vulnerability at any point of the recruitment and movement do not need to be present in the case of children[5] (unlike with adults), but are nevertheless strong indications of child trafficking (Calvani, 2009). In other words, children are considered to be victims of trafficking even where this has taken place without deception or coercion. Not only does this take into account their special vulnerability, it also makes it easier for law enforcement agencies and prosecutors to provide evidence ensuring that child traffickers are punished.

Other interpretations of what constitutes trafficking exist. In its annual *Trafficking in persons report*, the US Department of State (USDS, 2009) states that it does not believe that movement must be involved to define exploitation as trafficking. Under this interpretation, any child in a situation considered a worst form of child labour is considered trafficked. This eliminates special consideration that could be given to children who have been separated from their families and who are in need of special assistance vis-à-vis other children in situations of the worst forms of child labour who were not trafficked. In this regard, the ILO and the US Department of State have differing interpretations.

The ILO further considers the end results of child trafficking to be broader than those outlined by the Palermo Protocol. This lists the end results, under 'exploitation', as including: 'the exploitation of the prostitution of others or other forms of sexual exploitation, forced labour or services, slavery or practices similar to slavery, servitude or the removal of organs'. Yet the ILO (2007) considers that hazardous work (that is, agriculture, domestic work, organised begging, etc) and even non-hazardous work can be an unacceptable end result if the child is below the minimum working age for the particular type of work.

Although the end result of child trafficking invariably includes the denial of basic human rights (and a form of exploitation), the process of child trafficking can take many forms. It is a series of events that may take place in a child's home community, at transit points and at final destinations. There is invariably a third party that intends to exploit the child involved, yet the make-up of these third parties varies. The majority of trafficking is executed by small networks of people who are each trained in one aspect of trafficking, such as recruitment, advertising, transportation and retail. Yet in some areas (in particular Eastern Europe, Hong Kong, Japan and Colombia), trafficking is controlled by large criminal organisations (IOM, 2009). The next part of this chapter examines the magnitude (by region) and nature of the problem of child trafficking, addresses what factors put children at risk and explores different types of demand for child trafficking.

Magnitude and nature of the problem

Like any other illicit activity, child trafficking is a clandestine practice carrying many difficulties for collecting reliable data. Despite problems in recording cases of trafficking, in identifying trafficking victims and of standardising criteria for trafficking, all available data suggest that the number of children trafficked each year is large, covering every continent. The ILO's global report on forced labour (ILO, 2005) estimated a total of 12.3 million people in forced labour, including an estimated 2.45 million who were trafficked into forced labour. Of the latter, approximately half were children. Their vulnerability, as well as economic hardships that may make family members complicit or hopeful of better prospects in cities, results in a greater risk of being trafficked. Both boys and girls can be sold multiple times and in multiple ways for profit. This process can, and often does, include both legal and illegal activities. Routes are complex, ranging from domestic to cross-border trafficking, or even global trading. Countries can at the same time be sending, transit and receiving countries.

Regional overview

Although information regarding specific regions is scarce, the ILO's 2005 global report provides a regional breakdown. It estimates that Asia has the highest number of victims of child trafficking, followed by industrialised countries, Latin America and the Caribbean, the Middle East and North Africa, transition countries, and finally, Sub-Saharan Africa (ILO, 2005). Several important global trends in trafficking are also reported. In general, the US, Western Europe and Japan were the main destination countries for child trafficking. This reminds us that trafficking is not a problem limited to 'developing' nations. In fact, it occurs in every country, and every country has the responsibility to fight it. Since 2000, more than half of all countries have implemented laws banning all forms of human trafficking. Despite this, much work remains to be done in countries implementing laws outlawing child trafficking, as well as in countries that have not set up the legal infrastructure to prevent and outlaw child trafficking.

One problem that persists is the popular myth that child trafficking is limited to commercial sexual exploitation. Although around 43% of the world's victims are trafficked for sexual exploitation, an estimated 32% are trafficked for economic exploitation (ILO, 2005). Boys are typically trafficked for labour in agriculture, plantations, mines, armed conflict, the drugs trade and other illicit activities, while trafficking of girls often relates to domestic service or, indeed, sexual exploitation (ILO, 2009). Traffickers can exploit children in begging, street hawking, car window cleaning and other street-based activities. Some children are exploited as drug couriers or dealers or in petty crime such as pickpocketing or burglary. In larger cities, children with physical impairments are particularly vulnerable to being trafficked into organised begging. Because the factors that facilitate trafficking vary widely, some types of trafficking are prevalent in certain regions and practically absent in others. This has given rise to certain trends in child trafficking in different world regions.

Many African countries do not have legislation on human trafficking, and many of those that do have legislation only cover certain forms of trafficking (such as the trafficking of women) (Eisenstein, 2007). Poverty, war, disease, ethnic and religious conflicts – all root causes of trafficking – are prevalent in multiple areas of the African subcontinent, and most of the business of human trafficking occurs south of the Sahara (Eisenstein, 2007). Economic vulnerability and social exclusion resulting from the HIV/AIDS epidemic is one major barrier to preventing trafficking in Africa. According to the UNAIDS 2008 report on the global AIDS epidemic, 22 million of the 33 million people living with the virus are in Africa. As parents become ill, they also become unable to provide for their families. This causes many children to enter the labour force prematurely, where they lack parental support and are vulnerable to traffickers. Consequently, children may become double victims, as they lose their parents to the virus and may end up exploited.

Another widespread problem faced in the fight against trafficking is the refugee crises and the instability caused by wars and political conflicts. The problem is so widespread (Africa has experienced 186 coups and 26 major wars within the past 50 years) that in countries like the Democratic Republic of the Congo (DRC), the military is incapable of preventing trafficking violations committed by members of its own armed forces (Plaut, 2006). This is partially the result of the legislative and judicial infrastructure collapsing after years of civil war. Also because of the war, indigenous and foreign militia groups have actively abducted and forcibly recruited children into forced labour or sexual exploitation (USDS, 2009). The DRC government has tried to launch public awareness campaigns and has convicted an army major of forcibly recruiting children, yet an increased effort to prosecute trafficking offenders and to establish a judicial infrastructure is required to tackle the issue effectively.

Certain regions of the continent, especially Western Africa, also experience a form of child trafficking that delivers girls into domestic labour through a cultural practice called 'confiage' or 'entrustment' (Moens et al, 2004; see also Chapter Twelve, this volume). This traditional practice involves parents sending their children to a wealthier home of a relative or friend in a nearby town or region to improve their lives. Because this tradition of sending girls into domestic labour is seen in some regions as part of a girl's natural education to gain experience for eventually raising a family, traffickers, frequently extended family members themselves, can easily exploit children under the pretext of cultural apprenticeship. UNICEF reported that in Senegal, only 55% of girls who had been 'entrusted' to another household actually attended school, whereas 95% of girls who remained at home continued their education (UNICEF, 1999, cited in Moens et al, 2004). This study reinforces the theory that not only distant relatives but also close ones, including parents themselves, directly participate in their children's trafficking. In Asia, notably South and East Asia, governments preoccupied with growth have had to compromise the benefits of economic growth with the human rights violations inherent in child trafficking. According to the UN Office on Drugs and Crime (UNODC) global trafficking report of 2009, victims from East Asia were detected in more than 20 countries in regions throughout the world, including Europe, the Americas, the Middle East, Central Asia and Africa. Domestic trafficking is particularly troublesome in China. Speaking to *The New York Times* in June 2007, Hu Jindou, an economics professor at the Beijing University of Technology, said: 'Everything is about the economy now, just like everything was about politics in the Mao era, and forced labour or child labour is far from an isolated phenomenon. It is rooted deeply in today's reality, a combination of capitalism, socialism, feudalism, and slavery' (quoted in French, 2007).

Despite laws that outlaw child labour and trafficking, some Chinese employers have been able to get around these restrictions by implementing 'work-study' programmes, where there are no restrictions on age or working hours. According to the 2009 USDS *Trafficking in persons report*, under government-sanctioned work-study programmes, 'students had no say in the terms and conditions of their employment, and little to no protection from abusive work practices'. The report also notes that the conditions of these programmes were often dangerous and included mandatory overtime work with involuntary pay deductions. It is not uncommon for work-study programmes to bring children as young as 12 to places far from their families and communities to work in factories. Minority ethnic children, particularly girls, are known to be especially susceptible to trafficking under work-study programmes.[6] What exacerbates matters is that the traditional criteria for promotion of local officials are high growth rates and social stability. This has caused them to turn a blind eye or to point responsibility to other officials with overlapping jurisdiction. Although these programmes often include the consent of both the children's parents and the children themselves, they still qualify as trafficking.

Out of 29 countries in Asia, 14 have ratified both ILO child labour Conventions (ILO, 2007). India, which has the largest child population in the world, has not ratified either Convention. This is particularly alarming because even though India serves as a transit country for children trafficked from Pakistan, Nepal and Bangladesh, internal trafficking is more prevalent than cross-border trafficking (USDS, 2009). The ILO global report of 2005 notes that large numbers of poor children tend to move into the relatively prosperous urban centres such as Mumbai, Delhi and Kolkata.[7] During this migration, many are trafficked into labour exploitation and 70% to 80% of the trafficked children under the age of 14 are also physically and/or sexually abused (Calvani, 2009). Girls are particularly vulnerable to being trafficked and sold as brides, as the practice of female feticide results in skewed gender ratios in regions such as Punjab and Haryana. Another regional risk is post-disaster child trafficking. This has become common in India as man-made conflicts and natural disasters have increased. For example, seasonal floods in Bihar were followed by a surge in child trafficking (Bhalla, 2009).

Unlike in Africa and Asia, child trafficking in Europe has focused mainly on both child sexual exploitation and organised crime. Each year thousands of girls originating from Eastern Europe are trafficked into forced labour and sexual exploitation by gangs and criminal groups making enormous profits. These girls are frequently lured into trafficking by promises of lucrative job or educational opportunities in wealthier countries. The ILO has identified certain countries, in particular Albania, Moldova and the Ukraine, as major source countries of trafficked people. Since 2000, for example, the number of reports of children being trafficked across borders for labour and sexual exploitation has steadily increased in Albania. According to the Albanian government's initial report to the Committee on the Rights of the Child, about 4,000 of these children travelled unaccompanied by their parents to Greece or Italy, and in the process faced numerous risks jeopardising their health and well-being.

In addition, UNICEF et al (2004) report that as the international presence in the Balkans has decreased in the years following the 1990s wars, the force behind much of the trafficking of the region has shifted from international clients to local clients involved in organised crime. However, traffickers are rarely sentenced or are sentenced for lesser charges. The report also contends that the problem may be that many Eastern European law enforcement agents are not interested in prosecuting small-scale criminals, but rather seek to prosecute high-profile cases involving members of organised criminal groups.

Risk profiles and vulnerability

One common thread found in trafficking across all regions is that human traffickers target vulnerable men, women and children, using myriad methods of deception to gain their trust. Furthermore, the general public often misunderstand the circumstances that lead to trafficking. Poverty is undoubtedly an important factor in explaining why some children are trafficked, yet poverty alone cannot explain why some countries have more child trafficking than others; traffickers are active in some places and not in others; some communities face more child trafficking than others; some families are more at risk of trafficking than others; girls are more at risk in some instances and boys in others. Since many poor children do not fall victim to trafficking, understanding the differences between those who are and those who are not trafficked can help protect children at risk.

Children often simultaneously experience several risk factors creating vulnerability to trafficking, one of which may act as a trigger setting the trafficking event in motion. This is sometimes called 'poverty plus', a situation in which poverty does not by itself lead to being trafficked, but where a 'plus' factor such as illness combines with poverty to increase vulnerability. There are, for example, family disruptions that can be considered as vulnerability or 'plus' factors: men in the family going off to war or being killed in conflict, or one or both parents dying of AIDS, leaving children with no adult support. There are also wider social/economic factors disrupting family finances, such as drought or floods leaving a rural family with no food stocks or income.

Discrimination on the basis of sex, ethnicity or disability increases vulnerability to trafficking as well as to other forms of violence and abuse. These 'plus' factors show that vulnerability is not a static state. It changes over time, often the result of factors coming into play only in certain circumstances, and may or may not result in vulnerability. One example is given in the UN Office for the Coordination of Humanitarian Affairs (UNOCHA) *Youth in crisis* report (UNOCHA, 2007), which notes that the children of sex workers are subjected to increased vulnerability to trafficking, as girls are often forced into the sex trade by mothers who need funds to pay for their children's education. Sex workers' children are also more vulnerable to abuse by the customers who visit their mothers, as they can readily propose abusing children instead. These factors often result in societal exclusion of the children of sex workers, affecting access to education and further increasing their chance of being exploited.

Supply and demand of child trafficking

To understand the risks of child trafficking, it is vital to understand what fuels the need for traffickers to seek victims. A concept borrowed from economic analysis is often used in connection with trafficking: supply and demand. This has been adopted to look both at the issue within the context of labour market realities and to acknowledge that the people involved in trafficking – traffickers and victims – are in many ways two sides of an equation. Trafficked people, the 'supply' side of trafficking, are a factor of production when their labour is exploited. For example, a rural community with high levels of unemployment may have a 'supply' of young people desperate to find work and these adolescents may be recruited by traffickers into exploitation in a nearby city in factories producing clothes. The community impacted by unemployment is effectively 'supplying' the children while the people buying the clothes are creating 'demand' (although this demand is for the clothes, not the children). The true 'demand' for the children comes from traffickers hoping to make money and from factory operators who, trying to keep prices low and therefore profit margins robust, are willing to take trafficked children.

It is important to distinguish between consumer (or primary) demand and derived demand by exploiters, recognising that they occur at different points of the trafficking chain. Consumer demand is generated directly by people who actively or passively buy the products or services of trafficked labour, for example the tourist who buys a cheap t-shirt made by a trafficked child in a sweatshop. Research suggests that most of this kind of demand does not directly influence the trafficking – for example, the tourist buying a cheap t-shirt does not specially ask traffickers to exploit children and so cannot be said to be an 'accomplice' in the trafficking.

Derived demand is a very different matter because those who profit from trafficking generate it. These include pimps and brothel owners, various intermediaries involved in trafficking and corrupt factory owners or farmers who exploit trafficked labour to keep costs down, prices low and profits flowing.

Understanding demand is important in order to target the right people in the right way. The current economic crisis is affecting supply and demand and is expected to significantly change global trends in human trafficking. The economic crisis affects countries through reduced trade flows, declining commodity prices, tightened credit markets, decreased remittance flows, a decline in Foreign Direct Investment and reduced Official Development

Assistance. The resulting growth in poverty will contribute to more people becoming more vulnerable to trafficking, effectively increasing the supply-side of human trafficking globally. All this will affect some countries more than others. Open economies, for instance those that rely heavily on remittances of migrant workers, and those that do not have social safety-nets, are more likely to be affected. The 2009 ILO global report echoes these predictions by saying that at least 200 million workers, most of whom live in developing nations, are at risk of extreme poverty if the crisis continues. In general, this will result in a rise in the number of vulnerable households and increased poverty. As a coping strategy, families – in particular those without access to social safety-nets – may let their children drop out of school and send them to work prematurely. This puts many children at risk of trafficking and labour exploitation, particularly if these children migrate away from their families in search of work.

The ILO predicts that Asia will be the continent most affected by the crisis, with a worst-case scenario involving 113 million unemployed in 2009. This is particularly alarming given that the Organization for Economic Co-operation and Development (OECD) places 70% of the unemployment in the region as part of the informal sector (where exploitation is most likely). In addition, the World Bank has revised previous estimates on the decreases of remittance flows to Asia, changing its estimate to an approximate 5% to 8% decrease for 2009. This increase in financial stress will likely cause many families to seek alternative options for income, increasing their vulnerability to trafficking.

Learning and applying lessons; towards effective responses

With multiple international legal frameworks[8] in place to eliminate child trafficking, why does this form of slavery remain so predominant? What can be done better to advance the fight against child trafficking? While most states condemn forced labour and the worst forms of child labour, national laws often lag behind international commitments, and in many countries legislation remains vague in defining trafficking, resulting in ambiguous prohibitions. For instance, many states have criminalised human trafficking, but remain reluctant to improve the legal status of current and potential victims. Only a few countries allow identified victims to seek permanent resident status in the country of destination, and in most regions national laws do not cover all forms of trafficking, lack specifics on children or exclude certain groups of people. Anti-trafficking legislation may thus be limited to sexual exploitation, ignoring other aspects of labour exploitation.

Stronger law enforcement tools, such as stricter, less ambiguous laws, labour inspection, corporate social responsibility (CSR) mechanisms, specialised knowledge and outreach to workers' and employers' organisations, can all contribute to the protection of families whose children are at risk of (re-) trafficking.

Actors in the fight against child trafficking

Governments have prime responsibility to coordinate effective policies to fight child trafficking, being obliged by international law to apply ratified Conventions such as ILO Convention No 182. Articles 34 and 35 of the CRC say that the government should use 'all means possible' to make sure that children are not trafficked. It is, however, unimaginable that a problem of this magnitude can be entirely solved by any one government. Individual governments, international coalitions, regional agreements, private corporate initiatives, workers' and employers' organisations, NGOs and ordinary individuals must tackle the problem together.

Corporations and companies can also help in the fight against child trafficking. Industries that rely on cheap and low-skilled migrant labour are those most likely to be at risk of contributing to trafficking, and some of them have taken steps through their own CSR programmes. However, the number of actual companies with a CSR policy including a focus on fighting child trafficking is limited, and even some of those that do may not verify that their subcontractors do not employ trafficked children.

Finally, the participation of children in the fight against trafficking is an important protection mechanism not to be overlooked: it offers learning opportunities to children and reinforces their understanding, self-awareness and empowerment. Children who have been trafficked in the past possess much of the information needed to identify both risk factors and the processes traffickers put in place to entrap children. Their experience is a rich source of information.

Partnerships and collaboration

The multidimensional issue of trafficking requires a multi-partner response in which a range of different actors work together around a common platform. National action plans (NAPs) can provide effective frameworks for diverse actors to collaborate in the fight against child trafficking and work to their respective strengths, ensuring that responses to child trafficking are comprehensive.

The development of a NAP should involve national debate to ensure that existing frameworks or plans relating to areas relevant to child trafficking, such as child labour or forced labour, are taken into account. Additionally, considerations should be taken for children at special risk, while referencing known gender dimensions among children at risk. NAPs or other integrated planning frameworks should also list exploitative sectors known to exist in the country, and the sectors in which children trafficked out of the country end up, and recognise the differences of internal versus cross-border trafficking, as well as the source, transit and destination areas; each require different interventions.

Planning frameworks should include age-specific actions and target the specific rights and needs of specific subgroups of children. For example, children under 15 should be offered free basic education (under the Education for All initiative), whereas children aged 15+ should be allowed to work, if in decent conditions (and would benefit from skills training, job placement services, safe [internal] migration and youth employment interventions). Regardless of what planning framework is being used, actions should include broad protection to prevent trafficking of children at risk and former victims, prevention of the crime of trafficking as well as law enforcement and victim assistance.

Suggested interventions

Although the ultimate goal of anti-child trafficking programmes is to eliminate all forms of child trafficking, beginning by targeting the children at the highest risk of trafficking is a good initial step. Once a child, family, community or workplace has been identified as being in a high-risk situation, they should become the primary focus (target beneficiaries) of the actions to be undertaken. The focus, of course, should be on addressing the specific risk factors that created vulnerability. These factors might relate to risks at source, in transit and/or at destination, and are critical to preventing the crime of trafficking itself. It is vital that the measures included in broad protection apply not only to trafficking victims and potential victims, but also to the community and families within it.

Broad protection is about building a world fit for children, which is the best way to reduce and eventually eliminate threats to their livelihoods, and ultimately all threats to their and their family's well-being. This is the over-arching goal that supports all actions for and with children, including actions that are designed specifically to fight child trafficking. Broad protection includes ensuring access to basic socioeconomic services – such as education, training, healthcare, birth registration, job placement services, bank accounts and access to credit – which reduce vulnerability to trafficking. Access to these services is often impeded by the lack of an identity card (Blakeley, 2009). Simple measures, such as providing an identity card to children at risk, may be taken to reduce the vulnerability of potential victims. Also, targeting the socially excluded through programmes that offer rural skills training, micro-finance, business development services and job placement services to poor families whose children are at risk of the worst forms of child labour, can help generate income to expand a family's employment opportunities, lifting people out of the cycle of poverty that they would otherwise be unable to escape. In order to ensure institutional sustainability, these programmes must be supplemented by a legal framework to incorporate micro-finance within the formal banking system. Outreach programmes should furthermore assist families that are dysfunctional and where the children are at risk of running away (and thus of being trafficked) due to abuse, such as domestic violence or alcohol misuse.

Protective actions in anti-trafficking work are essentially focused on children and contribute to preventing these particular children from being trafficked. However, this does not mean that the crime of trafficking is stopped. The traffickers may move their operations elsewhere or focus on other groups. Preventative actions are therefore generally focused on addressing the problem of trafficking itself, including the demand for exploitation in all its forms. Interventions include legal instruments to pursue traffickers and those who facilitate – or demand – children's work at destination, and also the promotion of safe, legal migration for young people of legal working age. This enables them to seek out decent work or training if it cannot be found in their place of origin. Furthermore, migration and job placement services should be made accessible to the target group and relevant to their needs.

Effective law enforcement is a major deterrent to trafficking. Prosecuted traffickers may desist from trafficking again if the losses incurred (or the sanctions imposed) make trafficking no longer seem worth the risk. Even large-scale, organised trafficking rings may be at least temporarily interrupted by law enforcement actions if the penalties meted out are strong enough to be seen as significant by traffickers, particularly in relation to the substantial profits to be made. The sanctioning of traffickers presumes unequivocal laws that can be used not only to bring them to justice but also, through asset confiscation, to dismantle the mechanisms they use to traffic and exploit children. In addition, public reporting of prosecutions is important, because it helps to break down social indifference – often a result of apathy and ignorance rather than a positive tolerance of criminal activity. Reporting and a consequent belief that law enforcement against traffickers is successful also helps address the fears that people may have that 'nothing can be done' to stop trafficking or bring traffickers to justice. Law enforcement in relation to trafficking applies to the implementation not only of criminal law but also of labour law, a potent weapon in anti-trafficking efforts. Labour law cannot, however, reach into the underground economy or unregulated workplaces. It is also important that those working in the legal professions understand trafficking and appreciate issues relating to victim protection and rights.

Awareness of a victim's needs and rights is essential to providing adequate assistance and to providing protection to make sure that the child's rights are safeguarded. Identifying victims and referring them to appropriate services is the responsibility first of government services such as immigration officials, labour inspectors and police. One of the most important reasons for having specific national anti-trafficking laws is so that the status of 'trafficking victim' is enshrined in law. Trafficking victims – children in particular – have very specific needs because of the nature of the crime committed against them. For example, the fact that they are removed from family and support networks greatly increases their suffering and means they are likely to feel particularly isolated. Support services should include psychosocial counselling, legal assistance (where needed), shelter/housing, life skills training, (re)training and education, and return and reintegration where this is in the best interests of the child. Once the status of 'trafficked person' is clear in law, then it is much more likely that the provision of appropriate support services will be on the political agenda. The identification of trafficking victims is not, therefore, simply a matter of picking them out of a crowd at a transport hub, or recognising them in a clandestine workplace (although of course these forms of identification are also important). It is more than anything recognising their specific needs and knowing how these grow out of the very fact that they have been trafficked.

Finally, when dealing with cross-border trafficking, countries should collaborate to address the specific cross-border aspects of child trafficking, and work towards coordinated solutions that are in the best interest of affected children.

Conclusion

To avoid overlooking any aspect of child trafficking, the issue must be put into the broader context of children's rights, labour markets and migration dynamics. Again, the complex nature of child trafficking underlines the need for comprehensive multidimensional responses. Yet doing so provides us with key challenges that must be overcome adequately in order to assess and execute appropriate responses. Gathering data on child trafficking through a variety of methods and from a range of sources is necessary so as to improve the focus and effectiveness of responses and to monitor progress. Improving data-gathering techniques includes not only more and better data-gathering methods, but also a political will to initiate proper research. Few states, however, ever collect and publish data on the problem of child trafficking, and often NGOs researching the topic are bound by particular sub-topics. Even if countries undertook this research, variations in definitions regarding trafficking would make it difficult to extract trends in trafficking from statistical data. For this reason, multilateral collaboration on research methods and standards needs to be improved.

Governments, NGOs and other agents fighting child trafficking should be familiar with the concept of vulnerability, that is, moving beyond the idea that poverty is at the root of all trafficking, and understanding that there is a range of risk factors affecting the level of vulnerability of each child: at individual child, family, community, institutional and workplace levels, and in source communities and at destination. In responses to trafficking, we should be clear about which children are (most) vulnerable and who creates the demand for exploitation (and where), targeting our actions accordingly. Discrimination (including by gender) and marginalisation of socially excluded groups deserve special attention. Children without birth registration, children from minority ethnic groups, children with disabilities, homeless children, orphans and migrant children often lack access to basic social services, and are at particularly high risk of trafficking.

It is also vital for governments to address the demand for labour exploitation at all levels of the market, especially in the informal sector, where government regulation is either lacking or non-existent. Another area that demands government inspection and corporate action is the web of subcontracts in increasingly complex global supply chains that make child trafficking possible. Governments should establish legislative procedures that ensure that people participating in even one aspect of child trafficking (such as irregular recruitment) are indeed traffickers and should therefore not be prosecuted for lesser crimes.

Finally, authorities should work towards encouraging the engagement of labour organisations, trade unions, the private sector, local communities and national governments to help address the factors facilitating child trafficking. At a minimum, such programmes would create dialogue to highlight the problems of public indifference or ignorance of the problem. It is vital to recognise the 'cause and effect' of the response actions under consideration. Many promising policies have been put in place, but ultimately have had less impact than desired, because they did not address the crux of the problem. Understanding labour-related issues can thus help make us better anti-trafficking professionals.

The key to fighting trafficking is to stop it from being profitable through strict law enforcement (including in the informal economy where most of the demand is generated), to confiscate the profits of traffickers and to increase protection (and reduce vulnerability) of children. It is only when children and their families everywhere are aware of the dangers that they may face from trafficking, whether on a local, regional, national or international level, that the work of all other actors who are fighting child trafficking can be effective. The Roadmap for achieving the elimination of the worst forms of child labour by 2016, adopted during the 2010 Global Child Labour Conference,[9] offers clear guidance on priority actions to be undertaken to fight child slavery. It is now up to us all, led by governments, to follow through on these priority actions to end the worst forms of child labour including child trafficking.

Notes

[1] This chapter draws heavily on recent ILO publications on child trafficking, in particular *Combating trafficking in children for labour exploitation: A resource kit for policy-makers and practitioners* (2008) and *Training manual to fight trafficking for labour, sexual and other forms of exploitation* (ILO et al, 2009). The views expressed in this chapter are those of the author.

[2] Written with the assistance of Manus McCaffery (ILO intern from Stanford University, California).

[3] These can be individuals or groups, often a chain of people involved in one or more aspects of the trafficking process.

[4] Protocol to Prevent, Suppress and Punish trafficking in persons, especially women and children, supplementing the UN Convention against Transnational Organised Crime, Annex II, UN Doc A/RES/55/25/Annex II (15 November 2000).

[5] According to the Palermo Protocol and ILO Convention No 182, children are defined as 'any person under the age of 18'. The UN CRC uses the same age threshold, but with the exception that national laws can set a lower age of majority. This means that if authorities in one country decide that the age of majority for girls is 16, then the rights of the child shall only apply to those girls who are under 16.

[6] International media reported one case where 300 children were labouring in a shoe factory in eastern China as a part of a government labour transfer programme. Many of the children were Uighur girls, whose families were reportedly coerced, and in some cases threatened, by government officials to participate in the programme using fake or swapped identification cards provided by the government.

[7] See also the report of a study tour on modern slavery in India, 2009, available from the editor at G.Craig@hull.ac.uk

[8] As of 1 October 2009, all countries (save two) have ratified the UN CRC, 172 countries have ratified the ILO's Forced Labour Convention No 29, 165 countries have ratified the Worst Forms of Child Labour Convention No 182 and 117 nations have ratified the Palermo Protocol.

[9] For full text of the 'Roadmap to 2016', see www.ilo.org/ipecinfo/product/viewProduct.do?productId=13453

References

Belser, P., de Cock, M. and Mehran, F. (2005) *Minimum estimate of forced labour in the world*, Geneva: International Labour Organization (www.ilo.org/wcmsp5/groups/public/---ed_norm/---declaration/documents/publication/wcms_081913.pdf).

Bhalla, N. (2009) 'Traffickers prey on disaster-hit children in India', *Reuters*, AlertNet, 23 March (www.alertnet.org/db/an_art/55867/2009/02/23-145911-1.htm).

Blakely, R. (2009) 'India to issue all 1.2 billion citizens with biometric ID cards', *The Times*, 15 July (www.timesonline.co.uk/tol/news/world/asia/article6710764.ece).

Calvani, S. (2009) 'Children's exploitation and women's condition: the issue of human trafficking', Speech (Director of UNICRI [Interregional Crime and Justice Research Institute]), Scuola d'Applicazione, Institute of Military Studies, Turin, 12 June (www.unicri.it/wwa/staff/speeches/090612_dir.pdf).

Eisenstein, Z. (2007) 'Africa says world must fight human trafficking', *Reuters*, 15 July.

French, H. (2007) 'Fast-growing China says little of child slavery's role', *The New York Times*, 21 June (www.nytimes.com/2007/06/21/world/asia/21china.html).

ILO (International Labour Organization) (2005) *A global alliance against forced labour: Global report under the follow-up to the ILO Declaration on Fundamental Principles and Rights at Work*, Geneva: ILO.

ILO (2006) *The end of child labour: Within reach. Global report under the follow-up to the ILO Declaration on Fundamental Principles and Rights at Work*, Geneva: ILO.

ILO (2007) *Child trafficking: The ILO's response through IPEC*, Geneva: ILO.

ILO (2008) *Combating trafficking in children for labour exploitation: A resource kit for policy-makers and practitioners*, Geneva: ILO.

ILO (2009) *The cost of coercion: Global report under the follow-up to the ILO Declaration on Fundamental Principles and Rights at Work*, Geneva: ILO.

ILO, UNICEF, UN GIFT (2009) *Training manual to fight trafficking for labour, sexual and other forms of exploitation*, Geneva: ILO.

IOM (International Organization for Migration) (2009) 'Counter-trafficking' (www.iom.int/jahia/page748.html).

Moens, B., Zeitlin, V., Bop, C. and Gaye, R. (2004) *Study on the practice of trafficking in persons in Senegal*, Bethesda, MD: Development Alternatives Inc.

Plaut, M. (2006) 'Africa's hunger – a systemic crisis', BBC, 31 January (http://news.bbc.co.uk/2/hi/africa/4662232.stm).

UN (United Nations) General Assembly (1948) *Universal Declaration of Human Rights* (www.un.org/en/documents/udhr/).

UN General Assembly (1949) *Convention for the Suppression of the Traffic in Persons and of the Exploitation of the Prostitution of Others* (www2.ohchr.org/english/law/trafficpersons.htm).

UN General Assembly (1989) *UN Convention on the Rights of the Child (CRC)* (www2.ohchr.org/english/law/pdf/crc.pdf).

UN General Assembly (2000) *Protocol to Prevent, Suppress and Punish Trafficking in persons, especially women and children, Supplementing the United Nations Convention against Transnational Organised Crime* (www.uncjin.org/Documents/Conventions/dcatoc/final_documents_2/convention_%20traff_eng.pdf).

UNAIDS (2008) *Report on the global AIDS epidemic 2008*, Geneva: Joint UN Programme on HIV/AIDS (www.unaids.org/en/KnowledgeCentre/HIVData/GlobalReport/2008/2008_Global_report.asp).

UNICEF (United Nations Children's Fund) (1999) *Etude sur le travail domestique non-salarié des enfants*, Geneva: UNICEF.

UNICEF, UNOHCHR (United Nations Office of the High Commissioner for Human Rights) and OSCE (Organisation for Security and Cooperation in Europe)/ODIHR (Office for Democratic Institutions and Human Rights) (2004) *Trafficking in human beings in South Eastern Europe* (www.unicef.org/media/files/2004Focus_on_Prevention_in_SEE.pdf).

UNOCHA (United Nations Office for the Coordination of Humanitarian Affairs) (2007) *Youth in crisis: Coming of age in the 21st century*, UNOCHA (http://newsite.irinnews.org/pdf/in-depth/Youth-in-crisis-IRIN-In-Depth.pdf).

UNODC (United Nations Office on Drugs and Crime) (2009) *Global report on trafficking in persons*, Vienna: UNODC (www.unodc.org/documents/Global_Report_on_TIP.pdf).

USDS (United States Department of State) (2009) *Trafficking in persons report*, Washington, DC: USDS (www.state.gov/documents/organization/123360.pdf).

six

Clarity and consistency in understanding child exploitation: a UK perspective

Aarti Kapoor

Introduction

The acute problem of child exploitation is increasingly coming to the attention of child protection workers and policy makers. This is due to the ubiquitous use of the word 'exploitation' within national and international legislation, mainly in regard to human trafficking. 'Exploitation' (of persons) itself may be loosely defined as where a person unfairly takes advantage of another person. Within the UK, it has been accepted that child trafficking and exploitation is a form of child abuse (Home Office, 2006). In order to intervene, as required by law, to safeguard and protect children, it is necessary to understand child exploitation as a distinct and serious form of child abuse.

The Child Exploitation and Online Protection Centre (CEOP) has identified numerous forms of child exploitation as the end purpose of trafficking (CEOP, 2007, 2009). These include sexual exploitation, domestic servitude, benefit fraud, cannabis cultivation, labour exploitation/forced labour, drug trafficking/smuggling/dealing, illegal adoption, servile/forced marriage, street crime and begging. As child trafficking can be defined as the 'movement of a child for the purposes of exploitation', there may be other forms of exploitation where the child has not been moved for that purpose. Although this would not be child trafficking, it would still be child exploitation and would need as serious and swift an approach.

Some forms of child abuse, such as sexual abuse or child labour, are clearly accepted by practitioners and policy makers as exploitation. However, there are some forms of child abuse where there is some debate as to whether they would fall within an understanding of child exploitation. The debate mainly focuses on whether unfair advantage of the child has been taken or whether there has been any harm to the child. Examples of such are benefit fraud, illegal adoption, child marriage and female genital mutilation (FGM). These activities would obviously be unlawful and are covered by other aspects of the law. There is also discussion as to whether such offences are adequately covered by other laws and offences and therefore do not need to be enumerated explicitly under child exploitation.

This chapter seeks to examine the laws and common understandings of child exploitation in order to draw together some key elements of what child exploitation, as a distinct type of child abuse, would consist of. This would ultimately help practitioners and policy makers in developing more consistent systems in response to this problem.

Why is it important to understand child exploitation?

As global awareness of child exploitation rises, international differences in understanding become increasingly acute. What is classed as child exploitation in one country may be seen as a normal activity or practice in another. The consequence is often a clashing of cultural and social values in a fast-growing mobile world. Child trafficking is essentially the globalisation of child exploitation, and thus, it is of utmost importance that a common and harmonised approach is adopted in response.

In the UK, as awareness of child trafficking increases and draws more public and government attention, there are increasingly different views as to what is, and what can be identified within trafficking as, child exploitation. Due to the discrete processes by which stakeholders in separate sectors both at policy and practice level have developed awareness about how child exploitation manifests itself, there has resulted an imbalance in approaches and responses to the problem. The inevitable consequence is confusion and discordance between policy and practice, and between law enforcement and child protection agencies.

Recent research undertaken by Pearce et al (2009) on how practitioners respond to child trafficking concluded that: 'trafficking is hard to define, as it is a process with no easily identifiable beginning, middle or end. It can, therefore, go unnoticed: practitioners are uncertain about definitions or how to recognise a trafficked child or young person' (pp 58-9). Revealingly, one practitioner commented: "I have looked at all the different definitions that they have and I realised that there isn't a full definition that everyone sticks to." These findings show a lack of a consistent understanding of child trafficking and exploitation, contributing to the difficulties in identifying and adequately responding to vulnerable children themselves.

Where there are different views of child exploitation, this inevitably results in inconsistent actions by government and other agencies. Some forms of exploitation may be more targeted, as in the case of sexual exploitation, than other forms of exploitation 'reminiscent of slavery but which are nevertheless condoned or accepted by the public' (Dotteridge, 2004, p 19). General public disgust at child sexual abuse draws a more targeted response compared to child labour exploitation or criminal exploitation, for example.

These questions highlight the need for some harmonisation between the way child exploitation may be manifesting itself in reality and the way laws legislate around the issues.

International framework

International law delivers a framework within which we can best apprehend the globally set common standards surrounding child exploitation. This section examines key legislation, drawing out the main intentions and characteristics of 'child exploitation'.

Palermo Protocol

The Protocol to Prevent, Suppress and Punish trafficking in persons, especially women and children, supplementing the United Nations (UN) Convention against Transnational Organised Crime (hereafter the Palermo Protocol) delineates the international accepted definition of human trafficking, within which it necessitates the purpose of exploitation (Article 3(a)) (see Chapters Two and Five, this volume). The term 'exploitation' itself is not defined, however, only that it shall 'include at a minimum, the exploitation of the prostitution of others or other forms of sexual exploitation, forced labour or services, slavery or practices similar to slavery, servitude or the removal of organs'.

Where this involves a person under the age of 18, the Palermo Protocol states that the 'means' set forth in the definition do not need to be present (Article 3(c)). These are: threat or use of force or other forms of coercion, of abduction, of fraud, of deception, of abuse of power or of a position of vulnerability or of the giving or receiving of payments or benefits to achieve the consent of a person having control over another person. Under international standards, a person under the age of 18 cannot consent to his or her own exploitation. The very fact that exploitation is in itself not defined allows for flexibility in relation to contextual circumstances in each country.[1] Further, it also implicitly recognises the pre-existence of exploitation in its own right independent of there being *trafficking for the purposes of* exploitation.

Interestingly, the Protocol does not make a distinction between exploitation of children and that of adults. The *travaux préparatoires* records discussions and the proposal for making a special case for children in terms of sexual exploitation; this was not finally included, however.[2] It only draws the distinction in regard to consent. This also leads us to question whether, when we are talking about an adult, that even where they consent they could still be in an exploitative situation.[3] This can then lead us to conclude that there can be lawful and unlawful exploitation in regard to adults, depending on whether consent has been given or not.[4] In regard to children (those under 18), however, there is no such thing as lawful exploitation because consent is invalid.

International Labour Organization (ILO) Conventions

The ILO Conventions give the most detail on understanding child exploitation through Convention No 182 on the Worst Forms of Child Labour (1999) and Convention No 138 on Minimum Age for Admission to Employment (1973). The ILO International Programme on the Elimination of Child Labour (ILO-IPEC) has specifically distinguished the element of child exploitation in their work against child trafficking from these Conventions. For these purposes exploitation includes (ILO-IPEC, 2007):

(a) all forms of slavery or practices similar to slavery, such as the sale and trafficking of children, debt bondage and serfdom and forced or compulsory labour, including forced or compulsory recruitment of children for use in armed conflict (Convention No 182, Article 3(a));
(b) the use, procuring or offering of a child for prostitution, for the production of pornography or for pornographic performances (Convention No 182, Article 3(b));
(c) the use, procuring or offering of a child for illicit activities, in particular for the production and trafficking of drugs as defined in the relevant international treaties (Convention No 182, Article 3(b));
(d) work which, by its nature or the circumstances in which it is carried out, is likely to harm the health, safety or morals of children (Convention No 182, Article 3(c) and Convention No 138, Article 3);
(e) work done by children below the minimum age for admission to employment (Convention No 138, Articles 2 and 7).

Convention No 182 also states that all the types of work that would fall under the worst forms of child labour should be determined by the national laws and regulations, reviewed periodically (Article 4(1) and (3)). This confirms the room for flexibility given to individual countries in respect of their particular circumstances.

Points (a)–(d) above are applicable to all persons under the age of 18 (Convention No 182, Article 2). Convention No 138 states that the minimum age for employment should not be less than that for the age until which education is compulsory, but in any case not less than 15 (Article 2). However, in circumstances where the education system of a country is not so developed, the state may, in consultation with its employee and employer organisations, agree that the minimum age may be 14 (Article 4).

It is again pertinent to note that IPEC state that for their purposes exploitation *includes* the above forms of child labour but they do not limit it to these categories. Another question also arises as to whether child exploitation can include any form of activity that is not 'work', labour or income earning. Given that the worst forms of child labour consist of instances or scenarios where a child is in a 'work' or income-earning situation that is abusive and harmful to the child, the finding of exploitation, in terms of unfair advantage, is very clear. Article 3(d) of Convention No 182 outlines a general catch-all clause stating that any work likely to harm the health, safety or morals of children is considered a worst form of child labour.

UN Convention on the Rights of the Child (CRC) and Optional Protocol

The UN CRC is the most ratified UN Convention among member states and forms the global standard for responsibilities of governments towards children. Article 31(1) of the CRC delineates that 'States Parties recognize the right of the child to be protected from economic exploitation and from performing any work that is likely to be hazardous or to interfere with the child's education, or to be harmful to the child's health or physical, mental, spiritual, moral or social development'. Article 32 of the CRC refers to child exploitation in a broad sense and says: 'States Parties shall protect the child against all other forms of exploitation prejudicial to any aspects of the child's welfare'. These two Articles imply that children can be exploited in more ways than merely where economic gain is made.

The Optional Protocol to the Convention on the Rights of the Child on the Sale of Children, Child Prostitution and Child Pornography (OPSC) deals with the subject of the commercial enterprise in children. Article 2 states:

> For the purpose of the present Protocol:
>
> (a) Sale of children means any act or transaction whereby a child is transferred by any person or group of persons to another for remuneration or any other consideration;
> (b) Child prostitution means the use of a child in sexual activities for remuneration or any other form of consideration;
> (c) Child pornography means any representation, by whatever means, of a child engaged in real or simulated explicit sexual activities or any representation of the sexual parts of a child for primarily sexual purposes.

Article 3(1)(a) elaborates on Article 2(a) regarding the sale of children:

(i) The offering, delivering or accepting, by whatever means, a child for the purpose of:

    a. Sexual exploitation of the child;
    b. Transfer of organs of the child for profit;
    c. Engagement of the child in forced labour.

(ii) Improperly inducing consent, as an intermediary, for the adoption of a child in violation of applicable international legal instruments on adoption.

The OPSC clearly outlines the global standard that any exchange of the services, including sexual abuse, transfer of organs, forced labour or consent to adoption of a child, for remuneration should squarely fall within the criminal laws of member states. It can be concluded that these would evidently fall within the domain of child exploitation.

Slavery Convention

Article 1 of the 1956 UN Supplementary Convention on the Abolition of Slavery, the Slave Trade and Institutions and Practices similar to Slavery (the Slavery Convention) describes institutions and practices similar to slavery. Article 1(d) states that slavery is 'Any institution or practice whereby a child or young person under the age of 18 years is delivered by either or both of his natural parents or by his guardian to another person, whether for reward or not, with a view to the exploitation of the child or young person or of his labour'.

As with the definition of trafficking under the Palermo Protocol, this includes a reference to 'exploitation' without defining it. Nevertheless, further indications can be drawn from its context. First, the child may be delivered 'whether for reward or not' with the intention to exploit 'the child or his labour'. This alludes to the fact that children themselves can be exploited distinct from their labour or services rendered. It is pertinent to note that this describes an 'institution or a practice' rather than occasional one-off events within a community or society. Bokhari (2009) argues that forced marriage and child marriage is a practice similar to slavery. It is open for debate as to whether Article 1(d) could also include FGM within this definition.

As the main purpose of international law is to give a framework within which member states should develop laws in more detail, it may be helpful to examine the specific case of UK national legislation.

UK legal framework

Under UK legislation, 'exploitation' is mentioned in regard to offences of trafficking. These are enshrined in the 2003 Sexual Offences Act, Sections 57, 58 and 59 on 'Trafficking for sexual exploitation', and the 2004 Asylum and Immigration (Treatment of Claimants etc) Act, Section 4 on 'Trafficking for exploitation' (as amended by Section 54 of the 2009 Borders, Citizenship and Immigration Act). Section 5(1) of this Act enables it to cover Scotland. Further, for Scotland, the 2003 Criminal Justice (Scotland) Act makes 'traffic for prostitution' an offence.

The 2003 Sexual Offences Act offence of trafficking for sexual exploitation is where any person arranges or facilitates the travel of another whereby the offender or another person would commit a 'relevant offence' on that person. A relevant offence is any sexual offence under the laws of England, Wales and Northern Ireland. Given that trafficking of humans is for the purpose of exploitation, any relevant offence under the Sexual Offences Act would count as exploitation. This clarifies very neatly what could be classed as sexual exploitation within the UK legal system. Furthermore, other parts of the law are also relatively clear on what sexual offences are specific to children, for example, the production of indecent photographs of children is a specific offence under Section 1(1)(a) of the 1978 Protection of Children Act (c 37). The fact that there are specific and broader sexual offences that can be committed against children than against adults automatically broadens the legal definition of sexual exploitation of children vis-à-vis adults. To this extent UK law is in accordance with international law.

National legislation is not so clear when it comes to all other (non-sexual) types of exploitation. As mentioned, the relevant offence of 'Trafficking for exploitation' is delineated under the 2004 Asylum and Immigration (Treatment of Claimants etc) Act immigration legislation. Section 4(1)-(3) of this Act states that a person commits an offence if they arrange or facilitate the entry, travel within or departure from the UK of an individual and they intend to exploit that person or believe another person is likely to exploit that person.[5] Section 4(4), as outlined below, then gives an outline of what is meant by exploitation (for all persons, including children):

(4) For the purposes of this section a person is exploited if (and only if):

(a) he is the victim of behaviour that contravenes Article 4 of the Human Rights Convention (slavery and forced labour),
(b) he is encouraged, required or expected to do anything as a result of which he or another person would commit an offence

under the Human Organ Transplants Act 1989 (c 31) or the
Human Organ Transplants (Northern Ireland) Order 1989 (SI
1989/2408 [NI 21]),

(c) he is subjected to force, threats or deception designed to induce
him -
(i) to provide services of any kind,
(ii) to provide another person with benefits of any kind, or
(iii) to enable another person to acquire benefits of any kind ...

Section 4(4)(d) of this Act has been amended under the 2009 Borders,
Citizenship and Immigration Act (c 11) to:

(d) a person uses or attempts to use him for any purpose within
sub-paragraph (i), (ii) or (iii) of paragraph (c), having chosen
him for that purpose on the grounds that –
(i) he is mentally or physically ill or disabled, he is young or he
has a family relationship with a person, and
(ii) a person without the illness, disability, youth or family
relationship would be likely to refuse to be used for that purpose.

Section 4(4)(a) refers to European law and relies on international legal
definitions. Article 4 of the European Convention on Human Rights
(ECHR) states that: (i) no one shall be held in slavery or servitude; and (ii)
no one shall be required to perform forced or compulsory labour.[6] The
ECHR does not define 'slavery' or 'compulsory labour'. The UN Slavery
Convention, Article 1(1) states that 'slavery is the status or condition of
a person over whom any or all of the powers attaching to the right of
ownership are exercised'. The ILO Forced Labour Convention No 29,
Article 2(1) defines 'forced or compulsory labour' '[as] all work or service
which is exacted from any person under the menace of any penalty and for
which the said person has not offered himself voluntarily'.

This UK interpretation of the offence is consistent with international
law, which sees slavery and forced labour squarely as exploitation, whether
regarding adults or children.

Section 4(4)(b) deals with offences committed under the 1989 Human
Organ Transplants Act (c 31) and its equivalent Northern Ireland law. This
in essence covers the removal of an organ for the purposes of transplantation,
or the supply of an organ for money or the payment of money for an organ
(1989 Human Organ Transplants Act, Sections 1 and 2). The purpose of this
law was to prevent a market in human organs for medical needs, essentially
covering the demand and supply of human parts for traditional medicine as
has been known to occur in some parts of the world. Significantly, this does

not cover the removal of an organ or human tissue for other purposes, such as for cultural reasons. This would therefore not cover the activity of FGM.

Section 4(4)(c) is broader, as it can include any activity where the victim is induced to provide services, rendering benefits of any kind or enabling another person to acquire benefits of any kind. The Act does not define the meaning of 'services' or 'benefits' and leaves open what can be defined as the procurement of benefits. However, the use of the words 'benefits' and 'services' can be interpreted to mean where there has been some kind of resultant economic or commercial advantage.

Section 4(4)(d) goes more widely in describing 'exploitation' as any activity described in the paragraph above as long as the person has been chosen due to specific circumstances, which, between them, signify vulnerability. These circumstances are limited to where the person is mentally or physically ill, has a disability, is young or has a family relationship with the offender. In such circumstances the person would not need to have been forced, threatened or deceived for the purposes of inducing them into that activity. These circumstances are seen as making the person vulnerable where had they not been in such circumstances they would have refused. This can be seen as an attempt to codify those instances under 'means' as described in the Palermo Protocol definition where there is an 'abuse of power or position of vulnerability'.

Significantly, it does not codify any precise age that would make the person 'young' or have 'youth'. Therefore, given international legislation, including the Council of Europe's 2005 Action Punishing Trafficking in Human Beings Convention to which the UK is now a signatory, it is deemed that this would, at minimum, include any person under the age of 18.

Commonly identified forms of child exploitation

In arriving at a better understanding of child exploitation, it would also be prudent to examine types of abuses commonly identified as child exploitation. Both CEOP and ECPAT UK (see the Resources section at the end of this volume) have identified various forms of child exploitation manifested in the UK (CEOP, 2007, 2009; ECPAT, 2007, 2009). These forms can be categorised into four broad types: (i) sexual exploitation; (ii) labour exploitation; (iii) exploitation in illicit activities; and (iv) other practices/institutions where benefits are gained, whether to an individual or a group, from an activity detrimental to the child's safety, welfare and development.

Sexual exploitation is seen as a form of sexual abuse. Government guidance (DCSF, 2009) uses the following description:

> ... sexual exploitation of children and young people under 18 involves exploitative situations, contexts and relationships where

young people (or a third person or persons) receive 'something' (for example, food, accommodation, drugs, alcohol, cigarettes, affection, gifts, money) as a result of them performing, and/or another or others performing on them, sexual activities. Child sexual exploitation can occur through the use of technology without the child's immediate recognition; for example being persuaded to post sexual images on the Internet/mobile phones without immediate payment or gain. In all cases, those exploiting the child/young person have power over them by virtue of their age, gender, intellect, physical strength and/or economic or other resources. Violence, coercion and intimidation are common, involvement in exploitative relationships being characterised in the main by the child or young person's limited availability of choice resulting from their social/ economic and/or emotional vulnerability. (para 1.3)

Interestingly, this description focuses on some benefit being received by the child or young person instead of the exploiter.

Labour exploitation would cover all types of 'work' where at worst the child is held in servitude, including where the child is in debt bondage, and at best where unfair advantage is taken of the child and the child suffers adverse impact. This could be because the work may be risky or hazardous, because it is detrimental to the welfare and development of the child or where remuneration for the work does not match its normal value. In terms of the identified forms of child exploitation in the UK, this would broadly cover where children and young people are put to work in the construction industries, restaurants or nail salons, as well as where they are in domestic servitude within households.

Exploitation in illicit activities would broadly incorporate those activities where the child or young person is put to 'work' in criminal enterprises such as cannabis cultivation, drug trafficking, street crime and pickpocketing. Although many of these manifestations, such as cultivation in the illegal cannabis industry, can also be classed as labour exploitation, the distinct criminal nature of the activity even outside the sphere of trafficking and exploitation calls for a separate category, notwithstanding the fact that children and young people are often chosen for these activities precisely because they are young and therefore more amenable and dispensable.

The final category of *other practices or institutions where benefits are gained etc* consists of all other types of child exploitation. This would contain sale of children for adoption, child and underage marriages and may even involve practices such as FGM. In such practices, benefits accrued to a couple wanting a child, or a family acting for their 'honour' or a community attempting to control the independence of the child result in widespread practices that are at worst abusive, and at best detrimental to the best interests of the child. This grouping would also contain the phenomenon of benefit fraud where adults use children in order to fraudulently claim state benefits.

Key characteristics in any understanding of what is child exploitation

Having examined key international and UK laws and principles as well as commonly identified forms of child exploitation, it is possible to draw together common themes and characteristics. All the main elements presented below should in principle be found in any activity regarded as child exploitation.

Age

International conventions as well as UK national legislation clearly outline that a child includes all persons under the age of 18. It is universally accepted that children have special rights given their developmental status and their relative lack of choice. The CRC and the UK (1989 and 2004) Children Acts outline the basic rights and responsibilities owed towards every child. It is due to this principle that the boundaries of what should be seen as exploitation of children exceed those defined for adults. This is explicitly outlined in international frameworks such as the Palermo Protocol, which distinguishes between those under and over 18 years. Furthermore, the ILO Conventions, particularly Convention No 182, make a specific distinction in regard to children. In UK legislation, the issue of age is raised less explicitly but is nonetheless relatively clear. The 2003 Sexual Offences Act clearly outlines various types of sexual abuses that are criminal offences specifically relevant to the age of the victim. The 2004 Asylum and Immigration (Treatment of Claimants etc) Act (as amended by the 2009 Borders, Citizenship and Immigration Act) outlines where a person is 'young' and has been chosen to provide benefits etc, where these would have refused had it not been for their 'youth'. Although it is yet to be seen how this legislation will be applied in practice, it is deemed that this would include at a minimum any person under the age of 18. The other aspect key to the understanding of child exploitation and relevant to the issue of age is the minimum age for work.

Economic and other benefits

Generally, the term 'exploitation' when applied to people denotes some kind of commercial aspect. The interpretation of what is gained in terms of benefit or unfair advantage has been widened, especially in regard to sexual exploitation. For example, sexual gratification to the abuser may be seen as the benefit or unfair advantage taken from the child. It is argued that unless there were some other tangible benefits being acquired, that is, credibility within a community, provision of sexual services within a slavery-like practice, then this would not fall within an understanding of child exploitation. Otherwise, child abuse emanating from sadistic acts and torture could also then become inclusive under an 'exploitation' banner, given that the abuser would be deriving psychological pleasure from their actions.

Where there has been an exchange of money or other remuneration, the transaction in itself *commodifies* the child as a product. This in itself attaches the characteristic of *property* to the child and the transferring of *ownership* by the buyer and seller. This is clearly covered by international legislation as described earlier, including the Palermo Protocol, the CRC, the OPSC and the Slavery Convention.

The rendering of some profit, benefit or services, whether economic or otherwise, is also an important element in child exploitation. This is confirmed by the interpretations of the definition of trafficking in the Palermo Protocol as well as Section 4 of the 2004 Asylum and Immigration (Treatment of Claimants etc) Act (as amended by the 2009 Borders, Citizenship and Immigration Act). Where a child or young person is exploited for their labour, both within the wider or criminal economy, the abuser is gaining profit from the enterprise. Where a child or young person is held in domestic servitude, the exploiter gains directly from the labour and services provided. Servile marriages also come within this domain, given the victim provides unremunerated services to the spouse and family.

Abuse of power or position of vulnerability

An important element of exploitation of another person is the abuse of a position of power by the exploiter, and the corresponding abuse of a position of vulnerability on the side of the exploited. This is particularly acute where the exploited is a child. A child or young person has a developmental status, is at the mercy of her/his carer or guardian and has little choice in or alternative to events in her/his life. Therefore, the abuse of power over another's relative vulnerability should generally be taken as a given when understanding child exploitation. To take an example, in the UK there is a trend of young people being trafficked into the country to work in cannabis farms under a debt bondage system. There have been cases where these young people have been identified by police on raids and have been arrested and prosecuted for crimes related to cannabis cultivation. There has been some debate as to whether this is child exploitation or not, within the trafficking sphere. Despite the fact that these young people may know what they are doing, it would be unarguable that they are vulnerable and that another person has abused their position of power to put them to work in a far-off country in hazardous physical conditions in a criminal enterprise.

Where there is a family relationship between the exploited and an offender, there is a particularly acute and complex interplay of positions of power and vulnerability. In the practice of child or underage marriage, young people are often coerced, unbeknownst even to them, into marriages, which they would otherwise have refused had they not been so easily influenced. For this reason, family relationship has been specifically codified under Section 4 of the 2004 Asylum and Immigration (Treatment of Claimants etc) Act (as amended by the 2009 Borders, Citizenship and Immigration Act) as a position of vulnerability, independent of age. Furthermore, Article 1 of the Slavery Convention describes the delivering of a child for exploitation by parent or guardian as a practice similar to slavery.

Child abuse

In order for a child to have been exploited, there is a question as to whether it is a necessary prerequisite that the child has been abused in some way, or that the child's morals, safety, health or development have in some ways been adversely affected. One typical case is where a person illegally claims and receives state benefits using the identity of a child several times but where the child is leading a normal life, going to school, etc. In such a scenario it can be argued that, although this is exploitation of the child, as a person is deriving benefits from improper use of the child, the exploitation is not directly prejudicial or detrimental to any aspect of the child's welfare,[7] as outlined in Article 32 of the CRC. Another example is where a child has been illegally adopted. The adoption may well have been in the best interests of the child;[8] therefore, even though this has been undertaken without due legal process, this cannot be called child exploitation although it is possible that other laws and regulations have been broken.

Both international and UK frameworks imply that there should be some detrimental impact on the child for there to be some direct exploitation to the child. Child exploitation should clearly be treated as a form of child abuse. It follows that if child exploitation can be non-abusive, that trivialises the concept of child exploitation as something less than of the utmost seriousness.

Conclusion

The phrase 'child exploitation' involves many connotations and meanings, and is used in various contexts. However, as we have seen earlier, there is no full definition given of child exploitation in international or UK legislation. Notwithstanding this, child exploitation is a term commonly used to cover numerous types of abuse.

Having examined legal and common understandings around child exploitation, it seems the necessary elements would be:

- that the victim is under 18
- that some benefit is derived to the exploiter
- that the exploiter has taken unfair advantage of the child
- that the child is adversely affected or abused.

When talking about *child exploitation*, most practitioners and policy makers have a particular idea in mind, whether child sexual abuse or child labour. In terms of all non-sexual forms of child exploitation, this has been increasingly focused through work undertaken in response to child trafficking. This has somewhat skewed the general understanding of what child exploitation is. The term 'child trafficking' denotes movement, although by definition that movement must be for the purpose of exploitation. However, the emphasis taken by many stakeholders is to focus on the 'movement' part of the trafficking continuum. Although doubtless the movement of the child is very important, it should be the 'exploitation' element that receives more attention because it forms the major part of the abuse the child suffers. The current concentration on 'movement' has, unfortunately, resulted in policies and responses having more of an immigration than a child protection emphasis. This has had the positive effect of raising child protection issues in regard to migration in general. However, this has specifically resulted in much of the response to child trafficking focusing on national borders. Child trafficking is actually very difficult to identify at international borders for various reasons (CEOP, 2007). There is still a dearth of capacity in identifying those children being exploited in our communities. There needs to be a more equal focus on the actual abuse of the child that takes place in the form of child exploitation, whether sexually, in labour or criminal exploitation or other types of harmful practices.

As categories of child exploitation types develop and further types of exploitation come about, it becomes even more important to have a consistent standard and understanding of what is meant by child exploitation. At the same time, it is just as crucial to preclude locking ourselves into a legal definition. This would merely seal a contemporary understanding of child exploitation that would not allow flexibility in fast-changing times. The importance of this becomes all the more significant when dealing with the responses to child exploitation in dynamic communities, as evidenced by the new and emerging forms of child exploitation worldwide. By using the main elements of child exploitation as outlined earlier, tools, policies and practices can be better developed. In applying these, both from a law enforcement and a child protection perspective, a clearer and consistent understanding helps more efficiently to take the best possible approach to combating the varied abuses of children. Furthermore, it helps to consistently deliver messages against child exploitation to all communities in order to raise awareness.

Notes

[1] *Travaux préparatoires:* UN Convention against Transnational Organised Crime (p 343, footnote 22) highlights the intention to leave definitions of what constitutes exploitation to member countries.

[2] 'Several delegations supported having a clear reference to trafficking in children for the purposes of prostitution, pornography and pornographic performances. This language follows the language of the ILO's Worst Forms of Child Labour Convention. An alternative way to criminalise trafficking in children might be to state that children could not consent to certain activities (UN Convention against Transnational Organised Crime, p 343, footnote 17).

[3] In fact, this was a specific concern in the drafting of the Protocol. It was eventually held that where there were findings of any of the means, then any 'consent' would be invalidated. This became Article 2(b) of the Protocol.

[4] Where there are findings that a person has been subjected to forced labour, slavery, practices similar to slavery or servitude, the *travaux préparatoires* suggests that the very finding of this would inevitably have included means set forth in the definition (force, threat, deceipt, abuse of a position of vulnerability) and therefore any suggested consent would be invalidated (UN Convention against Transnational Organised Crime, p 344, footnote 26).

[5] This offence has been paraphrased here. See the legislation for full wording.

[6] Section 4(3) of the ECHR states some exceptions: 'For the purpose of this article the term "forced or compulsory labour" shall not include: (a) any work required to be done in the ordinary course of detention imposed according to the provisions of Article 5 of this Convention or during conditional release from such detention; (b) any service of a military character or, in case of conscientious objectors in countries where they are recognized, service exacted instead of compulsory military service; (c) any service exacted in case of an emergency or calamity threatening the life or well-being of the community; (d) any work or service which forms part of normal civic obligations'.

[7] This does not, however, apply to the many cases of benefit fraud where children have been sold, bought and brought to the UK only so that benefits can be claimed. In such cases children are commodified and may be taken away from their parents and guardians, grow up not knowing anything of their heritage and suffer other abuses at the hands of their exploiters. Often such children are passed between households impacting on their care and development. This is clearly child exploitation and a form of child abuse.

[8] It is accepted that legal adoption processes are designed to ensure that the best interests of the child are followed and therefore where due legal process is not followed, the potential for an adverse impact on the child is heightened.

References

Bokhari, F. (2009) *Stolen futures: Trafficking for forced child marriage in the UK*, London: ECPAT UK/WISE.

CEOP (Child Exploitation and Online Protection Centre) (2007) *A scoping report on child trafficking in the UK*, London: CEOP.

CEOP (2009) *Strategic threat assessment of child trafficking in the UK*, London: CEOP.

DCSF (Department for Children, Schools and Families) (2009) *Guidance on safeguarding children and young people from sexual exploitation*, June, London: The Stationery Office.

Dotteridge, M. (2004) *Kids as commodities? Child trafficking and what to do about it*, Geneva: International Federation of Terre des Hommes.

ECPAT (End Child Prostitution, Child Pornography and the Trafficking of Children) (2007) *Missing out: A study of child trafficking in the North-West, North East and West Midlands of the UK*, London: ECPAT.

ECPAT (2009) *Bordering on concern: Child trafficking in Wales*, London: ECPAT.

Home Office (2006) *Safeguarding children who may have been trafficked*, London: The Stationery Office [Supplementary to HM Government's Statutory Guidance *Working together to safeguard children*].

ILO-IPEC (International Labour Organization-International Programme on the Elimination of Child Labour) (2007) *Child trafficking: The ILO's response through IPEC*, Geneva: ILO.

Pearce, J.J., Hynes, P. and Bovarnick, S. (2009) *Breaking the wall of silence: Practitioners' responses to trafficked children and young people*, Luton: University of Bedfordshire/ NSPCC.

seven

A human rights approach to preventing child sex trafficking[1]

Jonathan Todres

Introduction

Despite worldwide condemnation of slavery, human trafficking – a modern form of the slave trade – persists today. Trafficking of persons for any purpose (for example, forced labour, sexual exploitation, domestic servitude etc) is a gross violation of human rights. Among the most heinous abuses here is the trafficking of children for commercial sexual exploitation, involving thousands of children annually. An estimated one million children enter the sex trade annually in Asia alone, many of them trafficking victims. The prostitution of children and child pornography are thriving trades that call for immediate and concerted government action (UN Development Fund for Women, 1996).

In the past decade, governments, international organisations and civil society have mobilised to address these gross violations of children's rights and dignity. Through the promulgation of international and regional conventions, the international community has agreed on a three-pronged mandate that requires governments to: (1) criminalise and prosecute acts of sex trafficking; (2) implement prevention programmes; and (3) provide assistance to victims.[2] To date, most governments have focused primarily on law enforcement-related aspects of this mandate, while also providing assistance to select victims. Few have undertaken comprehensive prevention measures, even though prevention is the ultimate goal.

For policy makers to achieve their ultimate goal of preventing child sex trafficking, they must address the root causes of the problem. That is, they must focus efforts on addressing the reasons underlying why so many children are vulnerable to such exploitation (the supply issue) and why so much demand exists for services that exploit children (the demand issue). Both the supply and demand issues must be addressed if governments and civil society are to make meaningful progress in protecting children.

This chapter suggests that human rights, when fully implemented, provide a foundation to strengthen communities and reduce the vulnerability of children to sex trafficking. It calls on governments and civil society to focus on rights that can further the goal of *preventing* child sex trafficking. In particular, the following rights offer significant potential for reducing vulnerability and protecting children from sex trafficking: (1) the right to be free from all forms of discrimination; (2) the right to birth registration; (3) health rights; (4) the right to education; and (5) labour rights. Importantly, while the focus of this chapter is sex trafficking, these rights when fully ensured can help prevent other forms of trafficking and exploitation of children.

Rights that address root causes

The right to be free from all forms of discrimination

Discrimination, whether on the basis of 'race', ethnicity, sex, religion, disability or another protected trait, operates both to drive the demand for prostitution globally and to heighten the vulnerability of marginalised children to trafficking and commercial sexual exploitation (Bond, 2003).

Discrimination occurs across many settings, including housing, employment, healthcare, education and social services. It marginalises poor and minority individuals, pressing them into more economically vulnerable situations. In these circumstances, traffickers are most successful at 'recruiting' into the sex trade. Not surprisingly, the majority of children targeted by traffickers are from historically marginalised populations. In India and Nepal, for example, caste discrimination underlies the sex trade. Dalits, or untouchables, constitute a sizeable portion of the women and girls forced into prostitution in rural areas or sold into urban brothels (HRW, 2001; see also Chapter Fifteen, this volume). Similar dynamics play out throughout the world, leaving racial and minority ethnic populations at heightened risk of exploitation.

Woven into this discrimination are additional burdens experienced by women and girls, the result of gender-based violence and discrimination. Because of gender inequalities, many young women and girls face challenges exerting control in relationships and may have little power to decide whether and when to have sex and with whom. This power imbalance often results in young women and girls being forced to have unprotected sex even when they know it endangers their health. Young girls are particularly vulnerable in this context because they are not fully developed physically and have more limited verbal skills, leaving them less capable of protecting themselves. Many young girls are forced to trade sex for school fees and other basic items (ILO, 2001; UNAIDS et al, 2004).

Inequality in property rights and control over the family's financial resources also makes women and girls more vulnerable to abuses of power. In certain countries, widows are prohibited by law or custom from inheriting property, leaving many women and children homeless or without financial resources following the death of, or separation from, husbands and fathers (UNAIDS et al, 2004; HRW, 2005). Local customs also may leave married women with little or no control over the marital property, whether or not they brought some of those resources to the marriage (HRW, 2003). Without access to the family's economic resources, women are at significant risk of ending up impoverished. In turn, poverty may push women and their children into risky behaviour, including engaging in sex work, in order to survive.

While discrimination operates to heighten vulnerability to trafficking, it also serves to fuel the demand for prostitution. For example, the sex tourism industry in Europe, Australia and the US plays on crude stereotypes of Asian women, emphasising the 'submissiveness of Asian prostitutes and the [supposed] complicity of their families in their situation' (Lyons, 1998, p 102). Advertisements for sex tours 'build on the patriarchal and racist fantasies of European, Japanese, American, and Australian men by touting the exotic, erotic subservience of Asian women' (Lyons, 1998, p 104). In these settings, gender-based discrimination intersects racism, as white men from the Global North are willing to take advantage of underage girls in Thailand, the Philippines or other poorer countries, when they would not treat girls in their home countries similarly. Racial, ethnic and gender stereotypes drive demand for sex tourism by simultaneously enticing men from the Global North while easing any guilt they may have over exploiting children from poorer countries. Moreover, when states fail to police these practices, preferring tourism revenue over the protection of marginalised populations, they allow such exploitation to persist.

Demand for prostitution in many poor countries is not driven by foreigners alone. For example, in Thailand, the sex trade is fuelled not only by tourists but also domestic demand – in rural Thai locales, where tourists generally do not travel, there is still prostitution. In these remote areas of Thailand, traditional values and customs still prevail, including the view that by the time men and women are of marrying age, men should be worldly and experienced, but women should still be virgins (Thianthai, 2005). So in relatively closed communities, this dichotomy works only by having another group of women, considered unsuitable for marriage, with whom men can gain the requisite sexual experience, and thus a market for prostitution is formed. Again, gender-based discrimination is evident here. But that is not all, as some women are deemed 'good' marriageable women while others are relegated to 'other' status. Other forms of discrimination are apparent, reflected in part by the fact that poor and minority ethnic women and children are at greater risk of ending up in prostitution (Burke and Ducci, 2006).

To all forms of discrimination, the response of human rights law is unequivocal: discrimination is prohibited and must be eliminated. The major international human rights instruments contain non-discrimination provisions that prohibit discrimination in the implementation of the rights enumerated in each treaty (CRC, CEDAW, ICCPR, ICESCR).[3] These human rights conventions require states parties to 'respect' and 'ensure' the rights of each individual covered by each convention without discrimination. The former obligates governments not to infringe individuals' rights, whereas the latter obligates states to take affirmative steps to protect individuals from any threat of human rights violations, including sex trafficking (Buergenthal, 1981).

In seeking to address discrimination, two steps should be considered. First, there must be greater accountability among governments that encourage or even tolerate the discrimination that fosters child sex trafficking. The law exists at the international level. Advocates must ensure that it is implemented and enforced at the national and local levels.

Second, states must address the rights of their populations in an holistic manner. The symbiotic relationship between women's rights and children's rights provides an example of the value of this approach. Often the rights of particular populations are treated as unrelated to each other. In certain instances, distinctions are understandable, for example, women confront special issues and abuses that children may not, and vice versa. However, women's rights can do much to further children's rights, and children's rights can improve the lives of girls so they develop better positioned to exercise their full range of rights as adult women.

As a threshold matter, women's rights law, which requires equality among men and women, applies to all stages of life and should be used to ensure that girls and boys have equal opportunities. At the same time, children's rights law covers a broad range of rights that can help ensure that young girls grow into adult women able to exercise all of their rights. Ensuring equality for girls from early childhood will help address a host of issues ranging from female infanticide to education preference for boys. As trafficking networks prey on girls and boys as young as five and six years old, early intervention is vital.

Education preference offers an important example of the need to address gender-based discrimination early. Education preference manifests when poor families elect to keep sons, rather than daughters, in school. Girls then obtain lower levels of education, enter the workforce at younger ages with more limited skills and thus are physically and mentally more vulnerable to exploitation, including via the sex trade. When these girls become women, they are more likely to be disadvantaged and less able to exercise their rights.

Moreover, if women's rights are suppressed, this has indirect effects on all children. In the overwhelming majority of families around the world, women are the primary caretakers of children, and thus children's well-being affects women's opportunities. In addition, women in many parts of the world also do work more than men outside the home (UNPF, 2005). Impeding the rights of women (for example, through employment discrimination, denial of bank loans and other forms of credit, and other means) will negatively impact on the children in their care. Accordingly, ensuring the rights and well-being of children (both girls and boys) requires due regard for women's rights.

Addressing individual rights holistically across different groups can facilitate the advancement of all individuals. Furthering women's and children's rights simultaneously can enable girls to have greater opportunities and develop into adult women positioned to exercise their rights; empower women and girls to exercise greater control over their bodies in sexual relations; and facilitate women's access to economic opportunities and equality in property rights, reducing their and their children's vulnerability to exploitation.

Tackling the various forms of discrimination is a major endeavour. However, ultimately, its far-reaching impact requires that discrimination be addressed in order to make progress on the supply and demand issues underlying the incidence of sex trafficking.

The right to birth registration

Traffickers prey on easy targets, such as undocumented children. It is easier to falsify their age and identity, making unregistered children more susceptible to sex trafficking and other forms of exploitation (see Chapter Ten, this volume). Consequently, the right to birth registration – the official recording of a child's birth – is an integral step to ensuring a child's well-being, as it establishes the child's existence under law, providing the basis for many rights of the child. It is essential to establishing a child's nationality and citizenship. It also helps prove a child's age, thereby allowing children to avail themselves of all legal protections available (UNICEF, 2002).

Birth registration is a basic step that most people in industrialised countries take for granted. Yet globally, an estimated 50 million children go unregistered each year (UNICEF, 2002). Without birth registration, a child does not exist in a government's records, and establishing citizenship can be problematic. Failure to register a child's birth also means community health workers may not know a child is missing essential immunisations, and schools may be unaware of a school-age child not enrolled. Equally important, many children are denied access to healthcare and education because their births are not registered and thus they do not have proper identification. If children do not have access to healthcare and education, they begin a downward spiral that increases vulnerability to the worst forms of child exploitation.

The child's right to birth registration is enshrined in several human rights treaties (CRC, ICCPR, African Charter),[4] and is considered a civil and political right. Accordingly, a state must ensure the right to birth registration to every child subject to its jurisdiction without discrimination of any kind. Of course, birth registration alone will not guarantee children's subsequent rights; however, failure to register births increases the likelihood that children suffer human rights violations. Therefore, comprehensive birth registration campaigns must be a part of any strategy aimed at combating child sex trafficking. It is a simple, low-cost step, yet the dividends can be great, especially for marginalised children who risk going unregistered and being left vulnerable to traffickers.

Health rights

Health rights are another foundational component in ensuring every child has the opportunity for a fair start in life. When health rights are jeopardised, the realisation of other rights – such as education rights – are put at risk, prompting a downward spiral that leaves the most vulnerable children exposed to potential human rights violations, including sex trafficking.

At the most basic level, a child's survival is at stake when health rights are in doubt. Even when interference with health rights is not fatal, the effects can be dramatic. Poor health hinders children's performance in school. Malnourished and ill children miss more days of school, often under-perform when at school and are at greater risk of falling behind their peers (UNESCO, 2001). This increases the likelihood that a child will drop out of school earlier. When children leave school early, they enter the workforce earlier with fewer skills and are at greater risk of exploitation.

Under international law, children's health rights include three key components: (1) the right to the highest attainable standard of health; (2) the right to access healthcare services; and (3) states' obligations to address particular healthcare issues relevant to children (ICESCR, Article 12; CRC, Article 24).

First, the major economic and social rights instruments each use a similar formulation related to health, requiring that states parties work to ensure each individual's 'right to the highest attainable standard of health' (ICESCR, Article 12(1); CRC, Article 24). In ensuring the right to the highest attainable standard of health, states must address all aspects of health, including both physical and mental well-being (ICESCR, Article 12(1)).

By affirming that every individual has the right to the 'highest attainable standard of health', international law acknowledges two important variables – differences among individuals and among countries. First, not all individuals are able to enjoy the same level of good health. Human rights law recognises that, at best, states can only ensure their populations will have the opportunity to enjoy the best health possible for each of them as individuals. Second, human rights law acknowledges that countries differ from each other in terms of available resources (CESCR, 2000). Chad does not have the means to provide the level of health services that Canada can afford (Canada's per capita healthcare expenditure is US$3,173, whereas Chad's is US$42; UNDP, 2007). International law recognises that certain countries have more limited resources and utilises flexible language to make health rights meaningful in all countries. In all cases, however, the obligation remains one of progressive realisation of every child's rights.

The second legal requirement incorporated in the right to health is that states ensure individuals' access to healthcare, treatment and facilities (CRC, Article 24(1); ICESCR, Article 12(d)). A fundamental component of this requirement is ensuring access for all without discrimination of any kind, as mandated by international law on discrimination. In this regard, the Committee on Economic, Social and Cultural Rights – the body responsible for monitoring states parties' compliance with the relevant international Covenant – has emphasised that the ICESCR prohibits all forms of discrimination in access to healthcare. Similarly, the CRC's requirement that 'no child [be] deprived of his or her right of access to such health care services', when combined with the prohibition on discrimination, obliges states to ensure that children in the most marginalised communities receive access to healthcare services as other children do (CRC, Article 24(1)).

Third, international law requires states parties to take steps to address specific health issues, including infant and child mortality, pre- and post-natal care and the provision of primary healthcare services (CRC, Article 24(2)). The expectation is that states will demonstrate progress over time, providing better healthcare to all children in these areas vital to survival and development.

Given the requirements of international law and the ongoing health challenges confronting states, especially poorer countries, greater efforts are needed to foster full implementation of children's health rights in order to help children minimise their risk of exploitation. One important component of this work is identification and allocation of sufficient resources, given that states' obligations under economic and social rights law are tied to available resources (CRC, Article 4).

Determining whether a state is meeting its obligations to identify and employ the maximum extent of its available resources is a fact-specific inquiry. For countries with more limited resources, the obligation remains progressive implementation of these rights. A commitment to progressive realisation of health rights can be reflected, at least in part, in government spending trends. For example, if a state's gross domestic product (GDP) is increasing each year, but its healthcare budget is not, one could argue that the state is not using its 'maximum available resources' to achieve the progressive realisation of these rights and is therefore failing to meet its international obligations. Budget analysis can help monitor states' practices to ensure they do not use the resource-qualifying language of economic and social rights law as an excuse to not pursue full implementation of children's rights (Fundar et al, 2004).

Budget analysis can also suggest areas in which there may be discrimination in the provision of healthcare services. Prohibitions on discrimination are not qualified by available resources. Additionally, budget analysis can highlight the areas where government has failed to spend allocated funds. Although budget analysis has limitations (for example, it does not reveal whether a state is utilising resources effectively), it can provide useful information that is a starting point for determining whether a country is using its 'maximum available resources'. Combining budget analysis with the content of specific provisions, such as health rights, can enable scholars and advocates to assess with greater precision states' compliance with human rights law.

Holding states more accountable for ensuring economic and social rights will lead to greater implementation of health rights. In turn, if states implement and enforce health rights, it will foster better health for at-risk populations. With better health, children can pursue their education more successfully, leading to greater opportunities in the future, and adults can pursue employment opportunities that will hopefully keep their families out of poverty and away from the dangers of trafficking and the sex trade.

The right to education

Despite the importance of education in ensuring that children have economic opportunities in adulthood, more than 70 million children of primary school age are not enrolled in school (UNESCO, 2007). Education keeps children out of exploitative environments (in addition to providing long-term benefits). An estimated 218 million children work for a living, with 126 million of them engaged in hazardous work (ILO, 2006). Children are pressed to work in a variety of settings, including as prostitutes, domestic servants, agricultural workers and factory workers. The less education a child receives, the earlier they enter the workforce and the more limited their skills are, making them a prime target for traffickers.

International law recognises every child's right to education (CRC, Article 28(1); ICESCR, Article 13(1)). Under international law, states' obligations with respect to education include three essential components: (1) ensuring access to education for all; (2) complying with the different requirements for each of the three levels of education (primary, secondary and higher education); and (3) progressively providing better educational opportunities over time.

A central tenet in education is that it be truly accessible for all. One notable obstacle to education is discrimination. Marginalised populations suffer most, resulting in their children being out of school and more likely targets for sex traffickers. Successful implementation of education rights requires states to combat discrimination and also to ensure birth registration, health rights and related rights.

As discussed earlier, the non-discrimination clauses of human rights treaties guard against discriminatory practices in all societal sectors, and they must be taken into account in the context of education. Even in situations where children are not prevented from attending school because of discrimination, they may still be forced to drop out of school for financial reasons. Children of poor families forced to miss school because they must earn money to support themselves and their siblings require additional support from the state to realise their right to education. States must eliminate obstacles that force children to leave school, to make education accessible for all and to comply with their obligations under international law.

Second, international law imposes different levels of obligation on states parties for primary, secondary and higher education. States are required to make primary education 'compulsory and available free to all' and secondary education 'available and accessible' to every child (CRC, Article 28(1)). With respect to higher education, states are required to make it 'accessible to all on the basis of capacity by every appropriate means' (CRC, Article 28(1)). For many poorer countries with large numbers of young children out of school, higher education is a secondary priority. The less stringent obligation under international law is an acknowledgment of that situation.

Third, states must fulfil the critical requirement of progressive realisation of the right to education. In other words, although the strongest obligation resides at the primary education level, states cannot stop after providing the minimum. There must be a concerted effort to enable children to achieve higher levels of education. This is essential to breaking the cycle of poverty and enabling families to live beyond mere subsistence and survival.

Full implementation of the right to education is of paramount importance as education is a foundation on which other rights are built. If children do not receive an education, they will be less equipped to exercise other civil, political, economic, social and cultural rights, and at greater risk of exploitation. Moreover, education is an important component of development, and its realisation strengthens communities.

As with health rights and other economic and social rights, states' obligations vis-à-vis education rights are subject to available resources. Therefore, budget analysis can again prove to be a useful tool in determining what a country is able to provide and, accordingly, must provide. Education can be a vehicle for breaking the cycle of poverty and reducing the incidence of sex trafficking. If governments see their mission only as ensuring basic literacy and providing primary school education to all, it will be more difficult for children to break the cycle of poverty. Children must have opportunities beyond primary education, for their full development and the development of their communities and countries. And human rights law requires it.

Labour rights

In seeking to ensure the rights and well-being of children, we must consider the context in which they are situated. Children, especially young children, rely on parents, guardians and other adults to help ensure and safeguard their rights and well-being. Therefore, as parents suffer, so often do children. Ensuring children's rights requires an holistic approach not only in terms of rights considered but also in terms of attentiveness to family well-being. A key component of this is ensuring that parents and guardians have economic opportunities enabling them to support and provide for their children.

Labour rights are a core component of fostering opportunities for adults that, in turn, enable them to be able to provide for their children. More broadly, they are important to the sustainable development of communities. Labour laws that protect against exploitation and provide special family-related protection measures, such as appropriate leave and job protection for pregnant women, help ensure the financial well-being of families and their children (IADB, 1999).

In the context of trafficking, many who are trafficked initially leave their home and community because there are no opportunities for work at home and thus they need to move to find work in order to survive (*The Economist*, 2000; Dinan, 2008). They subsequently get trapped by trafficking networks. Labour rights and economic opportunities and development are keys therefore to strengthening communities and making families and their children less vulnerable to exploitation.

Preventing sex trafficking of children

Preventing sex trafficking of children will require a comprehensive, multisector approach. States must redouble their efforts to combat sex trafficking and to comply fully with the requirements of the international law on child sex trafficking. In addition, states must reorient their focus to address the root causes of this issue.

An holistic human rights approach offers the prospect of addressing the root causes of child sex trafficking. The task is not easy. In the multi-billion dollar industry of sex trafficking, the incentives for perpetrators of these abuses are great. The challenge for governments and child advocates is enormous. However, a human rights approach can reduce vulnerability of at-risk children, foster development and strengthen communities. The rights discussed here are central to a human rights approach to addressing child sex trafficking. That they are enshrined in human rights law means that these rights are not merely moral principles but that they impose legal requirements on states to act. These legal obligations are ones that states have undertaken voluntarily. Advocates for children must press their governments to implement these rights fully to help ensure the well-being of children and reduce their risk of exploitation from sex trafficking.

Notes

[1] This chapter draws on Todres (2006).

[2] The Palermo Protocol (2000), entered into force in 2003 (see Chapter Five, this volume); and Optional Protocol to the Convention on the Rights of the Child on the Sale of Children, Child Prostitution and Child Pornography (OPSC) (2000), entered into force in 2002 (CRC Protocol).

[3] CRC: Convention on the Rights of the Child (1989), entered into force 1990; CEDAW: Convention on the Elimination of all forms of Discrimination Against Women (1979), entered into force 1981; ICCPR: International Covenant on Civil and Political Rights (1966), entered into force 1976; ICESCR: International Covenant on Economic, Social and Cultural Rights (1966), entered into force 1976.

[4] CRC and ICCPR, see note 3; African Charter on the Rights and Welfare of the Child (1990), entered into force 1999.

References

Bond, J. (2003) 'International intersectionality: a theoretical and pragmatic exploration of women's international human rights violations', *Emory Law Journal*, vol 52, no 1, pp 71-186.

Buergenthal, T. (1981) 'To respect and to ensure: state obligations and permissible derogations', in L. Henkin (ed) *The International Bill of Rights*, New York, NY: Columbia University Press, pp 72-91.

Burke, A. and Ducci, S. (2006) *Trafficking in minors for commercial sexual exploitation: Thailand*, UNICRI, Torino (accessed 2009 from www.unicri.it/wwd/trafficking/minors/docs/dr_thailand.pdf).

CESCR (Committee on Economic, Social and Cultural Rights) (2000) *The right to the highest attainable standard of health*, E/12/2000/4, CESCR General Comment 14.

Dinan, K. (2008) 'Globalization and national sovereignty: from migration to trafficking', in S. Cameron and E. Newman (eds) *Trafficking in humans: Social, cultural and political dimensions*, New York, NY: United Nations University Press, pp 58-79.

Economist, The (2000) 'Trafficking in women – in the shadows', *Editorial*, 26 August, p 38.

Fundar – Centro de Análisis e Investigación, IHRIP (International Human Rights Internship Program) and IBP (International Budget Project) (2004) *Dignity counts: A guide to using budget analysis to advance human rights*, Mexico City: Fundar, IHRIP and IBP.

HRW (Human Rights Watch) (2001) *Caste discrimination*, New York, NY: HRW.

HRW (2003) *Double standards: Women's property rights: Violations in Kenya*, New York, NY: HRW.

HRW (2005) *A dose of reality: Women's rights in the fight against HIV/AIDS*, New York, NY: HRW.

IADB (Inter-American Development Bank) (1999) *Facing up to inequality in Latin America*, Washington, DC: IADB.

ILO (International Labour Organization) (2001) *An ILO code of practice on HIV/AIDS and the world of work*, Geneva: ILO.

ILO (2006) *The end of child labour: Within reach*, Geneva: ILO.

Lyons, H. (1998) 'The representation of trafficking in persons' in H.J.M. Johnston and S. Khan (eds) *Trafficking in persons in South Asia*, Calgary: Shastri Indo-Canadian Institute, pp 100-19.

Malone, L. (1997) 'Protecting the least respected: the girl child and the gender bias of the Vienna Convention's adoption and reservation regime', *William & Mary Journal of Women & the Law*, vol 3, no 1, pp 1-28.

Thianthai, C. (2005) 'Gender and class differences in young people's sexuality and HIV/AIDS risk-taking behaviours in Thailand', *Culture, Health and Sexuality*, vol 6, pp 189-90.

Todres, J. (2006) 'The importance of "other rights" in preventing sex trafficking', *Cardozo Journal of Law and Gender*, vol 12, pp 885-907.

UNAIDS et al (2004) *Women and HIV/AIDS: Confronting the crisis*, New York, NY: UNAIDS.

UN (United Nations) Development Fund for Women (1996) *Trafficking in women and children*, UNIFEM Gender Fact Sheet No 2 (www.unifem-eseasia.org/resources/factsheets/UNIFEMSheet2.pdf).

UNDP (United Nations Development Programme) (2007) *Human development report 2007-2008*, New York, NY: UNDP.

UNESCO (2001) *Focusing resources on effective school health* (www.freshschools.org/Documents/FRESHandEFA-English.pdf).

UNESCO (2007) *Education: Regional sum of primary school age children out of school*, Institute of Statistics (http://stats.uis.unesco.org/unesco/ReportFolders/ReportFolders.aspx).

UNICEF (2002) *Birth registration: Right from the start* (www.unicef-icdc.org/publications/pdf/digest9e.pdf).

UNPF (United Nations Population Fund) (2005) *State of the world population*, New York, NY: UNPF.

eight

Child rights, culture and exploitation: UK experiences of child trafficking

Farhat Bokhari and Emma Kelly

> It is vital to listen to children, as well as involving them as actors in efforts to enhance child protection. (Dotteridge, 2008, p 11)

Introduction

The plight of children trafficked across or within countries has recently been headline news in the UK and internationally. Increasing awareness has seen a concurrent rise in policy and practice responses by government, practitioners and civil society groups. In the UK, international legislation has been ratified, multiagency national and local protocols developed, advocacy campaigns conducted and research reports published. Yet contradictions remain, and at the heart of these lie problems in listening to the views of children, attitudes towards different cultures and what constitutes exploitation and inconsistencies in best practice when applying child protection principles to safeguarding migrant children, including trafficked children.

The true magnitude of child trafficking in the UK is difficult to gauge given its covert nature, the difficulty in identifying children and the lack of a systematic and centralised data collection system. According to an analysis by the Child Exploitation and Online Protection Centre (CEOP) (see Chapter Six, this volume), 325 children were trafficked into the UK between March 2007 and February 2008 for a multitude of purposes including: sexual exploitation, domestic servitude, forced marriage, drug trafficking, unregulated adoption, cannabis cultivation and other forms of criminal activity, benefit fraud and other forms of labour exploitation (CEOP, 2009).

Despite these varied forms of exploitation the media have tended to focus on children being trafficked for sexual exploitation to the exclusion of more hidden forms of trafficking. These more invisible forms include child trafficking for domestic servitude, mainly through unregulated private fostering arrangements, and child trafficking for forced marriage. These trafficked children are hidden because they live in a domestic family environment rather than being exploited by organised criminals. Their exploitation may be seen as 'normal' and for their betterment, by their exploiters, their community and sometimes the children themselves. British experience has shown that professionals may also view these types of cases as acceptable cultural practices within certain communities. These attitudes, although borne out of government multicultural policies to respect diversity, have had contradictory effects, leading to a homogenised view of migrant and UK minority cultures to the disadvantage of protecting children in such cases. The result has been confusion and professional paralysis where child rights and child protection principles should be paramount.

Furthermore, despite sometimes harrowing accounts of abuse at the hands of traffickers, agencies appear to be sceptical of migrant children's experiences of trafficking. Whether this is because such children are largely seen as economic migrants, or criminals falsely seeking asylum, or even adults pretending to be children, the consequences of official disbelief are serious for children. Their ages can be disputed, thus denying them child services support and leaving them vulnerable to continuing abuse. They can be detained and then deported without any risk assessment as to the situation to which they would be returning. However, the vast majority of trafficked children remain hidden within specific communities and it continues to be a challenge to identify and protect them (UNICEF, 2003).

We draw on our research and fieldwork experience in a reflective attempt to analyse these dilemmas and move forward using a child rights perspective based on the UN Convention on the Rights of the Child (CRC) (1989). The overarching principle of the CRC is to ensure the best interest of the child and for a child 'who is capable of forming his or her own views, the right to express those views freely in all matters affecting the child, the views of the child being given due weight in accordance with the age and maturity of the child' (CRC, Article 12).

Children trafficked from West Africa into the UK

The first professional recognition of child trafficking into the UK was specifically in relation to West African children trafficked for the purposes of commercial sexual exploitation. In 1995, West Sussex Social Services identified a trend of young Nigerian girls arriving at Gatwick airport, claiming asylum, being accommodated by the local authority and subsequently disappearing (AFRUCA, 2007). Some children went missing soon after arrival and others later on while in public care (Beddoe, 2007). Seemingly, some were trafficked out of the UK to Italy and Spain to be exploited there (Harris and Robinson, 2007). By 2001, West Sussex Social Services had a list of 71 missing children, including 40 West African girls and 14 boys; all were probably trafficked for commercial sexual exploitation (McFaydean, 2001). While Nigeria was the first identified source country and remains a key starting place for children trafficked into the UK (CEOP,

2009), other children have been discovered from Ghana, Benin, the Ivory Coast, Mali, Cameroon, Guinea, Liberia and Sierra Leone.

Further evidence of West African children being trafficked into the UK has emerged with a particular recognition of female child victims being trafficked for sexual exploitation or domestic servitude. These trends were made explicit in the 2007 government study into the extent of child trafficking in the UK (Kapoor, 2007). Sixty-one West African girls were identified aged between 12 and 17. The youngest child, aged 12, was trafficked for domestic servitude and a girl of 14 identified as the youngest victim of sexual exploitation. Although a number of West African countries were represented as source countries, by far the largest source country was Nigeria.

By 2009, the number of West African children identified by statutory authorities had reduced, perhaps reflecting reductions in the number of West African children entering the UK, a result of changes to accompanied minors visa policy (CEOP, 2009). In 2009, 33 West African children were identified, 27 of them female. A similar age range was noted, the majority of the girls being in the mid- to late teens, with three children entering the UK at eight or nine years of age. Male victims were much younger at point of entry, with ages ranging from 4 to 16. As well as being brought into the UK for exploitation, some West African children were also then trafficked on to other countries.

Vulnerabilities in source country

The reasons for children leaving their source country are both simple and complex. The simplest driving force for many of these children and their parents is the desire for a better education and a better life. The complexity of the situation lies in the uniqueness of each child's circumstances and while some children are sent abroad by their parents or primary carers, others act independently. Some may enter into agreements with agents knowing that they will be required to perform labour; others will entrust themselves into the care of strangers genuinely believing the stories of the likely benefits to them (Blagbrough, 2008: and see also Chapter Four, this volume). The problems of survival and success are manifold, with children being put under significant pressure economically to support their natural families as well as to improve their own life chances (CEOP, 2009).

Within West Africa, two key factors contribute to creating opportunities for children to be recruited and exploited through trafficking – migration and 'fosterage' (see Chapter Twelve, this volume). These factors play a role in the perception and identification of victims in the UK. Large numbers of children migrate in West Africa, either alone or with their families, within their country of origin or to a neighbouring country (UNICEF, 2005). Most children migrate to find work, often moving from rural communities to areas that have a specific demand for labour, or to cities. While the primary driver may be the need to obtain work, it has also been argued that migration forms part of a socialisation process (UNICEF, 2005; Hashim, 2006). For instance, in Ghana's northern region, some girls will feel it necessary to save and provide for their wedding, so 'they migrate to seek work to purchase these items' (ECPAT International, 2008, p 14). The fact of moving to another area means that they will end up living with no parental or community supervision, rendering them more vulnerable to recruitment by agents and traffickers.

Girls are also subject to a well-established practice that is known as fosterage, where a child finds work with another family, usually some distance from their own family. Their role within the family is to cook and clean, as well as looking after other children. These arrangements may be made among families, between distant friends or by recruitment agents, often termed 'aunties' (Blagbrough, 2008; Dotteridge, 2008). If formal agents are involved, they can be either a protective factor in the girl's life or a primary source of abuse (UNICEF, 2005). The potential for exploitation in these situations is well documented (Blagbrough, 2008; ECPAT International, 2008) with some children then being passed or sold on to families living in the UK or other European countries.

Mr and Mrs Quainoo, an accountant and teacher respectively, were recently imprisoned for 18 months for trafficking a Ghanaian girl into the UK. The couple created a false birth certificate, changed the girl's name and claimed she was their daughter to assist with her visa application in Ghana. The girl, 14 years old at the time, thought she was coming to the UK for an education, as did her mother who had given her consent to the arrangement. In the UK, the girl was made to work in the Quainoo's house and to look after their two children. She was never paid. She was not allowed to go to school, could not make any friends and was given second-hand clothes to wear. After two years, she managed to escape and went to her local social services department. On discovery, the couple claimed that the girl tricked them by using 'voodoo'.

Source: Howe (2008)

Exploitation in the UK through domestic servitude

Significant anecdotal information exists about girls brought to the UK for the purposes of domestic servitude (Beddoe, 2007; CEOP, 2009; Kelly, 2009). While some children have been identified as domestic slaves, the majority may go undetected for many years (CEOP, 2009; Kelly, 2009). A typical narrative involves a girl recruited from home to work and live with a family in a European country. Once in the UK, having entered often as an accompanied child on a visa, she is forced to work for a family while locked up in their home. The promises of an education and a better life are replaced with the reality of looking after someone else's children and home, and not being allowed to leave the property. Some children will be subject to physical and sexual abuse and suffer from many of the typical characteristics of neglect: no education or healthcare, lack of food, inappropriate or no sleeping arrangements (Ayrio, 2007). In the main, these children are identified only after many years of exploitation, either because they are told to leave or they manage to escape (AFRUCA, 2008). Even then, many are fearful of reporting their experiences.

Vulnerabilities in the UK

Within the UK, children trafficked from West Africa remain hidden and exploited. In large part this stems from the domestic nature of their exploitation; the fact it happens in a home behind closed doors makes it near impossible to detect. This invisibility is furthered by a tacit acceptance of migration to and fosterage in the UK as customary practices; acceptance is both from local communities and the professionals tasked with safeguarding children.

Private fostering

Private fostering arrangements in the UK echo the fosterage systems of West Africa with children living with other families in unregulated environments. Utting's comment in 1996 remains as valid today: 'this is a situation that cannot be tolerated. These must surely be the most vulnerable of children living away from home' (quoted in Stuart and Baines, 2004, p 74). It has long been recognised that West African children are particularly likely to be privately fostered in the UK (Bostock, 2003), although historically this has involved West African children being placed with white families from the 1960s onwards (Peart, 2005). By 1991, a study into private fostering in London showed that 6,000 to 9,000 children were privately fostered and that 80% to 90% of these children were of West African origin (Bostock, 2003). The majority of these children are likely to be protected and cared for but where are the mechanisms for identifying risk given that the practice is perceived to be one of custom? Identification of exploitation through domestic servitude of West African children arguably rests with the UK West African communities, and this is one of the challenges. It relies on community members recognising that a situation is abusive and a violation of a customary practice, and then having the courage to report it. Some of the barriers to such identification are the myth that domestic work is important training for later life and that it is a safe practice as the child is within a family context (Blagbrough, 2008). A recent survey for the British Association for Adoption and Fostering (BAAF, 2009) illustrated that 22% of the public would not do anything if an unknown child moved in next door and 7% would not act if that child then disappeared. Research with young people who had been trafficked for domestic servitude reiterates the lack of opportunity for identification; in their opinion the only possible place where someone could identify their situation earlier would have been in a place of worship (Wirtz, 2010).

Migration

The Climbié Inquiry[1] made reference to the customary practice of sending children to live with a family in another country, with the Inquiry chair, Lord Laming, noting that: 'I have seen evidence which shows that entrusting children to relatives living in Europe who can offer financial and educational opportunities unavailable in the Ivory Coast is not uncommon in Victoria's parents' society' (Laming, 2003).

Lord Laming declined to comment on the appropriateness of this practice, thus denying the opportunity for professional debate on the safeguarding measures required for West African children migrating to the UK. It is the perceived normality of such arrangements that makes it far harder for UK professionals to challenge families who have a non-related child living with them. As a result the practitioners who are in a position to identify West African children who have migrated to the UK are often afraid to report these arrangements to the local authority for fear of being accused of a breach of confidentiality and losing all contact with a family already perceived to be on the margins of society (BAAF, 2006). Practitioners may well recognise these dilemmas but choose not to investigate further for fear of discovering a situation that they do not feel confident of responding to (Kelly, 2009; Pearce et al, 2009).

Child trafficking for forced marriage in the UK

The UK government recognises forced marriage as a form of domestic violence and child abuse, but it is also argued that 'forced marriage, where it involves the movement of a child for exploitation, is a manifestation of human trafficking' (Bokhari, 2009, p 7). Children, mainly girls, forced into marriage experience a number of human rights abuses including sexual assault and rape, enforced pregnancy and abortion, physical and emotional violence, domestic servitude, isolation and being prevented from leaving the house. Ways of preventing such marriages from taking place and ensuring the safety and well-being of children who are already in forced marriages are two key challenges with which practitioners are faced.

Forty-eight cases of this nature, including suspicions of the intent to force a child into a marriage, were documented covering a period of three years, from 2006 to 2008 (Bokhari, 2009). This research shows that British-born children have been trafficked out of the UK to be forcibly married abroad, and migrant children have arrived into the UK (sometimes on forged identity documents making them appear older) having been forced into a marriage in their country of birth to a UK citizen. In the most hidden cases of all it is believed children may be forcibly married in the UK. British girls – 13- to 15-year-olds – were taken mainly to countries such as Bangladesh and Pakistan but also to Iraq, Iran, Somalia and in one case to France. Migrant girls from Somalia, Iraq, Iran and Bangladesh were forced into marriage in their country of birth, then brought to the UK to live with their British spouse. Due to a combination of factors, these migrant girls can be particularly invisible in the UK and often live in harsh circumstances of domestic servitude and violence (Bokhari, 2009). Other studies have identified suspicions of underage marriage involving Somali females (Beddoe, 2007) and Romanian Roma children (CEOP, 2009) brought into the UK for marriage. The government agency designated with forced marriage casework and policy, the Forced Marriage Unit (FMU), deals with about 300 or more cases of forced marriage per year, of which 30% comprise children, mainly girls, under 18 years old (Home Office, 2007).

Why children are vulnerable

British and migrant children are vulnerable to trafficking for forced marriage for a number of interconnected reasons. For UK families, their child's marriage may be motivated by wanting to maintain kinship ties, control female sexuality and prevent unwanted relationships, improve their economic position both in the UK and abroad, and/or for close kin spouses to gain permanent residence in the UK (Brandon and Hafez, 2008; Bokhari, 2009). The pressure to marry a child may come from relatives outside the UK and for British families this combines with a strong sense of obligation to take precedence over a child's choice or consent (Shaw, 2001; Eade and Yunas, 2002).

Whereas deception and coercion are widely used in forcing British children into marriages abroad, migrant children may be coerced and also may obey their parents out of a sense of obligation and not see themselves as being exploited. Families and communities may hold a different view of childhood and see children of a certain age as mature enough to marry or see marriage as protection in a culture that connects their daughter's virtue with family honour.

European studies have also shown how child marriage has been used to recruit girls for sexual exploitation (ECPAT UK Law Enforcement Group, 2004). In regions where child marriage is widely practised, traffickers find it relatively easy to convince girls and their families into agreeing to a child marriage or the promise of one in the hope that marriage and travel abroad in a new country will improve the child's life. In other cases children and adolescents may be motivated to accept such offers to escape familial violence and abuse.

It is important to note the existence of diversity among family formations and marriage practices even within the same community to avoid received views of family orthodoxies and cultural practices. While bearing this in mind, in certain communities in the UK, arranged marriages are prevalent. In describing an arranged marriage the UK government has stated, 'the families of both spouses take a leading role in arranging the marriage. The spouses have the right to choose – to say no – at any time', whereas in a 'forced marriage there is no choice' (Home Office, 2000). In practice it is a challenge to distinguish between a child of legal marriageable age forced into a marriage and one whose marriage is arranged, if the child does not self-identify as having undergone a forced marriage, but instead sees the marriage as arranged and culturally acceptable (Gangoli et al, 2006). It is widely acknowledged that children under the age of 18 are emotionally, physically and financially dependent on their parents and thus vulnerable to parental coercion and manipulation, key methods employed by parents and families in cases of forced marriage.

Further research into structural and material processes, such as the impact of globalisation on transnational marriage patterns, would help to widen the debate on the vulnerabilities children face in trafficking for forced marriage.

UK as a source country

A typical scenario is where British girls, predominately from a South Asian or Middle Eastern background, are taken abroad, either unaware of an impending marriage or having been coerced into agreeing to a marriage. Once abroad they often face physical and psychological violence, documents are removed and movements closely monitored so they cannot leave or seek help. After the marriage ceremony they may be left in the country abroad, sometimes never to return to the UK. Many, however, are brought back, some expected to sponsor their husbands to live in the UK.

Detecting children or young people at risk of a forced marriage at ports of entry or exit can be challenging given that they are travelling with their family and often unaware of the real reason for the trip. When a child is reported as missing the FMU will try to trace their location and repatriate them to the UK. This is not, however, always possible because of problems of access in destination countries or lack of information. This is why women's rights agencies and the FMU stress that all child safeguarding agencies need to prioritise identifying children vulnerable to a potential forced marriage before they are taken out of the UK. These children are particularly invisible but agencies that are trained and familiar with forced marriage and child trafficking indicators are better equipped to identify these cases (HM Government, 2009; LSCB, 2009). This invisibility is compounded by multifaceted factors where children may be too afraid of the repercussions to themselves or their family and thus not seek help, communities may consider these practices as acceptable and 'normal' or be afraid of calling attention to themselves for fear of 'Islamaphobia' by the wider British community (Eade and Yunas, 2002) and not report cases they are aware of. Individuals and organisations may fear ostracism and other repercussions in speaking out against such practices and even though forced marriage has been integrated into domestic violence and child abuse policy, professionals may continue to view it as a cultural and private family matter and fail to take appropriate action when cases do present.

'Sakina' is 19 years old, born and brought up in the UK:

I first left home on March 19th. My dad wanted to get me married. So I ran away.

The guy I was supposed to get married to was my cousin. I saw him for the first time on a video. My mother said 'that's him – that's the one you're going to marry. You're gonna marry him, you are'. Since such a young age you get told that you'll get married. You think that it worked out for everyone else and so it'll work out for you. But I told my parents 'no, I don't want to get married' and they didn't listen. My mum said 'what's wrong with my cousins?' They put the guilt on you.

Because I didn't get married to him, they gave him my sister instead – that's what it's like. She's in Pakistan now. She's 16 and she's pregnant. They had promised me verbally to him and his family when I was born. But now because I've run away they've given my sister to him instead. My sister blames me because she's in this situation – she's three months pregnant and has been married for four months. My dad won't bring her back 'til she's had the baby. He's afraid that she'll have an abortion. It doesn't matter to them what happens to her – they got what they wanted – they got the land that his family had.

After I went back I wasn't allowed out; I wasn't allowed to do anything. The community thinks that if you do a runner, you're sleeping around. Sometimes I think maybe I'll just go back and do whatever they say – just because it's easier.

Source: Brandon and Hafez (2008, p 13)

UK as a destination country

Adolescent girls, particularly from Eastern Europe, have long been known to be trafficked into Western European countries, including the UK, on promises of marriage, as fiancées or girlfriends, but on reaching their destination are forced into sexual exploitation (ECPAT UK Law Enforcement Group, 2004; ECPAT International, 2008). They enter the UK accompanied by their trafficker 'boyfriend' or meet him soon after arrival. Since many belong to EEC member countries they have visa-free entry into the UK and do not raise any concerns at ports of entry or exit.

Many of these girls are leaving situations of family breakdown and violence, existing sexual exploitation in the home country's sex industry or economic instability in their countries. Their aspirations are those of other children seeking to migrate for a better life and they are just as vulnerable to recruitment by traffickers who befriend them. Some girls may travel abroad independently with a marriage arranged through a marriage broker (ECPAT UK Law Enforcement Group, 2004). In the UK, these girls are sold and sexually exploited in suburban locations, typically locked up, controlled with threats of violence to themselves or their families abroad should they escape, and debt bondage involves them having to pay traffickers a 'debt' far higher than they can ever repay (Kapoor, 2007). Like the West African girls sexually exploited in the UK, a few of these girls may escape or be abandoned by traffickers if they become pregnant.

Girls from South Asian, Middle Eastern and African countries are also married to British men abroad and brought to the UK. Some of these are underage marriages, as legally defined by both UK law and the civil law of the country where the marriage takes place. In cases where the girl is older than the legal minimum age of marriage but still under 18 it is debatable whether she has given her free and informed consent to the marriage. It could be a case of exploitation where there is evidence that the marriage consists of domestic and sexual servitude, physical or psychological violence and severe restrictions on outside contact or movement. Often such cases only come to light when an adult woman seeks help for domestic violence and only later discloses her underage or forced marriage, which even she may have considered 'normal' at the time (Gangoli et al, 2006). This is partly to do with notions of honour and shame in some communities where disclosing family problems to anyone outside the family or community is considered shameful. This acts as a strong deterrent to girls disclosing domestic abuse (Izzidien, 2008) and makes such cases particularly hidden and difficult for professionals to detect.

Police, alerted by other agencies (non-governmental organisations [NGOs], social workers or the FMU) have investigated forced marriage cases involving domestic servitude and violence by husbands and in-laws. If these girls have an irregular immigration status they are deemed as unqualified for support (except for healthcare and employment) by the local authority and not provided with accommodation. Their options are limited: temporary accommodation in a women's refuge or deportation without a risk assessment (Amnesty International UK and Southall Black Sisters, 2008). Women's groups find that the legal and financial implications of obtaining residency are a major obstacle to these girls seeking help (Khanum, 2008).

Conclusion

Children, whether alone or accompanied by an adult, migrate within their countries and across borders for diverse reasons and circumstances. Not all of them will be exploited.

However, cultural traditions of migrating for domestic work within private fostering arrangements and child marriage do make children vulnerable to exploitation and abuse. Children exploited and abused through these practices are likely to remain hidden and invisible as long as families and local communities fail to recognise or report the abuse and child safeguarding professionals fail to take action. Trafficked children, in common with victims of domestic abuse, rarely self-disclose and may not see their experience as exploitative or use terms such as 'trafficking' when describing their experiences.

For the practitioner, the process of assessment and identification involves building trust with children to enable them to reveal their experience, history, family circumstances and journey of being trafficked. Core to this process is for adults to believe the child, however fantastical their account may be. British minority ethnic children forced into marriages abroad may be more aware of their rights, but still have a deep distrust of adults by whom they feel betrayed and be reluctant to approach mainstream agencies they feel may not understand their background or needs (Izzidien, 2008). Practitioners should apply their existing knowledge and expertise on child abuse to such cases with the aim of ensuring the safety of a child, whatever the child's background or family context. In the recent Laming report (2009) it is recommended that complex child protection cases be dealt with by experienced social work consultants who are supported by senior practitioners and for multiagency training across all services that work to protect children.

However, to be truly effective, community partnership building should be at the heart of anti-trafficking strategies in the UK. Communities and families are the source of a sense of identity for children; their involvement is therefore necessary in shaping debates on child rights and developing a culture that recognises exploitation and empowers children. However, communities in the UK are highly diverse, both within and between communities, and therefore a wide spectrum of groups and individuals should be engaged, certainly not just faith-based leaders. In recognition of the importance of partnership working between statutory agencies and local minority ethnic communities in safeguarding children, the government piloted a community partnership project in eight London boroughs between 2006 and 2007 (LSCB, 2007). The project found that isolation from mainstream services contributed to a lack of awareness of UK child-specific laws and standards by minority ethnic communities. This could be overcome through the work of a dedicated and permanent local authority community representative. What needs to be borne in mind is that engaging with local communities to influence attitudes is not the same as seeking mediation, reconciliation and family counselling through local community leaders on specific cases. Government guidance warns against facilitating mediation and reconciliation between the victim and the family (DCSF, 2006, p 151). In the past this has exposed children to further coercion and violence (Khanum, 2008). In the event that children do ask to speak to their natural family or to return home, a comprehensive risk assessment would be called for to ensure their safety.

Experience from other countries may suggest innovative and more effective ways in which to encourage community responsibility and engagement in the UK. Blagbrough (2008) provides examples of community action in cases of child domestic work. For example, similar in concept to the Neighbourhood Watch crime schemes in the UK, a childwatch community scheme operates in the Philippines to detect the recruitment of children by traffickers. This involves training individuals and groups within affected communities to help them act appropriately, and also includes local authorities 'maintaining a high profile in local communities to ensure that their services are well-known and accessible' (Blagbrough, 2008, p 29).

The trafficking of children is a multifaceted problem of global dimensions. The solutions too must be multidimensional, requiring coordination and cooperation between all child welfare agencies, both nationally and internationally. Tackling the underlying causes lags behind other initiatives, but if given the commitment and resources, can lead to real and lasting change for all children. The best way forward is to situate anti-child trafficking strategies within a broader child rights and child protection framework that promotes their participation in decisions affecting their life (Dotteridge, 2008; Pearce et al, 2009).

Note

[1] Into the death of a young girl from the Ivory Coast starved and beaten to death by her UK private foster carers, despite the involvement of many services.

References

AFRUCA (Africans Unite Against Child Abuse) (2008) *What is child trafficking: Safeguarding African children in the UK*, Series 2, London: AFRUCA (www.afruca. org/work_trafficking_african_children.php).

Amnesty International UK and Southall Black Sisters (2008) *'No recourse', no safety*, London: Amnesty International UK and Southall Black Sisters.

Ayrio, D. (2007) 'Trafficking of African children – domestic servitude, sexual exploitation, forced labour etc and implications for victims', in AFRUCA, *Modern day slavery of African children in the UK: Addressing the demand and supply nexus*, London: AFRUCA, pp 40-55.

BAAF (British Association for Adoption and Fostering) (2006) *Submission of evidence to the Home Affairs Select Committee* (www.baaf.org.uk/info/lpp/pf/hacom.pdf).

Beddoe, C. (2007) *Missing out: A study of child trafficking in the North-West, North-East and West Midlands*, London: ECPAT UK (www.ecpat.org.uk/downloads/ ECPAT_UK_Missing_Out_2007.pdf).

Blagbrough, J. (2008) *They respect their animals more: Voices of child domestic workers*, London: Anti-Slavery International/WISE.

Bokhari, F. (2009) *Stolen futures: Trafficking for forced child marriage in the UK*, London: ECPAT UK/WISE.

Bostock, L. (2003) *Effectiveness of childminding registration and its implications for private fostering*, SCIE Position Paper No 3, London: Social Care Institute for Excellence.

Brandon, J. and Hafez, S. (2008) *Crimes of the community – Honour-based violence in the UK*, London: Centre for Social Cohesion.

CEOP (Child Exploitation and Online Protection Centre) (2009) *Strategic threat assessment: Child trafficking in the UK*, London: CEOP.

DCSF (Department for Children, Schools and Families) (2006) *Working together to safeguard children: A guide to inter-agency working to safeguard and promote the welfare of children*, London: HM Government.

Dotteridge, M. (2008) *Kids abroad: Ignore them, abuse them or protect them: Lessons on how to protect children on the move from being exploited*, Geneva: Terres des Hommes International Foundation.

Eade, J. and Yunas, S. (2002) *Community perceptions of forced marriage*, London: Community Liaison Unit and Foreign and Commonwealth Office.

ECPAT International (2008) *Global monitoring report on the status of action against commercial sexual exploitation of children, Ghana*, Thailand: ECPAT International.

ECPAT UK Law Enforcement Group (2004) *Joint East West research on trafficking in children for sexual purposes in Europe: The sending countries*, Amsterdam: ECPAT UK Law Enforcement Group.

Gangoli, G., Razak, A. and McCarry, M. (2006) *Forced marriage and domestic violence among South Asian communities in North East England*, Bristol: University of Bristol and Northern Rock Foundation.

Harris, J. and Robinson, R. (2007) *Tipping the iceberg*, Ilford: Barnardos.

Hashim, M. (2006) *The positive and negatives of children's independent migration: Assessing the evidence and the debates*, Working Paper T16, Brighton: Sussex Centre for Migration.

HM Government (2009) *Multi-agency practice guidelines: Handling cases of forced marriage*, London: HM Government.

Home Office (2000) *A choice by right: The report of the Working Group on forced marriage*, London: Home Office.

Home Office (Border and Immigration Agency) (2007) *Marriage to partners from overseas*, Consultation paper, London: Home Office.

Howe, M. (2008) 'Accountant and teacher kept girl, 14, as slave', *The Independent online*, 12 July (www.independent.co.uk/news/uk/crime/accountant-and-teacher-kept-girl-14-as-a-slave-865802.html).

Izzidien, S. (2008) *I can't tell people what is happening at home: Domestic abuse within South Asian communities: The specific needs of women, children and young people*, London: NSPCC.

Kapoor, A. (2007) *A scoping project on child trafficking in the UK*, London: CEOP.

Kelly, E. (2009) *Bordering on concern: Child trafficking in Wales*, London: ECPAT UK & Children's Commissioner for Wales.

Khanum, N. (2008) *Forced marriage, family cohesion and community engagement: National learning through a case study of Luton*, Luton: Equality in Diversity.

Laming, Lord (2003) *The Victoria Climbié Inquiry: Report of an Inquiry by Lord Laming*, London: The Stationery Office (www.dh.gov.uk/prod_consum_dh/groups/dh_digitalassets/documents/digitalasset/dh_110711.pdf).

Laming, Lord (2009) *The protection of children in England: A progress report*, London, The Stationery Office.

LSCB (London Safeguarding Children Board) (2007) *Community partnership project report*, London: LSCB.

LSCB (2009) *London safeguarding trafficked children toolkit*, London: LSCB.

McFaydean, M. (2001) 'Human traffic', *The Guardian*, 9 March (www.guardian.co.uk/society/2001/mar/09/socialcare1).

Pearce, J., Hynes, P. and Bovarnick, S. (2009) *Breaking the wall of silence: Practitioners' responses to trafficked children and young people*, London: NSPCC.

Peart, E. (2005) 'The experience of being privately fostered', *Adoption and Fostering*, vol 29, no 3, pp 57-67.

Shaw, A. (2001) 'Kinship, cultural preference and immigration: consanguineous marriage among British Pakistanis', *Journal of the Royal Anthropological Institute*, vol 7, pp 315-34.

Stuart, M. and Baines, C. (2004) *Progress on safeguards for children living away from home*, York: Joseph Rowntree Foundation.

UNICEF (2003) *End child exploitation: Stop the traffic!*, London: UNICEF UK.

UNICEF (2005) *Trafficking in human beings especially women and children in Africa* (2nd edn), Florence: Innocenti Research Centre.

Wirtz, L. (2010) *Hidden children: Action research with separated children*, London: Children's Society.

Part II
Themes, issues and case studies

nine

Preventing child trafficking in India: the role of education

Jason Aliperti and Patricia Aliperti

Of 27 million slaves in the world today (Bales, 2004), India has the largest number – between 8 million and 10 million, most, including children, in some form of debt bondage (Bales, 2007). India also has the largest number of child labourers, the Indian government estimating it at between 11 million and 17.5 million, many highly vulnerable to trafficking (ADB, 2002), while unofficial estimates range from 60 million to 115 million (HRW, 2003).

The elimination of child labour and the international efforts to achieve Education for All and universal primary education by 2015 – one of the Millennium Development Goals – are inextricably linked (ILO-IPEC, 2007). On the one hand, education prevents child labour; children without access to quality education have few alternatives and may enter the labour market forced to work in exploitative and dangerous conditions. On the other hand, child labour is a major obstacle to achieve Education for All since working children cannot go to school. Those who combine school and work may suffer in educational achievement and may drop out to enter full-time employment. In addition, illiteracy is one of the strongest predictors of poverty, and so unequal access to educational opportunities is linked to income inequality (Suas Educational Development, nd).

This chapter explores how education can make children and communities less vulnerable to trafficking. The education referred to herein is not reduced to the treatment of letters and words in a mechanical manner. Instead, education is conceptualised as what Paulo Freire describes as 'the relationship of learners to the world, mediated by the transforming practice of this world taking place in the very general milieu in which learners travel' (Freire and Macedo, 1987, p viii).

Labour exploitation in India

Non-governmental organisations (NGOs) estimate there to be between 20 million and 65 million bonded labourers in India in agriculture, stone quarries, brick kilns, jewellery, beedi (cigarette) making, rice factories and carpet weaving (USDS, 2008). According to Human Rights Watch (cited in Shakti Vahini, 2004), out of 40 million bonded labourers, at least 15 million are children, the majority being Dalits with bondage passed from one generation to the next. Of these 15 million, 52% to 87% of bonded child labourers are in agriculture (Human Rights Watch, cited in Sen and Nair, 2004). Many are also in bondage as domestic workers; in industries such as silk, beedi, saris, silver jewellery, gemstones, handwoven wool carpets and footwear/sporting goods; and in services such as restaurants, tea shops and truck stops. They are also found in begging, drug selling, petty crimes and prostitution.

Poverty and illiteracy are major factors compelling parents to send children to work in addition to lack of awareness and educational opportunities. A 'culture of silence' in India prevails with the family's and community's passivity and inability to respond to the situation due to a lack of public awareness and action compounded by social indifference (Sen and Nair, 2004, p 316). Despite established laws and efforts through raid and rescue, prosecution and repatriation, overall enforcement of child labour is inadequate due to insufficient resources, poorly trained inspectors and social acceptance of child labour (USDL, 2008).

Methodology and data collection

The research described here was conducted through the NGO Bachpan Bachao Andolan (BBA), or Save the Childhood Movement, during two phases of field study in 2007–08 at its rehabilitation centres of Bal Ashram in the state of Rajasthan and Mukti Ashram and Balika Ashram in Greater Delhi. BBA's vision is 'to create a child-friendly society, where all children are free from exploitation and receive free and quality education', while its mission is 'to identify, liberate, rehabilitate and educate children in servitude through direct intervention, child and community participation, coalition building, consumer action, promoting ethical trade practices and mass mobilization' (BBA, 2007). BBA conducts raid and rescue operations of establishments that use child labour and rehabilitates the rescued children, including trafficked and bonded children. As part of their rehabilitation, children are provided with social development, formal education, vocational training, physical education, leadership development initiatives, cultural education and human rights education for six months or more (Bal Ashram, 2006). Of the 40 children interviewed at the centres, 20 were classified as trafficked for forced labour and 12 trafficked for bonded labour.

In addition, 10 communities were visited to interview community members on the role of education to prevent child exploitation, of which six were BBA's Bal Mitra Grams (BMGs), or child-friendly villages. BMGs are created by identifying villages with high levels of child labour. BBA then supports the community with the objectives of withdrawing child labour from the village, mainstreaming children into formal schools, ensuring the adult village (Gram Panchayat) or local government recognises and incorporates the voices of children, and aiding socioeconomic development of the village's marginalised section. These objectives are achieved through the formation of three groups in the community: a children's parliament, a women's group and a youth group. Members of these groups were interviewed.

Analytical framework

The case studies used the Freirean concept of critical pedagogy, which provides tools for educators and the educated to understand more fully and combat the complex relationship between education and unequal political, cultural and economic power (Apple, 1999), for conscientisation to prevent oppression and exploitation such as child trafficking and bonded labour. Fieldwork and interviews focused on the outcomes of BBA's educational process, creating empowered children and communities. Thus, critical pedagogy is referred to extensively as the desired pedagogy to teach the oppressed to achieve a critical consciousness and is used to examine the actions undertaken by children and communities to prevent child trafficking.

Critical pedagogy: education as empowerment

According to Berbules and Berk (cited in Keesing-Styles, 2003), critical pedagogy shares considerable historical and contextual territory with critical theory. Critical theory involves issues related to the socialisation of people for existence in society, a society usually defined by dominant discourses. In contemporary educational theory, being critical is desirable and is not only related to critical theory and critical pedagogy but also to the tradition of critical thinking. This encourages an analysis of arguments and situations to identify faulty or unreliable assertions or meanings, perhaps encouraging discernment for social and human conditions but not demanding social action. Critical pedagogy, on the other hand, while preoccupied with social injustice, examines and promotes practices with the potential to transform oppressive social relations or institutions, largely through educational practices. Furthermore, critical thinking is mainly aimed at the individual and ignores pedagogical relations between teacher and learner or between learners, while critical pedagogy is more interested in collective action. Both critical theory and critical pedagogy aim to investigate institutional and societal practices to resist the imposition of dominant social norms and structures.

However, critical pedagogy differs from critical theory as it is primarily an educational response to oppressive power relations and inequalities in educational institutions. It concerns issues related to voice, opportunity and dominant discourses of education, and seeks more liberating and equitable educational experiences to create critical people empowered to seek justice. Critical pedagogy is committed to the development of a culture of schooling, supporting empowerment of the culturally marginalised and economically disenfranchised, seeking to transform the practices and classroom structures that perpetuate undemocratic life. It analyses 'the manner in which traditional theories and practices of public schooling thwart or influence the development of a politically emancipatory and humanizing culture of participation, voice, and social action within the classroom' (Darder et al, 2003, p 11). It also addresses cultural politics by legitimising and challenging learners' perceptions and experiences that shape the socioeconomic realities and histories giving meaning to their daily lives and their constructions of what is perceived as truth.

Critical pedagogy includes the rejection of banking methods of education in favour of a dialogical education. This banking education turns students into 'receptacles to be filled by the teacher' (Freire, 2000, p 72). Therefore, instead of communicating, the teacher deposits what the students must patiently receive, memorise and repeat. Existing knowledge is produced and prepackaged far from students and transferred to them to memorise (Shor and Freire, 1987).

A final element of critical pedagogy includes its aim to achieve a critical consciousness in learners to create societal changes. The method for liberation is found within a praxis, or 'the link between knowledge and power through self-directed action' (Aronowitz, 1993, p 12). 'There is no conscientization if the result is not the conscious action of the oppressed as an exploited social class, struggling for liberation' (Freire, 1985, p 125). In other words, revolutionary consciousness involves changing structures in the larger social order (McLaren and da Silva, 1993). Precisely because Freire's pedagogy fights against domination that perpetuates oppression, it has the potential to serve as a catalyst for the emancipation of children affected by trafficking for forced and bonded labour in India.

Critical consciousness in action

This section explores the role of education and critical pedagogy regarding the following two research questions: what is it about villages vulnerable to child trafficking that makes a critical pedagogy appealing to achieve critical consciousness? How do villages and children demonstrate the likelihood of having attained a critical consciousness through education, becoming social agents for the transformation of their society?

Forms of oppression and the need for conscientisation in villages

In Ghina village the community reported lacking proper mid-day meals for school children, receiving 10 grams instead of 100 grams. They did not complain about corruption because they said they were illiterate and therefore could not pursue written claims. If they complained, officers blamed their higher administrators for not giving them enough money for the mid-day meal. The village leader said that if children were given food at school, they would not have to catch mice and snails to eat.

Many children work and are trafficked to Amritsar and New Delhi. They point to the lack of facilities in school and because they are illiterate no one tells them about the government schemes. One man said: "We don't complain because the government will not listen. We have no house, nothing to eat, where will we go to complain?" An elderly man said that the government is corrupt and leaders do not listen to the villagers at all. He said he would complain to the government if someone told him where to go and how to do it. Before leaving this village, a young man gave us a letter he had just written, signed by the young men in the village, to give to the authorities demanding the arrest of a nearby villager who had kidnapped four of their children to traffic them.

This village community demonstrated a form of fatalism. According to Freire (2000), self-depreciation occurs when they internalise the oppressors' opinion that they know nothing and are incapable of learning anything. Freire considers this kind of thought as intransitive, followed by semi-intransitive and critical thoughts (Shor, 1993). Freire considers intransitive thought as the lowest and most dominated, with people living fatalistically believing only luck or God can influence their fates; they are therefore disempowered, believing their actions cannot change their conditions. In semi-transitive thought, people exercise thought and action for change to an extent. Partly empowered, they act to bring changes but relate to problems one at a time instead of seeing the whole system underlying any one issue. They may naively follow strong leaders, hoping they can make changes rather than the people themselves having to make the needed changes. This type of thought was evidenced in the young men's production of the letter and their dependence on BBA to whom the authorities would listen. Freire considers critical consciousness as critical transitivity and the highest development of thought and action, with people thinking holistically and critically about their condition and seeing themselves making the changes needed (Shor, 1993). These thinkers are empowered to think and act on their conditions, relating them to the larger contexts of power in society.

Murlibharna BMG community members reported they were not very aware of their rights, but BBA is helping them by giving their children an education, and teaching them their rights. Children from the children's parliament were passive, and three interviewed were aware of their right to attend school but only saw its benefit as one for employment. The community members complained of not having electricity or roads and wanted support to learn vocational skills including hand knitting, pickle making and perfume making. The government provides below-poverty-line schemes but because of corruption, villagers do not benefit. A women's group member reported that they are supposed to benefit from employment, pensions and home-building schemes but the village chief is not 'very capable' and cannot manage the money well. She said teachers are not interested in giving a proper education or in making adults literate; because they are illiterate, the adults cannot stand up against the teacher. As demonstrated, this village also suffers from fatalism and intransitive thinking. They have demands to meet their needs but have never taken action.

These cases present various indicators such as extreme poverty, lack of access to quality education and facilities, illiteracy, corruption of the oppressors and not being aware of human rights and government schemes that make children vulnerable to trafficking. People clearly have a concrete vision of a better life and would indeed act affirmatively, especially if someone could help them understand their human rights, civic rights and government schemes. It is evident that these communities complain and demand their needs from those who listen, but because of corruption and exploitation by the higher castes of the lower castes, leaders ignore them. These communities must engage in dialogue to develop their own conscientisation and praxis[1] to then be able to affirm their vision and dream for which to fight effectively.

Villages assuming rising conscientisation

The following villages represent the struggles, actions and successes in demanding their children's right to education and the community's right to participate in actions to promote children's well-being so as to prevent child trafficking and exploitation of those who are vulnerable. In Swami Ki Dhani BMG, the women's group and children's parliament spoke with the doctor to request school toilet facilities for girls since they had to run home to relieve themselves and refused to return to classes. When issues arise, the children's parliament members try to solve the problems themselves first before going to the village chief. For example, the children told their chief that there were not enough classrooms at school, after which the doctor allocated money and the community donated the labour to construct additional rooms. They also requested and received stationery and blackboards, repaired a door and applied for a secondary school to be built.

Some children take their responsibility as members of the children's parliament seriously. One child in Maydagraghat BMG reported going to the fields regularly where other children were working to inspire them to go to school, becoming their friend to then help them understand that if they got an education, they would be good civilians and get better jobs. He said that he himself, as a literate man, would do many good things for his village, going to the district magistrate to request a road, electricity and construction of a bridge. At an early age, this child is already becoming political.

Although only five months old, BMG Mankot's children's parliament has mobilised with the priority of establishing an upper primary school, grades six to eight, in their village. They have also already held a rally to raise awareness on child labour, child trafficking, child marriage and education. Women's group members discuss hygiene issues, schemes and how to enrol more children in school. A woman reported that she talks to parents to make them realise that "if children rear cattle, all their life they will rear cattle, and their life will be spoiled. But if they go to school, they can have a better life." They succeeded in enrolling 28 children who were not in school before, greatly reducing the risk of child labourers being trafficked.

BMG Vijaypura's children's parliament members discuss school issues such as what facilities are needed and the shortage of teachers. They submitted an application with the BBA activist's help to the village chief, who stamped it to submit to the block office, requesting more teachers for their school. They also wrote a letter to the headmaster requesting water facilities. The women's self-help group members give 50 INR (approximately £0.73) each per month and plan to apply for a loan to help pregnant women eat nutritious food, to give school materials to children and to buy a buffalo.

Conscientisation of children from Bal Ashram

Aronowitz (1993) argues that the task of revolutionary pedagogy is not to promote critical self-consciousness to improve cognitive learning or self-esteem, nor to assist students' aspirations to fulfil their human potential. Instead, it is to transform history. This appears to have happened with some children from Bal Ashram. According to BBA, when initially rescued, children are afraid and do not want to go to a shelter. One child, for example, reported wanting to return to the stone quarry where he was bonded and refused to study. This demonstrates the adaptation to a culture of silence and fear of the possibilities because they represent a break from their known exploitation. When they realise the freedom they can have with their life at the rehabilitation centre, BBA reports that children do not wish to return to work. With teachers who were themselves bonded labourers, the children relate and begin to trust to overcome their traumatising experiences through counselling. Soon, they exchange openly about their experiences, determined that they do not want other children to undergo such negative experiences. Many of these children attain not only self-empowerment but also empowerment to transform the larger social order, which is Freire's goal of conscientisation, in regards to education, child exploitation and child rights.

Case studies: The children

Kanak is a 13-year-old who has been at Bal Ashram for two years. He has four siblings and his illiterate parents work in agriculture; they belong to a scheduled caste. He was six years old when he was trafficked by a man who promised him sweets, taking him from Bihar to Punjab. He did not like working because he was forced to do domestic work, tend cattle and work in the farm field daily for five years from 6am to midnight, sleeping in the cow shed. He was beaten when tired, threatened to not talk to strangers, not given enough food and given opium with tea for energy. He was aware that he was being exploited but did not know about child trafficking or children's rights as he does now. He was never in school until BBA rescued him. When rescued, he was initially very scared but soon made friends and started his education. He was in non-formal education for one year and is now in 5th grade at the local school. He would like to become a district collector (a local government official). At Bal Ashram, he likes the cultural activities and social class because he is learning to understand society. With an education, he believes his life would be secure, he would be able to get a job and he would be aware of society's 'evils' to fight. "If I am not educated, people will ignore me and will not give me value in society." He believes human rights education is "the route to everything" and helps children the most. Before Bal Ashram, he thought he would spend his life as a bonded labourer, without a life in freedom. At Bal Ashram, he can now choose from many opportunities, one that included his participation in requesting the Prime Minister of India to eradicate child labour in a letter and meeting the Education Minister to demand free and compulsory primary education because "it is a fundamental right but not fundamental in India now". When he visited his family, he spoke twice to other children about child labour and plans to work to convince parents not to send children to work, but says that first "I must be educated so I am an example to convince parents". He was selected as a jury member for the 2008 World's Children's Prize for the Rights of the Child and travelled to Sudan where all children wrote a letter for all governments arguing that education should be made a priority and child labour eradicated . He believes the government should establish a law against child forced labour and open more schools with more teachers.

Jinendra is a 17-year-old who has been at Bal Ashram for eight years. He has eight siblings and his parents work in agriculture. He was a bonded labourer with his father for two years, working in agriculture to pay off a loan his father borrowed to investigate the murder of his grandfather. Later, he was trafficked by a man who promised his father to educate Jinendra at a hostel.

After one year of forced labour cleaning from 5am to 10pm, he was rescued by BBA activists. He had never gone to school and was initially bored with non-formal education because he spoke only the local language and not Hindi. After six months of non-formal education, however, he was enrolled in formal education. He is now in 11th grade. He would like to become a social worker working with children, as he sees his mission beyond the present time, saying, "When people get educated and older, they forget other children, but they should remember the others and not only see their own future." He is also very aware of social issues and their implications in society:

"Indians do not think about the future. They only think about the present. Corruption and bribes are a big problem but it could change slowly. The government has the ability to help poor families and give them education, but officials keep about 90% in their own pockets and use only 10% for people. Also, a big portion of GDP is used for weapons.... Girls are trafficked from Nepal because their families are very poor and traffickers promise them things. Boys are trafficked to the Middle East as camel jockeys."

Putting his awareness into practice, he has participated in marches, the Mukti Caravan (or Liberation Caravan, a mobile campaign of former child labourers who travel throughout India raising awareness about child labour and education through folk art and street theatre), the Second Children's World Congress, the BMG Children's Parliament Congress and 'Cricket for Peace' in Pakistan to speak about children in Kashmir not getting an education because they fear terrorism and the governments fighting. He also went to Japan through NGO Action Against Child Exploitation to speak about BMGs and to the Netherlands to receive his Children's Peace Prize. This prize was awarded for his work in identifying and registering 550 children from Rajasthan state to receive their birth certificate. He undertook this task after he applied for a passport and realised he could not be given one without a birth certificate. He recognised its importance for children to enrol in schools and receive government schemes. When asked what inspires him, he replied, "I was a child labourer and now I am free and have learned lots." He wants to inspire others to work for change too.

Viresh is a 15-year-old who has been at Bal Ashram for seven years and who wants to become a doctor to help poor families: "The poor become poorer and the rich richer. If the poor get sick, they die but the rich are taken to the hospital as soon as possible. My priority is for poor, marginalised people in society whose needs are deprived." He participated in the Second Children's World Congress and in a month-long march of 2,500km across the Indo-Nepal-Bangladesh border called the South Asian March Against Child Trafficking, which inspired him by seeing so many people mobilised. He led a strike at his local school and demanded from the village chief and block officer that they establish a school for 8th to 12th grades. He also requested the school to provide a playground and tap water and succeeded in increasing the number of teachers from four to eight in the primary school. He realises that *change is difficult but it is possible*, by relating how BBA was started with many difficulties and problems: "We can start these organisations, we will face difficulties but then they can run smoothly to end this evil in society."

Common themes

A major theme for the interviewed children is their worldview of the necessity to end child labour in society and the importance of education and making parents and other children understand how education can help their lives. For the majority of children interviewed, a recurring theme was the ability to do a different kind of 'better job' that is not exploitative. It appears that in their re-reading of the world, these children realise that illiteracy is keeping millions in India in substandard conditions that perpetuate poverty, inequality and oppression by the dominant groups having control over cheap child and slave labour, and how illiteracy also affects their parents. The majority of the children also stated that their teachers at the formal school do not allow group discussions of issues, making it evident that their conscientisation comes from Bal Ashram's human rights education and its child-friendly environment, and not from the formal school's curricula. While some see formal education or vocational training as the most important for children, the majority view human rights education as the most important for children to understand their rights in society since they do not learn these in formal education.

Conclusion

The trafficking in children for forced and bonded labour is the result of myriad factors including economic globalisation and technological/scientific advances that lack ethics to serve the interests of all human beings. Freire sees a vital role for subjectivity and consciousness in the making of history. A critical education gives access to ways of thinking about the world and the tools to understand why it is the way it is and how it should be and the means to act to transform it. Therefore, in transforming society, 'the important task is not to take power but to reinvent power. Without falling into an idealistic view or a mechanical explanation of history … education … has a lot to do with the reinvention of power' (Freire, 1985, p 179). For this reinvention to occur, civil society and NGO activists can lead by tuning into people's voices from below.

History is not deterministic but made by individuals. The future does not have to follow the same path if the oppressed are able to remake their histories. As demonstrated, by providing exploited children with the opportunity of receiving a critical education, Bal Ashram children have developed into empowered citizens who act as advocates, activists and supporters for all children's rights. History has demonstrated how education is instrumental in combating child labour (Matsuno and Blagbrough, 2006). However, education is only one piece of prevention. First, it must be a *critical* education. Second, effective legislature, law enforcement, livelihood options, implementation of schemes and collaboration and participation of all stakeholders to prevent child trafficking are also essential – that could be demanded through conscientisation and thus, affirmation.

Note

[1] '[T]he action and reflection of men and women upon their world in order to transform it' (Freire, 2000, p 79).

References

ADB (Asian Development Bank) (2002) *Combating trafficking of women and children in South Asia. Country paper: India* (www.adb.org/gender/final_india.pdf).

Apple, M.W. (1999) *Power, meaning, and identity: Essays in critical educational studies*, New York, NY: Peter Lang Publishing, Inc.

Aronowitz, S. (1993) 'Paulo Freire's radical democratic humanism', in P. McLaren and P. Leonard (eds) *Paulo Freire: A critical encounter*, London: Routledge, pp 8-24.

Bal Ashram (2006) *About Bal Ashram* (www.bba.org.in/balashram/activities.php).

Bales, K. (2004) *Disposable people. New slavery in the global economy*, Berkeley, CA: University of California Press.

Bales, K. (2007) *Ending slavery: How we free today's slaves*, Berkeley, CA: University of California Press.

BBA (Bachpan Bachao Andolan) (2007) *About us* (www.bba.org.in/aboutus/index.php).

Darder, A., Baltodano, M. and Torres, R.D. (eds) (2003) *The critical pedagogy reader*, New York, NY: RoutledgeFalmer.

Freire, P. (1985) *The politics of education: Culture, power, and liberation*, South Hadley, MA: Bergin & Garvey Publishers, Inc.

Freire, P. (2000) *Pedagogy of the oppressed*, New York, NY: Continuum.

Freire, P. and Macedo, D. (1987) *Literacy. Reading the word and the world*, South Hadley, MA: Bergin & Garvey Publishers, Inc.

HRW (Human Rights Watch) (2003) 'Small change: bonded child labor in India's silk industry', Human Rights Watch, vol 15, no 2c (www.hrw.org/reports/2003/india/).

ILO-IPEC (International Labour Organization-International Programme on the Elimination of Child Labour) (2007) *Education as an intervention strategy to eliminate and prevent child labor. Consolidated good practices of the International Program on the Elimination of Child Labor (IPEC)*, Geneva: ILO (www.ilo.org/public/english/region/asro/bangkok/apec/download/edu_strat.pdf).

Keesing-Styles, L. (2003) 'The relationship between critical pedagogy and assessment in teacher education', *Radical Pedagogy*, vol 5, no 1 (http://radicalpedagogy.icaap.org/content/issue5_1/03_keesing-styles.html).

McLaren, P. and da Silva, T.T. (1993) 'Decentering pedagogy: critical literacy, resistance, and the politics of memory', in P. McLaren and P. Leonard (eds) *Paulo Freire: A critical encounter*, London: Routledge, pp 47-89.

Matsuno, A. and Blagbrough, J. (2006) *Child domestic labour in South East and East Asia: Emerging good practices to combat it*, Bangkok: ILO (www.ilo.org/public/english/region/asro/bangkok/child/trafficking/downloads/cdw.pdf).

Sen, S. and Nair, P.M. (2004) *A report on trafficking in women and children in India 2002-2003* (vol 1), New Delhi: NHRC, UNIFEM, ISS (http://nhrc.nic.in/Documents/ReportonTrafficking.pdf).

Shakti Vahini (2004) *Trafficking in India report-2004*, Faridabad: Shakti Vahini (www.shaktivahini.org/assets/templates/default/images/traffickingreport.pdf).

Shor, I. (1993) 'Education is politics: Paulo Freire's critical pedagogy', in P. McLaren and P. Leonard (eds) *Paulo Freire: A critical encounter*, London: Routledge, pp 25-35.

Shor, I. and Freire, P. (1987) *A pedagogy for liberation: Dialogues on transforming education*, South Hadley, MA: Bergin & Garvey Publishers, Inc.

Suas Educational Development (nd) *Why education?* (www.suas.ie/99.html).

USDL (United States Department of Labor) (2008) *The US Department of Labor's 2007 findings on the worst forms of child labor*, Washington, DC: USDL (www.dol.gov/ilab/programs/ocft/PDF/2007OCFTreport.pdf).

USDS (United States Department of State) (2008) *India: Country reports on human rights practices-2007* (www.state.gov/g/drl/rls/hrrpt/2007/100614.htm).

ten

Birth registration: a tool for prevention, protection and prosecution

Claire Cody

Introduction

This chapter draws on experience from Plan International's long-running campaign for universal birth registration, exploring the significant role that registration can play in protecting children, preventing exploitation and prosecuting cases of child slavery. It identifies and defines the wide range of child rights abuses falling within the broad definition of contemporary slavery. It explores the basics of birth registration, why it is important and why so many people go unregistered in developing countries. It then examines the key role that registration plays in accessing the building blocks of life, for determining proof of age and, in some cases, for establishing nationality.

Contemporary slavery

The word 'slavery' today covers many human rights violations. The United Nations (UN) Office of the High Commissioner for Human Rights (UNOHCHR) defines it as:

> … the sale of children, child prostitution, child pornography, the exploitation of child labour, the sexual mutilation of female children, the use of children in armed conflicts, debt bondage, the traffic in persons and in the sale of human organs, the exploitation of prostitution, and certain practices under apartheid and colonial regime…. (UNOHCHR, nd)

Traditional slavery, at one time legally permitted, has, in essence, been abolished, yet the fact that numerous international conventions and treaties continue to highlight the issue is a clear indicator that slavery-like practices are far from eradicated. Slavery practices have been acknowledged in the 1926 UN Slavery Convention, the 1948 Universal Declaration of Human

Rights, the 1956 Supplementary Convention on the Abolition of Slavery, the Slave Trade and Institutions and Practices Similar to Slavery, the 1966 International Covenant on Civil and Political Rights, the 1966 International Covenant on Economic, Social and Cultural Rights and the 1989 Convention on the Rights of the Child (CRC) and its Optional Protocols.

Despite the clandestine and illegal nature of slavery-like practices, which makes measurement and monitoring almost impossible (especially since different definitions are applied), Bales (2007) puts the number of people held in slavery worldwide at around 27 million. The International Labour Organization (ILO) estimates that six million children are held in slavery (van de Glind and Kooijmans, 2008; see also Chapter One, this volume).

The role of birth registration

Although it is inaccurate to say that one intervention alone can stop tomorrow's children from becoming exploited and abused through slavery-like practices, the process of registering the birth of a child, and therefore simply declaring their existence, may be a key measure in the fight against slavery.

Birth registration is a critical first step in ensuring the rights of a child, and is a fundamental human right laid down in Articles 7 and 8 of the CRC. The CRC (ratified by all countries except Somalia and the US) clearly states that: 'The child shall be registered immediately after birth and shall have the right from birth to a name' (CRC 1989, Article 7) and that 'States Parties undertake to respect the right of the child to preserve his or her identity, including nationality, name and family relations' (CRC, 1989, Article 8).

Despite the fact that the CRC is the most widely ratified UN treaty, and it could be argued that recognition of legal existence – birth registration itself – is necessary to gain protection and fulfilment of all the other rights in the Convention, around 51 million births go unregistered every year in developing countries (UNICEF, 2007). Plan International, a child-centred, international development non-governmental organisation (NGO) working in 48 developing countries, started promoting birth registration in 1998, when invited by the NGO Committee on UNICEF to support the unregistered children project in Asia. Plan International's work on birth registration subsequently extended to Africa and the Americas and became the focus of Plan International's first global campaign in 2005 – 'Universal birth registration!' (Cody, 2009).

Why births go unregistered

Through experience, Plan International has identified various reasons why parents do not register their children at birth. For many, there is simply a lack of awareness of the importance and the procedures of birth registration. High rates of illiteracy act as an additional barrier, impeding access to any available information; for migrants or those from minority ethnic groups who do not understand the national majority language, they are often further isolated when documentation is only presented in that language. Furthermore, there may be geographical barriers, when families are living in remote, rural areas with little infrastructure and poor public transport links; travelling to the nearest civil registry office may prove long, expensive and unsafe. This is especially the case when registration is centralised at state level and parents must travel to the capital city to register a birth.

For others, there are the economic pressures of the registration or the associated costs, namely, taking time off work and paying for transport to a registry office. In India, for example, in order to get a birth certificate, parents have to spend hundreds of rupees as well as take time off work to make several trips to the registry office (Plan India, 2008). For those struggling to survive, if the choice is between the next meal and a piece of paper, there is no contest.

Birth registration is not always a straightforward process. Research commissioned by Plan International in China identified the complex registration procedures and steps required simply to register a birth in the country. The birth of a child has to be registered in a local police station in the area where the father or mother's household is registered. In order to register, a medical birth certificate is required – produced by the Ministry of Public Health – as is a family planning service booklet or 'bearing certificate', along with the parents' household registration book. In some cases, if the child is not born in a hospital facility, they may not be able to produce a medical birth certificate, or if the child is 'out of plan', as determined by the 1979 One-Child Policy, the bearing certificate will not be issued. For China's growing 'floating population' – those who have migrated away from their rural homes in search for work in the country's thriving urban centres – registering their children means returning to their natal homes within a month of the birth, which in many cases is not an option (IPDS Xi'an Jiaotong University, 2005).

In some cases, there may be traditions or historical reasons why birth registration is not prioritised. Cultural or social norms, including naming ceremonies or other traditional rites of passage, may be seen as more significant than legal registration, as is the case in Burkina Faso. For some, it is the custom to wait for a period of time before naming the child and therefore when the law stipulates that registration must occur within the first month of the birth of a child, this proves problematic. In some communities in Sudan and Zambia, Plan International staff have reported that families and individuals use other forms of legal identification, such as citizenship certificates and identity cards to access services, and therefore the need for a formal birth certificate is not clear. In countries where child mortality rates are high, parents may wait to see if the child survives rather than registering the child immediately after birth, especially if the process is costly (Cody, 2009).

Birth registration may also carry with it negative associations. In the past birth registers have been used for taxation purposes and for compulsory conscription into the armed forces. Such information has also been used for far more sinister purposes. To escape persecution under the Pol Pot regime in Cambodia, many Cambodians destroyed their documents in an attempt to hide their identities (Plan Cambodia, 2005). In 2004, when Plan International started working on birth registration in Cambodia, less than 5% of the population were registered. After 10 months of a mobile birth registration programme initiated by Plan International and its partners, more than seven million Cambodians, or close to 56% of the population, received their birth certificates (Plan Cambodia, 2005). The Asian Development Bank estimates that 90% of the population of Cambodia are now registered (Vandenabeele and Lao, 2007).

Today, fears over persecution and penalties persist in some contexts. Human Rights Watch, for example, has documented that in China many children with Chinese fathers and North Korean mothers are going unregistered as there are fears that if they try to register the child, the mother's 'illegal' status will be revealed and she may face arrest and repatriation back to North Korea (HRW, 2008).

The obstacles highlighted so far relate to difficulties or concerns in accessing the civil registration system. But in some cases, such systems do not even exist. In Ethiopia, there is no civil registration system, and births, deaths, marriages and divorces are not legally recorded. Civil registration systems break down in fragile situations, especially during times of unrest and war. Social systems collapse, areas become inaccessible, registrars are among those displaced and records are lost or damaged in the looting and fighting. Rebuilding the system takes time and money and dealing with the backlog of records overwhelms the registrar's capacity.

There may be many reasons why a parent chooses not to register a child; however, it is the responsibility of every state to ensure that all children are registered at birth. In many countries, the limited resources for a free and functioning birth registration system are due to the lack of political will to allocate them or the general absence of funds in a resource-poor country. Civil registration is not seen as a priority or a 'vote-winning' strategy by some political parties and this leads to a general lack of registry staff with adequate training and the necessary information technology equipment, leading to insufficient or inaccurate registration records.

Despite the many barriers and competing priorities that parents and states face, a birth certificate is essential to a child's place in the world and for their access to legal, political, educational, social and other rights. Registration is not only critical for that individual, but also valuable for the state. Data from birth registration can assist countries to plan their services appropriately and enable them to monitor birth rate trends and identify progress as well as worrying patterns. Plan International's work on birth registration in India, for example, has been integrated with tackling the problem of female feticide in the country (Plan India, 2008).

A birth certificate is an affirmation of a person's legal identity – in many cases it is seen as the legal identity document, outweighing any other. It can confirm a child's nationality, place of birth, parentage and age. It is also a powerful legal document.

There are many critical details on a birth record and in a birth certificate that can be applied to protect children and to prosecute perpetrators in the context of slavery. We next explore some of these critical elements and their role in children's vulnerability and exposure to slavery.

The building blocks of life

In some countries, children are unable to access education and healthcare without a birth certificate. Education is generally thought of as a key that unlocks the door to many of life's opportunities. In some cases, a certificate is required to enrol in school and to take up these opportunities. In Nepal, where birth registration rates are low, Plan Nepal identified the lack of a birth certificate as a major barrier to school attendance (Plan International, 2005). Even if school principals allow unregistered children to attend, these pupils will not be eligible for scholarships, free books or uniforms, and their lack of a formal identification number means they cannot sit state-recognised exams. Plan International has been working to ensure that the lack of a birth certificate does not stop children from receiving an education; in Honduras, Plan International has worked with the Ministry of Education to ensure that unregistered children are not denied access to school.

As Todres has noted, education is not only important in the long term, but it can also keep children out of exploitative working conditions in the meantime (2006, Ch 8). The less education a child receives, the earlier they are likely to enter the workforce, and at a younger age their employment choices are slim, meaning they are more likely fall into 'informal', illegal or exploitative trades.

The ILO has estimated that in developing countries 250 million children between 5 and 14 years old are working (Ashagrie, 1998). Plan Nepal supported several in-depth studies on working children in the country. In 2005, 1,074 children between the ages of 5 and 16 working in brick kilns were interviewed in Nepal. Around one third had never attended school and, of those who had, just 20% had completed education to a grade three level. Children spoke of the reasons why they were not in school and for some this was due to migration-related problems and legal issues surrounding citizenship documentation (Concern, 2005).

The lack of education is not only a factor associated with child labour; it has also been linked with an increased vulnerability to trafficking. A UN Development Programme study into trafficking in South Asia found that lack of education was an important factor in increasing the vulnerability of individuals to trafficking, as most victims identified were illiterate or minimally educated (UNDP, 2007).

Access to healthcare is also crucial in a child's development and critical for their ability to learn. In countries including Kenya and Thailand, a child with no proof of identity can be denied access to free or subsidised vaccination programmes (Plan International, 2005). Poor health can have detrimental effects throughout one's life, and lead to poor performance in school and early drop-out rates. Todres states that: '… when health rights are jeopardised, the realisation of additional rights – such as the right to education and labor rights – are put at risk, prompting a downward spiral that leaves the most vulnerable populations exposed to potential human rights violations, including sex trafficking' (2006, p 899).

When children miss out on a good start to life, this may set their future path. Of course, even with a birth certificate these children could still have limited opportunities to access education and health services for a number of other reasons, including poverty, social exclusion or the state's lack of capacity to provide basic services for its citizens. In its analysis of the importance of legal identity, the Asian Development Bank noted that many states were unable to provide basic services and opportunities for their citizens, and therefore the perceived advantages and security that should come with registration were not guaranteed. However, the Asian Development Bank predicted that birth registration would become progressively more important as developing countries become increasingly able to provide basic services to their people. In the past few years, we have seen that states themselves are starting to see the importance of civil registration.

In Bangladesh for example, the government introduced a new law, the Birth and Death Registration Act, enacted in 2006. This requires Bangladeshi citizens to possess a birth certificate in order to access a wide range of benefits and opportunities, including marriage registration, admission into schools, a driver's licence, employment in the formal sector, utility connections and national identity cards (Vandenabeele and Lao, 2007). For those without these documents, their rights will be compromised in the future as new regulations come into force and social systems advance and become more bureaucratic in nature.

The benefits of having a birth certificate, in the here and now, are less nebulous in the area of child protection; here a child's age is a prerequisite to enforce those specific laws put in place to protect minors effectively.

Proof of age

A birth certificate documents age and as children under 18 are entitled to specific rights and legal protection not always afforded to those over the age of 18, proof of age can protect children who are exploited in slavery-like practices.

We know that hundreds of thousands of children are involved in armed conflicts around the world. Estimates in 2005 indicated that 300,000 children were directly involved in conflicts, 40% of whom were girls (SCF, 2005). The 2000 Optional Protocol to the CRC on the Involvement of Children in Armed Conflict deems the minimum age for recruitment and deployment of soldiers to be 18; without proof of age this protocol cannot be enforced.

In the case of Nepal, where child soldiers were identified among the Maoist rebel fighters, the Committee on the Rights of the Child in 2005, in its concluding observations, stated that: 'The Committee is concerned that children who have not been registered at birth are more vulnerable to abuse and exploitation, including recruitment into armed groups, as their ages cannot be established' (Committee on the Rights of the Child, 2005, p 8). This was supported by evidence from focus groups conducted by the Asian Development Bank in Nepal that found that the lack of birth registration among Dalits (a group of people traditionally regarded as 'untouchable') and internally displaced children had increased their risk of military recruitment (Vandenabeele and Lao, 2007). Although the research noted that conscription was likely to involve severe coercion, and possession of a birth certificate was unlikely to prevent recruitment, this does not mean that registration is irrelevant. If children are rescued from such exploitative conditions, proof of identity and age can aid in formal identification and tracing efforts, as well as assistance with repatriation and reintegration. Such support may not be available to those who cannot prove their identity or status as a child, which has been the case in Uganda for some children abducted by the Lord's Resistance Army (UNICEF, 2005). In addition, prosecutions will only succeed if there is proof that alleged child soldiers were indeed children at the time of recruitment.

The determination of proof of age is also key in the fight against the worst forms of child labour, especially to bring offenders to justice. Research commissioned by Plan International in Ghana investigated the link between birth registration, child trafficking and child labour in the cocoa industry.

Plan International's study illustrated that it was very difficult to monitor the implementation and effectiveness of child labour laws in the country or to prosecute employers known to be employing minors as in many cases, without birth registration, it was almost impossible to ascertain the age of a child. An interesting finding from this study was that many of the young people preferred to be working illegally rather than remaining in their villages and performing menial tasks. Many of these children perceived possession of an official document showing their age as limiting their chances of finding employment (Plan Ghana, 2004).

This finding highlights some of the difficulties in intervening in child labour cases, where poverty and lack of life opportunities are so pronounced that protection tools and mechanisms become insignificant for those that they are designed to keep from harm. In addition, the lines between trafficking, migration, slavery and child labour become increasingly blurred.

Determining proof of age is also essential in the context of trafficking for sexual exploitation cases. UNICEF (2001, p 6) has stated that:

> The failure to register the births of many thousands of children throughout East Asia makes it difficult to assess the ages of children who enter into prostitution and to mount cases against traffickers and their agents. Children whose births are not recorded and do not officially exist can easily 'disappear' into the sex industry without a trace.

Similar cases have been experienced by Plan International's partners. A public prosecutor in the Philippines informed Plan International that at least half the cases that go to court involving different forms of child abuse fail because documentation of the child's age is lacking:

> Particularly for children between the ages of 13–17 ... a birth certificate becomes a sine qua non for convincing the court of the child's true age. While oftentimes child victims may resort to late birth registration, the probative value of such documents is weakened and can even put the credibility of the child in question. The defence can easily present arguments questioning the purpose of securing a birth certificate for the child victim at this stage. One may even attack the validity of the document, arguing that some facts may have been altered to suit personal interests. (Dionela, 2003, p 32)

In Bangladesh, Plan International works with its local partner, the Bangladesh National Women Lawyers' Association, which rescues sexually exploited children in the commercial sector. The Association explains that in many cases, due to the lack of a birth certificate, these children cannot be identified as children and therefore the perpetrators are simply not charged (Plan International, 2008). It is clear that proof of age is essential in circumstances where prosecution rests on this very fact. Another important aspect of the birth certificate is proof of parentage and place of birth, which can, in some cases, lead to the establishment of a child's nationality.

Nationality and statelessness

Statelessness, defined as the lack of nationality, impacts on the daily lives of around 11–12 million people around the world. Birth registration does not necessarily confer nationality, and the majority of children who do not possess a birth certificate are not stateless. However, the lack of registration in some cases may lead to this precarious status (Refugees International, 2008).

Research commissioned by Plan International in the Dominican Republic and Thailand in 2007 investigated the relationship between birth registration, nationality and irregular migration (van Waas, 2006). The connection between birth registration and nationality in the Dominican Republic was very clear. The denial of birth registration had become the mechanism for not granting Dominican citizenship to children deemed ineligible, including those of Haitian descent. This was creating new cases of statelessness in the country. In early 2008, the UN Committee on the Rights of the Child noted its concerns about the Dominican Republic's policy on birth registration. It urged them to adopt a policy in which all children born in the country could access the birth registration system in order to stop more children from becoming stateless and forgotten (Committee on the Rights of the Child, 2008).

In Thailand, the issue of statelessness was found to be equally serious, although the connection between birth registration and nationality was not so clear-cut as in the Dominican Republic. However, in both situations, Thai- and Dominican-born children of migrants were at increased risk of statelessness due to the inaccessibility of the birth registration system. Research concluded that the motivation behind such restrictive policies for migrants were due to political and economical concerns. Children who are stateless face similar risks to those children without a birth certificate – limited access to services, rights and life's opportunities.

In terms of trafficking, several studies have highlighted the links between the lack of citizenship and vulnerability to being trafficked. UNESCO research into hill tribes in Thailand found that lack of citizenship was the:

> ... single greatest risk factor for a hill tribe girl or woman to be trafficked or otherwise exploited. Without citizenship, she cannot get a school diploma, register her marriage, own land, or work

outside her home district without special permission. Lack of legal status prevents a woman from finding alternate means of income, rendering her vulnerable to trafficking for sex work or the most abusive forms of labor. (Feingold, 2005, pp 30-1)

Vital Voices (2007), in their report on statelessness and human trafficking in Thailand, agreed. They concluded that by improving access to citizenship in the country this would help eliminate one of the most salient factors that contributes to human trafficking in the country. One of the key steps highlighted to improve access to citizenship was registering the birth of every child. In other countries, work by Refugees International has emphasised the fact that when stateless people have no legal tie to a state, employment in the formal sector is impossible and therefore they are more likely to find work in hazardous conditions (Lynch, 2007).

Proving nationality is equally essential when it comes to rescue and repatriation efforts. Plan Nepal have reported a case where police were unwilling to trace a girl known to have been trafficked across the border to a brothel in India because she had no birth record. This meant there was no proof or her age, nationality or even her existence. With the well-documented pattern of the trafficking of girls from Nepal into India (see Chapter Fifteen, this volume), this is cause for great concern.

Conclusion

As yet, there have been few systematic studies to assess the direct impact of birth registration on child protection outcomes (Plan International, 2008). Much of the evidence is anecdotal, and we know that it is not as simple as giving a child a piece of paper to protect them. As the Asian Development Bank accurately states: 'It is important to bear in mind that child rights violations are caused and perpetuated by a complex interaction of social, economic, political, and cultural factors. Therefore, providing birth certificates will not, by itself, guarantee child rights protection' (Vandenabeele and Lao, 2007, p 32).

What is clear from the evidence and experience highlighted here is that birth registration is not the end-all solution, but it is a tool, and when applied in the right context with the right level of political will, birth registration can go some way to protecting children from slavery-like practices.

A birth certificate is the basis of so many rights for a child. Although rights are interrelated, interdependent and indivisible, the right to an identity is fundamental in realising many other rights. Plan International has documented the benefits of birth registration in many circumstances: children orphaned by AIDS who are denied the right to inherit parental property; proof of age to prevent child marriage; protection under the juvenile justice system; eligibility for assistance in times of crisis caused by disasters, emergencies and war; and rights as an adult to marry, travel, vote, access credit and to inherit land and property. A birth certificate can act as a preventative measure against slavery-like practices. It can prevent children falling into the trap of hazardous work and exploitation at an early age, it can protect them and it can lead to prosecutions against perpetrators of crimes against children.

Through its work, Plan International has identified many strategies for increasing levels of birth registration across the world, which include: raising awareness, conducting mobile registration campaigns, influencing policy and legislation, supporting the decentralisation of civil registration, reducing fees, simplifying procedures and designing special programmes to reach the most marginalised. Despite all the work by Plan International and its partners, many challenges remain, including the need for further research into these connections between birth registration, legal identity and child protection.

It is evident that just as the issues around child slavery are complex, the causes and effects are difficult to unravel, and the challenges are great. As the Asian Development Bank's work on legal identity has emphasised, social, economic, cultural and political factors need to be addressed simultaneously to maximise the value of birth registration. Although birth registration is just a tool and not the solution to all abuses against children, it is a critical first step, as well as one of the simplest. As renowned anthropologist and campaigner David Feingold has noted: 'Many activists have never considered that a fix as simple as promoting birth registration in developing countries is one of the most cost-effective means to combat human trafficking' (Feingold, 2005, p 32).

References

Ashagrie, K. (1998) *Statistics on working children and hazardous child labour in brief (1997–98)*, Geneva: International Labour Organization.

Bales, K. (2007) *Defining and measuring modern slavery*, Washington, DC: Free the Slaves.

Cody, C. (2009) *Count every child: The right to birth registration*, Woking: Plan Ltd.

Committee on the Rights of the Child (2005) *Consideration of reports submitted by states parties under Article 44 of the Convention*, Thirty-ninth session, concluding observations, Nepal and New York: Committee on the Rights of the Child.

Committee on the Rights of the Child (2008) *Consideration of reports submitted by states parties under Article 44 of the Convention*, Forty-seventh session, concluding observations, Dominican Republic and New York: Committee on the Rights of the Child.

Concern (2005) *Child labour in brick kilns in Nepal*, Kathmandu: Concern.

Dionela, A. (2003) *Toward universal child registration: Mid-term assessment of birth registration initiatives in Bangladesh, India, Pakistan and the Philippines*, Bangkok: Plan Asia.

Feingold, D. (2005) 'Human trafficking', *Foreign Policy*, September/October, pp 30-2 (www.hrusa.org/workshops/trafficking/ThinkAgain.pdf#search=%22david%20 feingold%20%22greatest%20risk%20factor%22%20hill%20tribe%20 population%20citizenship%22).

HRW (Human Rights Watch) (2008) *Denied status, denied education: Children of North Korean women in China*, New York, NY: Human Rights Watch.

IPDS Xi'an Jiaotong University (2005) *An exploratory investigation of birth registration in China: Situations, determinants and promotion policies*, Xian: Plan China.

Lynch, M. (2007) *Child labor common among the displaced and stateless*, Washington, DC: Refugees International.

Plan (2005) *Universal birth registration: Permanent proof of identity in a turbulent world*, Woking: Plan Ltd.

Plan Cambodia (2005) *Birth registration campaign*, Phnom Penh: Plan Cambodia.

Plan Ghana (2004) 'Birth registration in Ghana: overview, impact, challenges study to inform Plan Ghana's campaign on birth registration', Unpublished.

Plan India (2008) *Count every child as every child counts*, New Delhi: Plan India.

Plan International (2008) *Reaching child protection aims through universal birth registration: The experience of Plan in Asia*, Discussion paper prepared for the East Asia and the Pacific Regional Preparatory meeting for the World Congress III against Sexual Exploitation of Children and Adolescents, 18-19 August, Bangkok: Plan Asia.

Refugees International (2008) *Futures denied*, Washington, DC: Refugees International.

SCF (2005) *Forgotten casualties of war: Girls in armed conflict*, London: Save the Children.

Todres, J. (2006) 'The importance of realising "other rights" to prevent sex trafficking', *Cardozo Journal of Law and Gender*, vol 12, pp 885–907.

UNDP (United Nations Development Programme) (2007) *Human trafficking and HIV: Exploring vulnerabilities and responses in South Asia*, Colombo: UNDP.

UNICEF (2001) *Children on the edge: Protecting children from sexual exploitation and trafficking in East Asia and the Pacific*, Bangkok: UNICEF.

UNICEF (2005) *Trafficking in human beings, especially women and children in Africa*, Florence: UNICEF.

UNICEF (2007) *Progress for children: A world fit for children, statistical review* (www.unicef.org/protection/index_birthregistration.html).

UNOHCHR (United Nations Office of the High Commissioner for Human Rights) (nd) *Contemporary forms of slavery, Fact sheet number 14*, New York, NY: UNOHCHR.

van de Glind, H. and Kooijmans, J. (2008) 'Modern-day child slavery', *Children and Society: Special Issue Child Slavery Worldwide*, vol 22, no 3, pp 167-79.

van Waas, L.E. (2006) *Is permanent illegality inevitable? The challenges to ensuring birth registration and the right to a nationality for children of irregular migrants – Thailand and the Dominican Republic*, Woking: Plan International.

Vandenabeele, C. and Lao, C.V. (eds) (2007) *Legal identity for inclusive development*, Manila: Asian Development Bank.

Vital Voices (2007) *Stateless and vulnerable to human trafficking in Thailand*, Washington, DC: Vital Voices Global Partnership.

eleven

'Bienvenue chez les grands!': young migrant cigarette vendors in Marseille

Brenda Oude Breuil

Introduction

Every year, an unknown number of boys from the Maghreb region arrive in the ports of Marseille after long and often hazardous boat trips. According to local social workers, Marseille is the jumping-off point for 'El Dorado' to these young migrants, a place of unlimited possibilities to realise a better life for their families or to find the consumerist lifestyle long dreamt of. Once in Marseille they are generally taken under the wings of young men from their own ethnic communities, living and trading in working-class neighbourhoods in the city centre. Labour migration from this region is not new; long-standing connections exist between the countries of origin and Marseille (Temime, 1997), aptly called 'Porte de l'Afrique' (or 'Porte de l'Orient'; see Dell'Umbria, 2006, p 75).

From the moment they leave their homesteads and in the course of finding their place in Marseille's cityscape, these boys and young men will cross several borders, physical and visible ones in the first place, such as national borders. But they also cross social borders, defining their place in the social hierarchy. Their income-earning activities as cigarette vendors obfuscates with their social status as children; they are easily seen as illegal, 'expellable' migrants, notwithstanding their minority. Even though the exploitation sometimes involved in their work might qualify them as child victims of trafficking, whom the state is obliged legally and socially to protect, this legal status is not even considered in local authorities' treatment of their cases. Where French authorities try to force young vendors into clear-cut social and legal categories (that best suit national interests), their lives are better described as being betwixt and between. They have no clear status, live in squats at the margins of city life and dwell between accepted social categories. Such liminal settings can be called 'borderlands'.

Borderlands are peculiar places. Being at the margins of one's own, known world (often experienced as safe and homely), borderlands may evoke feelings of freedom, excitement, adventure and anxiety (Löfgren, 2002). Old structures, hierarchies and rules that guide behaviour 'back home' no longer apply, and they are not yet replaced by new ones, creating a sense of being 'in limbo'. Being outside national borders and not (yet or fully) accepted as a member of another nation state may cause feelings of insecurity and danger. One cannot claim a physical, legal and social place 'of one's own', nor is one protected by authorities who feel responsible for one's well-being. The same can be said about metaphorical borderlands between accepted social categories; they withhold from a person a sense of 'belonging' to a group, a socially relevant role and guiding rules of behaviour. This liminal position in the social structure creates insecurities for the person residing in a borderland; citizens who are firmly integrated in the social order often fear individuals coming from borderlands, as the latter embody liminality, an attack on what is familiar and safe, and a threat to ordered (city) life.

This anxiety can be clearly recognised in the case of migrating and trafficked children. Migrating children are often perceived as deviating from western social constructions of childhood, which dictate that the proper place of a child is at home or at school (Stephens, 1995, p 13; Agustín, 2005; Terrio, 2008, p 880; see also Oude Breuil, 2008, p 225). When working in the informal economy on the street, they are often perceived of as dangerous and a threat to social security. Trafficked children, for their part, are approached as being in danger, as innocent victims, unable to fend for themselves. They evoke moral outrage and fierce sentiments of protection, according to O'Connell Davidson (2005, p 22), because child trafficking attacks socially constructed divisions that order social life. Even though juridicial definitions of child trafficking suggest clear dividing lines both between children and adults, and between voluntary and forced migration, empirical studies of child trafficking (for example, Ahmad, 2005; Bastia, 2005; Agustín, 2007; Oude Breuil, 2008) show that these categories are not so clear-cut. Moreover, children and young people may attach more complex and diverse meanings to their trafficking experience than the legal categorisation of 'victim' allows for. Child migration and child trafficking thus blur existing categories, as well as underlying norms, values, social roles and power hierarchies. Reactions to both phenomena may therefore be fierce and full of emotions.

The experiences of the young Maghrebi migrants are an almost perfect example of the blurring of physical and social demarcation lines. They are often not accepted into the national, legal or social setting of their choice, and they resist the (physical or social) place appointed to them. Here, we address the question of how they cross physical and social borders while trying to build a life in the cityscape and social hierarchy of Marseille. In the first two sections of the chapter we see how they occupy city space while trying to reconstruct their lives and the social and physical borders they cross in this process. Then we explore the interplay of their efforts to create a place in Marseille, and local policies to come to terms with their presence. Different disciplining strategies, often acted out on young migrants' bodies, aim at appointing them a 'proper' place, in accordance with existing social hierarchies. Finally, we suggest revaluating the narrative capacity of migrants' social bodies and listen anew to what their border crossing realities are really telling us.

Occupying city space: plying the trade in cigarettes

It is six o'clock in the evening and the informal market at Porte d'Aix is in full swing. It is situated around the metro exit and spreads out on the car park, even between parked cars. The market constitutes a diverse blend of people: a Roma woman selling second-hand clothes, young (Sub-Saharan) African men selling mobile telephones and sunglasses and older Algerian men vending chewing tobacco. "Ici tout est en vente" ("everything is for sale here"), one of my informants tells me, and I believe him immediately, watching indistinguishable merchandise being sold quickly underhand.

Near the metro exit are two cigarette vendors; two others are positioned a bit further away. The cigarette vendors are typically young Maghrebi boys of about 15 to 17 years old, dressed in spotless jeans and t-shirts, hair decently cut, mostly working in pairs. The first takes care of the actual selling, while the second surveys the marketplace, trying to spot potential clients, or the police, who pay occasional visits to the market. When his vending partner runs out of supplies, the second partner gets a new carton from the hiding place behind the wheel of an old Peugeot, which is parked on the edge of the market. The boys buy their cartons of contraband Marlboro for €23 from a third person, someone from "the local mafia", they vaguely indicate, unwilling to go deeper into the subject. They sell their carton for €30, making a profit of €7 per carton. They sell the whole carton at once, in which case they put it in a nondescript, brown paper bag and hand it over to the buyer, or one or more packages at a time. The packages are stored in their jeans pockets, with long t-shirts hiding them from view. When continuing the selling for some hours, they may earn up to €60 a day, that is, if they are not caught by the police, in which case they lose their supplies, at the very least, and have to pay their losses to the supplier. When police appear, they swiftly disappear via the metro exit.

The practice of selling illegal cigarettes in the informal markets is a fascinating play on being visible while being (partly) invisible. In order to sell cigarettes the boys have to make sure they are recognised by eventual buyers. They do this by whispering 'cigarettes, cigarettes' or just the name of the brand they sell, but they sell their merchandise without even naming it as well; they just scan the public for restless and searching glances that may indicate a want. They approach the individual, ask if they can help, and if the buyer is looking for cigarettes they do their sale quickly, seemingly indifferently and almost invisibly. If the client is after something else, they will helpfully indicate which vendor to approach. They take care to maintain smooth interpersonal relationships with other vendors, as well as with clients, as the former might refer buyers to them later on, and the latter might be looking for cigarettes next time. Selling contraband cigarettes thus demands some evident qualities: it requires a trained eye, to be socially skilled, unobtrusive in one's vending ways, be able to oversee the marketplace – its possibilities and its dangers – and to be 'cool', not showing excitement or nerves.

Cigarette vendors evidently have their own, meaningful place in the cityscape of Marseille, more particularly in the markets. They have been there for decades, according to a city official (Temime, 1997, p 68; Bouillon, 2001, p 241), and their trade is as common a view in Marseille as the sunset at the Vieux Port. Their place in the city's everyday life is officially witnessed by the cameras the city government has placed at the entrance in order to curb petty criminality. Some employees of the city government laughingly told me that the vending of cigarettes happens right under these cameras, sometimes in plain view. The local police do not seem to be too bothered by the illegal vending, or have other priorities. Moreover, the boys see to the demand for cheap cigarettes among all social levels of Marseille's population, thereby earning a (to them) acceptable income with which they provide for their families ... just like 'regular' citizens, one might be inclined to say. These observations may give the impression that cigarette vendors are an accepted, or at least publicly tolerated, socially integrated group in the Marseille cityscape.

Life in limbo: 'those who burn their papers'

But that would be too positive an interpretation. Even though some citizens, in particular locals of the same ethnic group, show solidarity with the young migrants and help them hide their merchandise or find a place to stay, the boys' 'belonging' to a social structure stops short here. Many citizens consider them to be a plague and associate them with pickpocketing and petty criminality. Temime (1997, p 69), author of several writings on the history of migration in Marseille, cites police reports and newspaper articles in order to illustrate the stigmatisation that always befell the illegal vendors here, as it still does: "Un lecteur du *Méridional* ne parle-t-il pas encore en 1985 de la place d'Aix 'rebaptisée place des Délits protégés'(...)?" ("Didn't a reader of the *Méridional*, even in 1985, speak of the square of Aix 'rebaptised square of the Protected offences'?"). Their position in the social hierarchy is betwixt and between, not only in Marseille but also 'back home'. A closer look at their backgrounds illustrates that.

The young migrants predominantly come from North African countries – Algeria, Morocco and Tunisia – living in families at the bottom of the socioeconomic ladder. Generally unemployment and insufficient education characterise the lives of parents and siblings, making their own future perspectives look gloomy. Families live in neighbourhoods that are deprived of possibilities to earn a decent living, and of structural social facilities. Although some of the boys encountered do come from families that manage to offer family members a source of material and emotional stability, most of them report tensions and conflicts with their parents or other family members. These can be poverty-related – overcrowded houses, illness, alcoholism, unemployment, financial crises – but are often 'normal' intergenerational conflicts. Many boys report that they have left because they wanted to lead an autonomous life and to escape parental authority (see also Keilland and Sanogo, in Whitehead and Hashim, 2005; EFUS, 2009, pp 49-52).

They leave home because they dream of foreign lands, most often 'Europe' – which we might as well call 'Eurotopia', considering their unrealistic, Utopian expectations of getting rich fast and joining a paradise-like consumerism. In order to achieve this 'land of tempting Otherness' (Löfgren, 2002, p 260), they are willing to go a great way, even risk their lives, hiding illegally in the cargo hold of huge vessels, paying a smuggler to take them on an organised boat trip or putting money together to buy a small craft and the necessary supplies. Once in Marseille, they live in squats in the more dilapidated parts of Marseille, for which they pay the local (illegal) squat 'owner'. Sometimes they give the 'owner' part of the profit of their cigarette vending in exchange for their dwelling. The files of the Association Jeunes Errants (AJE)[1] showed that in at least one case, shelter was being paid by providing sexual services to the patron.

It is hard to determine whether these boys fit into the category of (illegal) migrants, who voluntarily work in one of the only sectors accessible to them, or as victims of child trafficking. Juridically, the difference between the two categories is in the eventual exploitation of the child: if a cigarette vendor is exploited, one could legally speak of trafficking. According to Article 3(a) of the Palermo Protocol, 'exploitation shall include, at a minimum, the exploitation of the prostitution of others or other forms of sexual exploitation, forced labour or services, slavery or practices similar to slavery, servitude or the removal of organs'. However clear-cut that may seem, in practice it is hard to decide whether the working conditions of young migrant cigarette vendors can be qualified as exploitation, especially since the 'terms of employment' are not the same for all. Does selling cigarettes in exchange for a meagre, but in their view, acceptable income constitute exploitation? Or selling cigarettes in exchange for residence in a dilapidated shelter? Or selling cigarettes *and* offering sexual services in exchange for shelter and a meagre income? Such questions of the limits of a legal concept are important, because an eventual legal qualification of a young migrant as a victim of child trafficking entitles her or him to special rights and protection measures, such as emergency shelter and a (temporary) residence permit.

Their vague legal position is linked in a complex way to the adult/child divide. Whereas this divide is unambiguous on paper (unaccompanied minors are entitled to protection measures and cannot be expelled), it is not in legal practice. Authorities often (informally) delay legal procedures just until a young migrant turns 18 (a common practice in other European countries) so s/he can eventually be summoned to leave. But not only does the French government treat them ambiguously as far as their age is concerned; their self-image also does not correspond to western constructions of childhood. In western thought children are often 'seen as immature, irrational, incompetent, passive, vulnerable, and helpless' (Theis, 2001, p 100; see also Ariès, 1962; Stephens, 1995; Lee, 2001) and are therefore entitled to adult protection and special rights. Although young cigarette vendors might, in theory, legally and socially benefit from a categorisation as 'children', in fact they emphasise their independence and autonomy, illustrated in their common expression that they are "managing all right" ("Je me debrouille, moi!").

The young migrant vendors are not only betwixt and between in a symbolic sense, as far as legal and social categories are concerned. Their borderland existence is reflected in their physical place. The young migrants' working places, the illegal markets, are obviously physically real, but at the same time not officially there, a 'no-man's-land, [...] terrain vague, unchartered margins "in the middle of nowhere," [...] black holes, attracting a lot of energy and anxiety', as Löfgren describes it (2002, p 252). The square of Porte d'Aix was, after all, never meant to be an informal market, even though it has been for a long time. The addition of a car park should have curbed the commercial efforts of the illegal vendors (Bouillon, 2001, p 240), but it did not. The market is a liminal place in Marseille's cityscape. And although the cigarette vendors consider their work a real job, these jobs officially 'do not exist'; the vendors are not really 'there'. Their earnings do not appear in the city's economic statistics or generate tax revenues. Even though their faces and trade are caught on the surveillance video tapes, enforcement of the laws that forbid this kind of trade is highly ambiguous; when the police raid the market and catch a vendor, they usually just take his cartons and let him walk, without reporting the offence, as an employee of the bar in the middle of Porte d'Aix told me.[2] Even as *illegal* vendors the boys do not exist unequivocally: they are neither treated as legal nor as straightforwardly illegal.

It therefore cannot be said that young cigarette vendors are tightly integrated in Marseille's social city life. They are, however, not fully 'belonging to' the society they have left either. Disappointment about what their home country has to offer them, but also insecurity about their place in the family due to their sometimes unexpected leaving or parents' support of their migration and unwillingness to reintegrate their child in the family household, have cut them loose from their original 'homes'. They see no future there, as one clearly expressed: "Même si c'est la misère ici, c'est mieux que là-bas" ("Even if it's a misery here [in Marseille], it is still better than there ['back home']"). They find themselves in a liminal phase or borderland, belonging neither to society nor a social structure. The precariousness and hardship this position implies might be reflected in frequent drug abuse – "to forget", one of my informants said – and a high incidence of scarification. Their liminality is expressed in the name they give themselves: *harragas*, meaning 'those who burn their papers before leaving' (EFUS, 2009, p 50). Identity papers being the most tangible proof of a person's political and legal identity, this illustrates their (temporary) non- or semi-existence in physical and social borderlands. Their ambiguous position makes their position in Marseille insecure, vague and open to manipulation.

Dreaming sovereignty, fearing majority

Rue Gambetta, the broad, cheerful street in Marseille's centre, is leaving its daytime jumble for the cooler ambiance of nightfall. Damien,[3] a skilled social worker, has been touring nightshifts with me for several weeks now, riding the motorcycle up and down the street, trying to spot familiar faces in the snack bars. Groups of boys and young men, all similarly dressed in sportsuits, high quality t-shirts and baseball caps, crowd around the snack bars' chairs and tables, cheerfully talking, laughing and punching each others' shoulders. One of them sees us and leaves his peers to come out and talk.

Fuad looks cool in his white, shining La Coste sportsuit, golden necklaces and spiky hair, highlighted at the tops and peeping out from under his baseball cap. I remember Damien's remark a few days ago, following my question of how to recognise an isolated minor: "Just look for the latest mark sportsuit, often glazing white … expensive clothes, shoes … you name it." We discussed stereotype notions of street children, as wearing poor and dirty clothes. According to Damien, working with these boys for some time now, it is not like that any more. "Especially when coming from the *bled*[4] they take such care of their appearances … you wonder how they manage to keep their white pants so clean while living in squats and on markets! They want to be part of that western consumption culture so much…."

We shake hands and start to talk. Fuad travelled from Casablanca to Marseille by boat. "Hidden? Hidden on the boat?" asks Damien, who knows the usual story all too well. But Fuad frowns. "No, with a passport and everything!" Fuad did not come to Marseille illegally, as most boys from the *bled* do. He was spotted by a football trainer who wanted to introduce him to some scouts in France. The trainer paid his trip, as well as those of 13 other boys who travelled with him to Marseille. Fuad cannot clearly explain where his boy's dream went wrong, but it is clear that his fantasy of living a professional footballer's life in Europe did not come true. Fuad was left to the crowded streets of Marseille, and picked up by young Moroccan men like himself, who directed him towards an organisation for 'young errants' (the AJE).

The *éducateurs de rues* (streetcorner workers) of the organisation were willing to help him fight for a legal status in France. They were used to this; until 2003 foreign unaccompanied minors could be taken in charge by the Aide Sociale à l'Enfance (ASE, the French Child Welfare Agency) if found without parental supervision. On turning 18 they could apply for French citizenship, provided that they were registered with the ASE and could show that they were making efforts to become socially integrated in French society (Terrio, 2008). Fuad was registered at ASE and started off on the long and cumbersome road of regulations, procedures, intakes for projects run by different associations, screenings, paperwork and a lot of waiting. He got additional schooling and a work placement at a bakery, but he does not yet receive a salary, neither has he got a CDD or a CDI (*contrat durée déterminée/indéterminée*, respectively a temporary/indeterminate job contract), which would have certainly improved his chances of applying for French citizenship before 2003. But his chances for such a status have dramatically dropped since then, as a new law on immigration control (Terrio, 2008) has narrowed the legal advantages for such minors.

Fuad is worried sick and looks tense and weary, for tomorrow is his 18th birthday. Whereas for many this would be a festive occasion, a celebration of one's existence in time and place, for Fuad it is a nightmare. He will officially not be a minor any more and the protective measures for children, which have so far prevented his forced return to Morocco, will no longer apply. Immigration politics cut short his dreams to build an independent life in France; on becoming 18, the age signalling legal adulthood, Fuad finds himself dependent on a prefect who is known for his severe stance on young migrants, and sees his mature educational and job efforts go up in smoke. When I ask him whether he is considering going back to Morocco if the quest for a residence permit leads to a dead end, he clicks his tongue and vehemently shakes his head. "There is nothing there," he explains, referring to his home town. If he gets a 'quit', as young migrants call the official letter from the prefect requiring them to leave French territory within a predetermined period of time, he will probably try to reach England from the common jumping-off point in Calais – a dangerous endeavour. Fuad sighs as we prepare to leave and shake hands. "Don't pull a long face, tomorrow is your birthday!" Damien ironically remarks. The joke does not escape Fuad, who, for the first time, breaks into laughter. As we drive off, Damien shouts after Fuad, who raises his hand in a greeting: "Ciao, bonne fête! Bienvenu chez les grands…" ("Bye, have a nice party! Welcome to the grown-ups…").

Local politics of exclusion: no bones broken?

Age has become one of the main measuring rods by which decisions are made over the space that is granted young migrants to eventually build a life in France. Even though age, at first glance, may seem an impartial and clear-cut legal criteria, reality bites. It turns out to be a rather flexible concept that might be adapted according to political goals concerning immigration control. As Terrio illustrates, the moral economy (see also Fassin, 2008, p 215) of immigration policies concerning foreign unaccompanied minors has undergone a significant change in France since the country signed the Convention on the Rights of the Child (CRC) in 1990. There has been 'a substantive shift in the juvenile justice system from a focus on prevention, assistance and rehabilitation to an emphasis on accountability, restitution, and retribution' (Terrio, 2008, p 879). Moreover, two reports on unaccompanied minors from 2003 and 2005 have recommended restrictions on their legal advantages (Landrieu, 2003; Terrio, 2008, p 885; and see the report of the Inspection Générale des Affaires Sociales, 2005), such as the above-mentioned right to apply for French citizenship at the age of 18.

In Marseille, the actual juridicial practice on unaccompanied minors in the 15–18 age cohort appears to be particularly harsh, ignoring international conventions. This matter was discussed in a colloquium in Marseille in June 2009.[5] Part of the discussions between lawyers, social workers, judges, immigration workers and social scientists was about the use of skeletal tests in legal procedures for determining the age of foreign unaccompanied minors. This particular use of medical tests for legal purposes is medically and ethically highly controversial (Adamsbaum et al, 2008). The most commonly used method, the Greulich and Pyle method (determining the skeletal age by taking an X-ray of the left hand and wrist), can only measure how the skeleton evolves, not determine an absolute age. The individual variation in skeletal development is about one year, making the method imprecise for legal decision making.

Notwithstanding this controversy, local associations, judges and lawyers at the colloquium had reported how such tests were increasingly and unproblematically used to determine young migrants' legal age. Moreover, the general impression was that the tests were primarily used to escape legal obligations to protect foreign unaccompanied minors. Whereas a lawyer from the Paris region reported a decrease in the use of such tests there in recent years (see also Terrio, 2008), this could not be confirmed by lawyers and social workers from Marseille. As one lawyer reflected, "the skeletal test is still very common here [in Marseille] and it is taken by magistrates as a precise measure, with disastrous results for unaccompanied minors". She recounted the case of a young migrant cigarette vendor, 16 years of age, who voluntarily underwent a skeletal test and was legally treated as an adult on the basis of it. The court put everything to work in order to expel him from French territory, notwithstanding the legal birth certificate retrieved by social workers, which stated that he was 16 years old, and the child protection measure that the boy had been accorded earlier in juvenile court. According to the lawyer, and confirmed by social workers, this was not an isolated case.

The common use of skeletal tests in Marseille as instruments to justify expulsion of minors illustrates that children's rights, which ought to be granted to all persons below 18 years of age, are vulnerable to local and national reinterpretation. The importance of medical knowledge in decisions on which foreigners are and which are not 'good migrants' (Terrio, 2008, p 885) corresponds to Fassin's (2001, p 7) conclusion that 'the contemporary biopolitics of otherness in France rests on one major foundation: the recognition of the body as the ultimate site of political legitimacy'. However, Fassin's research suggests that medical knowledge might help (sick) immigrants to acquire a legal status in France, as 'it is more acceptable for the state to turn down an asylum claim ... than to reject a medical opinion recommending legal permit for health reasons' (Fassin, 2001, pp 4-5). In the case of young migrant cigarette vendors in Marseille we see how medical knowledge may turn *against* the young migrants. Medical knowledge is used to prove that a young migrant is 'undeserving' of what French society might have to offer him, notwithstanding his possible – and not even verified – victimisation from the offence of child trafficking.

Conclusion: silenced bodies, crossing borders of integrity?

A common notion among human rights workers and anthropologists alike is that the body is 'the site and surface of essential but otherwise obscured social truths' (Klinenberg, 2002, p 121). Bodies, be they dead or alive, narrate a story about the individual's being in the world, as physical and social contexts inscribe themselves in the body; individuals 'embody' their surrounding physical and social circumstances. Klinenberg, however, states that once bodies are treated solely as medical evidence, their social 'being in the world' gets obscured and the narrating capacity gets lost. The same can be said for the way young migrants' bodies are treated in juridical procedures in Marseille. Their position can be described as a life 'in the borderlands' after they have crossed national borders, city demarcation lines and borders between categories of legality/illegality, adulthood/childhood and illegal migrant/victim of trafficking. They remain stuck between national, legal and social borders, not fully belonging to any territory, age group or legal category. This makes their position insecure and open to manipulation. Minor, foreign, cigarette vendors are feared because they are outside of the normal social order. They are socially stigmatised and reduced to a category of 'unwanted' migrants, even though the exploitation some of them experience might lead one to legally interpret these cases as incidences of child trafficking.

In order to deal with the anxiety young migrants evoke, the French government submits them to strategies of control, comparable to border controls. In the case of cigarette vendors in Marseille these 'border controls' are exercised directly on young migrants' bodies. Their bodies are used in legal procedures as medical sites from which to gather evidence against their own claims to their identity. Skeletal tests inscribe the selective truth of Marseille politics on young migrants' bodies and point out on which side of the border they belong: 'child' or 'adult', 'deserving' or 'undeserving', 'in need of protection' or 'to be protected against'. By using medical knowledge, young migrant cigarette vendors' low position in the social hierarchy is exposed and they are appointed their 'proper' place in the social universe: go back home, is the general message, we do not want you here.

Whether such stoic efforts reconstruct (old) borders around physical and social space by applying harsh methods of 'border control' is very much the question. It may be more fruitful to return to what young migrants' bodies really have to tell us; it seems important not only to read from those bodies biological truths, but social truths as well. As described here, their social reality is often that of the borderland, of living between places and social categories. Forcing borders on them may make us miss a lot of useful information on structural social problems and inequalities that made them leave home in the first place. As O'Connell Davidson (2005, p 84) aptly states: 'If we want them to make different choices, we had better think how to do something about the nothingness of their alternatives'. Moreover, turning the gaze to the anxiety and fear that borderlands – and the people who dwell in them – evoke in those enjoying a secure position within national borders might give the latter useful insights into their own society and the moral principles defining it.

Notes

[1] This association was created in 1995 in order to provide a minimum of subsistence provisions for unaccompanied minors in Marseille. Its main clientele has always been young Maghrebi boys, many earning their income by vending cigarettes. (The association changed into a Federation in 2008.)

[2] Independently confirmed by a social worker and one of the young migrants themselves.

[3] For reasons of anonymity, all names are fictitional.

[4] French expression for 'the inland', used in the context of North Africa.

[5] The colloquium 'Mineurs Étrangers Isolés' was held at the occasion of the publication of the report *Jeunes en errance: Les conditions d'un retour* (*Wandering young people: The conditions for return*) (EFUS, 2009), a feasibility study conducted by AJE (Marseille), the Terre des Hommes – Aide à l'Enfance Foundation (Budapest Bureau) and the European Forum for Urban Safety (EFUS) (Paris), with the cooperation of the author (Utrecht University) as expert in the project, and the support of the European Commission.

References

Adamsbaum, C., Chaumoitre, K. and Panuel, M. (2008) 'La détermination de l'âge osseux à des fins médico-légales, que faire?', *Journal de Radiologie*, vol 89, pp 455-6.

Agustín, L. (2005) 'At home in the street: questioning the desire to help and save', in E. Bernstein and L. Schaffner (eds) *Regulating sex: The politics of intimacy and identity*, London: Routledge, pp 67-83.

Agustín, L. (2007) *Sex at the margins: Migration, labour markets and the rescue industry*, London: Zed Books.

Ahmad, N. (2005) 'Trafficked persons or economic migrants? Bangladeshis in India', in K. Kempadoo (ed) *Trafficking and prostitution reconsidered. New perspectives on migration, sex work, and human rights*, Boulder, CO: Paradigm Publishers, pp 211-27.

Ariès, P. (1962) *Centuries of childhood: A social history of the family life*, New York, NY: Vintage Books.

Bastia, T. (2005) 'Child trafficking or teenage migration? Bolivian migrants in Argentina', *International Migration*, vol 43, no 4, pp 57-89.

Bouillon, F. (2001) 'Des acteurs et des lieux: les économies de la rue à Marseille', in M. Peraldi (ed) *Cabas et containers. Activités marchandes informelles et réseaux migrants transfrontaliers*, Paris: Maisonneuve et Larose, pp 237-68.

Dell'Umbria, A. (2006) *Histoire universelle de Marseille. De l'an mil à l'an deux mille*, Marseille: Agone.

EFUS (European Forum for Urban Security) (2009) *Jeunes en errance: Les conditions d'un retour* (*Wandering young people: The conditions for return*), Paris: EFUS.

Fassin, D. (2001) 'The biopolitics of otherness. Undocumented foreigners and racial discrimination in French public debate', *Anthropology Today*, vol 17, no 1, pp 3-7.

Fassin, D. (2008) 'Compassion and repression: the moral economy of immigration policies in France', in J. Inda and R. Rosaldo (eds) *The anthropology of globalization. A reader*, Malden, MA: Blackwell Publishing, pp 212-34.

Inspection Génerale des Affaires Sociales (2005) *Mission d'analyse et de proposition sur les conditions d'accueil des mineurs étrangers isolés en France*, Rapport No 2005 010, Paris: IGAS.

Klinenberg, E. (2002) 'Bodies that don't matter: death and dereliction in Chicago', in N. Scheper-Hughes and L. Wacquant (eds) *Commodifying bodies*, London: Sage Publications, pp 121-36.

Lee, N. (2001) *Childhood and society. Growing up in an age of uncertainty*, Buckingham: Open University Press.

Löfgren, O. (2002) 'The nationalization of anxiety: a history of border crossings', in U. Hedetoft and M. Hjort (eds) *The postnational self. Belonging and identity*, Minneapolis, MN and London: University of Minnesota Press, pp 250-74.

O'Connell Davidson, J. (2005) *Children in the global sex trade*, Cambridge: Polity Press.

Oude Breuil, B. (2008) 'Precious children in a heartless world? The complexities of child trafficking in Marseille', *Children and Society*, vol 22, pp 223-34.

Stephens, S. (1995) 'Introduction. Children and the politics of culture in "late capitalism"', in S. Stephens (ed) *Children and the politics of culture*, Princeton, NJ: Princeton University Press, pp 3-24.

Temime, É. (1997) *Marseille transit: Les passagers de Belsunce*, Paris: Éditions Autrement.

Terrio, S. (2008) 'New barbarians at the gates of Paris? Prosecuting undocumented minors in the juvenile court – the problem of the "petits roumains"', *Anthropological Quarterly*, vol 81, no 4, pp 873-901.

Theis, J. (2001) 'Participatory research with children in Vietnam', in H. Schwartzman (ed) *Children and anthropology. Perspectives for the 21st century*, Westport, CT: Bergin & Garvey, pp 99-109.

Whitehead, A. and Hashim, I. (2005) *Children and migration*, Background Paper for DFID Migration Team, London: Department for International Development.

twelve

Child domestic labour: fostering in transition?

Evelyn Omoike

Introduction

There is an increasing degree of commercialisation associated with the practice of employing child domestic workers in Africa. As at 2001, there was a record of about 14 million child domestic servants in African cities (Andvig et al, 2001) with some brought across national borders. In 2007, Human Rights Watch recorded domestic work as the largest employment sector for children in Africa, 85% being girls (HRW, 2007). Various policies such as the International Labour Organization's (ILO) 1973 Minimum Age Convention No 138, and 1999 Worst Forms of Child Labour Convention No 182 (see Chapters One and Three, this volume) and the 1989 UN Convention on the Rights of the Child (CRC) were promulgated to protect child labourers (child domestic labourers) from exploitation and harmful work. Despite concerted efforts on the part of international organisations, children who work as domestics are often the most exploited and most difficult to protect due to their confinement, age, sex and invisibility (see Chapter Five, this volume). The most recent submission from the ILO and other international organisations, the Worst Forms of Child Labour Convention No 182, was borne out of consideration for the diversity of work undertaken by children around the world. This Convention acknowledged that not all child work is bad, thereby altering the focus from eliminating all forms of child labour to concentrating on the worst forms of child labour (slavery or slavery-like practices, prostitution, trafficking, work that by its nature or the circumstances in which it is carried out is likely to harm the health, safety or morals of children) (Liebel, 2007). The consensus was that what needs to be addressed is the nature of work that children undertake, not the simple fact that children work.

As with other policies on child labour, this Convention was followed by various debates. It raises a number of particular challenges for child domestic labourers and potentially reinforces their exploitation. One of the challenges is that in Africa, domestic labour is not considered harmful work for children and is often rooted in societal and traditional practices

(Blagbrough and Glynn, 1999). Another is that focusing on the nature of work alone excludes the process/circumstances through which children become child domestic labourers. Children are recruited, trafficked, bonded (as a means of debt repayment), fostered and voluntarily go into domestic service, but the trafficking of children (recruitment, transportation, transfer, harbouring or receipt of children for the purpose of exploitation) is the only circumstance that is recognised as illegal under Convention No 182. In many African societies, children are sent into domestic service through the means listed above for the benefit of the child or the entire family. This could occur with or without the child's consent but does not preclude exploitation of the child. Categorisation of child work primarily based on the nature of work children do without taking into consideration the process or circumstances through which children gain entry into domestic labour leaves a gap in the level of protection offered to child domestic labourers, particularly in societies where the culture of child domestic work is hidden within pseudo (false) relationships and the determination of the worst forms of child labour is left to national authorities.

The aim here is to examine the fosterage system, one of the routes through which children are recruited into domestic service. The gap in the protection offered to child domestic workers and the potential challenges from Convention No 182 will be highlighted through the account of child domestic workers' entry and experiences of the fosterage system. We argue that current child labour policies and interventions that focus primarily on the nature of work those children undertake fail to take into account the nature of domestic work in regions such as Africa. This consequently exposes and potentially reinforces the exclusion and exploitation that African child domestic labourers face.

Child domestic labour in Africa

Child domestic labour is one of the most common forms of occupation for children, particularly for girls. It takes place within households and is often informal and invisible. The term 'child domestic worker' refers to paid or unpaid domestic tasks undertaken by very young children, that is, 'those under the legal minimum working age, as well as domestic tasks undertaken by children above the legal minimum age but under the age of 18, under exploitative conditions ...' (ILO, 2004, p 7). Child domestic labourers are marginalised both economically and socially, as domestic work is often seen as a safe form of employment for children. In many African countries, a child undertaking domestic work within the household is an accepted practice and is rooted in societal traditions and culture. It is not uncommon to find children undertaking various domestic tasks within the household (Nieuwenhuys, 1996). The expectation that children would provide labour to their families and communities is also noted in the 1990 African Charter on the Rights and Welfare of the Child (Articles 31a and 31b).

Child domestic workers encounter a wide range of abuses, including physical or verbal abuse and sexual violence that routinely accompanies this type of work. Many child domestic labourers are subjected to slavery-like practices. They may have to use unfamiliar machinery, chemicals, acids and other materials considered health hazards, often with very little protection and no training on how to handle dangerous substances. They are expected to perform skilled tasks such as childcare with minimum training and are severely punished for their mistakes. They can be on call 24 hours a day and may be awakened during the middle of the night to tend to their employers' needs. They perform multiple tasks often under the supervision and discipline of different employers. Child domestic workers are predominantly girls due to the gendered nature attributed to domestic work. They are highly isolated due to their invisibility behind closed doors, and due to the hidden nature of the work, it is almost impossible to tell how many children work in domestic service. These categories of child labourers are particularly difficult to protect as their labour is not considered work, but rather a mere extension of their obligations in the household.

As a subset of child labour, child domestic labour is not impervious to the general debates and complexities surrounding children working. But the nature of domestic work, its invisibility, the sanctity of the household, culture, ideology and the acceptance of domestic work as a safe form of work for children further adds to the complexities surrounding this form of child labour.

One of the key challenges for child domestic labour is the low economic value accorded to child work. Albeit the ILO definition of child domestic labour covers paid and unpaid work, domestic work is barely regarded as a viable commodity (ILO, 2004). The economic underpinning (fiscal value) of child work excludes children involved in unremunerated work such as domestic labour. Based on this economic bias, previous interventions have been targeted at the structured formal sector, where it is relatively rare to find children working. This only impacted on some portions of the formal sector while sanctioning a variety of activities such as housekeeping, child minding, domestic service, seasonal work on the farm, the very areas where child labour commonly exists (Nieuwenhuys, 1996). Niewenhuys maintains that the low economic value placed on children's work makes them susceptible to exploitation. She further suggests that the dissociation of childhood from the performance of valued work, although considered a yardstick of modernity and a tool to condemn the incidence of child labour, further denies children's agency in the creation and negotiation of value. This lack of economic value is also reflected in the fact that child domestic labourers are often overlooked because they do not work in the formal sector, waged or organised places of employment.

In several African countries, for a child to perform domestic tasks within a nuclear and extended family is often regarded as an essential part of growing up, upbringing and the socialisation process (Nieuwenhuys, 1996). Myers and Boyden (1998) point out that the role and importance of work for children's development is strongly influenced by their particular 'cultural system'. It could be argued that this idea of work as socialisation and training lends legitimacy to the distinction between child work and child labour. Child domestic labour is beleaguered with this notion of creating a distinction between child labour and child work, with the ILO focusing on the worst forms of child labour. The idea that not all work is bad as long as it gives children time for education and play could be an acknowledgement that not all work is harmful and some families depend on income provided by working children. Liebel points out that this is recognition of the wide spectrum of work children undertake and the need to differentiate between forced labour and need-oriented forms of work. He further suggests that UNICEF adopted this stance in acknowledgement that 'in every country, rich or poor, it is the nature of the work children do that determines whether or not they are harmed by it and not the plain fact of children working' (Liebel, 2004, p 18). The challenge with this over-neat formulation is that there is no consensus on the basic definition of children's work or standards. It brings up the question of who determines what. The definition of work is often marked by moral attitudes that determine which activities should or should not count as work. This formulation conveniently hides behind the African idea of child work as socialisation, education, training and play, which does not need to be eliminated. It further harbours problems for child domestic work in societies where domestic work is considered the safest form of work for children. However, this distinction between work that is harmful and work that is suitable has become a frame of reference for contemporary governmental and bureaucratic approaches to children's work.

Legal protection of child domestic workers: Convention No 182

Over time, the discourse on child labour (child domestic labour) has seen a number of shifts from policies and interventions originating from the assumption that child work itself is bad and should be abolished to a focus on exploitative and hazardous forms of children's work. Seabrook (1997) refers to this as a movement from the abolitionist stance that all child work is bad and must be abolished, to a new acceptance of child work under the banner of realism. This has led to a reduction in the urgency to eliminate child labour and a move to the recent stance of gradualism, which looks at long-term goals and aspirations to abolish child labour while targeting now the most intolerable forms of child labour. This seems like a justification for 'tolerable' child work, considering that the outright abolition of child work is seen as an impossible objective for both practical and humane reasons.

Traditional interventions such as minimum age laws, public sector inspection of workplaces and labour practice, control of children's work through work permits and compulsory school attendance up to a stipulated age failed (Myers and Boyden, 1998) to protect children from exploitation. This brought about a rethink of the goal of abolishing child work. Liebel (2004) argues that it was the lack of success of these efforts and the worldwide increase in diverse forms of children's work that led to the realisation that a differentiated approach was required. With a broader appreciation of the place of work for millions of children and their families, the 1999 Worst Forms of Child Labour Convention No 182 was introduced. The focus is on the abolition of unconditional worst forms of child labour, which include slavery, trafficking, bonded labour, forced recruitment into armed conflict, prostitution, pornography or illegal activities such as the sale and trafficking of drugs (ILO, 2004). Rather than exclude children from work, the ILO refocused on the immediate elimination of work that is hazardous and harmful to the health and physical and moral development of children.

It is pertinent to note that the focus on the nature of work that children do still reflects the difficulties in grasping the contexts of child work in various societies and the interpretation given to child work in such societies. Convention No 182 lists forms of child labour that should be eliminated immediately and contains a blanket prohibition of work that by its very nature is hazardous and harmful to the health, physical and moral development of children. The emphasis on the nature of work directly excludes children in societies where domestic work is regarded as a safe form of work for children. The interpretation in such societies potentially excludes child domestic labourers from the protection offered by Convention No 182 and sanctions a range of activities referred to as domestic work. Child domestic labourers are recruited, trafficked, bonded (as a means of debt repayment), fostered and voluntarily go into domestic service but in societies where child domestic work is considered safe, it is only children trafficked or held in slavery-like conditions that would constitute the worst forms of child labour that need to be protected immediately. Although in international treaties child domestic labour has achieved recognition as a subset of child labour, in a number of societies the acceptability of child domestic work still makes it challenging to categorise it as an exploitative or hazardous form of child work. In addition to this, child domestic labour takes place within the confines of the household, making it less visible and less open to scrutiny.

African fosterage system

There are a number of push and pull factors attributed to children entering domestic service, including family crisis (parental demise, orphaned through famine, divorce and HIV/AIDS), rural–urban migration and migration across borders to find work, to obtain dowry, independence or material possessions. For others, leaving the village to gain economic independence is simply a rite of passage (HRW, 2007). In line with the expectation that girls are expected to perform domestic tasks and to marry at an early age, some parents voluntarily send their children to work as domestics. Many children are also involved in debt bondage, the practice of pledging children's work against a loan (Nieuwenhuys, 1996; see also Chapter Fourteen, this volume). Children are trafficked for domestic labour, agriculture, market labour, street begging, prostitution and sexual exploitation (HRW, 2007). Many recruiters – traffickers in reality – go to rural areas, collecting girls from poorer areas of a country or from a neighbouring state to supply demand for cheap domestic labour in towns or cities in better-off areas (Anti-Slavery International, 2005). Recruiters, most of them women, often visit villages and negotiate a girl's placement and terms with her parents. Sometimes these women recruit directly for themselves or act as intermediaries for other women.

One other factor attributed to child domestic labour is the practice of fostering where children are sent by their parents to live and be raised by close or extended relatives, godparents, friends, acquaintances and in some cases, complete strangers where connections have been made through other villagers (Goody, 1982). This practice is quite common, as anthropological literature provides evidence of fostering of children between families as an established practice in many parts of West Africa (Goody, 1973, 1982; Fiawoo, 1978; Isiugo-Abanihe, 1985). Fostering is defined here as the 'relocation or transfer of children from biological or natal homes to other homes where they are raised and cared for by foster parents' (Isiugo-Abanihe, 1985, p 53). The African extended family network often includes children from other households, making it acceptable for members of the extended family to bring up children of kin. It is common practice for wealthier family members, or those who live in urban areas, to bring up children of disadvantaged family members and to act as guardians in exchange for the provision of domestic services or an apprenticeship. The parental task is delegated to a 'non-parent' and by the performance of that task the non-parent establishes the associated claim to support, allegiance and labour from the child (Goody, 1982). For many African cultures, this is an accepted ancient practice, and as Meillassoux pointed out in Schlemmer (2000, p 317), 'In the traditional, formerly self-sufficient, domestic family each child belongs not just to a couple – its parents – but to the whole family group'. Andvig et al (2001) also point out that it is well established empirically that a larger share of African children live away from their parents than children in other continents. These 'fostered' children provide predominantly domestic services for their 'guardians' and are compensated in various (but hardly ever monetary) forms. Goody (1982) refers to the labour of the child as a reciprocation of the teacher or guardian's efforts and this ancient custom practised throughout West Africa is one that creates solid (family or other) networks.

Although most fostering takes place within the kinship framework, it can be extended to non-kin when there are no members of kin willing to take on the fostering role or when a non-kin member can provide opportunities such as schooling or vocational training that kin members are unable to provide. In the Ivory Coast, children are taken to work in the household of a family member or someone from their village on the basis of the ancient practice of fosterage, and these girls are referred to as 'little nieces' (Jacquemin, 2006). Children are also sent to non-relatives such as friends and acquaintances of respected social standing to strengthen social, economic or political alliances (Isiugo-Abanihe, 1985). Isiugo-Abanihe (1985) refers to fostering as a consequence of the need to reallocate resources within the extended family or the kin group, ensuring maximum survival for the unit and strengthening kinship ties. He sorts African fostering arrangements into five categories: crisis fostering resulting from the dissolution of the family either by divorce, separation or death of a spouse or HIV/AIDS; alliance fostering, which often occurs with non-kin and is frequently used to establish and strengthen ties and alliances between friends or acquaintances; apprenticeship fostering where children are fostered out to artisans to learn a skill/trade; domestic fostering, when children are fostered to redistribute availability of resources within households; and educational fostering, where children are fostered for the provision of formal education.

The fostering system offers a number of benefits to the parties involved as the motivation or reasons for fostering determine the level of benefits to be derived from the arrangement. Kielland and Tovo (2006) point out that the benefits of the decision to foster the children out depend on how badly the family needs to send the children away, and how good the alternatives or how big the losses will be if they do not. Children benefit from the opportunity of a better life, schooling (although this is more common for boys than girls), vocational and skills training, apprenticeship with an artisan, homes in times of crisis, protection, living in more prosperous areas and hopefully developing social skills, dowries or better opportunities of finding a husband (this applies more here in the case of girls). Parents are assured of a better way of life, a trade or apprenticeship for their child, are relieved of their responsibilities of caring for the child, create alliances, obtain goodwill from the host parents and receive gifts or remuneration for the child's services. For the guardians, it is a source of status and prestige as they receive domestic help, and in some cases, companionship for grandparents and childless couples. Child fostering also occurs primarily to benefit family kinship, strengthening mutual interdependency of the family or to reallocate labour resources where there is a demand (Kielland and Tovo, 2006).

The safeguard of the fostering arrangements is the significance of the personal contacts involved; the children maintain contact with their families as networks are paramount. Bales points out that 'traditional societies, while sometimes oppressive, relied on ties of responsibility and kinship that could usually carry people through a crisis' (1999, p 13). Kielland and Tovo (2006, p 31) report that this kind of fostering is what ensured that many of today's government officials, professionals and teachers in Africa received the education that enabled them to attain their current positions.

In certain parts of Africa, however, the practice of fosterage has assumed new dimensions as societies become more diversified and complex. There is evidence that the African child placement (fostering) systems increasingly conceal the exploitation of 'in-fostered' child labour (Kielland and Tovo, 2006). Goody (1982), Isiugo-Abanihe (1985), Niewenhuys (1996), Jacquemin (2004) and Kielland and Tovo (2006) all draw attention to its changing patterns and the potential for exploitation, particularly in paternalistic African societies. Research has shown a pattern of recruiting girls from rural areas to work as 'housemaids' in the cities (Goody, 1982). Jacquemin (2006) and Goody (1982, p 183) particularly draw attention to the shift away from kin as foster parents and the transformation of fostering by kin into various forms of apprenticeship and domestic servitude: 'there has evolved the institution of the "housemaid", I say evolved, because there does not appear to have been anything similar in the traditional societies of West Africa, with the possible exception of children who were lent to a creditor as surety for a debt'.

The existing traditional practice of 'fosterage' is exploited by recruiters to place children for work in non-kin homes. A huge number of children are then placed in households with no kinship ties under the guise of extended familial relationships for the benefit of their domestic labour. Over the last 20 years, fostered children have been replaced by waged maids, and the number of recruitment agencies has significantly increased in response to this (Jacquemin, 2006). From the late 1970s, discovering that hiring out little domestics could be a very lucrative activity, some women (notably natives of the North-East region of the Ivory Coast) have been meeting a growing demand from Abidjan's women in need of cheap domestic help (Jacquemin, 2006, p 393). The notion of upbringing or socialisation is used to mask the fact that the child is employed even though this relatively new form of 'upbringing/employment' conveniently relieves the employer/patron/benefactor of the obligation to provide the child domestic with care, nurture and developmental support. This open-ended relationship creates an ambiguity and confusion as to the child domestic's place in the household. In these situations, there are no regulations, terms or conditions except those agreed by the employer and parent or recruiter, not necessarily adhered to by the employer. Children living and working in such households are in a limbo somewhere between fosterhood, employment and servitude. Bass (2003) argues that this is an outcome of modern work relations where rural families allow their children to work in urban areas with non-kin employers. The children often refer to their employers as 'aunt' or 'uncle'. This masks the nature of their work; the idiom of kinship can be used to hide exploitative relationships.[1]

The economic conditions in many countries in Sub-Saharan Africa led to a decrease in the number of salaried jobs, an increase in the 'informal' sector of the market, an increase in the number of women who had to go to work as income from women became indispensable for many families, and the breakdown of traditional family structures. Increased pressure on women brought about an outsourcing of domestic activities to the cheapest available options. This is not to deny the fact that the outsourcing of domestic activities is also a status symbol in a number of African societies, but socioeconomic conditions led to an increase in the demand for cheap domestic labour that resulted in the commercialisation of domestic work. This commercialisation has emerged as a survival strategy for poor families and metamorphosed to a form of unregulated employment and exploitation of young children. Schlemmer (2000) points out how the cash economy and urbanisation are among the factors that have combined to undermine family structures in traditional African societies.

Black (2002) observes that the ambiguities surrounding children's working situation often leads to confusion about traditional types of fosterhood or 'alternative upbringing'. She also highlights that the fostering practice may typically be regarded as socially acceptable, even benign. Furthermore, the ILO (2007), while redefining child domestic labour as work carried out by children in the employer's household rather than within their own family, points out that care should be taken not to allow an over-extended notion of 'family' or of a disguised 'adoption' to camouflage a situation that may be equal to the worst forms of child labour in domestic work. There are many cases in the literature of children taken in by members of the extended family only to be put to work as domestic workers under highly exploitative conditions (ILO, 2007).

This analysis does not claim the absence of the traditional fosterage model based on kinship but the trend shows that the model has become a basis for the recruitment of child domestics in Sub-Saharan Africa. It could also be argued that the increasing number of child domestics in Sub-Saharan households is simply the ancient practice of fosterage, but a number of complexities surrounding child domestic labour in the last few decades raise questions about the legitimacy of this practice and the forms in which it currently exists.

Conclusion

The fosterage system for domestic labour is an institution that exists in many African countries and is obviously fraught with various complexities. But, as pointed out by Oloko (in Kielland and Tovo, 2006), the main point of difference between fostered children providing domestic services and children providing domestic services under the guise of kinship is the change of environment and the absence of support networks (kinship), which are meant to offer some form of protection for such children. In the absence of this form of protection, however bogus, children living under these conditions are open to multiple forms of exploitation including 'assumed pseudo-kinship' protection that is non-existent and international protection that does not include them because of the focus on the nature of the work that they do, which is often considered safe, and a lack of understanding or acknowledgement of the potentially exploitative conditions under which they work. As rightly stated by Blagbrough (2008), the exploitation of children arises from the situation in which they live and work, and not just the work they do.

There is no specific international convention or policy targeted at child domestic labour. Protection of child domestic labourers is generally covered under child labour policies that are often subject to national interpretation and implementation. Reynolds et al (2006), writing on the refraction of children's rights, point out that the reality in the implementation of policies tends to yield a different result when applied to local contexts. Jacquemin (2006), in her research on the work of the International Catholic Child Bureau's work with child labourers in Abidjan, uncovered how the practice of children's rights excluded 'little nieces' (fostered child domestic workers) from their programmes. Their interpretation of child domestic labour excluded unpaid domestic workers, on the one hand, and, on the other, sanctified it as an expression of ancient forms of African solidarity and kinship.

This shows a need to obtain a better understanding of the lives of child domestic workers caught in such situations and, if required, to promote interventions and strategies that are drawn out of an understanding of the unique situations of these child domestic workers. Domestic work might not be considered harmful by some, but the circumstances under which children enter domestic service only serve to reinforce their exploitation, and there is a need for policies to reflect this.

Note

[1] It is relevant to note that Victoria Climbié, the little girl tortured to death in London in 2006, came from the Ivory Coast to stay with an 'auntie', with the promise of a bright future. This process may be becoming internationalised.

References

Andvig, J.C., Canagarajah, S. and Kielland, A. (2001) *Issues in child labour in Africa*, Africa Region Human Development Working Paper Series (No 14), Human Development Sector, Africa Region: The World Bank.

Anti-Slavery International (2005) *Child domestic workers: A handbook on good practice in programme interventions*, London: Anti-Slavery International.

Bales, K. (1999) *Disposable people*, Berkeley, CA: University of California Press.

Bass, L. (2003) *Child labour in Sub-Saharan Africa*, Boulder, CO: Lynne Reinner Press.

Black, M. (2002) *A handbook on advocacy: Child domestic workers: Finding a voice*, London: Anti Slavery International.

Blagborough, J. (2008) *They respect their animals more*, London: WISE/ASF.

Blagbrough, J. and Glynn, E. (1999) 'Child domestic workers: characteristics of the modern slave and approaches to ending such exploitation', *Childhood*, vol 6, pp 51-6.

Fiawoo, D.K. (1978) 'Some patterns of foster care in Ghana', in C. Oppong et al (ed) *Marriage, fertility and parenthood in West Africa*, Canberra: The Australian National University Press, pp 273-88.

Goody, E. (1973) *The character of kinship*, Cambridge: Cambridge University Press.

Goody, E. (1982) *Parenthood and social reproduction: Fostering and occupational roles in West Africa*, Cambridge: Cambridge University Press.

HRW (Human Rights Watch) (2007) 'Bottom of the ladder: exploitation and abuse of girl child domestic workers in Guinea', Human Rights Watch, vol 19, no 8 (A).

ILO (International Labour Organisation) (2004) *'Helping hands or shackled lives': Understanding child domestic labour*, Geneva: ILO-IPEC.

ILO (2007) *Hazardous child domestic work: A briefing sheet*, Geneva: ILO.

Isiugo-Abanihe, U.C. (1985) 'Child fosterage in West Africa', *Population and Development Review*, vol 11, no 1, pp 53-73.

Jacquemin, M. (2004) 'Children's domestic work in Abidjan, Cote D'Ivoire: the petites bonnes have the floor', *Childhood*, vol 11, no 3, pp 383-97.

Jacquemin, M. (2006) 'Can the language of rights get hold of the complex realities of child domestic work?: the case of young domestic workers in Abidjan, Ivory Coast', *Childhood*, vol 13, pp 389-406.

Kielland, A. and Tovo, M. (2006) *Children at work: Child labour practices in Africa*, Boulder, CO: Lynne Reinner Press.

Liebel, M. (2004) *A will of their own? Cross cultural perspectives on working children*, London: Zed Books.

Liebel, M. (2007) 'Opinion, dialogue, review: the new ILO report on child labour: a success story, or the ILO still at a loss?', *Childhood*, vol 14, pp 279-84.

Myers, W. and Boyden, J. (1998) *Child labour: Promoting the best interests of working children*, London: Save the Children.

Nieuwenhuys, O. (1996) 'The paradox of child labour and anthropology', *Annual Review of Anthropology*, vol 25, pp 237-51.

Reynolds, P., Nieuwenhuys, O. and Hanson, K. (2006) 'Refractions of children's rights in development practice: a view from anthropology – introduction', *Childhood*, vol 13, pp 291-302.

Schlemmer, B. (ed) (2000) *The exploited child*, London: Zed Books.

Seabrook, J. (1997) *Children of other worlds*, London: Pluto Press.

thirteen

Extreme forms of child labour in Turkey

Serdar M. Degirmencioglu, Hakan Acar and Yüksel Baykara Acar

Introduction

The literature on working children or children who are forced to work in Turkey is growing in terms of both size and coverage. The literature now covers children who work on the streets in urban areas, children who collect waste material that can be recycled from rubbish bins and children who accompany their parents to the cotton fields in the south of the country (Atauz, 1990; Acar and Baykara Acar, 2007). Most published work uses the legal definition of a child (a person under 18 years of age) in line with the Convention on the Rights of the Child (CRC). Sometimes it is not possible to identify the ages of the children studied.

The coverage, however, does not necessarily reflect the scale or urgency of the matter, or the number of children at risk. A relatively large number of studies focus on children who work on the streets in urban areas (Duyan, 2005). These children are traditionally the most visible working children and the visibility often translates into public attention, in turn becoming an issue that the public administration has to address. A few tragic events over the last decade, such as the killing of an army officer and that of one of the country's wealthiest industrialists in a cemetery, made 'street children' almost a household term. In the former case, several youths under the influence of solvents were responsible for the death of the officer. In the latter, there was actually no proof that 'street children' were involved, but the press found a convenient scapegoat. These events and very exaggerated, ill-informed media attention have led to further public scrutiny in the last five years, including a parliamentary investigation, resulting in a relatively comprehensive report on the conditions of children working on the streets.

The gaps in the literature reflect how not being visible translates into lack of attention, as in the case of cotton-picking children who work alongside their parents for extended periods of time. The gap also reflects the fact that 'hard-to-reach' children are the least often studied – the well-known bias of 'convenience samples' in the social sciences. Among these neglected children are children who are forced to work in slave-like conditions.

Here we focus on the less visible and less-studied forms of child labour. The process through which these children are made to work has parallels with the experiences of slaves in history or people who work under slave-like conditions elsewhere today. The process through which child labour examined here becomes possible involves parents abandoning their parental responsibilities and duties, and hiring their children out to complete strangers. Just as with slave trades, the transaction results in income for the selling party and in misery for the child. Again, just as with slave trades, the transaction and the ensuing labour violate the fundamental rights of the child. The violation is often not short-lived, but rather a long-term loss of fundamental rights.

The kind of child labour that can be described as work under slave-like circumstances is a serious matter, needing close attention. Here, we examine first the long-standing practice from northwestern Turkey of hiring children to better-off farmers. It is poor parents who hire out their child, invariably a boy. This practice appears to be disappearing but new forms of child hiring are emerging in other areas. One such pattern can be found in recent reports regarding children hired to streetwise employers, who take children away to large urban areas and make them work on the streets or in criminal rings. This is sometimes carried out with the consent of the parents. Here, the main actor is a person who lures boys away from home into a very difficult life.

In all of these examples, there is very little or no reliable information available in the literature or from official sources such as the Statistics Institute or the police. Forensic implications of the individual cases, institutional tendencies to protect the institution in cases of negligence and inaction, and sometimes attempts to protect the children in question lead to the withholding of information or possibly official cover-ups. Therefore, we rely primarily on secondary data sources, journalistic reports and a few interviews with well-placed informants to describe the state of affairs. We then examine the factors that are associated with child labour in general and extreme forms of child labour. A large number of children in Turkey are faced with these issues on a daily basis. This chapter concludes with a call for a coherent rights-based policy.

Background

Turkey has a large population, now estimated to be around 72 million. The population is clearly young, with a median age of 22. The economy has had a major crisis every five years until recently. Current economic 'stability' involves about 20% unemployment. During the 1990s, persistently high rates of inflation reduced the purchasing power of most families in Turkey (Government of Turkey and UNICEF, 1998, pp 4-6). The unequal income distribution became even more unequal, and poor families were clearly the hardest hit: households living in poverty were estimated to be around 30% in the mid-1990s. Current unofficial estimates put the rate at around 50%. Within the population living under very difficult economic circumstances, children often suffer the greatest brunt of deprivation (Libal, 2001).

The situation becomes clearer if economic growth and human development indices from the 2000s are considered together. In comparative terms, Turkey has a sizeable economy – it was the world's 21st biggest economy in 2004. However, the growth of the economy has not improved the lives of all. Official estimates indicate that more than 20 million people are poor, and about 25% of families and 38% of pre-school children live under the poverty line. The United Nations Development Programme (UNDP) Human Development Index captures the difference between economic growth and welfare indicators, Turkey ranking low particularly on indices related to child welfare.

In history, child labour has been commonplace (ILO, 1996). Traditional life in Turkish rural areas always involved children contributing to household work. In the case of farm labour, children were effectively considered as part of the labour force. Large-scale migration, beginning in the 1950s, from poverty-stricken rural areas to urban areas did not improve conditions for most children. Migrant families faced problems related to housing, employment and earning adequate incomes. Most children had no option other than joining the labour force to supplement the family income (Acar, 2000). By the mid-1990s, almost 1 in 10 children were working: the 1994 Child Labour Survey indicated that of the 11.9 million Turkish children between 6 and 14 years of age, 1.07 million were working (Duyan, 2005). Recent economic changes included a shift away from agriculture to a more industry-focused economy. The majority of the population now live in urban areas. This shift has not altered most children's living conditions, given the high rate of poverty and unemployment in urban areas.

Children for hire in the 'child market'

If children are considered part of the farm labour force, perhaps it is not too surprising that there is a marketplace for child labour. Until recently, a 'child market' (*cocuk pazari*) operated in Bafra and Alacam, and possibly in a similar fashion in nearby towns. There is very little documentation of what appears to be long-standing practice of parents hiring children to better-off families in some small towns in the province of Samsun, in northwestern Turkey. Existing information indicates that the market operated for a long time and children from poor and large families in villages located in mountainous areas of the province were hired by families located on the nearby plains.

There was always a need for cheap labour on the plains, and children from poor mountain families provided a convenient and cheaper labour force.

The hiring was based on an unofficial agreement between respective parents that a child – invariably a boy – would stay with the hiring family for an extended period of time. Payments were made on a monthly basis to the parents and not to the boy. Local people considered the practice as completely acceptable and normal. In their view, the benefit was mutual: this practice was not very different from any other mutually beneficial business transaction (Kantoglu, 1998).

Depending on the family's circumstances, the hiring might involve more than one child. For instance, two boys from a family with five children in a mountain village near Bafra were hired one after another when they were between eight to ten years old. The older brother was hired by a car mechanic and the younger by a farmer. It is common in Turkey for disadvantaged parents to send their sons to mechanics' shops and have them start working early. It is also common for boys who have difficulty with staying in school for financial and/or academic reasons to start working early as mechanics' apprentices. This practice is often considered beneficial for the boy because he gains marketable skills and the prospects of steady gainful employment. The younger boy was asked to work as a shepherd and a small monthly payment was delivered to the father. His father asked the hiring parents to treat his son well and also to send him to school. By 1998, when Kantoglu's research was published, the boy had been enrolled in a local elementary school for two years. The report also revealed how difficult this transition was for the younger boy and how emotionally shaken the eight-year-old was in his relatively more comfortable 'new home'.

Hiring agreements often took place at the 'child market'. Fathers would take the children to the market so that potential employers/fathers could see and examine the children. After the agreement was made, the children might go back home to prepare for their new lives. It is also not clear what happened if the new 'home' proved to be unfit for the children to stay or whether there had been instances where the children ran away either back to their parents or to some other location. It is also unclear how long the hiring arrangement lasted.

This practice of hiring or trading children came under close scrutiny from the governor's office in Samsun and neighbouring provinces, and there were indications that the 'child market' ceased its operation in Bafra by the end of the 1990s. It is not clear, however, whether the practice has completely been eliminated in northwestern Turkey.

Children trafficked to the cities

Towards the end of the 1990s there was an increase in the number of children involved in grab-and-run type robberies on the street and burglaries in major cities, particularly in Istanbul and Diyarbakir. There was a parallel increase in substance abuse and addiction (Ögel and Aksoy, 2007). The Istanbul police administration, while not denying an increase in the numbers, rejected claims this was a major increase. However, in following years, there were occasional reports in the media regarding trafficking of children by organised crime for the very kinds of cases that appeared to be on the increase. The Ankara Trade Chamber released a report on children being forced to work on the streets in 2004. Beginning in 2004, investigative journalists uncovered well-organised trafficking operations by gangs located in major cities (Tezel and Bel, 2004).

The picture emerging from these records was consistent with the observations of social workers and psychologists in social services practice, and researchers studying migration-related issues. The children who were involved in many cases of crime on the streets were aged 11–12 or older, physically strong enough to stand the harsh conditions they were forced to endure. They did not have family in the area and did not know anyone in the area other than the group they were working with. They did not have contact with other young people involved in crime in the same area, again indicating that they were newcomers. Some of them did not speak Turkish well. Further reports indicated that some of these children were forcibly trafficked from their cities of origin, particularly in southeastern Turkey where internally displaced families were having a very difficult time surviving, let alone keeping children off the streets. For some families, survival included letting children earn some money through petty crime. For others, even hiring children to organised crime became an option.

One example illustrates this emerging pattern: two men were arrested for forcibly trafficking six children from Diyarbakir to Istanbul. Three of the children (aged 13, 15 and 16) were actually 'hired' from their parents for a small amount of money. The other boys, aged 13, were first lured into coming to Istanbul but then changed their mind. They were threatened with a knife, taken to the train and were kept in the train compartment during the entire journey. The parents of one of the kidnapped boys heard about what had happened and contacted their older son who lived in a province located on the railroad. The brother informed the police and boarded the train with them to identify his kidnapped brother. One of the two men was arrested but the other one escaped with the other boys, only later to be arrested in Istanbul. The boys with him denied any charges and tried to convince the police that they were only taking a trip to see Istanbul (Tezel and Bel, 2004).

There are currently no reliable estimates of the numbers of children trafficked to the cities and very little documentation of their working and living conditions. Interviews with psychologists who have worked with these children (in or outside of the legal system) suggest that the more challenging or dangerous the task (for example, breaking into a flat in daytime), the more likely the child is to use substances to brave the risks involved. The substances are provided by the person(s) who runs the criminal ring and the addiction that often ensues is the fault of the ringmaster. As with most criminal groups, a child cannot leave the criminal ring without the consent of their master. Further work is clearly needed to address the needs of these children and to intervene in the trafficking mechanisms that take them into a form of slavery.

Children working on the streets

There is still an absence of scholarly work on the lives of these children working and living in slave-like conditions, but we can examine two better-documented forms of child labour in Turkish urban areas. As noted earlier, children working on the streets, particularly as beggars, *simit* (bread) vendors or shoe shiners, have been well-known for at least three generations. A more recent activity for children working on the streets is selling paper tissues, chewing gum or similar handy items. There are again no reliable estimates of the numbers of children living and working on the streets of big cities. Government estimates are markedly low – often because the institutional approach relies on very stringent criteria – and non-governmental estimates are much higher (250,000 children by the end of the 1990s, according to Libal, 2001). Until detailed work is done to estimate numbers, it will be very difficult to assess how widespread the practice is.

Atauz (1990) notes the linkage between families as a whole struggling with hardship in trying to integrate into a new life, and children working in the street. Duyan (2005) identifies poverty, unemployment, illiteracy, extended family structures, poor family function and migration as major factors. The work experience often involves vulnerability to exploitation and various forms of violence (Duyan, 2005). For most children, work displaces time for leisure activities and leaves little time to rest. Most children work very hard and beyond their capacities. This often leads to ill health and psychological problems. Work also leads to a degree of isolation from peers and the local social milieu (Bulut, 1996; Acar, 2000).

Children collecting recyclables

A considerable number of children who are working on the streets in many cities sort and collect recyclable waste material from rubbish bins. Collecting recyclable waste material is certainly not unique to Turkey (Medina, 1997) but it has emerged in the last 20 years as a very difficult form of child labour. The collection of such material becomes particularly difficult when a given collector visits many rubbish bins throughout the day and collects the material in a big bag attached vertically to a metal cart. When the cart is partly or fully loaded, pulling the cart becomes back-breaking work. The collector has to navigate through the streets and traffic, in all weather conditions, and the job becomes even more difficult (Altuntas, 2003).

A recent estimate puts the total number of recyclable waste collectors, adults and children combined, at around 200,000 (Soykan, 2007), with around 10,000 working in the capital city Ankara (Alkan, 2007). Several studies have recently been conducted on the working conditions of recyclable waste collectors (Altuntas, 2003; Acar and Baykara Acar, 2007; Saltan and Yardimci, 2007). These not only illustrate how difficult this type of labour is for children, but also reveal, to some extent, the dynamics leading large numbers of adults and children into collecting recyclable waste. An emerging pattern is the linkage between poverty and internal displacement due to forced migration from southeastern Turkey to all major cities in the country, a process long overlooked by researchers (Alptekin and Sahin, 2001).

Factors related to extreme forms of child labour

There is now clear evidence linking poverty to child labour. In a large-scale study, Tunali (1996) found that age and gender, parental education and residential region were related to child labour among children aged 6–14 years (that is, elementary school years). In particular, older male children and those with lower parental education were more likely to work. Dayioglu (2006) investigated the determinants of child labour in urban Turkey, particularly low household income or poverty as a root cause. She found that children from poorer families were clearly at a higher risk of exploitative employment. This finding was confirmed using various measures of household income. Not surprisingly, then, extreme forms of child labour are clearly linked to extreme poverty. The two forms examined here illustrate how poor parents can give up their children in return for a relatively small amount of money even though there are no guarantees regarding the child's well-being. Poverty has increased in Turkey, affecting almost half of the population; recent work indicates that concentrated urban poverty is a particular problem in major cities (Sonmez, 2007).

The extent of the problem has been underestimated for several reasons. One major obstacle has been the transformation of the welfare regime (Bugra and Keyder, 2006) and the changes in the way public administration views and addresses public issues. A related obstacle has been the dominance of the public administration in public life and the lack of agency on the part of local stakeholders, including non-governmental organisations (NGOs), voluntary community groups and the private sector. The lack of other stakeholders in public processes translates into a lack of diversity of opinion, unlike in the UK (Broadhead and Armistead, 2007), and allows the public administration to defer action with little pressure for accountability. Another major obstacle has been the ethnic and political nature of the dynamics leading to concentrated poverty. This obstacle is reviewed below.

Internal displacement due to forced migration

A number of studies now link forced migration to a large number of major problems, the primary one being poverty (Alptekin and Sahin, 2001; Kurban et al, 2007). In the latter study, Kurban and her colleagues describe internal displacement as follows:

> Some one million men, women and children were forcibly uprooted from rural areas in the east and southeast of the country as a result of the armed struggle from 1984 to 1999 between the [forces belonging to the Kurdistan Workers' Party (PKK), which now uses a different 'official' name] and the [government forces]. Large numbers fled to urban areas all over the country where they have long experienced poverty, poor housing, joblessness, loss of land and property, limited access to physical and mental health care services, and limited educational opportunities for their children. (2007, p 2)

Given the very sensitive, politically charged and almost 'untouchable' nature of the topic, debates on the impact of forced migration did not take place until very recently and research on the impact of internal displacement due to forced migration (IDFM) has been very slow to emerge. A number of studies now link internal displacement to psychological problems (Sahin, 1995; Bayram, 1998; Aker, 2002). Gün (2007) has recently done the same specifically for children and adolescents. The impact of IDFM on the entire country or on the specific regions where the displaced used to live is more difficult to assess, but is perhaps as large as the impact of land enclosures in the British context (Humphries, 1990). A rough indicator may be the increase in the size of the population. Diyarbakir was the city closest to the homeland of the displaced and suffered the largest impact of IDFM: its population increased by 20% and the crime rate increased even more.

Yükseker (2007) reviews sociological work on the impact of IDFM in some detail. Unlike in the previous waves of migration, families who were forced to migrate to urban areas were not able to find available free land to build their own makeshift homes. In the new urban economy, regular jobs with social security were not available for newcomers. There was therefore very little room for social mobility and newcomers often became the poorest of the urban poor. Survival in the city was particularly difficult for this internally displaced group because their relationship with their villages had been completely severed, with no resources to draw on, and they had no preparation or transition – their displacement was sudden, traumatic and involuntary.

Women and children appear to be the most disadvantaged groups as the displaced join the crowds of urban poor. If men cannot find employment, then women and children end up bearing the responsibility to earn some income and become part of the paid labour force. Yükseker (2007) notes that women have had to undertake the greatest responsibility in meeting the family's basic needs. The new life alters the balances at home and can strain relationships between the spouses and may even lead to domestic violence. This, and strained relations at home, often pushes children onto the streets (Duyan, 2005). On the basis of her review, Yükseker identifies IDFM as one of the major factors leading to the increase in child labour in the 1990s. Several studies indicate that children working on the streets of Istanbul report coming from internally displaced families and that they needed to work, dropping out of school in the process, because their parents could not find employment. Altuntas (2003) reports a similar pattern for working children in Ankara. A large number of school-age children report working on the street to contribute to family income, coming from internally displaced families.

The evidence thus indicates that IDFM is a major factor to consider in child labour and particularly in regard to extreme forms of child labour. There appears to be a direct relationship between urban poverty, the inability of parents, particularly the fathers, to find regular employment, and children having to work on the streets. Urban poverty is a major reason for school drop-out and school failure, and there might be a reciprocal link between child labour and school problems.

Conclusion

The forms of child labour described here deprive children of their fundamental rights and effectively place them in slavery. The long-standing practice from northwestern Turkey of hiring children to better-off farmers appears to be disappearing. However, the trafficking of children from southeastern Turkey to major cities to a criminal environment appears to be on the increase. The particularly troublesome aspect is that the trafficking is sometimes carried out with parental consent. Parents are hiring or, in effect, selling their sons to criminal employers. Both forms of child labour are consequences of poverty. In the light of scholarly work on the lives of children working on the streets across the country, the circumstances that give rise to child trafficking and parents letting their children be trafficked appear to be related to extreme poverty and internal displacement of masses from their villages.

Debate and research on the impacts of IDFM have only just started because of the very sensitive nature of the topic. So far, state agencies have been eager to engage in improving services without an explicit recognition of forced migration as a root cause. The current volatile political climate in the country will probably not foster more debate on the impact of internal displacement on families and children in particular. Poverty and IDFM are clearly major factors to consider from a policy vantage point. Reducing poverty and mitigating causes of poverty alone, however, may not be effective in reducing and ultimately eliminating child labour. There is a clear need in Turkey for social policy on child labour and on children's issues in general. The relevance of social policy is evident with respect to migration-related problems. As noted earlier, internal migration has been a persistent reality and it has direct relevance to child labour. If the state fails repeatedly to generate a policy to address migration-related problems, the failure is not a policy failure but a failure on the part of state institutions and public administrators. The current practice of policy making treats childhood essentially as an educational matter and very quickly excludes children outside of the school system as a residual category. A related point is the still marginal status of children's rights in service delivery and most policy discussions. A rights-based policy for children is urgently needed, particularly for children at greatest risk.

References

Acar, H. (2000) 'Working children on the streets and in the service sector: Hacettepe University Institute of Social Sciences', Unpublished MSW dissertation, Ankara (in Turkish).

Acar, H. and Baykara Acar, Y. (2007) 'Enformel bir sektör olarak Türkiye'de atik maddelerin geri kazanimi ve kente tutunma stratejisi olarak toplayicilik' ('Waste material recycling in Turkey as an informal sector and waste collecting as an urban survival strategy'), Paper to be presented at the 10th Congress of Social Sciences, Ankara.

Aker, T. (2002) 'Zorunlu ic göc: ruhsal ve toplumsal sonuclari' ('Internal displacement: psychological and social consequences'), *Anadolu Psikiyatri Dergisi*, vol 3, pp 97-103.

Alkan, A. (2007) 'Cope dusmek' ('Dropped in garbage'), *Radikal Iki*, 6 May.

Alptekin, M.E. and Sahin, N. (2001) 'Ihmal edilmis bir sosyal calisma alani olarak zorunlu göc' ('Forced migration as a neglected field of work'), *Sosyal Hizmet Sempozyumu 1999, Bölgesel Kalkinma Sürecinde Sosyal Hizmet,* Ankara: GAP Idaresi ve H.Ü. SHY Yayini.

Altuntas, B. (2003) *Mendile, simite, boyaya, cöpe: Ankara sokaklarinda calisan cocuklar (Dealing tissue, simit, shoeshine, garbage: Children working on Ankara streets),* Istanbul: Iletisim.

Atauz, S. (1990) *Ankara ve Sanliurfa'da sokak cocuklari (Street children in Ankara and Sanliurfa),* Ankara: UNICEF.

Bayram, Y. (1998) 'Zoraki ic göcün ruh sagligina etkileri üzerine bir ön calisma' ('A preliminary study on the impacts of internal displacement on mental health'), *Klinik Psikiyatri Dergisi,* vol 2, pp 83-8.

Broadhead, P. and Armistead, J. (2007) 'Community partnerships: integrating early education with childcare', *Children and Society,* vol 21, pp 42-55.

Bugra, A. and Keyder, C. (2006) 'The Turkish welfare regime in transformation', *Journal of European Social Policy,* vol 16, pp 211-28.

Bulut, I. (1996) 'Psycho-social dimension and implications of child labour', in E. Kahramanoglu (ed) *The problem of working children and ways of solution,* Ankara: Hacettepe University School of Social Work and Friedrich-Naumann Foundation, pp 135-46.

Dayioglu, M. (2006) 'The impact of household income on child labour in urban Turkey', *Journal of Development Studies,* vol 42, pp 939-56.

Duyan, V. (2005) 'Relationships between the sociodemographic and family characteristics, street life experiences and the hopelessness of street children', *Childhood,* vol 12, pp 445-59.

Government of Turkey and UNICEF (1998) *The situation of children and women in Turkey: An executive summary,* Ankara: UNICEF, pp 4-6.

Gün, Z. (2007) 'Kurdish internal displacement and mental health: children and adolescents', Paper presented at Internal Displacement in Turkey and Abroad: International Principles, Experiences and Policy Proposals, Istanbul, Turkey: TESEV.

Humphries, J. (1990) 'Enclosures, common rights, and women: the proletarianization of families in the late eighteenth and early nineteenth centuries', *Journal of Economic History,* vol 50, pp 17-42.

ILO (International Labour Organization) (1996) *Child labour: What is to be done?,* Geneva: ILO.

Kantoglu, F.D. (1998) 'O bir "satilik çocuk"' ('He's a "boy for sale"') (http://arsiv. sabah.com.tr/1998/05/11/r01.html).

Kurban, D., Yükseker, D., Celik, A.B., Ünalan, T. and Aker, A.T. (eds) (2007) *Coming to terms with forced migration: Post-displacement restitution of citizenship rights in Turkey,* Istanbul: TESEV.

Libal, K. (2001) 'Children's rights in Turkey', *Human Rights Review,* October-December, pp 35-44.

Medina, M. (1997) *Informal recycling and collection of solid wastes in developing countries: Issues and opportunities*, UNU/IAS Working Paper No 24, Yokohama: United Nations Institute of Advanced Studies.

Ögel, K. and Aksoy, A. (2007) 'Substance use in delinquent adolescents', *Journal of Dependence*, vol 8, pp 11-17.

Sahin, D. (1995) *Zorunlu göce ve siddete bagli ruhsal sorunlar* (*Psychological problems related to internal migration and violence*), Ankara: TIHV.

Saltan, A. and Yardimci, S. (2007) 'Geri dönüsümün görünmeyen yüzü: sokak toplayicilarinin is ve yasam kosullari üzerine bir degerlendirme' ('The unseen face of recycling: an appraisal of the working and living conditions of street collectors'), *Toplum ve Bilim*, vol 108, pp 206-38.

Sonmez, I. (2007) 'Concentrated urban poverty: the case of Izmir inner area, Turkey', *European Planning Studies*, vol 15, pp 319-38.

Soykan, T. (2007) 'Copteki servetin fakir iscileri' ('Poor workers of the riches in the garbage'), *Radikal*, 31 August.

Tezel, R. and Bel, Y. (2004) 'Kiralık kapkaççı'ları kurtarma operasyonu' (http://arsiv.sabah.com.tr/2004/12/08/gnd110.html).

Tunali, I. (1996) 'Education and work: experiences of 6- to 14-year-old children in Turkey', in T. Bulutay (ed) *Education and the labour market in Turkey*, Ankara: SIS, pp 106-43.

Yükseker, D. (2007) 'Research findings on internal displacement in Turkey: national reports', in D. Kurban, D. Yükseker, A.B. Celik, T. Ünalan and A.T. Aker (eds) *Coming to terms with forced migration: Post-displacement restitution of citizenship rights in Turkey*, Istanbul: TESEV, pp 145-57.

fourteen

Haliya and *kamaiya* bonded child labourers in Nepal

Birendra Raj Giri

Introduction

Debt bonded labour,[1] a contemporary form of slavery, remains a global concern. Out of 27 million globally, some 15 million South Asian people are reportedly in bonded labour (Bales, 2004). In Nepal, Anti-Slavery International, in association with the United Nations (UN) Working Group on Contemporary Forms of Slavery, estimate that there are between 300,000 and two million bonded labourers under the so-called *haliya* and *kamaiya* systems[2] (Lowe et al, 2001; CWA, 2007); there is no estimate regarding the number of children in bondage (Giri, 2004, 2009).

The term *haliya* means 'one who ploughs', but is understood to have the broader sense of an agricultural labourer, working on another person's land on the basis of daily or short-term fixed wages. As *haliya* workers find it hard to support their large families all year round from seasonal labour, they are forced to take loans from their 'landlords' (known locally as *kisan* or small landholders). In the long term, many of them may end up in debt due to high annual interest rates (up to 6%) and lack of work opportunities. They may eventually have to work as bonded labourer (Rankin, 1999). *Haliya* workers belong to many ethnic and caste groups, being found mostly in the far western hills and eastern Tarai district (Sharma and Sharma, 2002; CWA, 2007).

Likewise, *kamaiya* refers to a hired worker in the ethnic (Dangura) Tharu language. In Nepali it means a hired worker, remunerated for their labour. However, the *kamaiya* system is commonly known as an agriculturally based bonded labour system in which a *kamaiya* makes a verbal contract with a *kisan* (moneylender) to work for a year. People's bondedness may start like this: getting a part of the produce rather than wages barely allows a *kamaiya* to make a living from a mono-cropped land. In times of crop failure or family hardships the hired worker's family will be forced to take high interest rate loans, which can only be paid off by working. If his family ends up in a vicious cycle of debt, the next generation – his children – have to work as *kamaiya* labourers. This is why non-governmental organisations

(NGOs) argue that many of the *haliya/kamaiya* child workers are working in conditions of servitude or slavery. In some cases, they may be paying off a debt incurred earlier by parents or relatives (Lowe et al, 2001; Daru et al, 2005).

After widespread media coverage and lobbying by NGOs, the so-called *kamaiya* system of bonded labour was banned in 2000, and a law introduced in 2002 for the workers' 'systematic' rehabilitation. (Daru et al, 2005). Although each family received 2-5 *katth*[3] (0.0338–0.169 hectares), meant to terminate the *kamaiya–kisan* relationship once and for all (Daru et al, 2005), children increasingly came to act as replacements for adults (Giri, 2004, 2009). Most of these children, employed in rural areas, are initially hired as domestic helpers, but end up carrying out both household and agricultural activities. (Giri, 2009). This combination not only makes children's lives hard, but they are also vulnerable to physical, psychological and sexual maltreatment. Based on their reports on pre-2000 *kamaiya* practices, NGOs and human rights activists claim that working children, no longer monitored by their family, are likely to be badly abused. This leads them to consider *haliya/kamaiya* work as 'unconditional worst forms of child labour', enshrined in the ILO Worst Forms of Child Labour Convention No 12 (see Chapters One and Three, this volume).

Although NGOs have led awareness campaigns against *kamaiya* labour and the subsequent introduction of anti-*kamaiya* law has reportedly altered the terms of contract between *kisan* and *haliya* labourers, it has only attracted patchy media reports. Likewise, there are hardly any studies done with regard to *haliya/kamaiya* child workers (Sharma and Sharma, 2002; ; Giri, 2009). This chapter is based on extensive fieldwork[4] aimed at filling this gap, focusing on how *haliya/kamaiya* children themselves understand their everyday world of work (Woodhead, 1999).

We first describe how children become *haliya/kamaiya* labourers; we then discuss how they spend their daily lives and under what conditions, examining what factors lead them to terminate the terms of contract, and finally, what their future prospects are once they leave *haliya/kamaiya* work.

Becoming a haliya /kamaiya labourer

One of the main reasons that lead Musahar and Tharu families to send children to work as *haliya/kamaiya* labourers is extreme poverty, namely, shortage of daily foodstuffs. Because of household circumstances, most children agree to follow parental advice to accept *haliya/kamaiya* work. For instance, Lalu, a 15-year-old *kamaiya* girl, felt she must help her family in whatever ways she could:

"Our family is very big [eight members], but we've no land, except 5 *kattha* given by the government, and my father is the only person working to support us. I didn't want leave my family, but I had to think about the shortage of food and clothes at home."

Both Musahar and Tharu families in the field research village[5] are either virtually landless or the land is too small to grow foodstuffs for the family. As Lalu explained, the government-given land is just enough to build a 'house' and to plant vegetables, so they have mobilised their labour power to make their living.

"If we go for *majduri* [manual labour] we get NPR 60 [€0.69] per day. This is not enough to feed our large family daily, besides we can't find a regular work. If we work for a *kisan*, we get NPR 40 and a kilo of rice and seasonal vegetables. When we send our children to a *kisan*, we can also ask for loan in times of crisis and also *adhiya* [sharecropping] land." (Daate, 63, *haliya* man)

"I sometimes think working as a *kamaiya* was okay because we didn't have to go hungry. We had debt, that was bad, but we got land to work, and also a loan when desperately needed. Now, a *kisan* doesn't want to give us any loan or *adhiya* land without our commitment to provide labour. At the moment, my two grand-daughters are working for two *kisan* families." (Base, 59, ex–*kamaiya* man)

Despite the anti-*kamaiya* law, these stories illustrate the severe state of poverty that still forces many families to believe that being a bonded labourer was acceptable as their basic needs were 'provided' by their *kisa*.

Thousands of Musahar and Tharu families had been working as *haliya/kamaiya* labourers for generations, but NGO activists (often forcefully) removed *kamaiya* families from the *bukura/kothar* (a family hut within their employer's property) after the 2000 government decree. *Haliya* labourers also felt its indirect impact across Nepal, although they did not abandon annual contracts like their *kamaiya* counterparts. Many families have found it hard to live in their new huts away from their 'care taker' *kisan*. Since employers virtually controlled them, they have neither a social network nor the knowledge to deal with the outside world (Robertson and Mishra, 1997; Bales, 2004). At the same time, government and NGO support has been limited to short-term issues such as building a house, setting up a water supply and so on. They are unable to get bank loans as they have little or no land or property. So, whether Musahar and Tharu families like it or not, the only (economic support) network that they can fall back on remains their previous/current *kisan*, who is willing to provide *adhiya* land as well as loans (even if at highly inflated interest rates). In fact, some adults expressed happiness that they could maintain contacts with their former employers, allowing them to send their children to work in return for food/clothes, loans and *adhiya* land. The *kisan* community, on the other hand, avoid hiring adults due to the fear of anti-*kamaiya* laws with potential exposure to media and NGOs. In such a situation, children increasingly become intermediaries between parents and *kisan*.

> "After government banned the *kamaiya* system, we received land, but it's not enough. Most of us adults are engaged in seasonal *majduri* [unskilled labour] to earn daily meals, similar to being a *kamaiya*. To support our large family, we still need *adhiya* land to grow food, and loans to buy clothes or pay for marriage or illnesses. Except for a few adults, it is children who work as a *kamaiya* to get *adhiya* land and loans from the *kisan*." (Tike, 43, ex-*kamaiya* man)

As Musahar and Tharu parents struggle to feed their family all year around, the offer of an employer to 'take care' of their children, along with certain cash/kind remuneration or *adhiya* land, seems acceptable. Additionally, if the *kisan* 'promises' to provide certain years of formal education, as one parent said, it is like *ke khojchhas kana aakho* ('finding an eye for the blind man') for parents and children alike.

Notwithstanding this promise of education, children accepted their parents' idea of becoming a *haliya/kamaiya* labourer because of extreme poverty at home. However, a number of children, especially from Musahar families, also left their families because of difficult relationships they had at home; becoming a bonded labourer in the nearby village appeared to be the only available survival option. Jibe, a 10-year-old *haliya* boy, said "I give my earnings to my parents, but they finished in *daru/raski* [homemade alcohol] and quarrels with each other." Another 16-year-old, Shive, complained: "there's no food to eat, but only to hear scolding and sustained beating". In some cases the use (or abuse) of *daru/raksi* was so bad that children lost their father (or even mother). For instance, Bhabu, a 13- year-old girl, said "my parents were alcoholic and they died when I was six/seven years old; I used to stay with my uncle's family but got scolded and beaten so I went away to work as a *haliya*." For children like these, living with a *kisan* family to work as a *haliya/kamaiya* was a better option than staying with their parents or other relatives in a hostile environment.

Being a haliya /kamaiya labourer

As noted, Musahar and Tharu children come from very poor families owning little or no land and few domestic animals. Their daily workload is minimal at home when shared among many members of the family. For instance, two nine-year-old boys from Musahar and Tharu families would be doing the following activities in a day:

"I wake up at around 7 am. I drink tea or eat snacks if it's available. Sometimes I go to the forest to collect a bit of grass/fodder for the animals. During the day I attend the nearby school. I play with my friends and do some homework in the evening. At around 7, I go to bed after dinner. As I've many older siblings, I don't do much work at home." (Tule, *kamaiya* boy)

In both groups, however, gender discrimination is widespred. (Maslak, 2003). Kitchen work remains exclusively the girls' domain and girls carry out more tasks than boys; their chances of studying are very low, and they are likely to be married much earlier. A 10-year-old girl, Babu, illustrated this gendered division of labour:

"I get up at around 6 am (7 am in the winter) and take goats outside the house and give them some grass/fodder. I sweep/ brush both inside and outside the house, and clean the dishes of last night. After that I cook morning meal for the family (normally rice, vegetable curry, and lentil soup). In the afternoon, I bring the goats to the forest to graze and also to collect some grass/fodder. I prepare evening meal and go to bed at around 7 pm after the food. I follow this routine only if my mother and older sisters are working elsewhere. If I also go for *sakhaina* [labour exchange with neighbours], then, my routine also changes."

Once children leave their family to work as *haliya/kamaiya* labourers, which often particularly overwhelms 'spoiled' boys, they have to carry out numerous tasks daily. For instance, Thage, a 16-year-old *kamaiya* boy, reported doing the following activities in a day.

"I had to wake up at 5 am to clean animal shed, milk the buffalo, and give grass/fodder and water to cows and buffaloes. Then, I'd go out to collect grass and fodder. I also have to take the bullocks to the field for ploughing and take all animals to graze. If there is no planting work, then I've to collect firewood or help construction of animal sheds, *tanga* [oxen or male buffalo-drawn wooden wagon], etc. At the beginning of our contract, I was told that I just had to take care of the buffaloes and look after the children during their school holidays, but when I started work, they made me do everything, from planting to harvesting. Although I entered the home at 6 or 7 pm for food, I normally went to bed after 10 pm … I had to help with household work and also find out what work will be done in the coming days.… They give 2 quintals of unprocessed rice for my family, and two pairs of trousers/shirts and sandals for me in a year."

If Thage was in his family home, he could at least avoid working in the kitchen, but he has no choice at his employer's house. Likewise, Saru, a 15-year-old *haliya* girl spent her day as follows:

I get up at 5.30 am and make tea for my *malik*'s [male boss's] family. Then, I cook *khole* [soup from let-over food] and feed it to the animals. I again make the *khole* for the afternoon and store it. Then, I prepare *kuti* [fine chopping of grass] and give it to the animals after mixing with *bhus* [rice skin] and hay. I eat food and leave for school at around 10 am. During the short afternoon break at 1.30 pm, I come back home to give *khole* to the animals, and prepare snacks for my *malik*'s family. Then, I go back to school till 4 pm. After school, I give food to *bhai* ['small brother' – the baby son of her *malik*], and go to cut the grass. Then, I play with *bhai* until dinner is ready. After eating, I clean the utensils, and watch television for a while. I study for about 30 minutes before going to bed at around 8 pm …, I do not get anything extra than lodging, food and attending school."

Saru accepted becoming a *haliya* labourer because she was promised a chance of formal education instead of cash/kind remuneration. Saru may be considered lucky because she is at least able to obtain some form of public education. Despite assurances from their *kisan*, many of her *haliya/kamaiya* counterparts do not often get the chance to go to school. However, Saru's daily tasks make it clear that she is unlikely to pass her final examinations and will possibly drop out (providing a good excuse for her *kisan*) in the following year. The only thing Saru cannot do is cooking food – her 'low caste' status bars her from entering the kitchen.

Like Saru, the vast majority of children are promised education while entering into a *haliya/kamaiya* contract. Acknowledging their lack of chance to study at home, the idea of studying as well as working appealed to children.

"Since we have food shortage at home, my father wanted me to become a *kamaiya* to get food, clothes and study. He said, 'if you go to work for *kisan*, we'll also get land to farm on the basis of *adhia*'. I didn't want to go, but I have to listen to my parents, and I liked the education offer." (Anju, 12, *kamaiya* girl)

Unfortunately, these employers either give them much more work than was contracted or do not permit them to attend school at all. The few children like Saru, who are allowed to attend a local public school, often find it extremely difficult to sustain the 'double trouble' of work with study (Giri, 2007).

> During the day [10 am to 4 pm] I attend a nearby school, but I've no time to do homework because I must work other times. In the evening, even if I've free time, I can't study because I become so tired from working all day that I want to go to bed as soon as I've eaten my evening meal. I've barely passed my exams." (Laxu, 14, *kamaiya* girl)

Although she received no free time to study, Laxu was able to attend school, but other children, like Samju, eventually had to give up.

> "Sometimes they let me go to the school and other times I was not allowed. They often told me to go to cut grass so I couldn't study. So, I had to stop going to school." (Samju, 12, *kamaiya* girl)

> "Our *malik* takes us with a false promise like 'oh, we won't send you out to work, it's just household work'. Once we are at their place, the reality is totally different. We don't only do domestic work, but agricultural work, which is too heavy for our body. They also say, 'you'll be studying and your future will be better if you come with us ... we can't even know how the alphabets look like once we start working'." (Basu, 16, *kamaiya* girl)

Children like Basu frequently reported that their employers cheated them not only in terms of the types and amount of work, but also with the promise of education; this is why more than half of all *haliya*/*kamaiya* children annually change their *kisan*. If their hope of better employers, who keep their promises and treat them better, does not become a reality, they continue changing or eventually abandon the bonded labour contract.

Clearly, all working children do not have the same life experiences: many of them were working just for food/clothes and/or other remuneration for their families:

> "I'm the oldest child so my father found a *kisan* as soon as I was able to do some household work. I didn't want to go, but I had to think about the poverty in my family and go to work. Besides food, I get two pairs of clothes and my parents take 3 quintals of unprocessed rice in a year." (Lalu, 15, *kamaiya* girl)

"My parents are getting old so they can't do outside work, and I've many siblings to take care of. We haven't got enough food to eat or clothes to wear. I didn't know where else to go so I followed my father's advice to become a *kamaiya* in the nearby village to earn foodstuffs for my family." (Gope, 15, *kamaiya* boy)

Although they were having a hard time, children like these hoped their efforts would not only relieve daily needs at home, but would allow some of their siblings to attend school for a 'better future' for the whole family.

In terms of food and living conditions, *haliya* children appeared to be more content than their *kamaiya* counterparts. Most claimed that the food and sleeping place they got was much better than at their own home.

"We can't always eat enough food at home and also we've no bed or sleeping materials. We've to sleep on a mat with a torn blanket. Here, I eat the same food as my *malik's* family and sleep on a bed with warm clothes in the ground floor." (Sume, 10, *haliya* boy)

In contrast, a 15-year-old *kamaiya* girl, Raju, complained, "I often had to eat leftover food; my sleeping place was near the kitchen so it was very cold in the winter". Of course, what children say about their food and living conditions is directly influenced by how well they are received by their *kisan* vis-à-vis their families. Despite having to work hard and eat *daal bhat* (very basic Nepali food), *haliya*/*kamaiya* children could be happy with their employers, if they were regarded positively. Likewise, if they had a difficult time at home, for example, being scolded or beaten), they also tended to favour their workplace. For instance, a 13-year-old *kamaiya* girl, Kamu, stresses, "the food and the sleeping place are much better than at my parents' house".

Since the vast majority of *haliya*/*kamaiya* children combined household work with agricultural work, it was not surprising that they often received physical injuries. Agriculture is one of the most dangerous occupational sectors for children, accounting for up to half of all work-related injuries or deaths (Ennew et al, 2003; Giri, 2009). It was clear from individual as well as group interviews that children are well aware of the physical risks their work entails:

"I got minor injuries from my work but once my leg was seriously wounded when I was washing *pathuwa* [jute plants] and I was unable to work for two months." (Katte, 14, *haliya* boy)

"Once I cut my fingers badly when collecting grass, and the other time the buffalo stepped on my feet." (Mite, 11, *kamaiya* boy)

"I've received several injuries while working. I've twisted my hands and legs, fallen off many times, and received cuts and bruises." (Mayu, 13, *kamaiya* girl)

Like their living conditions, however, the seriousness of injuries/illnesses often reflected how well they were treated by their *kisan*.

"I call my *maliknia* [lady boss] grandmother. Once I was suffering from fever I didn't want to sleep inside because of the heat so she also slept nearby and gave me water, medicine and food time to time. Also, the grandchildren of my *maliknia* behave with me like their own sister." (Bhabu, 13, *haliya* girl)

Like Bhabu, the majority of *haliya* children reported positive treatment, and their working and living conditions did not therefore seem to bother them. Although their *kisan* sometimes used derogatory names (for example, dog, donkey) when scolding, most of them had not faced serious punishments like beating. In contrast, *kamaiya* child workers claimed that they were badly scolded.

"My *maliknia* always complained, and she never believed in my work though I worked so much. She'd say, 'you're not doing what I've asked you to do' and get really angry. My *malik* doesn't stay home so I couldn't prove that I'm not as bad as she thinks. She also gave me one task after another to keep me busy for the whole day. I think being *kamaiya* is the worst thing, but I'm still doing it to support my family." (Bhagu, 16, *kamaiya* girl)

Unlike Bhabu, Bhagu made it clear that it is the attitudes of their *kisan* rather than the working conditions that make them dislike *haliya*/*kamaiya* work, but she accepted it as she had no better alternative. It should be emphasised that in Nepali culture, scolding or shouting is generally taken as a normal part of life, be it at home or at work. Indeed, children seemed to feel humiliated only when they were slapped, or worse, badly beaten. For instance, Raju, a 15-year-old *kamaiya* girl, shared her experience:

"My *malik* used to come home drunk late at night, and whenever my *maliknia* complained about my work or behaviour, then he'd beat me up by tying my hands behind my back to the point that I'd receive bruises and wounds. I'd also get smacked for cooking slowly or if the meal wasn't tasty enough. Many times I was slapped on my face, and once he poured hot tea over my body. This kind of treatment made me cry when I recalled my parents and home."

Besides work-related injuries, most *haliya/kamaiya* children did not recall being seriously ill from natural causes. As noted, however, minor injuries and illnesses are reported frequently, and children received varying degrees of care from their *kisan*. Thage, a 16-year-old *kamaiya* boy, had this experience when he became ill:

> "Once I was severely ill and my *malik* took me to the health post, costing him NPR 180 for a check-up and medicine. In the evening, my *maliknia* found out about it and she quarrelled with him by saying, 'why did you spend so much for others?'."

While Thage's *malik* appears to be more supportive than his *maliknia*, Saru, a 15-year-old *haliya* girl, explains how positively her *maliknia* treated her:

> "When I had cut my fingers, my *maliknia* said, 'if you lose one of them, you will not be able to join the police force' [later on], and she gave me medication, including tetanus injection. Then, she used to cut the grass and clean the utensils until my wound was healed."

Besides medical care, children felt even more happy and satisfied if their *kisan* allowed them to be in contact with their friends and families in times of sickness. However, although a few children were able to maintain this kind of relationship, it did not mean that their workload was reduced or fixed free times were allowed. Whether children worked within the house, in agriculture or in both, there were no scheduled working hours or better conditions.

As far as girls are concerned, some of them not only had to endure scolding and slapping, but also faced sexual mistreatment. Previous studies have shown that girl workers seem to be 'massively abused' worldwide. (Blagbrough and Glynn, 1999; Janak, 2000; Ennew et al, 2003; Jacquemin, 2004), which is why the Nepali government included domestic work as the worst form of child labour. During fieldwork, it was possible to gain the trust of some girls to talk about their experiences. A number of girls reported that they were touched indecently or persuaded to sleep with their male employers.

> "While I'd be sleeping alone in my room, my *malik* would come in. He'd start persuading me to let him sleep with me. He'd offer me money, but I refused. I think my *maliknia* knew his behaviour towards me, but she didn't react even when I talked to her about it." (Kalpu, 16, *kamaiya* girl)

It is often difficult to verify these accounts, particularly when the *maliknia* colludes with the abuse or even rape. Some girls reported a few instances they had heard about:

> "Last year, we heard that Tharu *kisan* raped a 15-year-old *kamaiya* girl, and forced her to get married with someone else when he found out that she was pregnant. She told other people about the rape only when her husband beat her up and forced her to leave him. Although villagers caught the *kisan* and made him 'pay fine' the girl was probably ashamed of herself because she disappeared from the village." (Lalu, 15, *kamaiya* girl)

Lalu, who had worked as a *kamaiya* labourer since the age of nine, commented that "it's not easy for girls to open up their internal pains [of sexual abuse] because they'll only be stigmatised by society instead of it punishing the culprit".

This evidence demonstrates how *haliya*/*kamaiya* children leave their families before adolescence to assume economic responsibility towards their family. They worry a lot about poverty in their families, and about being unable to attend school while staying at home. While some *haliya* children were happier working elsewhere than living with their alcoholic/abusive parents, many reported that they were sent away to work as a bonded labourer even when they had been beaten or abused by their *kisan*. All children gave their earnings to their parents to meet family needs; some parents spent it on alcohol and smoking rather than on food and clothes for the family. These pressures impacted on the children's psychological health alongside the physical ailments from work-related injuries.

Leaving *haliya*/*kamaiya* work

In a 'normal' *haliya*/*kamaiya* contract, children started working from about the age of nine and continued up to the age of 18. While a few might work throughout their lives, many had started to leave around the age of 15. Interviews showed that how long children worked depended on their treatment by employers. They accepted scolding and minor beatings like one or two slaps, but when they were beaten up, they would change their workplace or sometimes leave the *haliya*/*kamaiya* agreement altogether. Some girls had also left because of sexual maltreatment, as well as scolding and beating.

Most girls leave *haliya*/*kamaiya* work much earlier than boys because both Musahar and Tharu families arrange daughters' marriages quite early (sometimes as early as 12). Most parents appeared to send daughters to work as *haliya*/*kamaiya* labourers to learn household and agricultural skills, essential parts of adult life, rather than to earn family income per se. Even where girls complained about difficult working/living conditions at their *kisan's* home, it seemed they often got better food and were healthier than those who were not working as *haliya/kamaiya* labourers. Once girls leave *haliya/kamaiya* work and are married, their parents do not expect any income from them; they must then take care of their husband's family.

> "After working as *kamaiya* for six years, my parents asked me to come back home [in August 2007]. I didn't know that they were arranging my marriage. I couldn't refuse so I moved to my husband's family. Since his parents are also poor … we decided to go to the city to become construction labourers. My daily work involves carrying bricks, sand and cement, just for NPR 150. I don't know how long I can work here, but if I'm pregnant, then, I've to go back and live with my husband's family to carry out daily household activities like cleaning, cooking and rearing animals. My life will be all about taking care of my husband's family (and later my own children), and maybe working nearby as a seasonal farm worker." (Basu, 16, ex-*kamaiya* girl)

> "I stayed with my employer for five years, but had to leave because my parents arranged my marriage. Now, I'm staying with my husband's family. I continue to do *haliya* work, but now more on a seasonal basis or sometimes even for a daily wage. This is going be my life (although my husband wants to go to the city or to India to earn more money) … most girls spend their lives like this." (Ramu, 15, ex-*haliya* girl)

On the other hand, many boys must take the role of household head and other work to continue supporting their family. For a boy, bringing a wife home is one way to help his family because she carries out the household work. She may also earn something from seasonal labour while he is free to look for 'better paid' work elsewhere.

> "I worked as a *kamaiya* for nine years, but I wasn't able to pay the debt incurred in my marriage. So, I decided to move to the city to become a rickshaw pedaller. If there are no violent strikes, I earn about NPR 200 a day, excluding NPR 30 for renting the rickshaw. Pedalling is obviously very hard, especially during the summer heat/ monsoon rain, but I'll continue for the next few years. I don't know what I'll do in the long run." (Thage, 17, ex-*kamaiya* boy)

As Thage noted, continuing political instability, coupled with lack of jobs, forces post-*haliya*/*kamaiya* boys to move around different cities or even to India, with friends or relatives, for unskilled jobs. For some, working in India seems to be a better option because income is slightly higher than in Nepal,[6] and, moreover, they come home only once in six months or once a year, which allows them to save (although not for the future). Like their parents, however, both Musahar and Tharu children of Bayibab and Nayajib villages struggle to make a living because they cannot save.

> "I worked as *haliya* for seven years. After getting married, I've been working in brick-kilns as well as seasonal *haliya* for the last three years. It's necessary to combine two types of hard work, otherwise earnings won't be enough to buy daily needs. However, I don't like working either place. I want to become a driver, but I don't know who to contact and especially how to get the licence. If I can't, my life will continue like that of my father and elder brothers." (Bidhye, 18, ex-*haliya* boy)

All children hoped that if they could get help, they would be able to attend school and to learn certain locally useful skills such as tailoring, masonry or carpentry. Without this external support, children did not seem to see any other ways to free themselves from the *haliya*/*kamaiya* labour contract.

Conclusions

It is clear that the generational family-based *haliya*/*kamaiya* agreement has increasingly shifted towards children. When children work for the *kisan*, Musahar and Tharu parents are able to receive in-kind wages such as unprocessed rice, besides loans and *adhiya* land. On the other hand, *kisan* families are also eager to employ children after the promulgation of the 2002 anti-*kamaiya* law, which has made it difficult to hire adult *haliya*/*kamaiya* workers who can bargain for higher payment. In this context, the promise of education becomes attractive to parents and *kisan* as well as to children. This allows both parents and *kisan* to bypass the law and possible exposure to advocacy groups and media. The idea of giving a chance to study and work is openly accepted by communities and tacitly approved by government. The majority of children, especially from Tharu families, forge agreements with their *kisan* on the basis of schooling (rather than cash or kind income).

It is hardly surprising that work activities carried out by most *haliya*/*kamaiya* children were stressful, with long working hours over many years and physical and sexual abuse. The 'salary' they received for their parents was often very low (a few quintals of unprocessed rice, besides food/clothes); many did not receive the 'promised' education. However, they could not stay without work; their only hope of betterment was to change their employer after ending the annual contract with the hope of receiving better income and/or facilities. While some succeeded in meeting a more generous employer, others continued to change employers until eventually they migrated to cities or to India. Girls were well aware that they must spend their adult life taking care of their husbands' families and working locally as seasonal labourers. Both *haliya/kamaiya* children saw education and external support as the only ways to improve their current situation.

Notes

[1] 'A person enters debt bondage when their labour is demanded as a means of repayment of a loan, or of money given in advance. Usually, people are tricked or trapped into working for no pay or very little pay (in return for such a loan), in conditions that violate their human rights. Invariably, the value of the work done by a bonded labourer is greater that the original sum of money borrowed or advanced' (Anti-Slavery International, online).

[2] The *kamaiya* labourers belong to the Tharu ethnic group and are mainly concentrated in the five western districts. Robertson and Mishra (1997, p 15) report that 95% of *kamaiya* labourers belong to the ethnic Tharu community, whose total population is 1.2 million, or 6.5% of the total inhabitants of Nepal. On the other hand, the *haliya* (also known as *hali/haruwa*) labourers come from various castes/ethnicities scattered across Nepal. Dalits form 13.1% of the total population of 23 million (see Giri, 2009).

[3] This is a form of land measurement prevalent in southern Nepal in which, for instance, 5 *kattha* is about 0.169 hectares.

[4] During extended period field research in 2006–08 several cross-sectional interviews were carried out with about 40 children belonging to Musahar (in the Morang District) and Tharu (in the Bardiya District) families. Cross-sectional interviews were used so the life cycle of Musahar and Tharu children was followed, providing a detailed picture of their life worlds before, during and after they enter/leave *haliya/kamaiya* labour (see Giri, 2009).

[5] Participants' identities and village names have been changed to protect them.

[6] Often largely due to the Indian rupee having a higher value than its Nepali counterparts, that is, INPR 100 = NPR 160.

References

Bales, K. (2004) *Disposable people: New slavery in the globaly economy*, Berkeley, CA: University of California Press.

Blagbrough, J. and Glynn, E. (1999) 'Child domestic workers: characteristics of the modern slave and approaches to ending such exploitation" *Childhood*, vol 6, no 1, pp 515-16.

CWA (Child Workers in Asia Foundation) (2007) *Understanding bonded labour in Asia: An introduction to the nature of the problem and how to address it*, Bangkok: CWA.

Daru, P., Churchill, C. and Beemsterboer, E. (2005) 'The prevention of debt bondage with micro-finance-led services" *European Journal of Development Research*, vol 17, no 1, pp 132-55.

Ennew, J., Myers, W.E. and Plateau, D.P. (2003) 'The meaning, nature and scope of child labour', Draft for the Colloquium on 'Combating Abusive Child Labour', Iowa, July.

Giri, B.R. (2004) 'South Asian bonded labour system: a comparative perspective on institutional arrangements', Unpublished manuscript, Amsterdam: The University of Amsterdam.

Giri, B.R. (2007) 'A reflexive autobiography of child work', *Childhood Today*, vol 1, no 2, pp 1-21.

Giri, B.R. (2009) 'Bonded labour system in Nepal: Making a sense of haliya and kamaiya children's work', Draft manuscript, Milton Keynes: The Open University.

Jacquemin, Y. (2004) 'Children's domestic work in Abidjan, Côte d'Ivoire: the petites bonnes have the floor,' *Childhood*, vol 11, no 3, pp 383-97.

Janak, J. (2000) 'Haiti's 'Restavec' slave children: difficult choices, difficult lives… yet… Lespwa fe Viv', *International Journal of Children's Rights*, vol 8, no 4, pp 321-31.

Lowe, P., Whyte, T. and Kasaju, B. (2001) *Kamaiya: Slavery and freedom in Nepal*, Kathmandu: Mandala Book Point/MS Nepal.

Maslak, A. (2003) *Daughters of the Tharu: Gender, ethnicity, and religion, and the education of Nepali girls*, London: Routledge Falmer.

Rankin, K.N. (1999) 'The predicament of labour: *Kamaiya* practices and the ideology of freedom,' in H.R. Skar (ed) *Nepal: Tharu and Tarai neighbours*, Kathmandu: Bibliotheca Himalayica, pp 27-45.

Robertson, A. and Mishra, S. (1997) *Forced to plough: Bonded labour in Nepal's agricultural economy*, London: Anti-Slavery International.

Sharma, S. and Sharma, K. (2002) *Findings of debt bondage: Long-term farm labour systems in Kavrepalanchok and Sarlahi Districts, Nepal*, Kathmandu: National Labour Academy.

Woodhead, M. (1999) 'Combating child labour: listen to what the children say', *Childhood*, vol 6, no 1, pp 27-49.

fifteen

Sex trafficking in Nepal

Padam Simkhada

Introduction

Trafficking in persons, particularly the sex trafficking of girls and women, has generated much attention over the past decade (IOM, 2005; Tollefson, 2006; Segrava et al, 2009). The United Nations (UN) Protocol to Prevent, Suppress and Punish Trafficking in Persons recognises trafficking as a modern form of slavery and forced labour that relies on coercion, fraud or abduction in order to flourish (UN, 2000). Globally, it is estimated that between 700,000 (USDS, 2001) and four million (UNFPA, 2000) people are trafficked each year. The large differential in estimated numbers of people affected by trafficking reflects the difficulties in obtaining accurate data and agreeing definitions. Asia is seen as the most vulnerable region for human trafficking (Kempadoo et al, 2005; Asha-Nepal, 2006; Huda, 2006). India is a major destination country for sex-trafficked girls (HRW, 1995; USDS, 2005), with large numbers of Nepalese trafficked to Indian cities, particularly Mumbai (Bombay) (Nair, 2004).

Estimates suggest that around 12,000 Nepali girls are trafficked for sex work each year (ILO-IPEC, 2002), and 200,000 Nepali girls are working in the sex industry in India; accurate numbers remain elusive, however (Rozario and Rita, 1988; O'Dea, 1993; HRW, 1995). Since the early 1990s, trafficking has been identified as a priority issue in Nepal and many non-governmental organisations (NGOs) and government ministries have developed social, cultural and economic programmes to address it. Despite the development of these programmes, there has been more recent criticism of national and local level political apathy on the issue, and the continued chronic lack of law enforcement to address this problem. While the Nepalese government has expressed a commitment towards anti-trafficking activities, most initiatives have not been implemented and some are awaiting funding.

There is a dearth of quantitative data on the characteristics of trafficked women, partly due to its illegal nature but also because existing data sources have not been fully utilised. Much existing information about sex trafficking in Nepal is collated in NGO publications (HRW, 1995; Pradhan, 1996; ABC Nepal, 1996, 1998; Ghimire, 2001), which present anecdotal case studies, newspaper reports and commentary from anti-trafficking agencies. There are a limited number of unpublished reports on trafficking in the South Asia region (Poudyal, 1996; Huntington, 2002; Khatri, 2002); however, these largely focus on policy analysis rather than reporting empirical research. Very limited research has been published using data from trafficked women themselves, investigating the nature and process of sex trafficking in Nepal, the spatial context of trafficking and the complex issues surrounding community reintegration on return to Nepal (Hennink and Simkhada, 2004; Asha-Nepal, 2006). Comprehensive research is urgently needed to further understand the process of sex trafficking and to support the development of effective, comprehensive and feasible anti-trafficking measures within Nepal.

The objective of this chapter is to understand more fully the process and context of trafficking from Nepal to India for sex work. More specifically, it will investigate: (a) the characteristics of trafficked women; (b) methods and means of trafficking; (c) traffickers; and (d) the routes of exit from trafficking.

Methods[1]

Young women who have been trafficked for sex work are a hidden population, largely due to the illegal nature of trafficking and (often under-age) sex work. Employers of trafficked girls may keep them hidden from public view and limit their contact with outsiders. Trafficked girls may not identify themselves as such through fear of reprisals from their employers, fear of social stigma from involvement in sex work or their HIV positive status and shame of their activities being revealed to family members. Any interview with trafficked girls is therefore likely to be a 'post-event' contact, such as accessing formerly trafficked girls in transit homes, in rehabilitation centres or in their communities of origin after return. In view of these difficulties, the target population described in this chapter were girls who had been trafficked to India for sex work and subsequently returned to Nepal.

The first stage of data collection involved conducting eight in-depth interviews with key informants, in order to provide a broader understanding of health and social issues surrounding trafficking in Nepal. Informants included directors of NGOs working on sex trafficking issues, coordinators of rehabilitation centres for trafficked women and health workers whose clientele included former trafficked women. Second, quantitative data on 206 returned trafficked women were collated from the records of six rehabilitation centres in Kathmandu. These data included information related to the trafficking event, sociodemographic and health information. These data were collected using a quantitative survey form, to ensure consistency in the information collated. Findings from this quantitative data are summarised later. Further information was collected from in-depth interviews with 42 girls trafficked to India for sex work but who had since returned to Nepal.

Findings from in-depth interviews have been presented elsewhere (see Simkhada, 2008).

What the study showed

Who was trafficked from Nepal?

The sociodemographic characteristics of trafficked girls are shown in Table 16.1. Girls who are trafficked are typically unmarried, non-literate and very young. It is clear that the majority of girls trafficked are within the narrow age range of 13–18 years. One third of girls were trafficked when aged below 16 and almost half between 16 and 18. The youngest age was 12 and no girls were trafficked older than 25. Although the majority of trafficked girls are unmarried (62%), more than one third of respondents were married at the time of trafficking. Girls trafficked under the age of 16 are twice as

Table 16.1: Sociodemographic characteristics of trafficked girls

		%	Number
Ethnic group	Brahmin/Chhetri	16.7	34
	Mongoloid[b]	35.8	73
	Dalit (untouchable)	31.4	64
	Other	16.2	33
	Total	100	204
Religion	Hindu	72.1	147
	Buddhist	24.0	49
	Other	3.9	8
	Total	100	204
Marital status[a]	Unmarried	61.8	123
	Married	37.2	74
	Other	1.0	2
	Total	100	199
Age[a]	Under 13	3.5	7
	13–15	31.3	62
	16–18	49.0	97
	19–21	12.6	25
	22+	3.5	7
	Total	100	198
Education[a]	Non-literate	80.0	160
	Primary/informal	15.5	31
	Secondary	4.5	9
	Total	100	200

Notes: Data from records of trafficked girls from six rehabilitation centres and community interviews.

[a] At the time of trafficking. [b] Includes Gurung, Magar, Rai and Tamang ethnic groups.

likely to be unmarried (45%) than married (21%). The predominant ethnic group of trafficked girls was Mongoloid or Dalit (untouchable); however, trafficked girls originated from 25 ethnic groups.

Figure 16.1 shows the districts of origin of trafficked girls. The distribution shows that girls originated from 37 districts, most of which are in the Hill or Terai ecological zones. Half the trafficked girls originated from eight districts that are predominantly border districts in both the Western and Eastern Region or districts in close proximity to Kathmandu in the Central Region. The highest proportion of trafficked girls originated from Chitwan (12%) and Sindhuplachowk (11%) Districts. Chitwan District is worthy of note as this is a border district encompassing major transport routes both from Kathmandu and the western districts to India and is therefore a key strategic district for trafficking.

Figure 16.1: District of origin of trafficked girls

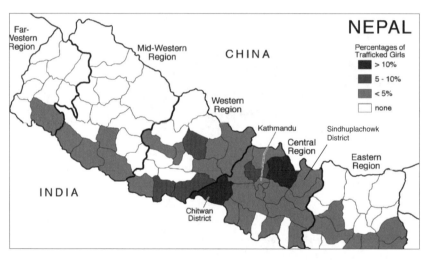

Note: Data from records of rehabilitation centres.

How were they trafficked?

Four key routes into sex trafficking were identified: (a) employment-induced migration; (b) fraudulent marriage; (c) deception, through false visits; and (d) force, through abduction (see Table 16.2). Girls and women may have entered sex trafficking either directly or indirectly. *Direct routes* into sex trafficking are the result of deception and force, whereby girls are deceived into fraudulent marriages or false visits for which travel out of the village is necessary, or they are abducted and taken directly to India for sex work. Girls who became part of sex trafficking through *indirect routes* typically migrate

Table 16.2: Routes into sex trafficking

	%	Number
Employment migration through *dalal* (broker)	62.6	122
Fraudulent marriage	13.3	26
False visits	17.4	34
Force (abduction)	6.7	13
Total	100	195

Note: Data from records of trafficked girls from six rehabilitation centres and community interviews.

from rural villages to urban areas for employment, often to work as cheap labour in carpet factories. The data identified that such employment-led trafficking often occurred through a *dalal* ('broker' or 'agent') working with a carpet factory owner or others. Carpet factories in Nepal are important recruitment centres for sex traffickers.

Those aged over 16 are more likely than younger girls to enter trafficking through such direct routes. In some cases traffickers conduct a fraudulent marriage ceremony and subsequently take the 'bride' to settle in India, or traffickers pose as marriage brokers for businessmen in India and persuade a girl to travel for marriage. Alternatively girls are offered the chance to visit India for employment as housemaids, actresses or to establish a small business. Brokers would often pose as potential boyfriends to gain the trust of girls before offering marriage or visits to India. Abduction was a less common means of trafficking young women.

Who were the traffickers?

A variety of people are involved in trafficking girls and women into sex work. The study showed that over almost half of traffickers were people familiar to the trafficked girls; these were often known, trusted members of their community or acquaintances. Girls trafficked by familiar people identified that job offers and, to a lesser extent, marriage offers led them to trafficking. One third of women were trafficked by people who were unknown to them prior to the trafficking. These strangers are most likely to deceive girls with offers of employment; trafficking by force is also most likely to be conducted by people unknown to the respondents. It is significant to note that 22% of girls identified that a relative was involved in their trafficking. These girls were most likely to be trafficked through offers of marriage or false visits. In most cases relatives included uncles, aunts, cousins, brothers or stepfathers who acted as brokers. In addition, some traffickers were women who were involved in sex work in India themselves, often former trafficked women or sex workers who are now brothel managers or owners (see Table 16.3).

Table 16.3: Types of traffickers

Trafficker	%	Number
Relative	22.2	44
Familiar person	46.5	92
Unknown person	31.3	62
Total	100	198

Note: Data from records of trafficked girls from six rehabilitation centres and community interviews.

How did they exit from brothels?

Three modes of exit from trafficking were identified: rescue, escape or release. The most common exit from trafficking reported in this study was 'rescue', after police raids for under-age sex workers (those aged below 18 years). Data from the rehabilitation centres in Nepal show that 80% of girls left Indian brothels after being rescued. However, this high figure may simply reflect the source of data collection, in that rescued girls often pass through a rehabilitation centre. Those who had been in the brothel for less than three years were more likely to have been rescued, perhaps because they were more likely to be aged under 18. Typically these girls were taken from the Indian brothels by social workers and/or the police, placed in an Indian transit home or rehabilitation centre and then transferred to a rehabilitation centre in Nepal.

The second mode of exit from sex trafficking was escape from the Indian brothels. Many respondents reported failed attempts to escape, but only 13% of girls reported a successful escape as their means of exit from sex trafficking. Escape from the brothel is much more likely among those who have been in the brothel for less than 12 months.

In fewer cases (7%) girls left the Indian brothels after being released by the brothel owner. In general, girls would only be released when they became too old to attract sufficient clients or when they tested as HIV positive. Table 16.4 shows that release by brothel owners was more common after five years

Table 16.4: Duration in brothels by mode of exit

Duration in brothel (months)	Mode of exit from brothel					
	Rescued		Escaped		Released by owner	
	%	no	%	no	%	no
Less than 12	27.2	41	50.0	12	0	0
12–36	44.4	67	20.8	5	15.4	2
37–60	19.2	29	25.0	6	38.5	5
More than 60	9.3	14	4.2	1	46.2	6
Total	100	151	100	24	100	13

Note: Data from records of trafficked girls from six rehabilitation centres and community interviews.

at the brothel. In some cases girls were permitted to leave the brothel for a visit to family in Nepal and then never returned. In addition, some trafficked girls exited the Indian brothels independently and did not pass through a transit home in India or a rehabilitation centre in Nepal. These girls either lived in India for some time or returned directly to Nepal. Some girls also returned to brothels in India after an independent return to Nepal; these were often trafficked women who had become brothel managers themselves. It was not possible to identify women who remained in India after exiting the brothel; however, key informants reported that these women sometimes married in India or continued with sex work independently.

Discussion and conclusion

In summary, girls trafficked from Nepal to India are typically unmarried, illiterate and very young. The key routes into sex trafficking include: employment-induced migration to urban areas, deception (through false marriage or visits) and abduction. Half of traffickers were people familiar to trafficked girls and over one fifth were relatives. Exit from trafficking was through rescue, escape or release; the majority of girls were rescued in police raids on Indian brothels.

Nepali and Indian literature points to hardships and the poor economic structure of the household that leads women to vulnerability to trafficking and their involvement in prostitution. Detailed case studies (Rajbhandari and Rajbhandari, 1997; ABC Nepal, 1998) indicate that poor economic conditions is the most common factor identified by the women. But the possibility of their involvement in other sectors of the economy is not detailed. The pimps' and brokers' assurance about earning without investment attracts women in the initial stages, and once they are in the sex market, the bonds of debt keep them within the profession. Women, once trafficked and forced to be in prostitution, often later accept their fate because of a lack of alternatives.

Some of the more frequently cited factors leading to trafficking were poverty, lack of employment opportunities, the low social status of girls, a general lack of education and awareness, corruption of officials, lax law and weak law enforcement machinery (Thapa, 1990; Pradhan, 1996; Rajbhandari and Rajbhandari, 1997; Acharya, 1998; ILO-IPEC, 1998; Asia Foundation and Population Council, 2001; Kara, 2009). All, no doubt, contribute towards the problem. However, they do not explain why only certain communities are affected, although all share similar socioeconomic conditions. Why are certain geographic, ethnic and ecological factors more significant in determining the magnitude of trafficking? This requires further research.

Some studies report that women and girls are attracted by reports of the wealth and fun to be had in the city and are easily duped into trusting the mediator. Likewise, some women are deceived into false marriages with the broker and are subsequently sold into the sex industry. Trafficking in women and girls reflects, possibly, weaker family structures, although the Nepali kinship bond is reportedly a strong one. Ironically, many brokers and pimps are reported to be relatives of the victims. Even the husbands and fathers of the women concerned are in some cases found to be involved in such flesh trade activities.

This study also revealed that brokers were increasingly operating within organised trafficking networks covering specific regions of Nepal and using sophisticated methods. For example, it is becoming increasingly common for trafficking to take place in stages, with women moved around to work in different sites before finally being sold into sex work.

A more refined analysis suggests that in many circumstances large disparities in income and wealth entice individuals to migrate, rather than absolute poverty pushing individuals away from their home communities; that is, inequality rather than poverty may be a key driver in some circumstances. Clearly a number of 'push' factors do exist that encourage individuals to migrate, including economic aspirations (looking for opportunities to better one's life) and a breakdown of family or social structure, in addition to the more frequently cited reason of absolute 'poverty'.

Migration more generally, which is easier now than at any previous time, is also playing an increasingly important part in Nepal's economy and social structure. As these factors lead to increased migration, more women and girls are found to be trafficked in the process. This finding is consistent with previous findings (O'Dea, 1993; ABC Nepal, 1996; Rajbhandari, 1997; ILO-IPEC, 1998; Asia Foundation and Population Council, 2001). Many misconceptions or over-simplifications of the underlying causes of migration obscure the resources that are available to trafficked people and their degree of resiliency. For example, poverty is often cited as the reason for migration or accepting employment conditions of debt bondage, despite the common occurrence of migrants actually paying for transportation or transit services. Migration policies in Nepal sometimes exclude the unskilled, particularly women, from legal migration and force them to seek alternative livelihood options through illegal means.

Implications for local anti-trafficking initiatives

The characteristics of trafficked girls and the various routes into trafficking identified in this study highlight a range of implications for community-level initiatives. Initiatives undertaken in local communities will target girls before trafficking movement has begun and therefore largely focus on reducing their vulnerability to trafficking and situations of entrapment.

There is a need, first, to widen the perception of the types of girls affected by trafficking. Trafficked girls in this study originated from a wider range of ethnic groups than indicated in previous literature, which suggested that trafficking was largely confined to Mongoloid ethnic groups (Rajbhandari and Rajbhandari, 1997). Both married and unmarried girls are vulnerable to trafficking. Second, trafficking is a more widespread geographic phenomenon than previously indicated. This study identified trafficking activity in 37 districts of Nepal, particularly those bordering India and adjacent to Kathmandu. Earlier studies identified the prevalence of trafficking in the Kathmandu Valley, while government and NGO activities focus on '19 danger districts' in which sex trafficking is thought to be prevalent (Pradhan, 1996; Rajbhandari and Rajbhandari, 1997; Ghimire, 1998; Frederick and Kelly, 2000). One of the major limitations of previous work is that districts considered as source areas for trafficking are identified informally rather than through analysis of existing data on trafficked women. There is a strong need to broaden the geographic reach of community-level anti-trafficking initiatives, in particular to include all border districts clearly affected by trafficking. The existence of well-defined networks of trafficking (for example, through carpet factories) has implications for targeting resources and the effectiveness of interventions.

There is a strong need to review the focus and format of information, education and communication (IEC) materials about sex trafficking used for community awareness. Much of the existing material is developed on the premise that the families of trafficked girls are passive innocents, and that girls are trafficked through direct routes such as kidnap and coercion (Asia Foundation and Population Council, 2001). However, this research has shown that in Nepal there is considerably more involvement of relatives in the sex trafficking process than previously identified (Bhatta, 1990). There is an urgent need to review current IEC materials to identify the full range of situations that may lead to trafficking as well as identifying possible traffickers. Such material should also draw attention to the vulnerability to trafficking after employment migration to urban areas.

In addition, the format of IEC materials on trafficking needs to be broadened to have greater impact at community level. Currently IEC materials are in the form of leaflets and booklets targeted towards a literate audience; however, the majority of trafficked girls are illiterate. There is a need for a broader range of IEC material and creative community initiatives to raise awareness of the risks of trafficking, not relying on written materials. Such strategies may include street theatre, community meetings and peer-led educational campaigns, targeted towards those most vulnerable to trafficking. Messages delivered through peers are more realistic and relevant to young girls and have greater impact.

Encouraging formerly trafficked women to share their experiences in community groups, schools or clubs may also sensitise the community to trafficking and help to reduce social stigma and discrimination towards trafficked women. It is important that community initiatives not only target individuals vulnerable to trafficking but also their carers, village leaders and the wider community, to raise general awareness of the practice of trafficking (Ghimire, 2001; CREHPA, 2003). Holding community meetings for local government officials, medical personnel, law enforcers, teachers and social workers will also contribute to increasing community awareness and empowerment. Utilising local and national media will not only raise awareness of trafficking among the community, but can play an important advocacy role in sensitising policy makers to trafficking issues.

Community initiatives to prevent trafficking need to adopt a more supportive, empowering approach to the urban migration of women. Employment migration to urban areas can have considerable economic benefits for the women involved and their families; initiatives that attempt to reduce trafficking by discouraging such migration are therefore likely to be ineffective (Walkowitz, 1980; Brandt, 1988; Asia Foundation and Population Council, 2001). There is a compelling need for interventions that empower women and girls in migration rather than seeking to protect women or discourage such movement. More sustainable community initiatives need to focus on strategies for safe migration by increasing women's awareness of the risks of urban migration, including increased vulnerability to trafficking (GAATW, 1999). There is also a need to establish support networks for women who have migrated to urban areas. Longer-term community initiatives to reduce trafficking need to address the push factors leading women into vulnerable situations to traffickers, such as the social and economic disadvantage of women in their home communities. Such initiatives may include women's leadership training, literacy programmes, micro-credit schemes and training in livelihood skills (Huntington, 2002).

Urban centres represent both a source and a transitory centre for sex trafficking. The indirect routes to trafficking identified in this study often involve employment in factories requiring cheap, unskilled labour before girls undertake migration to India. Interventions in urban areas urgently need to focus on carpet factories and similar establishments where girls are particularly vulnerable to exploitation by traffickers. Information and awareness campaigns need to alert young girls to the risks of sex trafficking and provide advice on how to seek assistance. This strategy targets efforts towards empowering those who are shown to be most vulnerable to trafficking from urban areas.

Initiatives at community level and in urban centres focus on measures to prevent trafficking through increasing awareness among those most vulnerable to entrapment. Once trafficking movement has begun, intervention activities become more complex and involve either (a) interception during the trafficking process or (b) rescue and repatriation from India after the trafficking movement has ceased. Interception of trafficked girls while in transit is a particularly difficult activity to manage without restricting valid migration, and is closely tied to effective border management (Salt and Hogarth, 2000). Huntington (2002) suggests that interventions during the transit stage of trafficking predominantly involve training and resources for border agents and local law enforcement officials. However, there remain difficulties in clearly identifying a trafficking case, those being trafficked occasionally not being aware of the deception surrounding their movement. The open border between Nepal and India makes border management activities difficult and past interception activities have been poorly coordinated among the various agencies involved.

Once trafficking movement has ceased, rescue and repatriation from the Indian brothels becomes the most pressing intervention. These activities are not straightforward and involve close cooperation between authorities in India and Nepal. Despite generally lax law enforcement, this research shows that rescue by law enforcement authorities is the most common exit mode from sex trafficking. Given that 88% of girls were under 18, police raids on brothels remain an important strategy for identification of under-age trafficked women. However, police corruption and the exploitation of girls in a vulnerable situation of trafficking needs to be carefully addressed. The concentration of Nepali sex workers in specific districts or brothels suggest that resources can be effectively targeted.

Kelly and Le (1999) suggest there exists no effective intervention model to prevent trafficking, partly because there is no suitable framework of trafficking from which to develop effective interventions. Awareness of trafficking and empowerment in the process of urban migration is required at the community level and a focus on urban carpet factories is particularly critical; during the transit phase, interception and rescue activities are required, while at the post-trafficking stage, activities focusing on both community integration and fostering social independence are needed. In addition, stronger political commitment in allocating sufficient resources towards implementation and enforcement of anti-trafficking policies remains critical. In summary, anti-trafficking measures need to focus on source, transit and destination locations, working with a range of agencies in a multiagency strategy based on education, social and economic empowerment, information and advice and effective law enforcement. These measures need to be targeted in a way that draws effectively on existing data and research findings.

Note

[1] This chapter is part of larger study and based fieldwork undertaken by the author in Nepal in 2000/01 and a follow-up visit in 2008/09.

References

ABC Nepal (1996) *Red light traffic: The trade in Nepali girls*, Kathmandu: ABC Nepal.

ABC Nepal (1998) *Life in hell: The true stories of girls rescued from Indian brothels*, Kathmandu: ABC Nepal.

Acharya, U. (1998) 'Trafficking in children and the exploitation in prostitution and other intolerable forms of child labour in Nepal: Nepal country report', Unpublished, prepared for ILO-IPEC, Kathmandu.

Asha-Nepal (2006) *A sense of direction: The trafficking of women and children from Nepal*, Kathmandu: Asha-Nepal.

Asia Foundation and Population Council (2001) *Prevention of trafficking and the care and support of trafficked persons: In the context of an emerging HIV/AIDS epidemic in Nepal*, The Asia Foundation and Horizons Project Population Council, Kathmandu, Nepal: Creative Press.

Bhatta, A. (1990) 'Cheliko vyapar sambandhi kes adhyayan' ('Case study of illegal trade girls'), in D. Ghimire (ed) *Cheliko abaidh: Yeska paksha* (*Illegal trade of girls: Its various aspects*), Kathmandu: ABC Nepal Kathmandu, pp 39-48.

Brandt, A. (1988) 'AIDS: from social history to social policy', in E. Fee and D. Fox (eds) *AIDS: The burdens of history*, Berkeley, CA: University of California Press, pp 147-72.

CREHPA (Centre for Research on Environment, Health and Population Activities) (2003) *The anti-trafficking program in rural Nepal: Assessment of change in awareness and communication among adolescent girls, peers and parents in Baglung District, 2002, An endline survey*, Kathmandu: CREHPA.

Frederick, J. and Kelly, T. (eds) (2000) *Fallen angels: The sex workers of South Asia*, New Delhi: Lustre Press, Roli Books.

GAATW (Global Alliance Against Traffic in Women) (1999) *The migrating women's handbook*, Bangkok: GAATW.

Ghimire, D. (1998) 'Chelibetiko abaidh vyapar' ('Illegal trade of girls'), in D. Ghimire (ed) *Chelibetiko abaidh vyapar: Yasaka vivid paksha* (*Illegal trade of girls: Its various aspects*), Kathmandu: ABC Nepal, pp 1-16.

Ghimire, D. (2001) 'Prevention, care, rehabilitation and reintegration of rescued girls (ABC's experience)', Paper presented at the Technical Consultative Meeting on Anti-trafficking Programmes in South Asia, Kathmandu, Nepal, September.

Hennink, M. and Simkhada, P. (2004) 'Sex trafficking in Nepal: context and process', *Asian Pacific Migration Journal*, vol 13, no 3, pp 305-38.

HRW (Human Rights Watch) (1995) *Rape for profit: Trafficking of Nepali girls and women to Indian brothels*, New York, NY: Human Rights Watch.

Huda, S. (2006) 'Sex trafficking in South Asia', *International Journal of Gynaecology and Obstetrics*, vol 94, no 3, September, pp 374–81.

Huntington, D. (2002) *Anti-trafficking program in South Asia: Appropriate activities, indicators and evaluation methodologies*, Summary report of a technical consultative meeting, New Delhi: Population Council.

ILO-IPEC (International Labour Organization-International Programme on the Elimination of Child Labour) (1998) 'Trafficking in children for labour exploitation, including sexual exploitation in South Asia', Synthesis paper (unpublished), Nepal: South Asian Sub-Regional Consultation.

ILO-IPEC (2002) *Internal trafficking among children and youth engaged in prostitution*, Kathmandu, Nepal: ILO-IPEC.

IOM (International Organization for Migration) (2005) *Data and research on human trafficking: A global survey*, Geneva: IOM.

Kara, S. (2009) *Sex trafficking: Inside the business of modern slavery*, New York, NY: Columbia University Press.

Kelly, P. and Le, B.D. (1999) *Trafficking in humans from and within Vietnam: The known from a literature review key informant interviews and analysis*, Research report prepared for ILO, Radda Barnen, SCUK and UNICEF.

Kempadoo, K., Sanghera, J. and Pattanaik, B. (2005) *Trafficking and prostitution reconsidered: New perspectives on migration, sex work and human rights*, Boulder, CO: Paradigm.

Khatri, N. (2002) 'Nepal: the problems of trafficking in women and children', Paper presented at the 7th Annual Meeting of the Asia Pacific Forum for National Human Rights Institutions, 11–13 November, New Delhi.

Nair, P.M. (2004) *A report on trafficking of women and children in India: 2002–2003*, **vol 1,** New Delhi: UNIFEM/ISS/NHRC.

O'Dea, P. (1993) *Gender exploitation and violence: The market in women, girls and sex in Nepal: An overview of the situation and a review of the literature*, Kathmandu: UNICEF.

Poudyal, P. (1996) 'Report of the South Asian workshop on trafficking in women and children', *Gender and Development*, vol 8, pp 74–9.

Pradhan, G. (1996) *Back home from the brothels: A case study of the victims of commercial sexual exploitation and trafficking across Nepal–India border*, Kathmandu: CWIN.

Rajbhandari, R. (1997) *Present status of Nepali prostitutes in Bombay*, Kathmandu: WOREC.

Rajbhandari, R. and Rajbhandari, B. (1997) *Girl trafficking: Hidden grief in the Himalayas*, Kathmandu: WOREC.

Rozario, S. and Rita, M. (1988) *Trafficking of women and children in India (Sexual exploitation and sale)*, Status of Women Series, New Delhi: Uppal Publishing House.

Salt, J. and Hogarth, J. (2000) 'Border control', in F. Laczko and D. Thompson (eds) *Migrant trafficking and human smuggling in Europe*, Geneva: International Organization for Migration.

Segrava, M., Milivojevic, S. and Pickering, S. (2009) *Sex trafficking: International context and response*, Cullompton: Willan Publishing.

Simkhada, P. (2008) 'Sex trafficking: life histories and survival strategies among trafficked girls in Nepal', *Children and Society*, vol 22, pp 235-48.

Thapa, P. (1990) 'Keti bechbikhan: lukeko aparadh' ('Trade of girls: a hidden crime'), in D. Ghimire (ed) *Chelibetiko abaidh vyapar: Yasaka vivid paksha (Illegal trade of girls: Its various aspects)*, Kathmandu: ABC Nepal, pp 21-5.

Tollefson, R. (2006) *Guide to reference sources on trafficking in women*, Cyprus: Mediterranean Institute of Gender Studies (www.humantrafficking.org/uploads/publications/traffickinginwomen_referenceguide.pdf).

UN (United Nations) (2000) *Protocol to Prevent, Suppress and Punish trafficking in persons, especially women and children*, Supplementing the UN Convention against Transnational Organised Crime, Annex II, UN Doc A/55/383, New York: United Nations

UNFPA (United Nations Fund for Population Activities) (2000) *State of the world's population*, New York, NY: UNFPA, September, p 5.

USDS (United States Department of State) (2001) *Victims of Trafficking and Violence Protection Act 2000: Trafficking in persons report*, Washington, DC: USDS.

USDS (2005) *Victims of Trafficking and Violence Protection Act of 2000: Trafficking in persons report*, Washington, DC: USDS.

Walkowitz, J. (1980) *Prostitution and Victorian society: Women, class and the state*, Cambridge: Cambridge University Press.

sixteen

The role of the arts in resisting recruitment as child soldiers and 'wives': experience from Uganda and Nepal

Bill Brookman and Katherine Darton

This chapter describes work with children associated with armed forces and armed groups by Bill Brookman for the International Labour Organization (ILO). It introduces the international laws on child labour and child soldiers, the ILO's SCREAM programme (Supporting Children's Rights through Education, the Arts and the Media) and Brookman's experiences when piloting his new SCREAM module with children and young people in Uganda and Nepal.

Introduction: the Bill Brookman Foundation

Bill Brookman is a performance artist and musician who has run his own street theatre company in Leicestershire for over 20 years (www.billbrookman.co.uk). In addition to events such as fêtes and carnivals, the company works with disadvantaged groups, using the arts for education. Some years ago, inspired by the work of Patch Adams, the American clown doctor, Brookman set up the Bill Brookman Foundation, which uses performing and circus arts for reconciliation and rehabilitation in places experiencing trauma.

The Foundation's first international project, in January 2002, provided street festivals in villages in Gujarat, one year after the devastating earthquake there. Since then, Brookman has run three arts-based projects with the United Nations (UN):

- in Kosovo (2003), teaching circus skills to local children and producing a street festival involving local dancers as well as volunteers from the UK;
- in Sierra Leone (2005), running a project after the devastating war there, using theatre and comedy to encourage civilians to give up their weapons, followed by a street festival in Rokel, featuring amputees as performers as part of the national celebration, *De war don don* ('the war is over');

- in Haiti (2006–07), recruiting and training a team of local performance artists forming *Caravane de la Paix*, a group that put on shows and workshops all over the country promoting a message of peace.

In August 2009 he began a similar project for the UN Development Programme in Somalia.[1]

Child soldiers and worst forms of child labour

The preface to the *Child soldiers global report* (CSUCS, 2008) says:

> An impressive and unprecedented number of international instruments are in place to support efforts to 'stop the use of child soldiers'.... The Optional Protocol on the Involvement of Children in Armed Conflict has been ratified by 120 states; special war crime tribunals and the International Criminal Court are becoming a more important means for bringing the perpetrators of crimes against children to justice.... Most recently, the Paris Principles and Guidelines on children associated with armed forces and armed groups have been endorsed by 66 governments ... pledged to work for the release of all child soldiers from fighting forces, and support programs which genuinely address the complex needs of returning child soldiers.

In order to further these aims by targeting children and young people themselves, in 2008 the ILO's International Training Centre (ITC) approached Brookman to write a new module for their SCREAM programme. The SCREAM programme is aimed at addressing children's rights generally: full details can be found on the ILO-IPEC website(www. ilo.org/public/english///standards/ipec/scream/on_the_web.htm).

The requested new module was to address the worst forms of child labour, and in particular, children associated with armed forces and armed groups, including child soldiers and those at risk of sexual abuse. Its aim was:

- to educate children in international law on child labour, including children in industrialised countries who are not at personal risk of recruitment;
- to teach children possible ways to resist recruitment;
- to help children rehabilitate and reintegrate into their societies if they had already been involved with armed forces and armed groups.

International law and conventions relating to child labour

The key conventions of relevance to this work are as follows:[2]

- UN Universal Declaration of Human Rights 1948;
- UN Convention on the Rights of the Child (CRC): this was adopted and opened for signature, ratification and accession by the UN General Assembly in 1989 and came into force in 1990. The Articles of particular relevance here are as follows: Article 32, protection from economic exploitation and hazardous work; Article 34, sexual exploitation; Article 38, involvement in armed forces; and Article 39, physical and psychological recovery and social reintegration of children who have been involved in any such work or exploitation.
- ILO Minimum Age Convention No 138: concerning minimum age for admission to employment (brought into force in 1976). This specifies a minimum age for work as the age for the end of compulsory schooling, or age 15, whichever is lower; and the minimum age for work that is 'likely to jeopardise health, safety or morals' as 18 years. Further Articles discuss the possibility of children undertaking light work that does not interfere with their education.
- ILO Worst Forms of Child Labour Convention No 182: concerning the prohibition and immediate action for the elimination of the worst forms of child labour (brought into force in 2000; see Chapters One and Three, this volume). For this Convention, the word 'child' includes everyone under the age of 18. The term 'worst forms of child labour' covers any form of slavery, sale or trafficking of children; any forced labour, including recruitment into armed forces or armed groups; any form of sexual exploitation; the involvement of children in illegal activities such as drug trafficking; and work that is likely to jeopardise the health, safety or morals of the child. It also imposes an obligation on countries where such use of children has occurred to take steps to provide them with the necessary care and rehabilitation to reintegrate them into society.
- ILO Declaration on Fundamental Principles and Rights at Work: this reminds member states that membership itself imposes an obligation to 'respect, promote and realise' its Conventions, even if not ratified individually.

SCREAM programme and working with children associated with armed forces and armed groups

The SCREAM programme uses the arts to educate children about their rights with respect to all forms of work. The exercises include role-plays, creative writing, drawing and painting, theatre projects, debates and so on.

Many can be extended to involve the whole community, depending on the context.

SCREAM is designed to be used as an educational tool in all parts of the world, including industrialised countries, and Brookman's module is no different; all exercises can be adapted for different cultural contexts, and to show European children, for example, the sorts of experiences children may have had and may encounter in the future in many parts of the world, and to educate them about international law on child labour. The module Brookman wrote adapted existing exercises in the SCREAM package. The exercises created were as follows.

Part 1: Recruitment

International legislation: 'Sabra says ...'. The group is introduced to the SCREAM programme with a fun, participatory exercise that also serves to provide information about the international laws and conventions that apply to and protect young people in conflict situations.

Peace processes: role-play. Discover that conflict is not formless but has a structure and that understanding and manipulating this structure can aid the quest for peace.

Who are they? The image. Young people will understand that, although they may face coercion to work with armed forces or groups, there are still worse and better outcomes. What they may face will be difficult, but knowledge of what to expect, or the opportunity to reflect on what has happened, can place the young people in better positions to manoeuvre themselves through these difficult situations. This exercise introduces the different roles that someone might be asked to take on in an armed group, such as scout, cook, messenger, 'wife', as well as fighter.

Why join up? One-minute mimes. Drama used alongside the transmission of information in order to assist the understanding of the consequences of joining an armed force or group. The group is introduced to dramatic expression as a means of education, preparing for later dramatic performances.

The Information Centre. Drama used alongside the transmission of information in order to show young people how to seek help and from whom.

Part 2: Reintegration

How might a person reintegrate? One-minute mimes. Drama used alongside the transmission of information to assist understanding of issues surrounding reintegration. The participants should be empowered by giving them the ability to contextualise their state of affairs.

Where to now? Backwards–forwards game. To show young people how to seek assistance and from whom. To know what it is realistic to expect.

Psychosocial issues: Let's make a picture! The group use artistic expression as a means of understanding how those who feel different or are treated differently because of their experiences may be perceived, and how this might differ from how they perceive themselves. They can also explore how they feel about the violators placing them in this position. This furthers the process of their rehabilitation and the self-assertion of who they really feel they are for their own and their communities' understanding and benefit.

Into work: Memory game! The group learns or understands what they must do to cover the transition from unemployment to employment. They use acting and presentation skills, which increases their confidence and self-respect.

Living positively: SCREAM timeline. The group use artistic expression as a means by which the young people and observers can understand and relate to young people made vulnerable by conflict.

Evaluation and reinforcement: Shout out! A means for evaluating how attitudes have changed and information has been digested; or to use the activity to reinforce what has been covered or needs modifying in the light of lessons learned.

Conclusion: Discussion. Followed by a concluding activity: let's make a picture! Sing songs! Dance ... and have some fun!

Images and equipment

One component of the SCREAM package is images of children working in different situations, used to promote discussion. Brookman tried to source images of child soldiers and other children associated with armed forces and armed groups from photographers. This proved very difficult, and there were, of course, issues of privacy and confidentiality for any children who might have been photographed. In the course of running pilot projects in Uganda and Nepal, he asked many of the young people to draw, and he kept many of the pictures. He then asked young people in his newly formed Young Foundation in Loughborough to create drawings based on those he brought back, depicting young people engaged in various tasks that children associated with armed forces and armed groups might be asked to do. Their drawings reflected the differences between the different cultural contexts of Uganda and Nepal, and the resulting collection of images proved very suitable for the new SCREAM module.

The suggested equipment needed includes a set of simple props, such as sticks, which may become guns; balls, which may be used as money or food; cloths, which may be used as bandits' masks or to carry loads; and paper and crayons for drawing and writing.

Piloting the module

In order to pilot this material with young people in Africa and in Asia, Brookman went to Northern Uganda in November 2008, and to Nepal in January 2009.

Uganda

Uganda has ratified the CRC, the African Charter on the Rights and Welfare of the Child (ACRWC), the Optional Protocol to the Convention on the Rights of the Child on the Sale of Children, Child Prostitution and Pornography, the Optional Protocol to the Convention on the Rights of the Child on the Involvement of Children in Armed Conflict and ILO Conventions No 138 and No 182.

The conflict in Uganda began in 1986, when Joseph Kony set himself up as the leader of a guerilla group, coming to be called the Lord's Resistance Army (LRA), with the aim of establishing a new state allegedly based on the Ten Commandments and the traditions of the Acholi tribe. The true aims of the group were never clear and one difficulty in negotiating with them was that they had no political agenda. The LRA operated mainly in northern Uganda, as well as southern Sudan and parts of the Democratic Republic of Congo. They were engaged in a long conflict with Ugandan government forces, during which more than one-and-a-half million people were displaced by the fighting into temporary camps; many suffered starvation and many more were mutilated or killed.

In 2002, the Ugandan People's Defence Force (UPDF) launched 'Operation Iron Fist' against LRA bases in southern Sudan. This was a complete failure, and led to a series of intense retaliatory attacks by the LRA, with a massive increase in them abducting and 'recruiting' children. Children were also recruited as soldiers to join local defence units as part of the UPDF, with promises of financial reward by the Ugandan government. In 2005, Ugandan President Museveni announced an 18-day ceasefire, backing away from previous commitments to sustain military operations until the LRA committed to withdraw from the bush. However, soon afterwards, the LRA's chief negotiator surrendered to the government. The situation has never been properly resolved; currently the fighting in northern Uganda has ceased, but Joseph Kony remains at large, and many people remain in camps as displaced persons (see HRW, 2003; ACPF, 2008).

During the period of intense fighting, the risk of abduction and forced recruitment caused many children to flee into the city of Gulu to sleep rough every night, seeking shelter in hospitals, churches and bus stations, as well as simply seeking safety in numbers. Children were recruited by kidnap both singly and in groups, as soldiers, and in many support roles, including as sexual slaves or 'commanders' wives'. Many girls became pregnant, and there was a high risk of infection with HIV and other sexually transmitted diseases. Once captured, children were brutalised by forcing them to inflict pain on, or to kill, other children or members of their own families and communities, to burn houses and to abduct other children. They were forced to carry heavy burdens and to walk long distances and those who fell behind were beaten and killed.

In November 2008, Brookman went to the area of northern Uganda, around the town of Lira, where there are a large number of children and young people who have direct personal experience of these events. He then tested various different aspects of his SCREAM module with different groups, including children aged 11 and 14 who remembered the fighting but who were not involved in it; groups of young people aged 18 and older who had been involved in the fighting and were still traumatised by their experiences; and young women who had been sexually abused during the fighting. The exercises included role-play, drawing, a 'backwards–forwards' game in which they aim to reach the goal of a home and a job, in the face of chance cards dealt out to them, and a mindmapping discussion of the advantages and disadvantages of various roles that a child might be tempted or be forced to take on in an armed group.

Brookman found that the exercise in the original SCREAM package called 'Shout out!', requiring children to shout out answers and give opinions, was not a success; Ugandan children are unused to expressing opinions openly in a school setting and thus were bewildered by it. Instead he substituted a game based on the English game 'Simon says' in which instructions are given but must only be carried out if preceded by the words 'Simon says'. (Of course, a local name should be chosen in place of Simon, and the final draft uses 'Sabra' as a generic name here.) This was much more successful and was used to teach international law on child labour and included in the final module.

In testing 'Who are they? The image', the 14-year-old children were very frank in their discussions of the roles, and, most shockingly, gave 'cooking people' as one of the disadvantages of the role of cook. They became excited when given the sticks representing guns, and immediately ran about playing at shooting each other. Brookman had to stop them and point out to them how seductive these 'guns' were, and how easily they could be caught up with and excited by the idea of being a soldier. After this incident, they role-played with much greater sensitivity, taking care of those who had been 'shot'.

The backwards–forwards game was tested with a group of young women who had been sexually exploited and violated. This exercise was, as expected, unhelpful for them, since it came too late to be useful, and merely served to emphasise their lack of support when they needed it.

In 'Let's make a picture', a group of traumatised young people with direct experience of the fighting drew pictures representing their lives now, the events that brought them there and what they foresaw for the future. Many of them had been unable to reintegrate into society because of the trauma they had experienced and the stigmatisation they still felt in their communities. One young man drew street drugs taken from a shared pot as his current situation, himself holding a gun as the experience that led to this, and his house in flames as what he foresees for the future – he believed that his community wished to be rid of him and might torch his house. Similarly, a young woman drew a star, and herself pregnant following rape – she believed she was as pure as a star despite the fact she had been raped; but her third picture was of a coffin, as she believed her community wished her dead.

Each group needed a careful concluding session, where they were encouraged to write and draw about the issues they had been working with in a kind of 'debriefing' so that they could leave the issues behind when they left the workshop. They made a simple exhibition of their work, giving value to their experiences and feelings. In many situations where this package is being used this might be extended to form a means of educating the wider community about what such young people may have been through and how they might be helped. This might help to increase sympathy for them and diminish the stigma many experience.

Field testing, Uganda: an impromptu exhibition to end the session

Source: Photograph by Bill Brookman

All the groups enjoyed the exercises and found them helpful; many said they would like more of this sort of input and really wanted Brookman to stay so that they could go on working in this way. This shows the value of such schemes, even four years on, emphasising the importance of training trainers to use this material in their communities.

Nepal

Nepal is a party to the CRC, as well as the second Additional Protocol to the Geneva Conventions of 1949, which governs situations of civil war such as those in Nepal. It ratified ILO Convention No 182 in 2002 and has also signed the Optional Protocol to the Convention on the Rights of the Child on the Involvement of Children in Armed Conflict, which came into force in 2002. This Protocol explicitly applies to non-state armed groups in addition to government forces, and, as with other armed forces, the minimum age for such groups is 18 years.

In Nepal the political situation was very different from Uganda. Nepal was a kingdom until 2008 when, after a 10-year period of violent unrest, followed by a peaceful protest by the people, King Gyanendra abdicated in favour of a democratically elected republican government.

The activities of the Communist Party of Nepal (Maoist) (CPN[M]) began in 1996 when they declared a 'people's war', an insurgency that began in the west of the country. As the movement grew, they acquired weapons, and in 2001 they attacked a military barracks near Kathmandu. A long period of unrest followed, during which an estimated 13,000 people, many of them civilians, were killed, both by the Maoists and by the army. The CPN(M) was accused of abducting children to be trained as soldiers.

After a ceasefire was negotiated in 2003, the Maoists continued to cause disruption by declaring general strikes in the country, requiring almost all businesses to stop trading and forbidding the use of road vehicles other than cycle rickshaws or ox-carts. People who were found breaking the strikes would have premises or vehicles torched. Trouble flared again, with serious fighting between the Maoists and the army. In 2006 an historic people's movement forced an end to the fighting, a coalition of seven opposition parties agreed a new ceasefire with the Maoists, and a comprehensive peace agreement included a commitment to stop the recruitment of children for military purposes (see HRW, 2007).

During the conflict, children were recruited by the Maoists by kidnap of individuals, abduction of groups and by propaganda, which attracted them as 'volunteers'. In some areas they operated a 'one family, one child' policy, which obliged each family to provide a recruit or face violent reprisals. Many children were not forcibly recruited but enticed to join by the offer of 'training' and financial reward; girls were attracted by the chance of escaping a culture that denied opportunities to women (see Chapters Fourteen and Fifteen, this volume); and many young people were drawn in by the lure of cultural activities including songs, dancing and theatre. Once recruited, they were afraid of surrendering to the Nepali army because of the risk of violence and sexual abuse from the soldiers.

After the conflict was over, the Maoists continued to hold children, claiming they were orphans unable to look after themselves. Not only did the Nepali government provide no assistance to the children to enable them to escape, but they treated those who were captured by security forces during the conflict as badly as they treated the adults.

Although educational and training programmes have since been put in place to help them, many children will not know of these, or of their entitlement to them. The Maoists' philosophy is such that they believe in gender equality and were therefore just as likely to recruit girls as boys into their ranks. For the same reasons, they were less likely than most militias to sexually exploit or abuse the young people they recruited. Although the Maoists have a place in the new coalition government, they continue to call strikes, and Brookman was unable to visit the town of Biratnagar in the south east of Nepal, as planned, because of a general strike there.

Brookman spent two days working with young people in Nepalgunj, a town in south west Nepal close to the border with India, and one day working with young adults in Bhaktapur, close to Kathmandu. This latter workshop replaced the planned visit to Biratnagar, which had been abandoned.

In Nepalgunj the first group were teenage children who were from bourgeois families and were all attending school. They were educated, and some of them spoke or wrote in English. After a warm-up session with a game of 'catch', the first exercise they did was 'Sabra says ...', introducing the different sorts of work a child might be asked to do, and the legality of each at different ages. This group refused to entertain the possibility that they might ever do labouring or other manual work; they said they would never need to. One of the local staff who was acting as interpreter suggested that they should nevertheless know about these roles, and which were legal and which were not, so that they could behave appropriately with people who were working for them.

This group were so interested and keen on this workshop that they returned the following day at their own request so that they could do some more. In this second session they did role-plays on the subject of conflict and conflict resolution. This exercise introduces ideas such as boundaries, peace negotiation and a demilitarised zone.

The young people enjoyed these improvised dramas and were very engaged by them. At the end of the session, unprompted, they initiated long lists of bullet points on flip chart paper, summarising what they had discussed

Field testing, Nepal: role-playing peace negotiation

Source: Photograph by Katherine Darton

and learned. The second group in Nepalgunj were six girls and two boys who had all been child soldiers with the Maoists. They explained that they had been kidnapped and trained to take various roles, including propaganda, cooking and fighting with guns. One girl said that she had been too young to be a soldier when she was first taken and worked as an 'artist'. Although they appreciated some aspects of the Maoist philosophy, they said they did not like having to kill people. They said they had not been sexually abused, telling a story of how a girl had been raped in one camp, and the rapist was caught and punished. However, one girl, asked to draw a picture showing a relationship between two people, accompanied her drawing with a short narrative (in Nepali) leading local ILO staff to suggest that she had in fact been sexually abused.

After the exercise, they all drew pictures illustrating the various roles, and wrote accompanying descriptions. They took time over this, and were focused and concentrated as they worked. Their work was then pinned up to make a small exhibition that was photographed.

In Bhaktapur, the group consisted of about 20 young people in their late teens and early twenties who had experienced various forms of social hardship and exploitation, including domestic slavery, drug dependency and being in an armed group. They were all attending training for work. The policy of the training providers was to make no inquiry into their background in order to avoid conflicts arising between them in relation to their past experiences or involvements, but it became apparent that they appreciated the opportunity to revisit past experiences that SCREAM material gave them, as they had never been given any kind of debriefing.

After a warm-up exercise, the module they used was the return to work 'Memory game', in which participants make up actions to illustrate the different steps on the journey to work, and then have to remember them in the right order. They can then be divided into teams, with a light-hearted competition to see who can get through the steps fastest, ending up accepting micro-finance to start their own business.

After this exercise they, like the ex-soldiers in Nepalgunj, were asked to do some creative writing and drawing. This group were asked to illustrate the best and worst moments of their lives. Best moments mostly showed them going from home to school; one boy drew himself on a swing at his home in the country. Worst moments showed people hiding while others nearby were kidnapped or shot; being in the gutter with a syringe; and witnessing homes being bombed. As with other groups, they worked with concentration and commitment and appreciated the opportunity to share something of their stories and to have them acknowledged.

Next steps

The SCREAM package is no good unless it is used. The young people who piloted it in Uganda and Nepal found it helpful and would have liked more of it. Some were disappointed that Brookman was not staying longer and doing more work with them. What should happen next is a training for trainers, so that teachers, advocates and peer educators can take the ideas and the material into their communities and use them to educate the children to resist recruitment and help to rehabilitate those who have been associated with armed forces or armed groups.

From experience to date, Brookman is of the opinion that it should also be used in areas where there is high risk of imminent conflict, as was the case in the Congo in the latter months of 2008. Extreme poverty means that children will do almost anything for food and for money. People providing SCREAM programmes in communities where there is a high risk of conflict and recruitment of children associated with armed forces and armed groups will need to provide food as well as training; what they offer must be at least as enticing at that moment as what is offered by the armed groups and their gangmasters.

International law obliges countries where children have been recruited and used as soldiers to provide them with special assistance to ensure their rehabilitation and reintegration back into society. This should happen immediately, regardless of the stage of any peace or security agreement that may be made between parties to the conflict. But Brookman's experience also shows that these sorts of workshops are very much appreciated by their target audience, even several years after the events they were caught up in. Children in industrialised countries should use this material to give them an insight into the consequences of war situations for children directly affected, as well as a knowledge of the law as it relates to child labour. There is urgent need for a programme to get this SCREAM material into all communities, but especially in those where children are still at serious and immediate risk of exploitation.

Notes

[1] For more information about these projects, see the Bill Brookman Foundation website at www.billbrookman.co.uk/foundation. See also the Resources section at the end of this book.

[2] These Conventions are available in full at http://learning.itcilo.org/ilo/ipec/scream/pack_en/pdf/International%20declarations.pdf

References

ACPF (African Child Policy Forum) (2008) *The Africa report on child wellbeing* (www.africanchildforum.org).

CSUCS (Coalition to Stop the Use of Child Soldiers) (2008) *Child soldiers global report* (www.childsoldiersglobalreport.org/).

HRW (Human Rights Watch) (2003) 'Stolen children: abduction and recruitment in Northern Uganda', *Human Rights Watch*, vol 15, no 7 (A) (www.hrw.org).

HRW (2007) 'Children in the ranks, the Maoists' use of child soldiers in Nepal', *Human Rights Watch*, vol 19, no 2 (C) (www.hrw.org).

seventeen

International adoption and child trafficking in Ecuador

Esben Leifsen

Introduction

Illegal circulation of children often draws on formal resources provided by public administration and the jurisdictional apparatus. In order to 'traffic' a child, actors involved need to translate crucial aspects of the process to recognisable and accepted forms, apparently following the requisites of law and administrative order: we refer to this as 'formalisation'. One context in which this happens is international adoption. This phenomenon has increased steadily since the 1970s, and today more than 30,000 adopted children move between over 100 countries each year (Selman, 2000). The practice of international adoption emerged from the orphan situation in Europe after the Second World War, but increased significantly as an effect of the Korean War; today, children are transferred predominantly from Asia, Latin America and East Europe, to North America and Western Europe. According to some observers, 'trafficking flourishes' within international adoption; 'a booming trade has grown in the purchase and sale of children in connection with [this practice]' (Saclier, 2000, p 57). International organisations have reported that adoption is linked to a child market (UNICEF, 1998), and is observed or suspected to exist in a range of countries such as Romania, Guatemala, Nepal, India, Brazil and Haiti. Acknowledgement of this situation from the 1980s resulted in international efforts to introduce mechanisms of control through the implementation of the Convention on the Rights of the Child (CRC) in national legislation (Triseliotis, 1999).

The trafficking dimension in adoptions is a complicated issue, challenging to define and involving value conflicts (Zelizer, 1994; Triseliotis, 1999; Leifsen, 2004). Two main approaches may be identified in relation to the perspective of child trafficking. One sees child trafficking as a parasitic activity on the formal care transference practice. The other sees the issue of trafficking as internal to the adoption practice in itself. This chapter draws on circumstantial evidence of irregularities in adoptions from the Latin American country Ecuador, since the 1990s, and on public discourse about these events (Leifsen, 2006). Data gathering on adoptions and irregularities

271

formed part of a more extensive multi-sited fieldwork carried out in Quito, Ecuador, from 1999 to 2003.

The formalising dimension in the events considered indicates very clearly an interrelation and exchange between external actors and internal, public functionaries and lawyers in facilitating irregular transfers. However, civil society representatives who are leading opinion makers and central policy formulators have drawn attention away from this connection and towards the external actors, acts and institutional connections. This focus became dominant from the 1990s due to successful alliances established between child rights advocates, public administration and the media. Their influence was strong in the period when the principles of the CRC were implemented into national law.

In dominant public interpretations of irregular international adoption occurrences, a marked tendency identifies ever more activities as trafficking, expanding its meaning even beyond its conceptual boundaries. Moreover, there is a clear tendency to singularise and personify the problem of trafficking, and also to externalise it, that is, to locate the source of the trouble in non-state and international actors and institutions. Hence, a complex issue is transformed into a singular and personified problem emerging as diffuse connections in what social scientists describe as the disorganised, uncontrolled and decentralised market channels of the globalised economy (cf Appadurai, 1996). As we discuss later, child trafficking has thus paradoxically become diffuse because of simplification. Moreover, the different interests and concerns held by the parties involved in policy formulation take the trafficking problem of international adoption in a direction that makes it almost impossible to address or regulate. A lesson could be learned from considering the dissonance between the dynamics of such policy formulation and the formalising practices of irregular child circulation carried out within the system. We argue that insights might be gained by looking at the child trafficking complex as a system that incorporates both the outrageous operations of profit seekers and the daily routines of bureaucrats. By thus widening the scope of analysis we might produce knowledge that could be instructive for the design of laws and regulations that could effectively combat what are morally disturbing practices. Let us consider first the main issue at stake, the logics and operations of 'formalising' the involuntarily separated child as an adoptable child.

Formalising the irregular

A serious adoption scandal in the Ecuadorian capital, Quito, in 1989 had a major impact on policy formulation and public administration in a crucial moment in the history of child rights implementation. A ring of illegal child circulators were identified by a young child rights activist and lawyer,

Farith Simón, and his findings were published (Simón, 1990) and exposed in the media. The disclosure coincided with the emergence of a strong civil society-based child rights movement promoting the principles of the CRC, and recruiting young professionals both to strategic positions in the National Directorate of Child Protection under the Ministry of Social Welfare, and to international and national non-governmental organisations (NGOs) forming alliances with this unit within public administration. Ecuador ratified the CRC in 1990 and implemented its main principles in a new Child Code in 1992. The 1989 scandal and its disclosure was one driving force in this developing process. It motivated the establishment of a new Technical Department of Adoptions under the National Directorate in 1990, leading to the elaboration of the first adoption regulation based on the legal principle of full adoption the same year. It also provided a backdrop to the elaboration of a new adoption law, part of the 1992 Child Code.

The police and an internal commission in the Ministry of Social Welfare investigated the adoption scandal, ending in a criminal court case, an internal process of dismissals and relocation of public judges and functionaries. A variety of irregular acts and strategies and a complex network of actors directly involved in or supporting illegal adoption were detected. Investigations identified three lawyers and several people employed in the private orphanage, Amparo y Hogar. Methods of persuasion and threats towards original parents were revealed, and people having stolen children in public places were exposed in the media. The report also detailed irregular and manipulative collaboration of state functionaries employed in child tribunals, in the Ministry of Social Welfare, the National Directorate and the Civil Registry. Such collusion was also found in maternity hospitals. What becomes clear from reading the report is that the legal–administrative adoption system consisted of people, within every department, willing to use the 'formalising' capacities open to them, to manipulate adoption procedures. The illegal and criminal acts detected formed part of a *production of legal formality*. Very few children were adopted out of the country without legal documentation.

The simple but determining operation enabling 'formalisation' of the children being involuntarily separated from their parents involved manipulation of their origins. Simón was surprised to learn that almost all adoption cases reviewed fulfilled legal requirements. But at the same time, 'in almost a total of the effectuated adoptions it was impossible to determine with certainty the origin of the minors, their family situation, and their parent's motivations for handing them over to adoption' (Simón, 1990, p 16). Simón received testimonies from women who had lent their name in order to appear as mothers for children. The rationale behind this fake identity construction was that these 'mothers', after ratifying the 'biological bond' in the Civil Registry by presenting a counterfeit birth certificate, gave consent to having them adopted in child tribunals. Hence, in the application of techniques for disconnecting the child from its social past and fabricating identities, state functionaries and informal institutional practices were involved.

Considering the massive attention this scandal received and the impact it had on policy formulation, the final outcome seems meagre. As Simón noted in 2002 (personal communication), concrete irregularities were finally established as offences by a lawsuit. The police investigation identified a trafficking network, but only one person was detained, the lawyer Roberto Moncayo Morales, identified as the mastermind behind the illegal adoptions, and broker to international adoption agencies. The other central people implicated fled the country, and were never traced or charged for their infringements, soon disappearing from public consciousness. Curiously, there exists very little information about the lawsuit against Moncayo. This never managed to prove allegations of child kidnapping and the judge was left only with the falsifications of identities. Considering the extensive trafficking ring detailed, and the well-documented participation of public functionaries and judges in facilitating the illegal circulation of children for adoption, the scandal underwent an extreme transformation. The most significant evidence of child trafficking was reduced to the manipulative creativity of one person. The scandal had been personified; it had a name and a face. Furthermore, the archetypical trafficker was identified – the external actor, the one connected to the international institutions and with access to large-scale profits that the transnational circulation of children supposedly produces.

External and personified explanation

There are many reasons why the 1989 scandal was personified. The media obviously played an important role in visualising people and their testimonies rather than highlighting systemic irregularities. Public functionaries had their own interest in externalising the problem with practices that, through their routine activities, they were aware of, implicated with or even directly involved in. Rights activists' concern for the child market and the scenarios of moral decay that international adoption seemed to embody directed their attention towards the 'real' profit seekers. Nevertheless, all these actors' contributions to public opinion building seemed to bear on an underlying legal logic, of establishing truth through lawsuit processes. Hence, only evidence of illegal or irregular practice confirmed through a final sentence could obtain a status as true and hence legal existence. Out of complex court cases emerged singular acts and people: the rest of it converts into a diffuse body of knowledge. The outcome is often a result of power struggles where truth is established through attacks and counter-attacks from legal players with specific interests and motivations. In this sense lawsuits tend to be politicised processes of truth establishment, contributing to the definition of what can be held as real in public (Sieder et al, 2005; Pérez-Perdomo, 2006).

One important consequence of this legal logic is the accumulation of diffuse knowledge, setting it in a kind of mysterious light, and enabling, even inviting, speculation to which child rights activists are major contributors. It was clear from activists that child trafficking was a desired theme, increasing the intensity of debate. Activists were attracted to the issue of trafficking by its negation, perhaps because of the contrast the trafficking scenario makes with their own moral ideals and political convictions. Their intense interest often fuelled speculation around cases characterised by secrecy and inaccuracy. In cases checked against reliable sources and available documentation, they expressed versions that clearly changed the content and meaning of what had occurred. In one of the best-documented and rehearsed cases, concerning the unsuccessful attempt at illegal circulation of a girl by a network of employees and ex-employees at the child tribunal in the costal city Machala (Leifsen, 2006), a serious reinterpretation emerged. What was really an internal problem of severe manipulation in the child tribunal was used by rights activists to evidence the need to combat and delimit the methods of the Ecuadorian representatives of international adoption agencies. In this case there was no such representative involved. The wrongdoings of public functionaries were, as a result, projected onto external actors.

A model case

Parallel to the Machala case, a new scandal in international adoptions made public in the following years had a far stronger impact on public opinion making and policy formulation. Although complicated, the incidence was not especially severe, and concerned manipulation of the legal procedure of adoption internal to one of the Quito child tribunals. Nevertheless, it contained the right ingredients. One of the most influential adoption lawyers in the country, Alfredo Barragan, was involved. His and his wife María José Buendía's ownership of an adoption orphanage, FAFECORP, and their parallel representative functions for the US-based adoption agency Alliance for Children, indicated possible conflicts of interests. In this case, the best interests of two girls adopted by two US families could have been endangered. Manipulation of adoption procedures, especially affecting formal matching of the girls to adoptive families, accelerated the process of adoption significantly and favourably for Barragan and the Alliance for Children. It implied at least specific collusion between him and a judge at Quito's child tribunal no 2. An assumed economic gain followed the two adoptions.

Because of a specific constellation of rights advocacy advisers and child welfare professionals in the National Directorate for Child Protection at this time, the documentation of the case circulated within a closed circle of people with good contacts to the media. The documents were handed to a journalist in the newspaper *El Diario Expreso*, and a series of reports under the title 'Children of nobody' were published in March 2001 (*El Diario Expreso*, 2001). These newspaper articles had a great impact on people's awareness within the child welfare milieu. Extensive investigation and the initiation of an administrative case within the Ministry of Social Welfare underlined the gravity of the case. It was the director of the National Directorate of Child Protection in this period, Glenda Yager, who initiated and led this action. However, as in the 1989 scandal, the outcome in legal terms was meagre. A report elaborated by a state administrative unit concluded that there existed no administrative, civil or penal irregularities. By a legal definition, the outcry concerning this adoption case was thus reduced to a storm in a teacup. Nothing grave had really happened.

What was hidden from the newspaper presentation and the public eye, however, was that this version of reality gained salience because of a legal counter-action taken by Barragan. Without doubt Yager demonstrated unusual bravery when, with the support of highly competent adoption lawyers and child rights activists, she started this process. Her chances of succeeding were not completely unrealistic; the National Directorate had a strong case to investigate. A problem occurred, however, when Yager expressed opinions concerning the case in an official memo before its resolution. By publicising her opinion, she broke with a basic legal principle of not giving what is termed previous criteria (*previcariato*) to a case under investigation. Barragan used this slip to his own advantage and accused Yager of *previcariato*, a legal offence. His access to the official memo with Yager's opinion offered a legal resource in his favour, eventually forcing Yager to refrain from the case to avoid a lawsuit against her, and driving the Barragan case in a new direction. The handling of the two international adoptions had received public justification, Barragan using the case to illustrate the hollowness of activists' warnings about child trafficking. In an interview in December 2001 (fieldwork notes), he exclaimed that "not one case of child trafficking is documented", and accused Yager and her followers simply of being hysterical.

Interestingly, this outcome put the Barragan case and the sequences of documented irregular acts outside the body of legal case law. This did not, however, withdraw the case from public awareness, but made it more opaque. This opacity had to do with the obvious possibility of doubting the evidence produced concerning the two international adoptions, and the equally obvious existence of irregularities. The status of the case passed from one of confirmed proof to one of suspicion. The case had been unusually clear because of exposure in the press, which still remains the only available public source. No other additional information or alternative interpretation has been presented. Instead there has been considerable use of the newspaper articles in policy making, such as the elaboration of adoption regulations and law proposals. In these uses there has been an astonishingly consistent emphasis on certain aspects of the Barragan case, aspects that were used to frame an 'ideal type' model of the irregular in international adoptions, linked to child trafficking. The model's main characteristics were as follows.

The model identifies actors, activities and institutional constellations. The *main actor* is the adoption agency and, even more specifically, the adoption lawyer. A characteristic of this protagonist is that s/he is a prominent person – socially significant, politically and professionally powerful and influential. The main actor is not a petty criminal, a little crook with low social status; rather, this is a person from the establishment, close to the normative authorities and to political agency on a national level. He or she is also a person with international experience and connections, in short, a person in Barragan's mould.

The *irregular acts* given relevance in the model are those initiated by the adoption agency and its lawyer. Other actors and their actions are made relevant as a result of the main actors' prior initiatives; they become effectively enrolled into a trafficking practice as a result of him/her. That means that the irregular actions others may take independently of this main actor do not count as part of the problem; rather they constitute other and less serious types of deviances (for example, irregular payments received by functionaries at the child tribunals). This distinction obviously has to do with the kind of acts focused within the model, namely those that connect the emotional value of a child to a monetary value (Zelizer, 1994). Other transactions that support this core undertaking are distinguished from it because they do not directly partake in the profit-gaining exchange; they signal, for example, economic survival within a bureaucratic system. As a consequence it is the international rather than the internal exchange of money occasioning the care transference that is identified as irregular.

The *institutional constellation* emphasised in the model is the agency–orphanage relationship. The problematic relationship between the adoption orphanage, FAFECORP, and the adoption agency, Alliance for Children, stands here as a model. This implies that the non-state institutions are seen as most heavily involved in the childcare transference business. Furthermore it focuses on the national–international link rather than the network engaged in the adoption, which crosses both state–civil society, public and private, national and international institutional borders.

Systemic considerations

The relevance and power of the model outlined above reflect a restricted part of reality. Its potential for explanation is based on the efficiency of reification. Aspects of irregular and illegal practices labelled as trafficking represent the whole of a complex phenomenon or problem. The basic elements of the model 'stand out' from an over-complex 'landscape' of practices, strategies and motivations; its visibility signals that there is more behind it. The sensation of being introduced to something more complex and difficult to grasp is often evoked in situations where the model is utilised, even if these connections are not made explicit. Furthermore, trafficking cases speak directly to the heart and moral consciousness of the people, as well as policy makers and administrators. As such, they lend themselves easily to singularising and generalising intents – because the problem seeks explanations suggesting immediate action. Nevertheless, some irregular cases serve better than others to undergo transformation from the particular to schematic representation. The most useful cases are those where it is possible to externalise the problem of the irregular, and localise the problem in a restricted set of actors, institutions and types of actions.

As Handelmann (2004) and Heyman (1995) both argue, reification and reduction of complexity into simple, ordered descriptions is a crucial aspect of bureaucratic codification and classification. The focus in their studies is on what bureaucratic codification does with complexity. Here, however, we ask what kind of irregular complexity lends itself to reification. Not all disorder on the ground or out in the field of actions and interventions is adequate for codification. The Machala case did not serve to inform a model of the irregular in international adoption, but the Barragan case did. What this difference illustrates is that bureaucratic codification such as that which enters into an adoption regulation or a law proposal is not a neutral or pragmatic process of transformation. As Mol (1999) argues, it forms part of political practices involving committed interests. Policy makers search for adequate or even ideal instances of disorder on which to build their models.

Idealisation, externalisation and the model's reference to a greater unspecified whole are characteristics of the thinking that influenced policy formulation concerning international adoption and child trafficking in Ecuador in recent years. These specificities indicate how the child trafficking concept, described earlier, has subsumed an increasing range of activities and operations within its boundaries of meaning. An observation from this field that has a much more general relevance is that trafficking is seldom defined but often declared. People – policy makers and social scientists included – tend to have a rather diffuse idea about what child trafficking is. The root of it is clearly connected to profit-seeking activity, to the commercialisation of exchanges involving children, to the generation of a price related to the value of a child and to the commodification of people. Furthermore, it implies a degree of exploitation and the disintegration of value schemes that protect children and secure their best interests. These characteristics are present in a peripheral way in the majority of the examples of irregular adoption practices in the Ecuadorian context and are far from central to the operations that are focused and identified as the crux of the problem. In fact, the central operations identified are basically about the manipulating dispositions of bureaucratic routine. Such dispositions often imply different kinds of compensational practices: small payments for extra services, gift giving or a trade in influences. These practices, however, could hardly be defined as profit seeking, commodifying or market driven in a child trafficking sense. Nevertheless, they are connected to the trafficking business. Hence, these activities are not relevant as separate acts or operations, but as connections that constitute systemic conditions for profit seeking.

The tendency to focus on particular acts, actors and institutional connections obscures the systemic dimension. This has a twofold consequence: first, trafficking is often rooted in bureaucratic activity that could hardly be labelled so and that is easily dismissed as such in legal trials; and second, the connection of the internal actors and acts to external profit-seeking actors and practices are not seriously scrutinised or understood. The rights activists' and policy makers' emphasis on the external actors and dimension, then, does not address the child trafficking problem in international adoptions from Ecuador and elsewhere. Hence, laws and regulations emerging from such policies create weak and inadequate instruments for combating the trafficking problem. This can be illustrated first by outlining some aspects of bureaucratic practice in the child tribunals, and then by looking at laws resultant on the application of the model of the irregular in international adoptions.

Small bureaucratic acts and gross policy generalisations

One of the leading Ecuadorian experts on international law and child rights, Arturo Marquéz detailed in an interview (fieldwork notes, 2003) the precarious situation of the child tribunals with a simple yet illustrative figure: the adult population in Ecuador amounts to 49% of the total population. For the whole country there are around 4,000 people employed in the judicial system serving this adult population. For the remaining 51% of children and youth, the legal administration is supported by 280 employees at the national level. It is inevitable, Marquéz concluded, that this inadequate situation generates deficiencies, shortages and delayed trials (Marquéz, 2000). Another lawyer, Guerrero, now working for an adoption organisation and an ex-president of one of the child tribunals, noted that disorganisation, a considerable volume of cases and a high level of activity characterise the daily life of the tribunals. Hence, systematic and goal-oriented work is necessary in order to make a representative visible to the functionaries and hence get one's own cases through the system. Advocates can be taken into account through various means, the most important of which is to build personal relations based on trust and empathy. Building up trust is a matter of experience and interaction and takes time. Those who also take jobs within the system gain an extra advantage.

In addition to the human capacities of each actor, personal relations are built and maintained through small gift giving. Material need at the offices is high – small office items like a package of clips change hands in return for a friendly attitude. But services are also exchanged for money, and relations of semi-dependency may develop. A practice has evolved among lawyers working in relation to the child tribunals to pay extra for services. Low monthly salaries are in themselves a driving force in this type of irregular exchange. The obvious inequality in economic power between state functionaries and external legal experts can generate a semi-clientelistic relationship. Service delivery, compliance to a case and even loyalty to an external user are bargained and exchanged for monetary compensations in these asymmetric relationships (Fox, 1997). The problem for those who refuse to accelerate procedures with money, Guerrero stated, is that there is always competition from lawyers who are willing to do so. 'If a functionary has five cases on his table, and a lawyer pays him US$20 for his case, he will take that for obvious reasons' (fieldwork notes, 2003).

The problem with the irregular procedures of international adoptions, then, is that they are woven into a structure of personal and informal exchanges. Adoptions of this kind do not implant bribes and semi-clientelistic relationships into the tribunals' practices; rather they make use of existing ones. Hence, they will not appear as separable from the general activity of the child tribunal or as exceptional. Any particular irregular act reflects the overall rationale, namely of speeding up procedures and generating small extra informal incomes. The possible outcomes of any informal arrangement functionaries may be involved in and the moral dilemmas it may produce are then evaluated against a generalised acceptance of a bureaucratic system. However, the acceleration of the adoption procedure could be what makes possible the kidnapping of a baby, the pressure put on a birth mother for accepting care transference for some kind of material compensation or a judge's tampering with legal administrative procedures. Irregular practices oil the wheels of a general bureaucratic structure. At the same time these practices facilitate deeply problematic actions.

What becomes clear here is that the internal bureaucratic dynamics of a public entity such as the child tribunals are intricately woven into external actors' and institutions' practices, which from time to time also involve child trafficking. It is surprising then that much policy formulation in the 1990s and early 2000s employed the externalising model, emphasising the irregular acts of the adoption lawyer (representing international adoption agencies) and the institutional link between adoption agency and orphanage. Of the many examples from the making of regulations, ministerial agreements, presidential decrees and law articles that reflect this externalising model, one example stands out as especially significant because of the implications it had for the legal reform process from 2000–03, ending in the implementation of a new Childhood and Adolescence Code (Registro Oficial, 2003).

Article 248 of the draft versions of this law was undoubtedly the most debated single article in the full law text. The article treated the *actividades vinculadas*. This concept, difficult to translate literally, broadly means 'coordinated activities'. The concept connotes an assumed problematic concerning the coordination of activities between adoption agencies and child welfare organisations. If a formal link was established between the two types of institutions, there was an inherent danger, it was assumed, that the interests of adopting would influence decisions concerning the optimal care solution for the child. In these coordinated activities, then, child rights activists seemed to have found the essential mechanism of conflicting interests between the economic interest implicit in care transference and the best care transference solution for the child. The route to trafficking in international adoption was limited by the possibilities that this specific institutional connection created. The explicit model behind it was the Barragan case and the connection between the adoption agency Alliance for Children and the adoption orphanage FAFECORP.

Before the issue of 'coordinated activities' entered Congress, the theme had been central to conflicts concerning the elaboration of principles, guidelines and instruments of regulation, in different units within public administration. A wide range of actors were engaged, including Congress representatives, spokespeople from the National Minors Court, child rights advocates from civil society organisations, including international NGOs, child welfare professionals and representatives of international adoption agencies. Different constellations of alliances of non-state and state actors confronted one another. In one of these constellations, child rights advocates were central, and in others adoption mediators had protagonist roles. These confrontations escalated through Congress, and the prolonged and surprisingly bitter conflict over Article 248 placed the theme of international adoption irregularities central to the whole field of childhood legislation.

Conclusion

Independent of the outcome of the law process in the Congress (Article 248 was eventually removed from the law because of serious disagreements), the focus in this debate and the turn it took teaches us an important lesson.

A focus on the external dimension and the orphanage–agency connection drove a fundamental aspect in irregular adoption activity – the formalising mechanisms and practices needed in order to blend illegal activity into public administrative and legal procedures – out of sight. All known examples of irregularities in international adoptions in Ecuador show that formalisation is a crucial mechanism in this sense. Regulations and laws introduced to control and combat irregular practice are hence created from a mistaken perspective. Governing instruments emerging from this perspective weaken possibilities for a relevant child welfare administration and do not eradicate the operations of the actor identified as the problem. These policies do not target the child trafficking problem as a system, but merely as individual/ external causes. As such they become too dependent on a legalistic logic concerning the possibility of establishing truth based on certain mechanisms of evidence making, identifying singular people, acts and institutional connections, and not systems.

This lesson, to do with the tendency to emphasise the particular and external at the expense of the systemic, has relevance beyond the particular Ecuadorian situation, and even beyond adoption as an irregular child circulation practice. Other countries' policies – and those of receiving countries concerning adoption as well as international organisations – should be examined for this kind of bias. If not, we could witness a continuous production of regulations, laws and controlling mechanisms that are inadequate in combating the problems of trafficking in international adoptions and other transnational undertakings. We should bear in mind that child trafficking generates a fundamental moral problem from which we need to distance ourselves. This may be why there is a strong tendency to embrace or accept the personal, singular and external explanations, among rights activists, policy makers and researchers, explanations that probably help them more than the children in question. An approach that would have a better chance of providing children with effective protection would have to focus differently, on the many small undertakings and irregularities that involve the formal system and its guarantors making possible the serious crimes of involuntarily separating children from birth parents in order to profit from childlessness in the West.

References

Appadurai, A. (1996) *Modernity at large: Cultural dimensions of globalization*, Minneapolis, MN: University of Minnesota Press.

El Diario Expreso (2001) 'Los hijos de nadie' ('Children of nobody'), 28, 29, 30 May.

Fox, J. (1997) 'The difficult transition from clientelism to citizenship: lessons from Mexico', in D.A. Chalmers, C.M. Vilas, K. Hite, S.B. Martin, K. Piester and M. Segarra (eds) *The new politics of inequality in Latin America: Rethinking participation and representation*, Oxford: Oxford University Press, pp 391-420.

Handelmann, D. (2004) *Nationalism and the Israeli state bureaucratic logic in public events*, Oxford: Berg.

Heyman, J.McC. (1995) 'Putting power in the anthropology of bureaucracy: the Immigration and Naturalization Services at the Mexico–United States border', *Current Anthropology*, vol 36, pp 261-87.

Leifsen, E. (2004) 'Person, relation and value: the economy of circulating Ecuadorian children in international adoption', in F. Bowie (ed) *Cross-cultural approaches to adoption*, London: Routledge, pp 182-96.

Leifsen, E. (2006) *Moralities and politics of belonging: Governing female reproduction in 20th century Quito*, Oslo: UNIPUB.

Marquéz, A. (2000) *Legislación internacional sobre derechos de los niños: Aplicación y obligatoriedad en el Ecuador (International legislation on child rights: Implementation and enforcement in Ecuador)*, Quito: Abya Yala.

Mol, A. (1999) 'Ontological politics: a word and some questions', in J. Law and J. Hassard (eds) *Actor network theory and after*, Oxford: Blackwell Publishers, pp 74-89.

Pérez-Perdomo, R. (2006) *Latin American lawyers: A historical introduction*, Stanford, CA: Stanford University Press.

Registro Oficial (2003) *Código de la niñez y adolescencia. Tribunal Constitucional año III, viernes 3 de Enero de 2003 (Code of childhood and adolescence: Year III Constitutional Court, Friday 3 January 2003)*, Quito: Editora Nacional.

Saclier, C. (2000) 'In the best interest of the child?', in P. Selman (ed) *Intercountry adoption: Developments, trends and perspectives*, London: British Association for Adoption and Fostering, pp 53-65.

Selman, P. (2000) 'The demographic history of intercountry adoption', in P. Selman (ed) *Intercountry adoption: Developments, trends and perspectives*, London: British Association for Adoption and Fostering, pp 15-39.

Sieder, R., Angell, A. and Schiolden, L. (eds) *The judicialization of politics in Latin America*, New York, NY: Palgrave Macmillan.

Simón, F. (1990) *Informe sobre las adopciones internacionales ilegales en el Ecuador durante el año 1988 (Report on illegal international adoptions in Ecuador in 1988)*, Quito: DNI/Sección Ecuador.

Triseliotis, J. (1999) 'Inter-country adoption: global trade or global gift?', in A.L. Dalen and B. Sætersdal (eds) *Mine – yours – ours and theirs*, Oslo: University of Oslo Press, pp 79-92.

UNICEF (1998) *Innocenti digest: Intercountry adoption*, Florence: UNICEF.

Zelizer, V.A. (1994) *Pricing the priceless child: The changing social value of children*, Princeton, NJ: Princeton University Press.

eighteen

Child slavery in South and South East Asia

Cecilia Flores Oebanda

Context

Despite the numerous conventions and protocols, national and local legislation protecting children and banning them from work, the challenge of ensuring freedom for the 218 million children trapped in child labour worldwide is ever growing. The issue is as complex and difficult as ever, particularly for those 126 million children still engaged in hazardous work. There continues to be widespread suffering for children from forced labour, slavery, trafficking and exploitation. While some countries experience progress, others that are still greatly affected continuously ignore the problem. Even where protocols have been ratified and laws initiated at national levels, many countries ignore the issue in practice, with the police, judiciary and local officials turning their backs on the problem, thus undermining these same laws. Thus, despite progress in some parts of the world, the scale of the violations of children's rights seems still to be in an upward trend, with many faces of child slavery being seen all around the world.

The human race has entered a phase in its history where rhetorical calls for equality and rights are stronger than ever. Children's rights are codified into international laws and conventions have their own counterpart legislations in state parties concerned. Yet again, despite some commendable progress on paper, child slavery, perhaps one of the most inhumane treatments of children, persists as a thorny issue all around the world. Socioeconomic, legal and even cultural forces in many countries tend to reinforce systems of exploitation, systems that can be both complex and nuanced.

While we live in an era of children's rights, the reality is that the issue of child slavery is still a complex problem. Many factors contribute to the massive exploitation of children and these vary from country to country. They include poverty, gender inequality, uneven development (driving migration between and within states), state oppression (as in Myanmar), the impact of climate change (also encouraging migration) and the pressures brought about by globalisation, in particular the tendency for suppliers to have to drive their prices down to achieve a market share of their goods.

The diversity of forms of slavery and the factors that cause them in South and South East Asia alone are so numerous that the appropriate strategic approach in addressing this issue is probably to see these problems not as an issue for any one country but as a system of interconnected issues, that is, that child slavery is a dynamic issue linking countries through migration, trade and development, for example.

A major factor that causes the perpetuation of abuse of children is widespread inequality and discrimination within the two regions. There are many social constructs that fuel exploitation of children in the areas. There are, for example, fault lines of class, gender, religion and economic capability. For instance, according to the International Labour Organization (ILO), the Dalits in India are generally more vulnerable to exploitation due to their treatment within wider Indian society as a result of their perceived inferior status. Here, national and state laws have banned both prostitution and forced labour for children, yet it is widespread and it is disproportionately carried out by children and young people from Dalit and Scheduled Tribe statuses. In other parts of Asia, the plight of minorities and refugees as vulnerable groups needs particular attention. They are often the ones not given ample opportunities for social mobility or even survivability. Migrants fleeing the effects of war, state oppression, climate change (desertification and flooding, for example) all find themselves in situations where they are 'outsiders', unfamiliar with laws and policies and thus more vulnerable to exploitation.

In the same manner, gender disparities contribute greatly to the widening problem of child slavery. There are also massive gender gaps in education and opportunities that make girls especially vulnerable to abuse (see Chapters Four and Seven, this volume, for example). Challenging these cultural aspects becomes extremely difficult in specific places where they are long entrenched. A complete change of mindset has to be espoused in order for these changes to really take place.

Visayan's perspective

In the experience of the Visayan Forum Foundation,[1] in partnering with other groups across two global regions, the processes of abuse and exploitation are being perpetuated in particular not by the lack of laws or policies, but by the weak political will and, in many instances, poor governance or implementation by those charged with acting on laws and policies to combat slavery. This is not therefore a drawback in the provision of social services to help victims of child slavery alone, but a problem further up the chain, in terms of poor enforcement.

The most exploitative forms of child slavery are thus still widespread even with existing labour laws in those countries. Much of the abuse happens in the private sphere, particularly, for example, in child domestic work and sweatshops where there is very little ability for the government to intervene, often because they know little about the situation.

As noted, the problems of child slavery in one country should not be seen in isolation because they are all intertwined. In every context, there is no singular 'root of the problem', although massive poverty is the usual reason that people point to. The fact of the matter is that it is a combination of economic, social, cultural and even political factors that come together to perpetuate child slavery. Therefore, even today, more than 10 years after the Worst Forms of Child Labour Convention No 182 was agreed in Geneva (see Chapter Three, this volume), no state or region is free from child slavery. The problem becomes even more complex as the face of this exploitation continuously evolves. The strategies of traffickers, illegal recruiters and abusers change over time, as they respond to a changing legal and policy context but also because new opportunities arise for children to be exploited.

As a result, we would argue that it is not only the problem that becomes more complex. The required solution and strategies for combating child slavery must never be simplistic and must be as inclusive as possible. This issue cannot be solved using a 'band-aid' solution of merely patching up the symptoms and assuming that this will somehow shift the balance irrevocably in the interests of children. An holistic, multi-tiered and multi-stakeholder strategy must be espoused.

In the Visayan Forum Foundation, our strategy is based on the belief that the way forward is through expanding the capabilities of the stakeholders and through finding innovative strategies and partnerships. The case of the Philippines provides a good example of this approach.

Migration and exploitation

The Philippines is known to be among the leading sources of migrant workers worldwide. From as early as the 1970s, the number of Filipinos abroad has been steadily increasing. The country's economy is heavily dependent on eight million Filipinos working abroad, many of whom send remittances back to families within the Philippines. So also are the economies of the countries where these migrant workers are employed. Many Filipino women work as nurses, carers and domestic workers in more industrialised countries of the North and South (including the Gulf States, Western Europe, North America and Hong Kong), while many men work in labouring and construction.

The three decades of migration practice and acceptance implies that there is an entire generation of young people already born into a culture where movement from one place to another is common. Over time, the culture of migration and the willingness to take any risk has been ingrained in the Filipino psyche, and especially in young people. This three decades of exposure to mass migration has led young people to explore the possibilities of work abroad and to disregard the potential consequences for them. This is reinforced by their immediate family and communities who provide an emotional and psychological support for these decisions. Many of these young people are, however, eventually trapped in exploitative and slave-like trafficking and forced labour situations. This exploitation may begin to take effect during the process of migration: for example, agents may charge migrants enormous sums of money to 'secure' a post for them. Workers thus arrive at their destination already deeply in debt to the agent and find themselves working in highly exploitative conditions in part to pay off the debts owed to the agents.

Janice is a native of Ilocos Sur, Philippines. She finished secondary education and undertook vocational training, including baking and dressmaking. Her cousins introduced her to a recruiter who offered her a job in Dubai as a sales clerk with a salary of PHP 18,000 (US$390). She used her life savings to pay the placement fee but that was still not enough to pay this exorbitant amount. The immigration officer discovered that her visa was fake and offered to refer her to an employer for domestic work. Because she was desperate, she agreed.

She was verbally and physically abused and was barely fed anything for 20 days. Eventually, she was sent away by her employer, leaving her to go back to her agency to beg for a new job. She was made to transfer to Al-Ain, Abu Dhabi, where she worked for only eight days before transferring again to Oman to another abusive employer. Eventually, she sought the help of the Philippine Embassy to file charges against her employer. The embassy officials dismissed her case because her employer was a powerful figure in the country. In retaliation, the employer charged her PHP 120,000 (US$2,660) for apparent breach of contract.

Fortunately, some friends from the UK came to her aid and gave her enough money to go back to the Philippines. On her arrival in the country, she filed a case against the employment agency. After a long legal battle, she won the case, which paid for the amount she had spent along with the damages incurred. It was only then that Janice felt that justice was finally served.

The Philippines continues to export its people abroad to acquire the much needed remittances of overseas contract workers to keep its economy afloat. The current strengthening of the Philippine peso is largely related to the amount of remittances that overseas Filipino workers (OFWs) return to the country from working abroad. In 2007 alone, OFW remittances reached US$13.1 billion, 14% higher than in 2006. While this is boosting economic progress at home and the government generally welcomes this development, it has a very dark side: thousands of Filipinos, working abroad in many countries (and many of which themselves have laws and policies against slavery and child slavery), fall into the crack of exploitative human trafficking situations.

Tens of thousands of these migrants, including many thousands of children, are recruited and trafficked, lured by promises of a better life in the urban centres within the Philippines and at a range of destinations abroad. These traffickers, together with their corrupt cohorts, have mastered the art of deception, coercion and fraud, with techniques that successfully exploit the vulnerabilities of people desperate to acquire an adequate income.

We have argued that the existence of slavery and slavery-like practices in one country has to be seen in a wider context. Thus, the internal dynamics of the problem of systemic slavery as it happens inside the Philippines is part and parcel of wider international dynamics. Even overseas recruitment relies on intricate processes and complex networks that start from far-flung, usually rural communities, where those recruited are completely unaware of what they are being recruited for. Traffickers thrive in known hubs and hotspots as they trade women and children in clubs and brothels. Many exploiters have perfected the art of deception, coercion, fraud and exploitation of victims' vulnerabilities. They control victims under conditions of fear, debt bondage, confiscation of documents and harassment, as well as threatening them with retaliation should they go against the traffickers.

Rina always dreamt of working abroad. Local headhunters in her community offered her a job in France as a hotel worker. There is an intricate network of traffickers connected to local and international criminals that starts in the far-flung communities. She travelled to Manila with dozens of other women and boarded a plane with these other women. On arriving at her new home, Rina found out that she would be forced to work as a prostitute: she had fallen into a human trafficking operation and she could not back out. By the time she turned 17, Rina had been forced to have sex with more than 80 strangers. Eventually, a foreign customer informed Rina she was not in France, but in the Ivory Coast – a war-torn country in West Africa. It was only when one of her customers found out that she was not prostituting by choice that an intervention happened. That customer tipped off an organisation that referred her case to the Visayan Forum Foundation. With a concerted effort from organisations and the International Police, Rina was rescued and given a chance to rebuild her life.

Gelyn, 17, was recruited to work in Manila along with 80 other children and adults from Davao del Norte. She was promised a monthly salary of PHP 2,500 (US$50) as a domestic helper in Manila. They were part of two big groups that crossed the islands using inter-island ferries carrying their jeeps. Each jeep was packed with 40 passengers, twice the number of the vehicle's 20-person capacity.

Mats were rolled over the floor of the jeep and their luggage was used to secure the ends. They were fed salted fish rationed by the recruiter. The trip took eight days to reach Manila.

When they reached the island of Samar, they boarded a ferry boat that brought them to the port of Matnog, the gateway to Luzon. Before they went onboard, the recruiter hid them from the authorities by covering them with sheets of tarpaulin. The recruiters declared them as 'cargo'. Some of the recruits vomited and urinated in the jeep because they were not allowed to go out.

When they reached Manila, the owner of the agency informed Gelyn that she owed the agency PHP 7,500 for the meals and transportation expenses for her trip and the PHP 500 advance payment that the recruiter gave to her mother. She had to work for three months without pay. She first worked as a domestic worker, then as a hostess in one of the owner's entertainment bars where she was physically and sexually abused. Eventually, one of the girls was able to escape and reported the case to the authorities. Freedom was restored to the victims. However, there is still no trace of the other victims trafficked with them.

It is imperative to address a number of dimensions of both internal and cross-border movements, and to recognise the complexity of the problem. This requires working across national borders and, within any one state, also working across departmental and organisational borders. For example, there is a clear struggle between the wants of the economically powerful and the rights of the child. Trade relations are often inconsistent with policies working towards the implementation of human rights that strongly emphasise consistency of all of a state's actions with the protection and promotion of human, including children's rights. The need to adhere to the ILO core standard (see Chapter One, this volume) and other international standards is important. It is even more important that these commitments translate into tangible actions and strategies on the ground. This requires that governments need to recognise that dealing with child slavery is not simply a social services problem but one that involves organisations responsible for trade, policing, education and social services, to name but a few.

This need for an interorganisational approach reflects the interconnectedness of the issues. Cultural, economic, social and political factors all reinforce the problem of trafficking. Trapped in it are many individuals whose lives have been destroyed and their freedom taken away. One critical example of this is given by the experience of domestic workers in the Lebanon. We have had countless stories reported to us of women domestic workers, trafficked there, who were trapped during the recent Lebanon civil war. Only around 3,000 out of the estimated 30,000 Filipino workers were evacuated. Many of these workers have reported to us that their employers treat them as slaves. Some of them had to jump from the building just to escape. Others were locked in houses to take care of the employers' dogs, properties and sick relatives while their employers' families fled the war. Some who were lucky to escape and stayed in church sanctuary have been forced by their employer to go back to their houses because they had already been paid and they had to work off their debts.

Child domestic workers

The culture of migration and trafficking has, of course, as noted earlier, a strong gendered dimension. The sizeable majority of victims of human trafficking are women. They are usually promised domestic work in the city centres, for example in Singapore and the Gulf States. Domestic work and even child domestic work is treated as a common practice in these urban centres. Again, the hidden face of exploitation is obscured by the illusion that just because they work in the household, it is automatically a safe occupation. We know, however, that this is far from the case and that children working in domestic situations are often among the most exploited of children (see Chapter Seven, this volume).

Again, although there is a plethora of laws banning exploitative child domestic work, the reality is that inside the Asian countries, the problem of slavery practices are still rampant in the sector of child domestic workers. There are cultural issues to be faced here: for example, domestic work has been accepted as a common cultural practice in the Philippines with slavery at its historical roots. This deeply rooted culture is a serious challenge to the Visayan Forum Foundation because domestic work is widely assumed to be a relatively safe occupation. Right up to the present day, however, thousands of Filipino domestic workers are still trapped in a cycle of immense abuse and practices of slavery that mirror these historic practices.

Long neglected by society, the child domestic worker's plight is characterised by lack of child rights, limited or no access to education and exploitative or hazardous labour conditions. This exploitation is worsened by the fact that child domestic work is recognised as one of the oldest forms of child labour that, over the years, in many Asian countries has relevant legislation banning it. Despite these laws, many child domestic workers and employees – as well as legislators, politicians and officials concerned with child protection – still believe this work to be safest for children because they are working inside households, a phenomenon common throughout Asia. This is, however, frequently not the case because numerous child domestic workers are reported to be victims of physical, verbal and sexual abuses. They suffer very long working hours and are always on call. They perform an almost endless list of chores, often with multiple employers. They are isolated from their families and peers. In many instances, their contact with their families is permanently severed. They rarely leave the household even when they suffer abuse because of either fear or coercion or just the simple fact that they have nowhere to go to. They have too few of the simple freedoms that a normal child would have, such as playing with other children (and indeed they are often prevented from having any social contact with employers' children). They are expected to perform all day doing even heavy adult chores and are also expected to work until late in the evening. They have too little or no pay or adequate compensation, usually not enough to cover the artificially high transport costs being imposed on them by their recruiters or traffickers. Many children who are trafficked into domestic work are also trapped in debt bondage situations that force them to endure the exploitative situations because they have been convinced that they will be prosecuted or that their families will bear the consequences should they decide to escape. More basic human rights such as access to education, to effective healthcare and proper working conditions are all denied them.

Mimi was only 15 years old when she was recruited to work in Manila as an all-round domestic worker. She went with the recruiter hoping to work in order to continue her studies. On reaching Manila, Mimi and her fellow recruits were immediately brought to the Caloocan office of her agency where she was picked out and chosen to work for a Chinese businessman. When she arrived at the employer's house, she was immediately locked up together with another domestic helper in the house. To prevent them from escaping, grills and locks surrounded the house. Even their sleeping quarters, where they were padlocked inside when resting, only being opened the following day, were surrounded by steel bars. During her five years employment, Mimi was never able to step out of the house. She was prohibited from communicating with her family.

Her monthly salaries were withheld from them because her employer claimed that he had paid the recruitment agency in advance. For five years of work, Mimi was unable to receive any remuneration. She had to endure the long hours of work with barely enough rest and no days off or rest time. She ate stale food, and often the leftovers in the house were passed on to them.

> Unable to withstand their situation, Mimi and her two other companions decided to get away from their abusive situation. They had no other means of escape but to climb down and jump from the third floor of the house. Although very much terrified, they were able to escape safely and undetected.

Most child domestic workers are working in conditions that can be considered among the worst forms of child labour as defined under ILO Convention No 182 and Recommendation No 190. Many are sold and trafficked, often ending up in conditions of bondage and forced labour. Many also work without pay, working excessive hours and in isolation or during the night. Child domestic workers are also commonly exposed to grave safety or health hazards, abused and at risk of physical violence or sexual harassment.

A strategy for ending child slavery

The Visayan Forum Foundation has been fighting for the rights of domestic workers for over a decade. We have been lobbying for a law that increases the minimum wage of domestic workers and protects them from abuse and exploitation. Yet beyond legislation, there is so much that we need to do. Legislation is just one of the battles we need to win, and without effective social movements that will serve as a civil society platform and focus for national efforts, pressurising legislators, judiciary and the police, legislation is bound to fail.

The complex and interconnected nature of the problems can also only be dealt with using strategies on various fronts: international, local and community-based. They must simultaneously target the many factors that perpetuate these abusive cycles.

On the international front, the plan of ASEAN (the Association of South East Asian Nations, the main economic forum for governments in the region) to create a programme to combat child labour should be included in the presently negotiated Free Trade Agreements and incorporated into the relatively better frameworks of human rights and governance that are being developed across South and South East Asia, best practice being disseminated between countries to put pressure on those which are lagging behind. ASEAN should adopt a stricter assessment of the implementation of the ILO child labour Conventions and monitor its progress in countries throughout the region. This monitoring must, where necessary, then be translated into local legislation.

Since implementation in itself can never be realistically done by only one group, and as we have argued, the Visayan Forum Foundation's strategy has been one of partnership and collaboration. This acknowledges a need to develop actions and services that draw in many stakeholders. Building alliances and networks of service providers is therefore a critical prerequisite for any rescue operation. Reaching out to and organising child domestic workers themselves is essential for the empowerment of the sector. Trade unions also have a role here.

It is important to involve the domestic workers themselves by creating structures that allow them to help themselves, thus reducing their isolation and their vulnerability. Acting collectively is also central to their ability to participate in advocacy, increasing their voice in matters that concern them. Given the size of the sector, it can be reasonably conceived that if they are organised well, they can form not only a support group for each other but also a critical mass that will represent their sector's interest. Again, they can learn from the experience of, and build links with, trade unions.

To address the problems created by the migration of domestic workers, in the ports where we work we have created a task force composed of law enforcers, port authorities, private shipping companies, faith-related institutions and ordinary members of the public to ensure that traffickers are brought to justice and the victims healed and reintegrated. The Visayan Forum Foundation has even partnered with corporations like Microsoft to give victims economic skills so that they will not be re-trafficked. To restate our approach, the dynamic nature of the problem requires multiple stakeholder cooperation and engagement.

What we have also learned is that there is a need to mobilise public–private collaborations by enlisting the ownership of private companies as in the case of Microsoft and the shipping companies. The government must play a role as the institutional support for these actions particularly in the field of evidence gathering and prosecution.

However, despite this kind of strategic approach, our efforts for rescue and reintegration will not be sufficient and sustainable if the scope of the problem keeps growing. The public has a stake and should be aware that women and children are sold into slavery inside and outside the country. Slavery thrives on social myths and asymmetric information created by abusers and the long practice of employing children. To break these mindsets, there must be aggressive advocacy and campaigns with materials and messages targeting the young who are particularly vulnerable, and at the same time the public in general, who should be vigilant not only as the source of the demand for this labour but also as vigilant players against abuse. Public education therefore has an important role in this strategy.

There is a need to engage the public by creating massive social awareness in order to develop commitment to the all-out war to end slavery of our children, especially as domestic workers. We do not need partial or staggered actions but a full-scale battle against the system and the people who exploit them. All over Asia, women and children domestic workers are deployed everyday all over the world. Many of them do not know their real destinations. We are talking here about generations of people that are sold, deceived, coerced and threatened and in particular, we are talking about the most vulnerable segment of our population, our children.

The real battle is not just what we do to rescue victims and to prosecute traffickers and abusers. The real struggle is one of hearts and minds. It is a fight against exploitative cultural premises and economic injustice. Therefore, attacking the problem of slavery should not be treated as a project to implement, a case that needs to be studied and statistics that need to be recorded. For us as freedom fighters, slavery is an important battle we need to win because it puts our people, especially our children, in hell, where abusers sell thousands of children and women into servitude, debt bondage and slavery. It is only through our concerted efforts that we can finally and truly abolish slavery.

Note

[1] Visayan Forum Foundation is a campaigning organisation based in Quezon City, Philippines, which works on issues of child trafficking and other aspects of child slavery. Since 2001, it has rescued and provided assistance to more than 32,000 victims and potential victims of trafficking. The author of this article, President and Executive Director of the Foundation, was the recipient of Anti-Slavery International's Anti-Slavery award in 2005.

nineteen

Routes to child slavery in Central America

Virginia Murillo Herrera

Central America is a region with high levels of poverty, violence and social inequality, which has undergone wars and armed conflicts that have had a terrible impact on its countries, its inhabitants and social and economic dynamics. This situation has made the transition to, and construction processes of, peace and democracy difficult. This is a region that, due to its geographic location, has served as a route to North America and Europe for drug smuggling, labour and sexual exploitation through the trafficking of people, and it is permanently exposed to natural disasters.[1] In the last decade, the portrayal of it being a suitable destination for the commercial sexual exploitation of minors has increased and has become more complex.

Central America has great natural wealth and an important indigenous and African-American population, with a population exceeding 40 million inhabitants, of whom over 55% are children. Fifty-one per cent of the total inhabitants are poor, and 23% of them are in a situation of extreme poverty.

Poverty directly affects children and adolescents. In the case of Central America, in Panama and the Dominican Republic, poverty is not only more widespread among children (60% of boys and girls between 0 and 14 years old are poor), but also a huge portion of the total of poor people are children and young people; 47% of Central American, Panamanian and Dominican people altogether are poor boys, girls and young people aged 14 or younger. That is why the expression 'poverty has a child's face' is so very true.

On the other hand, the continuing high level of violence present in all Central American countries without exception is affecting the lives of all Central America's population. Organised crime has unleashed responses from the various governments consisting of a tough approach and of a repressive and prosecuting style against the adolescent population, especially those linked to gangs and against those in situations of social discrimination. Furthermore, this violence has created an environment of citizenship insecurity that is very difficult to live with and it has also evidenced the lack of capacity of governments to respond to this context of violence.

Central America is also affected by natural disasters that generate impacts – physical, emotional, psychological and economic – on poor people, holding back the development of countries; these impacts add another twist to the spiral of difficulties these countries already face.

Children and adolescents, migrants and the route to slavery

Migration is a complex phenomenon in Central America affecting thousands within the population, and especially particular groups and individuals, who by virtue of the circumstances and their condition are much more vulnerable and more exposed to be victims of abuse, mistreatment and discrimination. This is the case particularly for women and children.

Latin America as a whole contributes a significant proportion of migrating populations in the context of international flows as a whole. In 2005, it was estimated that 25 million Latin American and Caribbean people migrated. This is more than 13% of the total of international migrants worldwide (CEPAL, 2006, p 1). Central American migrants (with Mexico) represent 4% of the regional population, followed by those from the group of countries of the Caribbean Community and Colombia, who represent the biggest quantity of the respective populations moving across national borders (exceeding one million people in each case).

However, in the last 30 years Central America has experienced big changes in migrating patterns. The causes of migration relate to a diversity of factors such as internal political confrontations, economic crisis and processes linked to natural and environmental disasters.

Contemporary international migration constitutes a dynamic that implies risk and brings migrating people to experience situations of vulnerability and lack of protection. The difficulties faced by migrating people range from racism, xenophobia and other intolerance and discrimination to abuse, violence and deceit in the case of various forms of slave trading, as well as threats to their physical and psychological integrity. These factors are also linked to their ethnic origin, nationality, gender and age, as well as the processes of labour insertion, the mechanisms of migration and the legal status of migrating people.

The slavery process in which children are involved, essentially responds to three types of settings:

- minors who remain in their country of origin when their parents emigrate (this group represent more than half of the children of those migrating and as a result has an enormous social impact); their parents usually emigrate for reasons to do with poverty in the first place;
- boys and girls who are migrants themselves (see also Chapter Eleven, this volume);
- sons and daughters born in the country of destination of the adults.

Causal factors associated with the migration of children

Contexts of social exclusion: for many Latin American children and young people, migration turns into an event that will substitute for education as a search for human development through better labour opportunities, and a generally better way of life (Cruz, 2005).

Characteristics linked to the status of childhood and adolescence: in Latin America, the reality of children and adolescents is difficult. Children essentially become adults at an early age because they acquire responsibilities that socially do not correspond to those of minors. Adolescents and young people who do not have the opportunity to study start working from 12 years old, and maybe even younger, and often face problems such as social insecurity, inhumane treatment and uncertainty in relation to permanence at work.[2] In summary, the conditions in which they live make them excellent candidates to be drawn towards the processes that lead people to migrate people abroad (Cruz, 2005).

Processes of family reunification: children seek to satisfy emotional needs derived from the absence of their father, mother or both parents, when the latter have already emigrated to the north. Their motivation then is also essentially to do with family reunification (Ramírez, 2005).[3]

Strategy of running away from situations of danger: in many cases, children and adolescents are actually escaping from situations of violence outside or within the family; this might take the form of physical, sexual and social abuse (Ramírez, 2005).

Process of migration for children

The lack of information on migrating flows of children nationally and regionally is a serious problem when addressing this issue. While the isolated and scarce data that already exist suggest that the number of mobilisations increases annually and that most of those people migrate in an irregular way, the trend appears to be for those migrating to have a younger profile each year and for the proportion of girls and older children to have increased .

A second characteristic is associated with the lack of basic integral protection of the rights of these people, despite many of the countries having ratified the international Convention on the Rights of the Child (CRC; see in particular Chapters One and Two this volume). In relation to this structural weakness in the framework of protection for children there has also been an increase in the tendency of migrating minors not to be accompanied by their relatives. This accentuates their vulnerability. The main features then are that they are young, that larger proportions of migrant groups increasingly comprise female minors and that they lack adult protection. These unaccompanied children are the ones requiring more urgent attention.

A fourth defining characteristic in this process is that the laws forbidding child labour are making a positive effect on the surface but are driving the process of exploitation underground. Children who migrate for labour are finding it difficult to obtain paid work in the formal economy, but are consequently driven into the informal sector where no regulation exists or is enforced. These children do not study, they do not understand their rights and they end up in activities that have a profound effect on their development and that violate their human rights.

Child and adolescent work represents a violation of economic, social and cultural rights and is associated with other violations. The nature of these depends on the characteristics of the activity and the particular conditions of the children.[4]

How trafficking occurs

It is difficult to estimate the current number of people who are child victims of trafficking and the slave trade more generally in Central America. In part this is because, as other chapters have shown, it is difficult to clearly define the boundaries of the problem. More importantly, however, there are no registration provisions or indicators that allow us effectively to measure the problem. There is also a lack of both resources to explore the issue as well as proper training for treatment and follow-up of cases that have been identified.

Most of the trafficking in the region occurs for the purposes of commercial sexual exploitation, but again there are no statistics available to quantify this phenomenon.[5] Deceit, international adoptions (see Chapter Seventeen, this volume) and illegal documents facilitate the trafficking of boys and girls in Central America. Trafficking for the purpose of sexual exploitation, however, requires the cooperation of many people:

- brothels and other organisations require specific and defined types of girls and boys for the purposes of prostitution for particular kinds of demand;
- corrupt officers counterfeit documents to guarantee the (false) identification of girls and boys as being of age to be migrated;
- trafficking agents (adults, often posing as relatives) are required to move with the children;
- corrupt lawyers produce a country's exit permissions;
- migration officers facilitate the passage of victims through borders; and
- in other cases, the counterfeiting of documents is unnoticed and girls and boys are passed through borders without the knowledge of the authorities, that is, they are smuggled as well as trafficked.

Once children have been trafficked to an unknown location, they do not have any options to escape. They are in an area with which they are not familiar and they have no resources. Not only do they not have money, but they also are informed that they are indebted financially to the traffickers. These girls and boys rapidly reach the conclusion that their only solution is to participate in forced labour, which usually involves their kidnappers putting them into prostitution.

Trafficking in its geographical, social and economic contexts

Costa Rica is one of the countries within Central America that is most prone to sexual tourism; a quick search on the internet provides enough evidence of this. Nicaragua is, in turn, one of the supply countries for trafficked girls and boys with destinations in Central America. In Nicaragua, it appears that documents are counterfeited quite easily: Honduras, Guatemala and Mexico are all countries of 'encounter' where girls and boys are deceived, manipulated, perhaps coerced and then sent for eventual transportation to a third country, usually the US or Canada. The map below (Figure 20.1) shows these processes in geographical form.

One of the characteristics on which many studies from different parts of the world agree (and that is confirmed elsewhere in this book) is that traffic moves from poor regions or countries internally or externally towards more prosperous regions or countries. The International Human Rights Law Institute (IHRLI, 2002, p 47) suggests that in terms of trafficking networks, the Central American region may be broadly divided along a North–South axis, with Nicaragua as the point of origin for flows of people traffic in both North and South directions. Thus, an experience of trafficking starting in Nicaragua can move through Honduras, possibly El Salvador, and end in Guatemala, Belize or the south of Mexico. Going on through that route, women and children are recruited in Honduras and then sent to El Salvador, Guatemala and Belize. El Salvador is a transit country for Guatemala, Mexico and Belize; Guatemala is a country of origin for the south of Mexico and Belize.

From cases and testimonials collected, the traffic from Nicaragua towards the north of Mexico mainly uses land routes. The movement towards the north is facilitated by free transit agreements (CA-4) between Nicaragua, Honduras, El Salvador and Guatemala; consequently monitoring is relatively weak at these national borders. Bearing in mind the economic development and the perception of better work opportunities in each country to the north of Nicaragua, the traffickers who recruit children and minors can easily make credible employment offers that attract children into the trafficking process.

Long-distance lorry drivers who travel along the Pan-American route contribute to meeting demand and also supply the necessary transportation.

Figure 20.1: Geography of the flow of people trafficking (Central America)

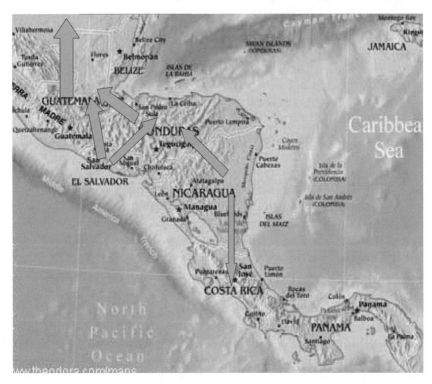

Source: Casa Alianza, Guatemala

The ports along the Pacific and Atlantic coasts also both generate demand and attract trafficking activities. Prostitution close to the border zones and in larger cities increases the demand even more, as a result of the additional effects of local patterns of demand, by male migration towards the north and by the migrating working populations in general.

The slave trade in children and adolescents then occurs when three conditions occur:

(1) the capture, transportation, transfer or reception of people;
(2) the 'capture' of children is associated with threats or the use of physical force or other forms of coercion, kidnap, deceit, abuse of power, of a situation of vulnerability or through the concession or reception of payments or benefits to obtain the consent of a person that has authority over others (except among those under 18 years old); and
(3) traffickers have the goals of exploitation, including essentially the exploitation of others through prostitution or other forms of sexual exploitation, work or forced services (including domestic work), slavery

or practices analogous to slavery, servitude or the extraction of human organs.

What has been done and what are the challenges?

During the first 10 years of the CRC, countries in the region started to harmonise their domestic legislation and to promote codes of childhood and adolescence as a response to the new focus based on human rights and shaped by what is called in the region the Integral Protection Doctrine. Some countries also elaborated supplementary laws in response to specific problems that required particular attention in their own jurisdictions.

In the case of child labour, work for the elimination of child labour, as well as platforms such as the Global March against Labour Exploitation of Boys, Girls and Adolescents, together with the activities of other prominent child-centred organisations such as Save the Children, DCI and UNICEF, among others, contributed to the development of national commissions for the approval of Convention No 182 (see Chapters One and Three, this volume) and its Recommendation No 190. This work also aimed at promoting the ratification of ILO Convention No 138 where relevant, and the implementation of programmes and projects to eliminate child labour in its different manifestations: for example, in the agricultural and fishing sectors, services, domestic work, construction and pyrotechnical games among others. National plans against child labour and the protection of working adolescents were also developed.

In the case of commercial sexual exploitation, it proved more difficult for states to accept that the problem existed and to take strict measures to address it. This situation then allowed Central America to be viewed by those engaged in trafficking as a destination for commercial sexual exploitation of minors throughout the last decade. However, campaigning by many national, regional and international social organisations put the problem firmly on national agendas and contributed to better understanding of the real size and nature of the problem as well as shaping recommendations for combating it. Some countries have reformed their criminal codes, and many key actors , such as the police, government officials and non-governmental institutions, have received training in migration. Criminal networks and in some cases, exploiters, have been put in jail.

In relation to the phenomenon of migration, many efforts have been made in the region; for example, the International Migrants Convention has been ratified. In recent years, important meetings have been conducted where the various states have agreed key declarations (such as the Ibero-American Summit 2006 on Migrations and Human Development). In Central America, discussions have been held with a view to regulating migration as a whole.

Despite all these efforts, many deficiencies continue, which means that efforts taken by states are found not to be sustainable. On the one hand, weak institutional structures in Central American states cannot respond effectively to the complexity of the problem. Not only are good intentions required, but also the reform of institutions and adequate social investment to fight the causes that generate the problem of modern slavery. More extensive efforts are required fully to protect children's and families' economic, social and cultural rights if the problem is to be prevented at source. And tools and much greater intelligence are required to be able to confront the organised networks involved in the sexual and commercial exploitation of children.

The Latin American region has valuable experience in relation to the recognition of the seriousness of the problems of human rights of all migrants, including refugees. This is expressed in the initiatives of the Inter-American Commission of Human Rights, in the 12 countries' ratification of the International Convention on Protection of all Migrant Workers and in reports and activities of the United Nations (UN) Special Rapporteur on migrant workers and their families. However, conventions and protocols are not enough on their own. The complexity of the interrelationship between the processes of migration, trafficking and modern slavery demands new and creative approaches and we need to understand more about the specific conditions under which migrant children find themselves that make them particularly vulnerable to this. Only then can we construct appropriate mechanisms to stop it.

Notes

[1] This chapter was completed shortly before the terrible earthquake in Haiti.

[2] It is worth saying that these conditions shaping labour insertion are produced in general among the economic activities of receiving societies. A reflection on this dimension is included on p 299.

[3] Most minors migrating through Central America and Mexico to reach the US do so for the purposes of family reunion. In a monitoring of the Forum for Migrations it was found that 90% of minors intercepted had relatives in the place of destination.

[4] Labour/work acquires different meanings and connotations according to the context in which it is produced. For instance, note that: 'in Costa Rica there is a distinction between child labour under 15 years old where legally it is not allowed to work but also child labour is the work that affects the social, psychological development of the child. Adolescent work is for those upwards of 15 years old

where legally it is permitted to work but there are some regulations that need to be implemented' (DNI/Marcha Global, 2006, p 32).

[5] Even though there are many cases of trafficking for forced labour purposes.

References

CEPAL (2006) *Migración internacional de derechos humanos y desarrollo en América Latina. Síntesis y conclusiones (International migration and the development of human rights in Latin America: Summary and conclusions)*, Thirty-first session, DNI and Plataforma Subregional Montevideo, Uruguay citado por Acuña Guillermo en Migración, Derechos Humanos y Trabajo Infantil.

Cruz, T. (2005) *Migración y juventud: Reflexiones en torno a los riesgos que implica estar en la frontera sur de México (Migration and youth: Reflections on the risks involved in being on the southern border of Mexico)*, Seminar on Border Migration, San José: Universidad de Costa Rica.

DNI/Marcha Global (2006) *Migración, trabajo infantil y derechos humanos: Apuntes para una agenda regional, foro de ongs cumbre Iberoamericana de Presidentes (Migration, child labour and human rights: Notes for a regional agenda, NGO Forum, Ibero-American Summit of Presidents)*, Montevideo: Uruguay.

IHRLI (International Human Rights Law Institute) (2002) *In modern bondage: Sex trafficking in the Americas*, in association with the Inter-American Commission of Women and the Inter-American Children's Institute of the Organization of American States, Chicago: IHRLI.

Ramírez, A.L. (2005) *Consulta regional sobre niños y niñas sin protección parental en las Américas: niños y niñas en migración, Antigua (Regional consultation on children without parental protection in the Americas: Children in migration, Antigua)*, Citado por Acuña Guillermo en Migración, Derechos Humanos y Trabajo Infantil, San Jose: DNI and Plataforma Subregional.

Resources

This is a listing of further sources for those interested in following up the issues raised in this book.

Useful websites

Organisations and resources for those working on trafficking

International Labour Organization:
www.ilo.org

ILO Mekong anti-trafficking project:
www.childtrafficking.net

ILO China anti-trafficking project:
www.preventtraffickingchina.org

Web resource on the fight against human trafficking:
www.human-trafficking.org

Child trafficking digital library:
www.childtrafficking.com

United Nations Global Initiative to Fight Human Trafficking:
www.ungift.org

Office of the United Nations High Commissioner for Human Rights:
www.ohchr.com

International Organization for Migration:
www.iom.int

Organization for Security and Cooperation in Europe:
www.osce.org/cthb

Child Exploitation and Online Protection centre:
www.ceop.police.uk

United Nations Inter-Agency Project on Human Trafficking:
www.no-trafficking.org/

Global March Against Child Labour:
www.globalmarch.org/

MTV End Exploitation and Trafficking:
www.mtvexit.org

ECPAT (see Chapter Eight): there are a number of associated ECPAT
organisations across the world, each with its own website. For example,
ECPATUK is at www.ECPAT.org.uk and ECPAT-USA (End Child
Prostitution and Trafficking) at www.ecpatusa.org/

Not For Sale Campaign:
www.notforsalecampaign.org/

Other general web-based organisational resources on child slavery

International Labour Organization (Programme on the Elimination of
Child Labour):
www.ilo.org/ipec

UN Committee on the Rights of the Child:
www2.ohchr.org/english/bodies/crc/index.htm

Free the Slaves:
www.freetheslaves.net

Global Alliance against Traffic in Women:
www.gaatw.net

United Nations Children's Fund: the United Nations International
Children's Education Fund (UNICEF) publishes widely on issues of
child trafficking and forced labour, including child domestic labour.
Reports may be downloaded from:
www.unicef-icdc.org

UNICEF Innocenti:
www.unicef-irc.org/

United Nations Office on Drugs and Crime:
www.unodc.org/

Child Rights Information Network (CRIN):
www.crin.org

2010 Child Labour Convention:
www.childlabourconference2010.com

Wilberforce Institute for the study of Slavery and Emancipation (WISE):
www.hull.ac.uk/WISE

International Slavery Museum:
www.liverpoolmuseums.org.uk/ism/

World Vision Research:
www.worldvision.org/content.nsf/learn/Publications-reports-research#child

Amnesty International:
www.amnesty.org

Casa Alianza:
www.casa-alianza.org.uk

Coalition Against Trafficking in Women:
www.catwinternational.org

Counter-Trafficking Service:
www.iom.int/jahia/Jahia/about-iom/organizational-structure/migration-management-services

Inter-Agency Project on Trafficking in Women and Children in the Mekong Sub-Region:
www.un.or.th/TraffickingProject/

Stop Trafficking:
http://secretary.state.gov/www/picw/trafficking/home.htm

Websites on bonded labour in South Asia

Resources on child labour and bonded labour practice: www.birendra.ws contains in-depth information about bonded labour and child labour practices in Nepal as well as in South Asian region

Nepal Research: website on Nepal and Himalayan Studies: www.
nepalresearch.com/human_rights/bonded_labour.htm links news clips
published by various newspapers concerning bonded labour practice in
Nepal

Bonded Labour in South Asia: www.bondedlabour.org/web/index.asp
contains information about bonded labour practices in Bangladesh, India,
Nepal and Pakistan. It also provides various reports prepared by local and
international non-governmental organisations (NGOs) on the topic of
bonded labour

Bonded Labour/Debt Bondage Resources: www.vachss.com/help_text/
bonded_labor.html contains various publications on bonded labour
practices in different parts of the globe. The site also lists a number of
national and international organisations working against the use of
bonded labour

Other key organisations and materials

Anti-Slavery International: www.antislavery.org

Anti-Slavery International works on all aspects of child slavery and
publishes a range of reports in English, French and Spanish. Reports
relevant to child domestic labour (Chapter Four), for example, include
the following:

- *Child domestic workers: A handbook on good practice in programme
  interventions* (Maggie Black, 2005)
- *Child domestic workers: Finding a voice, a handbook on advocacy* (Maggie
  Black, 2002)
- *Child domestic workers: A handbook for research and action* (Maggie Black,
  1997)

For details of the partners described in Chapter Three, see the following:

African Network for Prevention and Protection against Child Abuse and
Neglect (ANPPCAN)
Head Office
Wood Avenue, Off Argwings Kodhek Road
Komo Lane
PO Box 1768 – 00200 City Square
Nairobi, Kenya
Email: regional@anppcan.org
Website: www.anppcan.org

Defensa de Ninas y Ninos-Internacional (DCI) Costa Rica (see also Chapter Nineteen)
Apartado Postal 1760-2100
San José, Costa Rica
Email: info@dnicostarica.org
Website: www.dnicostarica.org

The Society for the Protection of the Rights of the Child (SPARC)
House 151-B
Street 37, F 10/1
Islamabad
Pakistan
Email: isb@sparcpk.org
Website: www.sparcpk.org

WAO Afrique
Rue des Frères Franciscains – Adidogome
BP 80242
Lomé – Togo
Email: waoafrique@cafe.tg
Website: www.waoafrique.org

Human Rights Watch: publishes reports from its different offices around the world: www.hrw.org

For example, publications on child domestic labour include:

- *Swept under the rug: Abuses against domestic workers around the world* (2006)
- *Inside the home, outside the law: Abuse of child domestic workers in Morocco* (2005)
- *Always on call: Abuse and exploitation of child domestic workers in Indonesia* (2005)
- *No rest: Abuses against child domestic workers in El Salvador* (2004)

ILO-IPEC: see website above under trafficking entry. ILO-IPEC also works on issues of forced labour and child domestic labour (www.ilo.org/childlabour). Relevant reports include:

- *Helping hands or shackled lives? Understanding child domestic labour and responses to it* (2004)
- *Child domestic labour in South East and East Asia: Emerging good practices to combat it* (2005)

UNICEF: the United Nations International Children's Education Fund publishes widely on issues of child trafficking and forced labour, including child domestic labour. Reports may be downloaded from www.unicef-icdc.org; see, for example:

- *Child domestic work*, Innocenti Digest No 5 (UNICEF-ICDC, 1999)

The Paulo and Nita Freire International Project for Critical Pedagogy: http://freire.mcgill.ca/

The Paulo Freire Institute at UCLA: www.paulofreireinstitute.org/

Asian Development Bank: www.adb.org/

Open Society Justice Initiative: www.soros.org/initiatives/justice/focus/equality_citizenship

Refugees International: www.refugeesinternational.org/

The International Observatory on Statelessness: www.nationalityforall.org/

Plan International – Universal Birth Registration Campaign: http://plan-international.org/birthregistration

Bal Ashram rehabilitation centre for rescued children (see Chapter Nine): www.bba.org.in/balashram/

Bachpan Bachao Andolan (Save the Childhood Movement: see Chapter Nine): www.bba.org.in/

SCREAM materials (see Chapter Seventeen): www.ilo.org/ipec/Campaignandadvocacy/Scream/lang--en/index.htm
Nepali organisations (see Chapters Fourteen and Seventeen):
Maiti Nepal
PO Box 9599
Gaushala
Kathmandu, Nepal
Website: www.maitinepal.org

Shakti Samuha
PO Box 19488
Gaurighat
Kathmandu, Nepal
Email: samuha@wlink.com.np
Website: www.shaktisamuha.org.np/#

ABC/Nepal: Anti-Trafficking, Basic Human Rights and Cooperatives
PO Box 5135
Narephat, Koteshwor
Kathmandu, Nepal
Email: abc@transit.wlink.com.np

Women Acting Together For Change (WATCH)
PO Box 11321
Battisputali – Maitiden
Kathmandu, Nepal
Email: watchftp@wlink.com.np

Women's Rehabilitation Centre (WOREC), Nepal
PO Box 13233
Balkumari, Lalitpur
Website: www.worecnepal.org

Other literature on aspects of child slavery

Note: See also the references for each chapter. The listing here includes the more recent literature only.

Ali, A.K.M. Masud (2005) 'Treading along a treacherous trail: research on trafficking in persons in South Asia', *International Migration*, vol 43, nos 1/2, pp 141-64.

Bales, K. (2004) *Disposable people. New slavery in the global economy*, Berkeley, CA: University of California Press.

Bales, K. (2005) *Understanding global slavery. A reader*, Berkeley, CA: University of California Press.

Bales, K. (2007) *Ending slavery: How we free today's slaves*, Berkeley, CA: University of California Press.

Bashford, P. (2006) *A sense of direction. The trafficking of women and children from Nepal*, Nepal: Asha.

Blagbrough, J. (2008) *Child domestic labour*, London: Anti-Slavery International/ WISE.

Casa Alianza (2003) *Trafficking in children in Latin America and the Caribbean. Documento preparado para el Instituto Latinoamericano de las Naciones Unidas para la Prevención del Delito y Tratamiento del Delincuente*, San José: ILANUD.

Cody, C. (2009) *Count every child: The right to birth registration*, Woking: Plan Ltd [available in English, French and Spanish] (http://plan-international.org/birthregistration/files/count-every-child-2009).

Craig, G., Gaus, A., Wilkinson, M., Skrivankova, K. and McQuade, A. (2007) *Contemporary slavery in the UK: Overview and key issues*, York: Joseph Rowntree Foundation.

DNI/Plataforma Subregional Trabajo Infantil/Marcha Global (2009) 'Migración, trabajo infantil y derechos humanos' ('Migration, child work and human rights', *Actualización*, San José: DNI.

Freire, P. (2000) *Pedagogy of the oppressed*, New York, NY: Continuum.

Global Rights and others (2005) 'La trata de personas en El Salvador, Guatemala, Honduras y México' ('Trade in persons in El Salvador, Guatemala, Honduras and Mexico'), Presentado en el marco del 123avo período de sesiones de la Comisión Interamericana de Derechos Humanos de la Organización de Estados Americanos, Mexico City.

Gupta, R. (2007) *Enslaved: The New British slavery*, London: Portobello Books.

IHRLI (International Human Rights Law Institute) (2003) *Study of trafficking in women, children and adolescents for commercial sexual exploitation*, National Report, Brazil: IHRLI.

ILANUD (2003) 'Trata de seres humanos, especialmente de Mujeres, Niños y Niñas' ('Trade in persons, especially women and children'), XII Sesión de la Comisión ONU sobre la Prevención el Delito y la Justicia Penal, Viena, 12-22 Mayo.

Innocenti Insight (2007) *Birth registration and armed conflict*, UNICEF (www.unicef.at/fileadmin/medien/pdf/birth_registration_and_armed_conflict.pdf).

LWF (Lutheran World Federation) (2006) *Baseline survey on anti-trafficking needs*, LWF.

LWF ONRT (Office of the National Rapporteur on Trafficking) in Women and Children (2008) *Trafficking in persons especially women and children in Nepal*, LWF.

OIT (2005-09) *Diversos trabajos OIT sobre Explotación sexual comercial de personas menores de edad en Centroamérica, Panamá y República Dominican*, OIT.

OMT (2003) '"Consideraciones finales" de la Consulta Regional realizada por la Organización Mundial del Turismo', San José de Costa Rica, Mayo.

Plan Ltd (2006) *Count me in: The global campaign for universal birth registration, Interim campaign report 2005-06*, October, Woking: Plan Limited (http://plan-international.org/birthregistration/files/count-me-in-english).

Quirk, J. (2008) *Unfinished business: A comparative survey of historical and contemporary slavery*, Paris: UNESCO.

Save the Children US (2005) *The movement of women: Migration, trafficking, and prostitution in the context of Nepal's armed conflict*, Washington, DC: SCFUS.

Todres, J. (2009) 'Law, otherness, and human trafficking', *Santa Clara Law Review*, vol 49, pp 605-72 [also available at http://papers.ssrn.com/sol3/papers.cfm?abstract_id=1362542).

UNICEF (1999) *Child Domestic Work,* Innocenti Digest No. 5, New York: UNICEF-ICDC.

UNICEF (2007) Innocenti insight: Birth registration and armed conflict: Italy UNICEF Innocenti Research Centre.

Winrock International (2008) *Best practices in preventing and eliminating child labor through education* (http://circle.winrock.org/circle_English/winrockenglish.pdf).

Literature on aspects of adoption and trafficking (see Chapter Seventeen)

Bowie, F. (ed) (2004) *Cross-cultural approaches to adoption*, London: Routledge.

Briggs, L. and Marre, D. (eds) (2009) *International adoption: Global inequalities and the circulation of children*, New York, NY: New York University Press.

Selman, P. (ed) (2000) *Intercountry adoption: Developments, trends and perspectives*, London: British Association for Adoption and Fostering.

Academic journals and special issues

Childhoods, vol 14, no 3, 2007: Special issue on 'The state and children's fate: reproduction in traumatic times', edited by Claudia Fonseca and Jessaca B. Leinaweaver.

Childhood and Society, vol 22, no 3, 2008: Special issue on 'Child slavery worldwide', edited by Gary Craig.

Forced Migration Review on Statelessness, issue 32 [available in English, French, Spanish and Arabic] (www.fmreview.org/FMRpdfs/FMR32/FMR32.pdf).

The International Journal of Critical Pedagogy: http://freire.mcgill.ca/ojs/index.php/home

Journal of Latin American and Caribbean Anthropology, vol 14, no 1, 2009: Special issue on 'The cultural and political economies of adoption in Latin America', edited by Linda Seligmann and Jessaca B. Leinaweaver.

Radical Pedagogy: http://radicalpedagogy.icaap.org/

Conferences and events

The Child Labour International Conference (sponsored by ILO/Netherlands government) was held in May 2010. The website will contain many relevant materials and remain in place for some time after the conference: www.childlabourconference2010.com

The UN, ILO and other international organisations sponsor other conferences from time to time on aspects of child slavery.

Afterword

The end of child slavery?

Kevin Bales

There has always been child slavery. There has not been a day in human history without the enslavement of children. In the past the accepted and permissible control of children within most cultures included their exploitation extending into slavery. The 'discovery' of childhood in the 18th century combined with concepts of innocence and vulnerability began to extend to children an interesting set of paradoxical rights. On one hand, what would today be called the worst forms of child labour began to be regulated, in law if not in practice. At the same time, parental and governmental controls over children's lives were extended. In the past and today, parental controls, especially, often come into conflict with both national and international norms and laws. The result is a little talked about but profound tension that is both conceptual and practical. The protection of children assumed in law requires vigilance, physical protection extending to physical domination, *de facto* and *de jure* controls, the rights of children regularly suborned by the rights of adults, and, in many cultures, the expectation that adults have rights and children have few or none. International norms, such as those stated in the Universal Declaration of Human Rights, may assign rights to children, but these continue to be controversial and not just ignored but rejected by many governments as well as individuals. It is worth noting that one of the strongest arguments against ratification of the UN Convention on the Rights of the Child by the United States government was that it would remove the right of parents and others to use corporal punishment on children. Whatever the state of international conventions, socially and culturally there is no agreement on the rights adhering to children. This is in contrast to the wide consensus rejecting all forms of slavery.

This paradoxical situation exists within a larger context of trends that confound the application of rights to children. All forms of enslavement are supported by two key factors: economic and social vulnerability, and a lack of protection by the rule of law. It is not too great a generalisation to say that, with very few exceptions among human cultures, women are more vulnerable than men, children are more vulnerable than adults, and girls tend to be the most vulnerable of all. Because the internal dynamics and power relations of families are seen as outside the regulation of law except in the most egregious circumstances, the rule of law often fails to

317

reach to minors. This pattern is typically embedded deeply within culture and reinforced by religious dogma. Indeed, all social institutions in most societies tend to assume the complete control of children by older family members. The result is both that children face possible enslavement within their family and that they are less likely to be protected from enslavement outside the family.

The enslavement of children within families is demonstrated in the ubiquitous practice of the forced marriage of minors. There is no reliable estimate of either the number of adult women or children in forced marriages. Indeed, in many cultures forced marriages are not defined as such, in spite of clearly violating the criteria in, for example, the 1956 UN Slavery Convention. Required minimum age at marriage varies from country to country, and is often ignored. Sub-groups within many societies jealously guard the 'right' to marry off minor girls, and their doing so is overlooked by governments as an 'ethnic' or 'cultural' practice. This relativistic approach opens the door to the commoditisation of children. As Dottridge (2004, p 20) notes:

> In some cultures it is still common for girls to be abducted by the bridegroom or his relatives, for example in parts of Bénin and Ethiopia. In others, notably in China, it is common for an intermediary to be involved in the abduction, in order to make a profit by delivering a young woman to her prospective husband: in this case it qualifies as trafficking. In addition to abducting women for marriage, however, marriage agents play a role in many societies in negotiating marriages and are remunerated for their efforts. On the whole this traditional role is regarded as perfectly acceptable.

In developed countries there is confusion and misapprehension over forced marriage, and the term is often used interchangeably, but wrongly, with 'arranged marriage'. The result is that while the result is slavery, it is not seen as such by the public or by policy makers. Those who see the disposal of minor children into forced marriage as a 'right' are happy to foster this confusion.

This concept of the 'right' to control and dispose of children extends beyond family arrangements to religious practice. Two examples from West Africa clearly demonstrate this. The first is the use of children by religious guardians in the *Madrassa* schools. Children, from a very young age, are handed over to such schools by their fathers. Ostensibly, this is an act of piety, but it is also used as an action to discipline a child's mother and a demonstration by the father of his complete control over the family. At the schools the children are expected to receive theological training and memorise the Koran, they are also expected to support the *imams* or *marabouts* who teach them. In reality, in many schools, the children, known as *talibé*, spend their days begging in the streets and are punished if they fail to bring in enough money. Their situation is one of complete control coupled with economic exploitation and little or no religious, or other, education. A 2010 Human Rights Watch report suggests that 50,000 children are 'forced to endure often extreme forms of abuse, neglect, and exploitation' in Senegal alone. In a second example, girls and young women in other parts of West Africa are given to *Trokosi* priests as an act of atonement for sins committed by male relatives. The priests use the girls as servants, to grow food and earn money, and for sex. All free will is lost. The enslavement will continue until the woman is incapable of further work and she is then disposed of and another girl is requested from her family to take her place. Any of her offspring remain the property of the priest.

Even when forced marriage or enslavement through religious practice is not a threat, patterns of discrimination and prejudice are compounded for children. The lack of access to education, health services, adequate nutrition, and legal protection is exacerbated for children who are members of a group suffering discrimination, and leaves them at a significant disadvantage. One of the most blatant indicators of this is the lack of birth registration, as Claire Cody makes clear in Chapter Ten. Nearly two thirds of all births in Africa and South Asia go unregistered and this lack of registration falls more severely on the poorest families or members of marginalised ethnic communities. Without a birth certificate a child is a non-person, unable to prove identity and easily dismissed as ineligible for support programmes. In the mountainous regions of Southeast Asia hill tribes are regularly denied government birth registration and with it citizenship. If a child from one of these groups is caught up in human trafficking and taken to another country it becomes very difficult to repatriate them upon rescue, as their home country will reject them at the border. Recent policies enacted by the US tie birth registration to aid, but the establishment of an open and comprehensive system will take time.

These few examples point to the many forms of child slavery, and that is what is so very welcome about this volume. Too often in the popular media, and by organisations and individuals that should know better, trafficking and sexual exploitation of children is presented as the sole form of child slavery. This book is important because it demonstrates the breadth and complexity of child slavery, how it fits within our global economy and how it replicates patterns of prejudice and exploitation in nearly all countries and cultures. In nearly every way that an adult can be enslaved and exploited, a child will be as well. What is more, this book helps to lay the false dichotomy that is often raised between 'sex' slavery and 'labour' slavery. If there is a universal theme across the history of slavery it is that slaves are sexually abused and that women slaves and child slaves are sexually abused with the greatest regularity.

Enslavement is a licence to rape whether the child is enslaved on a farm, a boat, in a shop, in the military, or in a brothel. Criminal slaveholders do not make this distinction, child slaves do not benefit from this distinction, and it is important to use the division of 'sex' and 'labour' slavery very sparingly or to drop it altogether.

This false dichotomy is illustrated in one dimension of child slavery not discussed in any of the chapters in this volume – the enslavement of children linked to environmental destruction. In many cases, a major by-product of the slave labour feeding into the global economy is environmental destruction. Not surprisingly, criminal slaveholders who destroy the lives of slaves don't mind wreaking havoc on nature as well. Forests are illegally cut, strip mines are carved into protected areas, reefs and coastal environments are destroyed, and it is slaves, often child slaves, who do the work.

Good examples of this are the mangrove swamps destroyed to build shrimp farms or fish processing camps which decimate vital ecosystems and remove the ecological 'sponges' protecting the coastline from being overwhelmed by a tidal wave. In the devastating tsunami of December 2004, the areas of Sri Lanka that suffered the greatest loss of life were those where natural coastal ecosystems had been ripped up to install fish and shrimp farms. This was especially the case when outlying coral reefs were broken up as well, thus removing a second natural buffer.

In early 2010 I visited the Sundarban Forest in southern Bangladesh, a UNESCO World Heritage Site. In this tapestry of islands and forests, the largest single tidal mangrove forest in the world, boys as young as eight are lured or kidnapped and taken to remote islands along the southern coast. Sold to the fishing crews for about $15, they are set to work processing fish on shore for 18 hours a day, seven days a week. If the boats return with a large catch they might work several days with no sleep at all. Like robots they clean, bone, and dry fish; shell mussels, shrimp and crab, and wash squid to remove the ink. At other times they sort, weigh, check, and load the haul, processing and preparing the fish for drying and shipment. The slaveholders sexually abuse the boys and beat them regularly. They get little food, no medical care, and sleep on the ground. If they sicken or are injured and die, they are thrown into the ocean (Anti-Slavery International, 1998). One larger island, Dublar Char, was raided and children freed in 2004 when researchers linked to the US anti-slavery group Free the Slaves discovered the situation. They worked with the US State Department's anti-trafficking office to bring diplomatic pressure on the Bangladeshi government, which led to a raid by military police. But that one raid was very much the exception not the rule, and the practice continues unabated on many of the small islands of the forest reserve.

The fish processing camps are carved out of the protected forests on many of the islands of the World Heritage Site. Hundreds of boys may be enslaved at any camp, held by one of several slaveholders running their own fish processing and drying crew. To build the camps the forest is cut back from the shore and the timber is used to construct drying racks and huts. As the camp grows it pushes deeper into the forest. With firewood needed every day, some children are sent into the forest to collect it, along with palm fronds and other useful materials. But in the forest the children are prey to the Sundarban Forest's most illustrious inhabitant, the Bengal tiger. In a day spent interviewing child slaves who had recently escaped from the fish camps I discovered that every respondent knew someone, had heard of someone in their camp, or had personally witnessed another child taken by a tiger. It seemed to be one of the top two causes of death for these child slaves, the other being diarrheal diseases. The fishing camps serve illegal and uncontrolled fishing boats that are depleting the fish stocks and damaging biodiversity. They are also systemically destroying a rare and protected forest, as well as using children as the hapless foot soldiers in this attack on the natural world. The great tragedy for the children is that in the Sundarban Forest nature fights back.

Child slaves are used in environmentally destructive work in other parts of the world as well. In Ghana, illegal gold mines strip forests away to the bedrock and pollute large areas, streams and rivers with the mercury used to extract gold. The health effects on the enslaved children are extremely destructive: mercury poisoning is common, as is silicosis from the constant inhalation of quartzite dust (gold traces are found in quartzite deposits). Similar destruction of the environment and deployment of child slaves occur in gold mining in Peru and Brazil. In the Kivu region of the Congo, children are enslaved in the mining of coltan, cassiterite and other minerals used in electronics. The mines are unregulated and operate without any environmental controls, the enslaved children are seen as disposable, and are likely to be victims of regular sexual abuse. If there is a theme to child slavery it is that children are used in virtually every type of slavery where adults are used, and this is certainly the case with enslavement that exploits the destruction of the environment.

Ending child slavery?

Given the breadth, depth, and horror of child slavery to be found in this volume, how is it possible to suggest that there could be an end to child slavery? Surely, this practice, as old as history itself, is a permanent part of the human condition. But while it is true that child slavery has emerged regularly in human societies, it is not a universal condition. In the same way that slavery is found in many societies, but is not ubiquitous or necessary, the state of being a child slave is not inherent in the child but a status and condition forced on an individual through their own actions and/or, especially, the actions of others. Children can be forced into slavery, but they can also be protected from slavery. There are two key reasons why we might feel hope that child slavery can be eradicated.

The first has to do with trends within child labour generally. In 2006 the International Labour Office published its second Global Report on child labour under the follow-up to the ILO Declaration on Fundamental Principles and Rights at Work. In it they reported on the extent of the problem: 'In 2004 there were 218 million children trapped in child labour, of whom 126 million were in hazardous work. Although the participation of girls in child labour and hazardous work is on a par with that of boys in the youngest age group (5–11 years), boys predominate considerably at older ages in both categories' (ILO, 2006). There is no clear estimate for the numbers of enslaved children, but they would fall within the group engaged in hazardous work. This is important because the headline finding of the ILO report was this: 'the number of child labourers globally fell by 11 per cent over the last four years, while that of children in hazardous work decreased by 26 per cent. For the age group of 5–14 years the decline in hazardous work was even steeper – by 33 per cent. The global picture that emerges is that child work is declining, and the more harmful the work and the more vulnerable the children involved, the faster the decline' (ILO, 2006).

If there is indeed a trend of children being removed from the worst forms of child labour, then child slaves will benefit. The report goes on to mark the most significant gains in Latin America and the Caribbean, with the least improvement in sub-Saharan Africa. These regions also reflect a lower and higher incidence of slavery respectively. There are a number of reasons posited why child labour has declined, including policy changes (e.g. reduction of corruption), economic growth, poverty reduction, decreased birthrates, industrialisation, and mass education. All of these have an impact on the occurrence of slavery as well, especially reducing corruption and increasing education levels. It is certainly the case that countries that today have very low rates of child labour, such as the UK, had very high rates in the past, suggesting that change is possible. In fact, child labour in Britain in the 19th century was more extensive than in any other country past or present, and included what would today be defined as cases of child slavery. The ILO research team also devoted significant energy to exploring what factors might 'tip' a country with a high level of child labour into the virtuous cycle where low child labour maintains itself. Not surprisingly, nearly all of the recommended actions also tend to reduce the incidence of slavery. The report points out that these actions rest on a growing international consensus that child labour must be radically reduced.

This idea of a global consensus highlights the second key reason why the eradication of child slavery can be seen as possible: the understanding that just such 'tipping points' apply to slavery, and child slavery, as well. Admittedly, it may seem naïve to assert that after more than 5,000 years of slavery, we can bring slavery to an end, but several factors support this assertion. One factor is the extent of slavery within the larger global population and economy. In slavery today, *more* is actually *less*. While it is a large number, today's 27 million slaves represent the smallest *proportion* of the global population to ever be enslaved. Likewise, the $30–$40 billion in goods and services slaves produce each year is the smallest percentage of the world economy ever generated by slave labour. In global terms slave output is a drop in the ocean. The same applies to the total number of slaveholders. While they may number in the low millions, for the most part they are isolated landowners and moneylenders, locally powerful but not part of a unified vested interest or organised industry supporting slavery.

There are a number of reasons why ending slavery is possible, and as with child labour a favourable social, political, and economic context can provide the foundation. There is a growing consensus for change; no government or organised interest group is pressing the case that slavery is desirable or even acceptable. The world is united in its condemnation of slavery. The Universal Declaration of Human Rights simply underscores this, placing freedom from slavery at the top of the list of fundamental rights. The moral challenge today is not how to convince people that slavery is wrong, but how we can *act effectively* on our universally held belief in the absolute and essential equality of human dignity.

Secondly, as Gary Craig reminds us in his Introducion, the legal framework tends already to be in place. Laws against slavery are already on the books in every country. Around the world some of these laws need updating and expanding, others need their penalties increased. Many anti-slavery laws are waiting for the allocation of funds needed to train police in their use. And given the international nature of human trafficking, nearly all national laws need to be brought into harmony with each other. Actual eradication needs the political will to enforce law, not campaigns to make new law. Probably the most important laws needing enactment are those appropriating the funds needed for eradication.

A third factor has to do with the economic arguments against slavery. As noted above, the actual monetary value of slavery in the world economy is extremely small. One estimate states that all the work done by slaves in the whole world in a year is worth about $13 billion. Another study estimated that global profits from human trafficking are about $31 billion a year. Given the date of those estimates and the rate of inflation, the total output in 2010 might be $40–$50 billion, still negligible. Put simply, the end of slavery threatens the livelihood of no country or industry. At the same time there are strong arguments that ending slavery is good for economies. While slaves may make money for slaveholders, they tend to be a drag on a community's or country's economy. They contribute little to national production; their work is concentrated on the lowest rung of the economic ladder, doing low-skill jobs that are dirty and dangerous. Economically, except for the criminals, slaves are a waste. They contribute next to nothing to an economy; they buy nothing in a country's markets. Slaves are actually an untapped economic resource. For poor countries, allowing ex-slaves significantly to increase their earning and spending would be a small but important improvement in the national economy. At the international level if you compare countries on the strength of their economy and how many slaves they have, the picture is clear – the more slaves, the weaker the economy. This is not surprising when one examines the 'freedom dividend' that comes with liberation. Freed slaves are more productive and consume more than they did in slavery; they are also likely to remove their children from the workplace and place them into schools. Increased productivity and consumption by adults coupled with education for children creates an upward cycle in communities where slavery has been eradicated, precisely the sort of virtuous cycle identified by the ILO as the path to the eradication of child labour.[1]

Dealing with the damage

No other country in the world so dramatically demonstrates the consequences of a botched emancipation as the US. It is important to remember that of the nearly four million slaves freed from legal slavery in 1865, about 45 per cent were aged 15 and younger. If we count children as those under the age of 18, then half of all slaves in the US were children. America has suffered, and continues to suffer, from the injustice perpetrated on ex-slaves. After liberation, generations of African-Americans were sentenced to second-class status, exploited, denied and abused. Without education and basic resources it was very difficult for African-American families to build the economic foundation needed for full participation and well-being in America. Today there are laws that force criminals to make restitution for what they have stolen, for the damage they have inflicted. No such restitution came for the stolen lives of millions of slaves.

If child slaves are freed only to live in destitution, without access to education and healthcare, then liberation holds little value. We've seen that helping freed slaves achieve full lives is one of the best investments a government or a society can make. The US experience shows the results of neglecting life after liberation, that way lies a horrible waste of human potential. It also gives birth to anger, retribution, vengeance, hatred and violence. In fact, one of the most profound questions about slavery and freedom that remains unanswered is this: even if there is restitution, can there be forgiveness?

Those who have suffered enslavement may well say that this is a crime beyond forgiveness. It is no momentary act of violence, no crime of passion, but a systematic brutality and exploitation that can stretch over generations. It combines within itself the most horrible crimes known – torture, rape, kidnap, murder and the wilful destruction of the human mind and spirit – crimes especially horrifying when perpetrated on children. It is exploitation, injustice and violence all rolled together into their most potent forms. The damage it does and has done is inestimable, and that damage includes the minds deeply injured by enslavement.

The minds injured by slavery include the minds of the slaveholders. By dehumanising another person in order to enslave them, slaveholders dehumanise themselves. Those of us with little direct experience of slavery find it hard to feel any concern for the slaveholder, especially that person who enslaves a child, but many of those who have lived in slavery recognise the damage slavery does to the master as well. A community that allows slavery in its midst is sick to its roots. For the freed child slave to grow as a person and a citizen, that sickness needs to be treated, especially because many freed slaves live in the same area where they were enslaved. Ex-slaves and their slaveholders may see each other regularly. If injustices are allowed to fester, it will be impossible for either group to move on. In the US, the ugly sickness of slavery re-emerged in segregation, discrimination and lynch law. In part, this was because most Americans sought to ignore the legacy of slavery. The immediate needs of freed slaves were not met in the years following 1865, and ever since there has been an attempt to draw the curtain over the past, to let bygones be bygones.

We can see a parallel in post-apartheid South Africa. Faced with the large-scale horrific murders and torture of the past, many people in that country argued that collective amnesia would best serve the reconstruction of a truly democratic state. But Desmond Tutu (1999, p 31) explained that: 'Our common experience in fact is the opposite – that the past, far from disappearing or lying down and being quiet, is embarrassingly persistent, and will return and haunt us unless it has been dealt with adequately. Unless we look the beast in the eye we will find that it returns to hold us hostage.' In the US that beast has been on the prowl for more than 100 years, and has evolved into new forms of discrimination, recrimination, and injustice. Putting down that beast is one of the US's greatest challenges. Ensuring that same beast never grows up when child slaves are freed today is a challenge for the whole world.

Note

[1] Supporting this virtuous cycle at the international level, existing patterns of research, policy, diplomacy and outreach can be easily transferred to ending child slavery. We know that when governments really get involved in collective international effort big changes can happen. In 1988 the Global Polio Eradication campaign began,

with nearly every government in the world promising to take part. In that year, the crippling polio disease was active in 125 countries. By 2003, there were only six countries left with vestiges of active polio. As with many diseases, it will be difficult to wipe out the polio virus completely, but millions of children and adults have been saved from being crippled by the campaign. Child slavery can also go from being global, pernicious and pervasive to being a rare crime on the watch list. But as the work of liberation goes on, great attention must be paid to the young survivors of child slavery so that what they have suffered does not shape their lives in freedom.

References

Anti-Slavery International (1998) *Indonesian Fishing Platforms*, Marlborough: Adam Matthew Publications.

Dottridge, M. (2004) *Kids as commodities? Child trafficking and what to do about it*, International Federation Terre des Hommes, Terre des Hommes Foundation, Lausanne, Switzerland and Terre des Hommes Germany.

Human Rights Watch (2010) *Off the backs of children: Forced begging and other abuses against talibes in Senegal*, New York: Human Rights Watch.

ILO (International Labour Organization) (2006) *The end of child labour: Within reach. Global report under the follow-up to the ILO Declaration on Fundamental Principles and Rights at Work*, Geneva: ILO.

Tutu, D. (1999) *No future without forgiveness*, London: Rider.

Index